THE SLUM A…

The Slum and the Ghetto

Immigrants, Blacks, and Reformers in Chicago, 1880–1930

Thomas Lee Philpott
University of Texas at Austin

Wadsworth Publishing Company
Belmont, California
A Division of Wadsworth, Inc.

History Editor: Peggy Adams
Editorial Assistant: Tammy Goldfeld
Production Editor: Donna Linden
Designer: Andrew Ogus
Print Buyer: Barbara Britton
Permissions Editor: Peggy Meehan
Copy Editor: Margaret Moore
Technical Illustrator: Guy Magallenes
Compositor: Scratchgravel, Auburn, Washington
Cover Design: Andrew Ogus

Printed in the United States of America 49

1 2 3 4 5 6 7 8 9 10—95 94 93 92 91

Library of Congress Cataloging-in-Publication Data
Philpott, Thomas Lee.
The slum and the ghetto: immigrants, Blacks, and reformers in Chicago, 1880–1930 / Thomas Lee Philpott.
p. cm. — (American society and culture series)
Includes bibliographical references and index.
ISBN 0-534-14742-9
1. Chicago (Ill.)—Race relations. 2. Afro-Americans—Illinois—Chicago—Social conditions. 3. Immigrants—Illinois—Chicago—Social conditions. 4. Afro-Americans—Housing—Illinois—Chicago—History. 5. Immigrants—Housing—Illinois—Chicago—History. 6. Housing policy—Illinois—Chicago—History. 7. Social settlements—Illinois—Chicago—History. I. Title. II. Series.
F548.9.N4P47 1991
305.896'073077311—dc20 90-46971

To the memory of my grandparents, Thomas F. Lee and Mary McCormick Lee

And for Anne and Paul, Tommy, and Sara

This edition is for Whitney, my granddaughter

Contents

Illustrations

FIGURES

MAPS

Tables

Preface to the Wadsworth Edition

I wrote this book about immigrants, blacks, and reformers in Chicago in an effort to understand American society. It is a scholarly book, which it needed to be. But it is a personal book, too, as it was bound to be. For American society was my society. Chicago was my city. And questions of ethnicity, race, and class were not scholarly abstractions for me. They were the wrenching questions of daily life. The great event of my lifetime was The Movement for civil rights and against the war, and I took part in it: This study is as much an expression of the passions of that cause as it is a product of the seminars I attended in graduate school.

My background is Irish Catholic. The grandfather who brought me up was an immigrant. He always kept a safety deposit box. When it was opened after his death, there was only one thing in it, a parchment certifying that the government of the United States had conferred on him, "formerly a subject of Gr. Britain," the gift of citizenship. He kept the contents of his box a secret, but he raised me teaching me the value of its gift.

Where I grew up, in the part of Chicago called South Shore, there were enough Jews for the area to be considered Jewish. But there were even more Catholics, and there was a sizable Protestant minority too. Still, with over thirty nationalities represented, everyone was white, and as I gradually caught on, that was the point: Race counted much more than religion or nationality. In my boyhood, I watched policemen arrest black people who tried to swim at Rainbow Beach, *our* beach, for "loitering" or "for their own protection." Since 1884, Illinois law had prohibited discrimination in public places. But I would learn that only later. The cops probably didn't know the law either. The code they were enforcing was not on the books; it was the unwritten law of the "color line." It took me some time to learn that, too.

My high school was miles from our neighborhood, on the other side of what was called the Black Belt. The Catholic schools were rigidly segregated. Two were for blacks, and all of the rest for whites only. So I rode the city bus back and forth between a white neighborhood and a white school. But the bus passed through six or seven minutes of streets where no one was in sight but "colored people."

The sharpest racial memory of my youth is of a Sunday Mass at my church, St. Bride's. No blacks ever came there. They had parishes of their own set aside for them. But this morning a black man entered and stood against the back wall. There was a troubled stir, and when I looked back I recognized him. He worked as an attendant at Rainbow Beach. He was on his way to work and had stopped off to hear Mass. At communion time, he stepped to the end of the line of people approaching the altar rail to receive the blessed sacrament. The priest was a brawny Irishman who bullied the altar boys. When he looked up over the communicants and saw the black man, he took the communion wafer he held between his thumb and forefinger and spiked it angrily into the chalice. Then, jabbing his finger at the man, he roared, "There are churches for your kind to go to. Don't come here making trouble. Go away, you. Go!" The man froze for a long moment, then hurried out. After Mass my grandpa, who did not want "the colored" coming into South Shore, said that what had happened was "a sin and a shame." From then on I was ashamed to face that man. When I went to the beach, we sometimes spoke, but never about that morning.

That was in 1955. I was thirteen. Black families trying to move into neighborhoods like mine were being mobbed and firebombed. And questions of race were crackling in the charged air. In Mississippi a black Chicago boy named Emmett Till was murdered for being "uppity." In Montgomery, Alabama, people were mobilizing to challenge and change what was wrong in the South. And that kept me thinking about what was wrong on the South Side of Chicago.

Later, after years of study on the streets and in the archives, I was talking about all of this with my mother. (She is the unnamed "woman from St. Columbanus" who is cited in this book.) The subject of Mercy Hospital came up. My parents were born there, so were my brother and I, and my father died there. It was a Catholic institution, but it accepted patients regardless of creed—as long as they were not black. The hospital refused service to "colored Catholics," even in emergency cases—proof again that the bottom line in Chicago was the color line. This longstanding policy stayed in effect long after 1916, when the area around the hospital "went colored." I told my mother the story of a member of the Colored Catholic Women's Club, Maude Johnson, who went to Mercy's emergency room with a heart attack in 1944. After examining her, the doctor explained, apologetically, that because she could survive the twenty-minute drive to County Hospital, she would have to go there. Mercy, he told her horrified husband, "just did not take colored." A Mercy nun called a priest to meet Maude Johnson at County, to administer the last rites. (It was all right to perform that ritual at the public hospital, but not at Mercy.) Fortunately, Mrs. Johnson got to the hospital in time to get the medical care that saved her life.

When I had finished the story—which had come out of my research—my mother said she had a story of her own, which was not recorded in any archive, and the time had come to tell it. Her story was about my father, who died of pneumonia in 1943, when I was one year old. He was a Mercy patient. His doctor told my mother he was dying, but sent him home briefly, instructing my mother to bring him back when it got bad, and they would try to make it easier for him at the end. When that time came, my father broke into a soaking sweat, his hair curled tightly, and his skin turned dark. My mother and my father's uncle drove to Mercy's emergency room and dragged him to the desk. The nurse stationed there asked, "Is that man colored?" My mother said, "Can't you see he's dying?" The nun replied, "Don't be impertinent with me, young woman. Is that man colored or isn't he?" My mother answered, "No, Sister." So he was admitted. He could have lived through the ride to County and died there. Instead, he spent his last hours in the care of the Sisters of Mercy.

That was all my mother had to tell, except that Uncle Jim was mad as hell that someone could mistake one of *us* for one of *them*. I remember him as a loving uncle. But in all affection I have to say he was a racist. Not that he would have denied it. He called civil rights "civil riots." And he relished telling me that he was not for segregation, he was for slavery.

Most Irish men and women of my generation who grew up in Chicago have memories like these and stories of relatives like Uncle Jim. But the Irish did not segregate black Chicagoans single-handedly. The South Side was no Little Ireland. The Irish didn't have any neighborhoods of their own to keep "Irish." No group, ethnic or native, had any area all to itself to protect on its own. The neighborhoods where whites lived were not ethnically homogeneous. They were mixtures of nationalities. When blacks came looking for someplace to live (and they looked on the West and North sides as well as the South), the Irish did not have to confront them alone. Catholics and Protestants, gentiles and Jews, immigrants and natives, whites of all countries, all creeds, and all classes, collaborated to keep their neighborhoods white. The result was the ghetto, and it was the work of all their hands.

The difference between the slum and the ghetto was that poverty alone defined the slum, whereas poverty combined with racism to create the ghetto. When white people were poor, they lived in districts of low-grade housing, the slums. Economic advances—better jobs with higher pay, and savings—enabled them to move out to better neighborhoods. The slum was a hard reality, but it was bearable when people believed that with hard work they could put it behind them. And that is what masses of immigrants managed to do, usually within one or two generations. The poverty and progress of the ethnic whites—people like my own—is one of the major themes of this book. But the experience of African Americans was different. They were the ones burdened most heavily by poverty and the slum. But it was their color, not their class, that confined them to a slum that was permanent and inescapable, the ghetto. The jobs people needed to make it out of the slums were available to immigrants but usually closed to blacks. And where employment was available, advancement was not. When, against all odds, a black family made some headway by working and saving, the homes they could now afford in better areas were denied to them. They were hemmed in by the color line, and money was not enough to buy their way out. The poorest whites continued to keep even the grimmest slums closed to blacks. The object of their wrath was the poor black, the figure lampooned in the longtime favorite vaudeville number, "Rastus, Roostus, Johnson Brown,/What'cha' gonna' do when the rent comes round?" For well-off whites in desirable areas, that stereotype was just a joke. What they feared was the black family that *could* pay the rent, *could* afford to live in decent housing in clean neighborhoods—white neighborhoods.

Crowding black people into a separate section of the city was a tremendous civic project. It involved every form of social action, from naked terrorism to economic discrimination to the might of the law. It was done by countless individuals, but also by banks and realty firms, neighborhood organizations, and government officials. Churches, hospitals, charity societies, and social agencies down to the Boy Scouts and Girl Scouts all took part in it. Even the progressive movements examined at length in this book—movements for housing reform and neighborhood betterment—drew the color line. The ghetto was forced housing. It was a civics lesson in systematic, sustained segregation. And the lesson was not theoretical: It worked. Against other groups, coercion of this kind and on this scale had never succeeded, in Chicago or any other American city. It had never even been attempted. "The city within a city," as the Riot Commission of 1919 called the Black Belt, was unique in Chicago history. Its only counterparts were the "colored districts" that took shape in other American cities after 1880. But the pioneer urban sociologists at the University of Chicago observed all of this and said it was natural, necessary, inevitable, and normal, no different from the experience of all other ethnic groups.

This book ends in 1930. Since then, six decades have gone by. Now Chicago is celebrating the centennial of Jane Addams's renowned settlement house, Hull-House. It was once a spearhead for reform; now it is a shrine. But there is another centennial that no one wants to celebrate. The ghettos of Chicago and of many another city are now about a hundred years old. And the ghetto is not a thing of the past. In Chicago today, the Black Belt covers thirty-three square miles. More than a million people live within it—almost 90 percent of Chicago's African Americans. Outside, in the city's remaining two hundred square miles, 98 percent of the people are Anglos, Asians, Hispanics, and others; blacks total only 2 percent. In the surrounding suburbs, the level of segregation is even worse. White developments command choice locations within the black boundaries, but it is as hard as it ever was for African

Americans to move into white neighborhoods. Chicago's ghetto is special in its sheer mass and magnitude. In other cities the segregation occurs in scattered sites, not in a megaghetto like Chicago's. But everywhere the separation of white families from black is close to complete.

All across metropolitan America today, the most successful inhabitants of cities and suburbs alike are Jewish and Catholic. They are the descendants of yesteryear's old immigrants. They have long since made it, and more than made it. They take pride in their achievements and understandably resent the lack of recognition they have received. But one part of the population, at least, seems inspired by their example: the new immigrants who have been pouring into the cities for the past two decades. These newcomers are following the path of the old white immigrants. They are far from well-off, but still they start off at an advantage over African Americans who go back five generations in the cities. When Asians and Hispanics advance in education, income, and occupation, they move into better housing, whereas blacks with comparable accomplishments cannot. It is a fact that new immigrants who are poor have more residential freedom than even the most successful blacks do. An Asian or a Hispanic with only three years of schooling has a better chance of moving into an integrated neighborhood than a black person with a Ph.D. does. An Asian or a Hispanic who makes under $2,500 a year is more likely to live in an integrated neighborhood than is an African American earning over $50,000. Statistics like these will come as a shock only to those who do not know the history of immigrants and blacks in the city. It is the same old story, happening all over again. And scholars in universities are still teaching that the black ghetto is just another ethnic enclave.

The ghetto is still complete, still compulsory, still largely a slum, still officially sustained, still for blacks only. It has proved to be permanent, not just something that is lasting, but possibly everlasting. There is a slum outside the ghetto whose residents and homeless people are not blacks, but the forsaken families and luckless loners of all the other groups. But this kind of racial "equality" compensates African Americans not at all.

The slum and the ghetto have endured for a century. They have outlasted the Jim Crow system of formal segregation, and they are likely to last at least as long as slavery itself did, which would mean they will continue well into the twenty-second century. Unless some people, some time, act with purpose and persistence to persuade their fellow citizens to change, the slum and the ghetto will be with us for a very long time, possibly forever. But there can be no action without understanding, and Americans today (including many scholars) do not even know that *slum* and *ghetto* are two different words defining two social worlds that both make a travesty of democracy.

And democracy is the issue. Abraham Lincoln once said that as he would not be a slave, so he would not be a master. "This," he said, "expresses my idea of democracy." Moreover, he explained, any society that differed from this idea was "no democracy." He was speaking of his own society—a slave society—especially. After generations of denial and delay, which made the cost of doing it so terrible, Lincoln's contemporaries finally confronted slavery. It did not just go away. Neither will the slum and the ghetto. Jane Addams and her fellow reformers worked, and worked long and hard, to improve living conditions for the poor, white and black, but they would not face the basic problem of the slum, which was economic injustice, or of the ghetto, which was economic injustice compounded by racial injustice. Instead of challenging poverty and racism, they tried to make the slum and the ghetto safe for democracy—almost as though Lincoln had recommended food stamps for slaves, instead of emancipating them. Only in the 1950s and 1960s did the activists of the civil rights movement begin to say with great force that a society with official segregation, economic inequality, and pervasive racism was no democracy. They defeated legal segregation in the South. But when they came North in 1966 to confront the ghetto head-on, in Chicago, they met an opposition they could not overcome. There has been no progress from that time to now.

And what now? The time of a new generation has come round. It is their turn, if they will take it. The college students among them are notorious for "looking out for themselves." But that is no reason to lose hope, for as Rabbi Hillel said ages ago, if people are not for themselves who will be for them? But if they are only for themselves, Hillel asked, what are they? "And if not now, when?" I am grateful to the people who have made my book available to students and teachers. Maybe reading it will prompt some of them to think about the slum and the ghetto and the idea of democracy. That might help to make a beginning. Without some beginning, the future will only prolong the past and present. The past is Chicago, 1880–1930. Read it and weep. The present is every American city today. Look around. In the meantime there is what Meister Eckhart wrote in the Middle Ages for us to contemplate: "God waits on human history, and suffers in the wait."

TLP
Austin, Texas
December, 1990

Preface

In the years following 1880, Chicago, more than at any time in its history, was a magnet for masses of poor European immigrants. Like other cities of the time, Chicago sweated their labor, stacked them in shambling tenements, and seemed to mock the promise that had lured them to urban America. Still, they streamed to Chicago. And in the slums that they had to occupy, they managed to create neighborhoods to sustain themselves, in which they could take pride, even while they worked to move up the social ladder and out to the zone of emergence beyond the slums. Many of them made it, and there were members of "the better classes" who tried to lend a hand. That is part of what this book is about.

Settlement workers like Jane Addams, philanthropists, and progressive businessmen and politicians launched movements for better housing, neighborhood centers, and open spaces—efforts that, over the years, proved helpful, but did not confront the central problem of the people in the slums, which was the simple fact that they were poor. The reformers' motives were a mixture of sympathy and fear, a paternalistic desire to help the ethnic poor and a determination to control them. The reformers were socially concerned but, for the most part, economically conservative, looking to private enterprise to solve the housing problem and never advocating legal measures that would violate the business creed. Their ultimate goal was the assimilation into the American social system of the slum-born youngster, scrubbed clean of his foreignness, indistinguishable from all other Americans, or rather, all other *white* Americans.

For there was one group of slum dwellers whom reformers had no intention, or at least no hope, of incorporating in this way.

Blacks had always lived in wretched housing in Chicago, but it took a major race riot to bring the Black Belt to the attention of the reformers. By then it was the city's most appalling slum, and it was something else as well: a ghetto—the only one the city had ever had. Unlike the ethnic clusters, it was a place where segregation was practically total, essentially involuntary, and also perpetual. This book traces the process of ghettoization and the role of reform within it. The process involved not only white realtors and residents' groups, who contained the blacks by using violence and such devices as restrictive covenants, but also progressives, who established settlement houses and model housing projects "for colored" like those they had provided outside the ghetto for whites. Reform was benevolent, benign, an effort to compensate for past neglect and make life better for the people of the Black Belt. It also aimed to keep them contentedly confined inside. As one reformer put it, providing the ghetto with the needed housing and social services was "the real way to concentrate the negro population."

In contending that assimilation was for whites only, I am not charging that all reformers were conscious racists. There were some who complied with segregationist policies with reluctance and regret, challenging certain forms of segregation. But in housing reform and neighborhood work they nonetheless followed these policies. This study also shows that the same white ethnics whose plight had inspired the housing movement were themselves active segregationists. Again, I do not mean to suggest (as so many commentators on the contemporary resistance to residential integration have done, without any justification, over the past dozen years) that the ethnics were somehow more bigoted than the natives. The immigrants were assimilated—on their own terms as much as the reformers', without forfeiting their identity—and by the 1920s they were fanning out across the metropolis. Wherever they lived, in old neighborhoods or new, Catholics and Jews of foreign stock joined together with their native neighbors in drawing and holding the color line. This was one matter in which Irish Americans, Polish Americans, and Jewish Americans really were indistinguishable from all other white Americans.

The Slum and the Ghetto, then, without setting out to undermine reputations, makes a critical assessment of middle-class reform, and it addresses the question that ethnic Americans have so often asked:

"If *we* did it, why can't *they*?" The answer, as I hope this book shows, is that contrary to popular and academic tradition, "we" (I am ethnic, raised on Chicago's South Side, of Irish Catholic stock) never experienced the ghetto and therefore never had to escape it. In Chicago and all across urban America, blacks continue to face, after all of these decades, a kind of residential confinement that is unique. To turn the familiar question around, "If we didn't have to do it, why should they?"

TLP
Austin, Texas
September, 1977

Acknowledgments

This book is a revision of my doctoral dissertation, "The House and the Neighborhood: Housing Reform and Neighborhood Work in Chicago, 1880–1930," which I submitted—"finally," as everyone who knew me said, friend and foe alike—to the University of Chicago in 1974. I first thought of writing it when, as a student in Professor Richard Wade's class on the American city, I watched his slide lecture on tenement life. That was nearly twelve years ago, and from that day to this, I have had more than a little help from my friends—much more. Writing is always a personal, private matter, yet there were times when the writing of this book resembled one of those community barn-raisings of frontier lore.

In the early years of research, the Ford Foundation and the National Institute of Mental Health granted substantial fellowships through the University of Chicago's Center for Urban Studies. Without this aid and the regular assistance of my wife's parents, Mary Anne and Robert J. Sugrue, I would have had to drive a CTA bus many more miles than I actually did. Driving the bus was a tremendous educational experience, invaluable for an urban historian, but you could do just so much of it and still get through the grind that is graduate school. Much later the University Research Institute of the University of Texas provided summer grants to assist in completion of the dissertation and then its revision for publication.

Among fellow students at Chicago who transcended the traditional cannibalism of Ph.D. candidates were Paul Green, Steve Trimble, Glen Holt, David Johnson, Perry Duis, Howard Rabinowitz, James Sanders, and especially Joel Schwartz. Professor Arthur Mann's criticisms sharpened the thesis and led to the emphasis reflected in the present title; his advice, "don't let them rush you into print," I followed too well, resulting in all that gnashing of teeth and tearing of hair in the offices of Oxford University Press.

At the University of Texas I have had the good fortune to serve under two thoughtful and patient chairmen, Clarence Lasby and Standish Meacham. Standish, along with Ronnie Dugger and Lisa Hazel, read the manuscript and suggested revisions. My friend James Curtis, now at the University of Delaware, was the most considerate of critics and an unfailing source of moral support. Brian Levack helped out with proofreading, and during prolonged crises, his wife Nancy helped my wife Anne with the shopping so that I could stay at my desk. Susan Bash typed a great deal of the original manuscript, and her husband Frank, an astronomer, kept assuring me that the stars were aligned in my favor when it really didn't look that way.

My students have been tolerant, kind, and helpful. I can list only a handful of those I want to thank: Shirley and Rodney Kelley, Craig Swearingen, Jean Kealing, Susan Rubin, Richard Tansey, Patrick Carroll, Cathy Brannon, and Gloria Goldblatt. Gloria volunteered to do a lot of the final typing, including most of the footnotes and the index: It is impossible adequately to thank someone who has typed footnotes and an index.

The people who granted me interviews are cited in the notes, except for the people of Garden Homes, who preferred anonymity. One original settler of Garden Homes told me he would not mind being thanked, as distinct from being cited. George McInerney, Jr., was a hospitable guide to his neighborhood. My favorite interview was with "the woman from St. Columbanus," who is my mother, Rose Mary Philpott. When she came down to Texas for a visit, she too did some typing.

In Chicago, Pat Ireland let me borrow his only copy of a manuscript he wrote forty-five years ago about a settlement house. The Metropolitan Housing and Planning Council let me prowl through their library and files. Louise C. Wade shared freely her knowledge of reform in the city.

At different stages of my life, I, like many who have become teachers, was deeply influenced by gifted and compelling teachers. In my case there were four in particular; and though only one of them was directly involved with this book I want to acknowledge my debt to the other three: Sister Mary Patrick Simpkin, Brother R. M. Coogan, and Robert W. McCluggage. The fourth teacher was Richard C. Wade. He inspired my research on this topic and guided it through to the end. In his commitment to scholarship and teaching, in his direct involvement in community issues, and in his ability to know at close hand conditions like those described in this book without losing either his hope or humor, he has been a unique example, and a great and special friend.

Another friend, Archie Motley of the Chicago Historical Society, gave indispensable aid with source materials. No one knows the sources as well as Archie. Along with the world's tallest building, Chicago can claim the world's greatest manuscript curator.

The last people I encountered in the process of publishing this book were the publishers. I am grateful to Susan Rabiner and Parke Puterbaugh of Oxford University Press for their proficiency, patience, and friendly consideration.

Finally, there is Anne. In my first four years of graduate school we had three babies, a record sure to stand at the University of Chicago and possibly a world's record. Over the next seven years she bore far more than her share of the task of tending to our three children, who have grown up asking, "Is Daddy still working on *that*?" Meanwhile she was typing draft after draft and doing much of the work on the tables and the maps. She kept our household from going under like the storied House of Usher, and she encouraged me to go on, even through those times when I was ready to give it all up and go back to driving the bus.

❧

Postscript, 1990

This book appears in paperback because of the generosity of Sheldon Meyer, of Oxford Press, and the zeal of David Nasaw and Jack Wilson of Wadsworth, three gracious men.

THE SLUM AND THE GHETTO

PART I ❧

The Slum

The house is very largely the standard of the neighborhood. It is the neighborhood social unit . . . the stability of the community depends upon this question of better housing. . . .

—Graham Taylor, "The House and the Neighborhood," *Proceedings of the Sixth National Conference on Housing,* 1917 (New York, n.d.), pp. 306–7.

Let us at least give our boys and girls a chance to be decent by starting them in the kind of houses where there is light and air, room for decency and delicacy, where life may grow normally, where ideals may be planted, where the right ideals of life may be fostered. . . .

—Harriet Vittum, "The House and the Delinquent Child," ibid., pp. 317–18.

Graham Taylor and Harriet Vittum were two of Chicago's leading neighborhood workers. Years of residence in the city's tenement districts made them housing reformers as well. Like most participants in the movement to improve the habitations of the working people, they had no illusions that decent dwellings would solve the problems of the slum population. They were aware that bad housing was not the cause of all evil. On the other hand, they knew that the misery they saw in the slums was connected in some way with bad housing.

"Our spot maps match," Harriet Vittum told fellow delegates to the National Housing Conference in 1917:

> . . . the highest infant death rate, the highest tuberculosis death rate, the greatest juvenile delinquency, exactly match the spot map indicating the greatest congestion, showing that all the evil conditions will unite in one great spot over the bad places.

How these conditions related one to another was not clear to Vittum, but she told her audience that she was certain they were "interrelated." "We cannot possibly separate them," she said.

Harriet Vittum, head resident at Northwestern University Settlement, then described for her audience the experience of one fifteen-year-old Polish resident of a slum neighborhood near the settlement. The girl took poison when she discovered she was pregnant. Learning what had happened, Vittum went to help her while the family awaited the arrival of an ambulance.

The girl's family lived up three flights of stairs in a building that occupied the rear of a lot. Another building stood in front of it. As Vittum entered the flat, she told her audience, the father "and two or three men boarders and two or three small boys" were asleep on the kitchen floor. The mother was awake, but she was lying on the floor of the next room. With her on the floor were "one or two little children and one or two women boarders." As Vittum glanced out the room's window she realized she was looking at the wall of the front building. She could have put her hand out and touched that wall.

In the remaining, third, room, on a bed that took up most of the floor space, lay the girl. With her were two small children, asleep. As Vittum stood there, waiting for the ambulance to come, she wondered if she had any right to bring the girl back "from the haven which she had tried to reach to the misery and hopelessness of the life she was living in that awful place."[1]

Scenes such as this moved settlement workers to fight for tenement reform. Graham Taylor believed that the people of the tenements had to be "better trained and disciplined" as well as better housed. He thought that housing reform was crucial because without it no amount of training and discipline could transform the people. A disorderly family could "unmake" a decent house, he told the audience of reformers, but a congested tenement could destroy a good family, too.[2]

When the National Housing Association met in Chicago in 1917, the city's tenement problem was already more than sixty years old. And the movement to control slum conditions—and slum dwellers—was in its fourth decade. An era of housing reform was coming to a close; another was about to begin.

The first era had begun with the labor riots of 1877. In response to that crisis the most powerful citizens of Chicago had exerted two forms of control on the turbulent masses. One was repression; the other reform. The great reform experiment of the period was the creation of a model town on the outskirts of the city. The features that would most clearly mark subsequent housing-reform efforts were present in the town of Pullman: privatism, environmentalism, paternalism, and racism. Pullman was reform on a strictly business basis. The industrialist who built the community believed that "everything depends upon surroundings," and he attempted to control every part of the physical and social setting. George M. Pullman ruled his town absolutely, or tried to, and said that the residents were his "children." And he drew the color line: The community was a crazy quilt of creeds and nationalities, but everyone in it was white.[3]

The Pullman experiment ended in disaster in 1894, when the townspeople rebelled against their industrial benefactor's rule. The upheaval at Pullman persuaded many members of "the favored classes" that reform, at least ambitious reform, was pointless. Other people questioned the place of paternalism in a society that was supposed to be democratic. Settlement workers and their allies tried to carry on reform along new lines. They did not seriously consider measures that would violate the business creed. Convinced that the "worst housing problem" was among the city's "foreign people," they paid little attention to the housing needs of blacks. They drew the color line almost unthinkingly, as a matter of course. What was new about their endeavor was their determination to work "with" the people of the slums, not "for" them, to solve the problems associated with bad housing.[4]

In practice the settlement workers failed to overcome their own tendency to be paternalistic toward the poor. Regulating tenement conditions, it turned out, involved regulating the tenement dwellers. And after a decade and a half of regulation, the tenements of Chicago were still miserable places to live in. They were more crowded than ever. When the National Housing Association convened in 1917, Chicago was on the brink of another crisis, the worst one yet.

CHAPTER 1 ❧

Tenements and Immigrants

The immigrants constituted at any early date a problem for the charitable and, of course, a housing problem.
—Edith Abbott, *The Tenements of Chicago, 1908–1935* (Chicago, 1936), p. 26.

THE GROWTH OF CHICAGO IN THE NINETEENTH CENTURY WAS A SPECTACLE that astounded the world. In 1830 the site was just a swamp near the southwest shore of Lake Michigan. Fifty people, living in a dozen log huts scattered along the banks of a sluggish river that emptied into the lake, had the place to themselves. By 1890 this inauspicious spot was the second city of the Western Hemisphere in population and in manufactures, and it was one of the five great metropolises of the globe.

At first the town grew slowly. It took eleven years for the population to reach 5,000. After that the number of Chicagoans soared (see Table 1.1), passing 50,000 in 1853, 100,000 in 1860, and 300,000 in 1871. For a while it looked as if 1871 would mark the terminal date in the career of the fastest-growing city in the history of the world. A fire roared out of control, consuming four square miles of densely built-up territory, leveling the downtown area, and leaving one-third of the people homeless.

TABLE 1.1. POPULATION OF CHICAGO, 1840–1930

Year	*Population*	*Year*	*Population*
1840	4,470	1890	1,099,850
1850	29,963	1900	1,698,575
1860	109,260	1910	2,185,283
1870	298,977	1920	2,701,705
1880	503,185	1930	3,376,438

Source: U.S. Census Reports, 1840–1930.

But Chicago rose from the ashes. By 1880 its population exceeded 500,000, and it doubled within ten years. The eighties was the first of five successive decades in which the city grew by half a million or more. Chicago's "I will" spirit was unstoppable. For Americans the city's dramatic rise gave proof of the inevitability of progress in the New World. Chicago was the ultimate American success story.[1]

"The dynamics of its rapid growth," St. Clair Drake and Horace Cayton would write in their classic *Black Metropolis,* were "the pull of the American Dream and the push of hunger and discontent and restlessness." In the eight years from 1848 to 1856, Chicago made itself the focal point of the continent's inland waterways and railways. It collected, processed, and distributed the produce and natural resources of Mid-America, potentially the most grain-rich, timber-rich, and mineral-rich area in the world. Chicago was always a marketplace, exchanging the raw materials of its hinterland for finished products. In the beginning it had to import those products from older cities. Increasingly after 1850 the city became a workshop, manufacturing goods for local and regional consumption and exporting the surplus all across the continent, and then around the world.[2]

The burgeoning steel mills, slaughterhouses, lumberyards, freight warehouses, mail-order establishments, and retail stores needed hands to do the lifting, hauling, slicing, stacking, selling. A vast city of houses, factories, stores, and streets was, literally, on the make in Chicago. It became *the* place to go for work, especially the kind of heavy, dirty work that required no more qualification than a strong back and a readiness to sweat for bread. The legend grew that if a man couldn't "make it" in Chicago, he couldn't make it anywhere. So the people swarmed to the city in hopes of making it.

TABLE 1.2. SOURCES OF INCREASE IN CHICAGO POPULATION, 1830–1900, 1860–1900

Decade	*Total Increase in Population**	*Increase in Foreign-Born Population**	*Increase in Black Population**	*Increase in White Population from U.S. Outside Chicago***	*Increase in Births over Deaths***
1830–1840	4,450				400
1840–1850	25,493		270		2,000
1850–1860	79,297	38,942	632		10,000
1860–1870	189,717	89,993	2,736	63,000	30,000
1870–1880	204,208	60,302	2,789	95,000	50,000
1880–1890	596,665	245,807	7,791	144,000	100,000
1890–1900	598,725	136,446	15,879	265,000	170,000
1860–1900	1,589,315	532,488	29,195	567,000	350,000

Sources: For columns marked *, *U.S. Census Reports,* 1840–1900; for columns marked **, estimates adapted from Homer Hoyt, *One Hundred Years of Land Values in Chicago* (Chicago, 1933), table 30, p. 284.
Note: Before 1850 no exact data are available for increase in foreign-born population.

They came from all over the world, but mainly from the countrysides of Europe and the prairies of America. In 1850 half of Chicago's inhabitants were immigrants (see Table 1.2). Fifty years later the foreign-born and their children comprised nearly four-fifths of the population. Immigrants accounted for 33.5 percent of the net population increase from 1860 to 1900. Fugitives from the farmlands and hamlets of the United States accounted for a slightly greater share, 35.6 percent.

Paradoxically, in the same decades when hundreds of millions of acres of land fell to the plow for the first time, millions of people abandoned the fields for big cities. The revolutionary new machines that mowed and reaped the plains—and displaced much of the rural population—were manufactured in Chicago. Many country lads unable to make a living in farming ended up in Chicago making agricultural machinery. In that industry, as in others, the American "buckwheats" competed for jobs against peasants uprooted from the soil of Europe. The excess of births over deaths added increasingly to the population, but migration was always the greatest source of growth, even in slack periods, when the economic pull of the city was weakest.[3]

A few years before the Great Chicago Fire, a journalist-historian named James Parton ventured from the East to appraise the new city. The frontier metropolis of 220,000 dazzled the much-traveled Parton. "In the heart of town the stranger beholds blocks of stores solid, lofty and in the most recent taste, hotels of great magnificence and public buildings that would be creditable to any city," he informed the *Atlantic Monthly*'s sophisticated readers in 1867. "As the visitor passes along," he declared, "he sees at every moment some new evidence that he has arrived in a rich metropolis." Nothing that met Parton's eye failed to delight him.

Chicago seemed to have everything that New York City had, or at least everything worth having. The older city exhibited the extremes of opulence and indigence, and in 1863 the poor had streamed out of their wretched tenements and staged a massive, murderous riot. But in the lake city, Parton encountered no one who was poor. Chicago, he concluded happily, was free of slums. The well-to-do occupied "the beautiful avenues" that bordered the lake, but ordinary workers lived nearby on "streets of cottages and gardens which have given Chicago the name of the Garden City." Thrifty workmen owned their homes, and the typical renting family had "a whole house" to live in, not a flat. "In all Chicago," exulted Parton, "there is not one tenement house." [4]

In a way the journalist was right. Instead of one tenement there were thousands. By "tenement house" Parton probably meant a building three stories tall or higher with more than one family living on each floor. That was the sort of tenement that blighted New York City, and Chicago, as yet, had few of them. At the time Parton wrote, the typical Chicago tenement was a frame dwelling of one or two stories, without water or plumbing, heated by a stove, and built for a single family, but occupied by two or more.

If Parton had looked more closely as he toured downtown, he would have seen some tenement houses. In those days State Street was "a narrow lane between rows of shanties." Preoccupied with the impressive façades lining Clark and Lake streets, Parton overlooked the run-down rooming houses and rickety two-flat shacks on State. Such crude dwellings had fronted on the better business streets, too, before grander structures preempted their space. Among the newer buildings were multistory barracks, some without windows on the sides. Although they stood in plain view, the visitor did not notice them. Behind the brick façades, hidden from sight, a jumble of old dwellings covered the ground. In the 1850s and 1860s photographers, interested—like Parton—in the visible signs of prosperity, climbed atop the County Court House to shoot a panoramic view of the emerging downtown skyline. What their prints revealed, besides the handsome street frontage, was the grimy network of shacks and shanties that clogged the interior of the blocks.[5]

Most of the tenements were outside the main business section where land prices were lower. From the late 1830s on, factories were located near the river, rimming the main channel, then following its branches north and south. As early as the 1840s shantytowns sprang up near the industrial sites. Respectable people believed that only immigrants inhabited these places. Kilgubbin, elbowed in between the river and its north fork, was supposed to be the exclusive preserve of the lowest sort of Irishmen, the "shanty" Irish. The slum whose boundaries overlapped it on the north was called Swede Town. Canal workers scratched out a patch for themselves beyond the city limits near the juncture of the south branch of the river and the Illinois and Michigan Canal. Known as Hard Scrabble, this suburban slum was a battleground where rival ethnic armies clashed incessantly—so the story went—until the scrappy Irish drove the Germans north across the river into the Lumber Yards region and south to a spot the refugees christened Hamburg. By the late 1860s, Hard Scrabble and Hamburg were inside the municipal borders, and they typified the territory in which six or seven out of ten Chicagoans lived.[6]

James Parton glanced down the "roads of prairie black" with their endless rows of "small wooden houses" and called them garden spots. "Prairie black" was his melodic euphemism for dirt and mud. "The land," another observer noted, "was thickly studded with one-story frame dwellings, cow-stables, pig-sties, corn-cribs, sheds innumerable; every wretched building within four feet of its neighbor, and everything of wood—not a brick or a stone in the whole area." The streets, which lacked sewers and water mains as well as pavement, trailed through a "forest of shanties." The Great Chicago Fire started in one of these huts, and the small frame houses fed the flames like so much kindling.[7]

Visiting journalists were not the only ones who failed to take a close look at "the homes of the humble." The poor neighborhoods, a local reporter commented after the fire, were "a *terra incognita* to respectable Chicagoans" and, he added with unintended irony, to most newsmen as well. This was true even though districts of extreme wealth and extreme "squalor" were often located "within a stone's throw of each other."[8]

The prairie about the city spread out limitlessly from the lake, but the population was concentrated close to the original town site on a particle of the vast landscape. In 1871 four out of five Chicagoans lived within three miles of State and Madison, the once-neglected corner that Potter Palmer was transforming into a thrumming intersection. Horse railways and steam locomotives had been providing commuter service for more than a decade, but Chicago was still a "walking city" because so many workers could not afford to ride.

The homes of the "luxurious classes" occupied three strips of land radiating outward from downtown to the west, north, and south like the spokes of a great half-wheel. Toward the rim of this residential wheel the spaces between the spokes were vacant, but close to the hub all the land was occupied. At the periphery the distance between the wealthy and the poor was spatial as well as social. Near the center the spatial dimension was reduced to the minimum: Residential belts only two to four blocks wide shielded the best districts from the worst. It was in these middle-class buffer zones that newsmen tended to live.[9]

Occasionally, reporters enlivened the front pages with lurid exposés of the dives in the downtown vice districts, but they rarely mentioned the nearby workers' neighborhoods unless there was a fight, a crime, or a fire to report. The day-to-day existence of the common people was not newsworthy. On the other hand, almost anything that the commercial leaders or "society" people did was fit to print. So the habitual beat of the newsmen followed the principal business streets and the finest residential lanes. Except on days when wealthy matrons dispensed their "basket charity" to the needy, society ignored the common folk. So did the press.

After the holocaust of 1871, when reporters trekked to the West Side to find the fire's starting point, they were amazed at the wretchedness of the warrens that had survived. To their eyes the area adjacent to the burned district was like a foreign city. "It had no look of Chicago about it," one man commented. The Chicago they knew was a city of riches; this was a city of rags. It even bore the name of a European capital, Prague, because the residents were not ordinary Americans, supposedly, but Bohemian immigrants.

As they surveyed the scene around 137 DeKoven Street, the reporters could not deny that this other Chicago—Prague—was pocked with tenements. But they comforted themselves with the knowledge that "the sickly tenement system" peculiar to New York City did not afflict the area. It was James Parton's logic all over again: Chicago did not have New York City's housing problem, therefore it had no problem at all. This would become Chicago's stock response to critics of its tenements.[10]

If these reporters had been so disposed, they could have found much to criticize. The property at 137 DeKoven was still largely intact. Everything else on that side of the street was destroyed. The lot was 25 feet by 100 feet. A common laborer named Pat O'Leary had bought it for $500 in 1864, a sum that probably exceeded his annual income by a substantial amount. He put up two shingled shanties with no space between them, so that the double huts looked like one. The front building, which faced the street and had more room in it, he rented out to help pay off the debt on the lot. Forty feet behind the rear building, near the alley, he erected a small barn and a shed for storing coal, stove wood, and wood shavings. At the time of the fire, O'Leary's tenants were Mr. and Mrs. Patrick McLaughlin and their brood of children. O'Leary, his wife, Kate, and their large family lived in the tiny rear tenement. The barn had seven more occupants: a horse, a calf, and five cows (one of which attained celebrity, perhaps undeserved, for kicking over a lantern, igniting her stall, and thus setting fire to Chicago).

The O'Learys stuck out from other families in Prague not because of their Irish origin—their tenants and many of their neighbors were Irish—or the shabbiness of their home—it was typical of the district. They were people of property and standing, with a lot and two houses they could call their own. Contrary to a rumor that circulated after the fire, they were never objects of charity. To augment her husband's meager earnings, Mrs. O'Leary operated an unlicensed dairy out of the barn and delivered milk through the neighborhood. She had a new wagon parked in the dirt alley. The O'Learys were not "lace curtain," but neither were they "shanty" or "pig-shit" Irish. They had ambition; they worked hard. They were landlords, and they were in business for themselves. They were rising in the world as they never could have risen in Ireland. By the standards of Little Bohemia, they were affluent. It was their progress, not their poverty, that was remarkable in Prague.

In the obscurity of DeKoven Street, Pat and Kate O'Leary were living out a version of the American Dream as authentic as the version Potter Palmer was enshrining on State Street. By their enterprise they had amassed holdings that would have been spread out over 160 acres on the countryside. The reporters saw nothing on DeKoven Street to shake their faith in the Chicago success story. Instead of pondering the O'Learys' experience, they wrote about Kate's cow.[11]

The trouble was that the O'Learys crammed everything they had, plus all the worldly possessions of another sizable family, into 2,500 square feet of space. That was all the ground they could afford. Indeed, they had to struggle like Trojans to pay for it. An ordinary Midwest family farm had room enough to hold their miserable lot and 2,787 more just like it. The whole of Prague, with its twenty congested blocks, covered only 62.5 acres (street, alleys, and all). It could have fit into an average-sized farm site two times over with 35 acres to spare. Out on the prairies a homestead like the O'Learys' posed no threat to health and safety. But in an urban setting, squeezed between two properties the same size, with the same sanitary facilities available to rural cabins—that is, none—it was dangerous. Pat O'Leary's Chicago was a slum, and it menaced not only its own inhabitants but those of Potter Palmer's Chicago as well. It took a catastrophic fire to alert the better-off citizens to that fact.

The holocaust engulfed both Chicagos. In dollars the wealthy classes lost the most, because their offices, factories, and residences were so valuable. In other ways the working classes were hit the hardest. Places like Kilgubbin and Swede Town disappeared. About half the territory occupied by low-cost housing went up in flames. Most of the dead, the maimed, the missing, and the displaced were from the slums. Substantial citizens set out at once to rebuild *their* Chicago, and they established a relief committee to provide temporary housing for the homeless poor. In two years the committee built four great frame barracks for the "class of permanent poor" and nearly eight thousand "small but comfortable homes," also frame, for "the better class of laboring people." These emergency dwellings equaled the worst jerry-built huts destroyed in the fire, and they proved to be permanent. Dilapidated yet durable, they stood for decades.[12]

Meanwhile, the merchants remade downtown on a scale far grander than before and built new mansions for themselves to boggle the beholder like nothing that had existed prior to the fire. And a year after the disaster the city fathers took a precaution that proved how much they had learned from the Great Fire. They established a legal perimeter around the city's core within which all new buildings had to be made of noncombustible materials. The ordinance came too late to ban all of the relief committee's emergency firetraps from the city core area, but the "fire limits" did push Pat O'Leary's inflammable Chicago farther away from downtown.

To the extent that the ordinance was enforced, it made the cost of building a house in "the brick area" prohibitive for common laborers. At the same time, land values were rising. Chicagoans of all classes felt the pinch. Until a few years before the fire, all but the poorest families lived on lots at least 50 feet wide. Now the average lot shriveled, as people said, to the width of a shoestring. Hence the name "shoestring lot" for a plot 25 feet by 125 feet. Few families could command more space than that. For most people, living on a lot any larger inevitably meant sharing it with one or more families.

To be able to afford a single-family dwelling, even if it was built of wood on a lot no wider than the shoestring, a middle-class breadwinner had to locate miles from downtown and bear the costs of commuting. The alternatives were to occupy a two-flat or three-flat building farther in or one of the new "apartment houses," which proliferated after 1878, still closer to downtown. The poor had fewer options. They could not afford commuter fare, so the new, outlying developments were closed to them. Land prices and building regulations combined to exclude them from most of the innermost zone as well.

The workers had little choice but to make their homes in the space between the fire limits and the outer zone of desirable subdivisions. In the decades following the fire, they crowded into a widening semicircular belt a mile to two miles across and nearly ten miles from north to south. It started on the North Side, at Fullerton Avenue near Halsted Street, then moved south and west, crossing the north branch of the river to cover most of the West Side up to Western Avenue. On the Lower West Side it extended as far west as California Avenue. Then it cut back, crossed the Illinois and Michigan Canal, swung past the stockyards and the region called Back a' the Yards, and came to a stop at 55th and State.

There were additional poverty areas, inside the "brick area" where the fire had not destroyed all the old frame housing, and in outlying industrial districts, such as South Chicago, where laborers could live and work without having to commute. But it was largely inside the growing semicircular belt that "the tenement system . . . engrafted [itself] on the life of Chicago."[13]

❧

In 1878 Chicago took its first official notice of the tenement problem. The Department of Health, following the New York City definition of a tenement as a dwelling occupied by "more than three families" keeping house in separate compartments, reported that there were 4,896 tenement houses in the city. For the most part these were the homes of "the poorer and dependent classes." Many of the buildings stood on streets without sewers. The contents of privy vaults—"slops and kitchen wash"—fouled the ground and ran through the gutters. Health officials suspected that the infectious diseases that scourged the city started in the tenement districts and spread from there.[14]

In 1881 the state legislature empowered the Department of Health to regulate the sanitary condition of buildings. Previously no health inspector could enter a domicile without the owner's permission unless there was a suspected case of cholera or smallpox on the premises. A year later, G. H. Genung, the department's chief of tenement and factory inspection, reported the initial findings of his small corps of inspectors. Their evidence was impressionistic and fragmentary, but pieced together it pointed unmistakably in the direction of a grim future for Chicago housing.

The inspectors found "dangerous overcrowding in all the poorer districts." They attributed this to "the great and rapid influx of population," which overwhelmed the existing stock of housing. Speculators were enjoying a lucrative business in "the building of tenements" on cramped lots along unimproved streets. Although the profit seekers threw these multistoried rookeries up as hurriedly as possible, they could not build them fast enough to meet the desperate demand of the mass of immigrants for cheap shelter. Homeowners, poor themselves, increasingly converted their meager dwellings into tenements by parceling out portions to renters.

The converted cottages were as "dense in population" as the new barracklike tenements. "Thousands of small houses and cottages arranged for one family are now packed with a family in each room," the chief inspector wrote. His investigators uncovered among Italians cases of even more extreme crowding: "several families living huddled together in one large room, with mere boards and curtains for partitions between their scanty household goods." Additional thousands of immigrant families, "swarming with children of all ages," had their "kitchen, dining room, sitting-room, and sleeping apartment" all crammed into two or three closet-sized rooms.

It seemed to the chief inspector that the tenement problem was an immigrant problem. He calculated that "the whole number of occupants of tenement houses" was "about equal to the foreign population." Germans apparently lived frugally but comfortably in their flats, but "the other nationalities, as a rule, live[d] in close quarters." The only "native Americans" who contributed to the tenement problem were Negroes, and their number was comparatively small. The whites in the slums were foreigners.

Inspector Genung suggested that it was the poverty of the immigrants, not "their nationality," which compelled them to crowd into buildings "unfit for habitation by civilized people." Still, he came close to putting the blame for tenement conditions on the poor immigrants themselves. He ventured the information that immigrants, especially those from Southern and Eastern Europe, had "hereditary peculiarities." Furthermore, he said, "in their trans-Atlantic homes" they customarily lived "in crowded quarters in close proximity to their domestic animals." In their new habitat, Genung reported, the foreigners tended to reproduce Old World conditions, even to the point of sharing their quarters with livestock. The immigrants, he thought, huddled together with their countrymen in "distinct and separate" colonies. Their habit of herding like (and sometimes with) cattle and swine aggravated the problem of overcrowding.

The Bureau of Tenement and Factory Inspection was powerless to correct the abuses it uncovered. Inspector Genung could do little but warn the city about the conditions that were developing. While

Genung was wayward with his ethnic statistics (his estimate of the Italian slum population greatly exceeded the Italian population of the city, for instance), his figures on tenement congestion were accurate. He was probably right when he said that the immigrant population (about 220,000 in 1881) and the tenement population were roughly equivalent in size. And he was right when he declared that it would take "thousands of new tenement buildings to accommodate properly those families who are now compelled to crowd together in homes too small for them."[15]

If Chicago had been willing to take action, and *if* the population could have been frozen at its 1881 level for some years, the city might have had a chance to eliminate the housing shortage and upgrade the stock of shelter. Even under those conditions, it would have been a tremendous task to house every Chicagoan decently and extend adequate services to every neighborhood. As it was, Chicago was not much interested in housing reform, and the population was skyrocketing. It was not until after Genung made his report that the tremendous waves of immigration from Southern and Eastern Europe came breaking in over the city. By 1900 the foreign-born would constitute a population larger than the whole of Chicago had been in 1882. And the poverty of masses of these people would consign them to the meanest streets of the city.

While the poverty belt was piling up with shambling tenements, crammed from cellar to rafters, the well-to-do were establishing certain avenues and boulevards as the showplaces of Chicago. The city had millionaires, almost all of whom had arrived in Chicago with nothing but ambition. To demonstrate their hard-won eminence, they built monumental mansions on Calumet Avenue, Millionaire's Row on Michigan Boulevard, and, later, on Astor Street and Lake Shore Drive. For decades the most spectacular stretch of residential real estate in the city was just south of downtown on Prairie Avenue. In 1873 Marshall Field (the department-store king), Philip Armour (the meat-packing king), and George M. Pullman (the palace-car king) all put up castles there. Within twenty years forty of Chicago's two hundred millionaires had their domains on Prairie between 16th and 21st streets, and all of them were members of the Commercial Club, which restricted its roster to the sixty richest men in town. Prairie Avenue was "the very Mecca of Mammon, the Olympus of the great gods of Chicago." Nowhere else in the world were there streets that presented more glaring contrasts than Prairie and the streets of the poor.

All of the millionaires' homes on Prairie cost upwards of $100,000. Marshall Field's mansion, designed by Richard Morris Hunt, the architect whose credits included the Astor and Vanderbilt estates in New York, was "said to have cost two million dollars," but the price was really in the range of $175,000 to $250,000 including furniture, horses, coaches, and stables. The Pullman palace, according to newspaper reports, was worth $350,000 to $500,000, and these reports were correct. As a rule the millionaires maintained elegant country estates as well. Pullman had three manor houses and a permanent hotel suite in different parts of the country; he journeyed from one to another in a specially built palace car, which cost $38,000.

The money Pullman spent on his personal railroad car would have paid the monthly rents on five thousand tenement flats. For what it cost to build and furnish the Prairie Avenue palaces of Pullman, Field, and Armour, a thousand workingmen could have bought homes of their own, complete with running water, clear of all encumbrance. Each of the "big houses with little families" on Prairie was worth much more than a whole block of "little houses with big families" on a working class street.[16]

In his classic study, *One Hundred Years of Land Values in Chicago*, Homer Hoyt compared the amount of ground covered by the homes of the rich and of the poor (see Figure 1.1). The rich block he selected was on Prairie, between 13th and 20th streets. Marshall Field's palace dominated the middle of the block. Immediately to the north of this block, commanding the northeast corner of 18th and Prairie, stood the three-story gray-stone residence of George M. Pullman. Philip Armour's house was one block south. Across the street, to the west, was another vista of luxurious homes. Behind the block, shading the coach houses at the rear of the lots, and separating the Prairie Avenue bluff from the low-lying Illinois Central train tracks, was a lush woodland. The poor block was on Des Plaines Avenue, about two miles to the northwest, across the river, near the site of Pat O'Leary's humble but celebrated cottage.

At the time of the Great Fire, the poor block was 356 feet wide and covered nearly six and one-half acres of ground. After the fire gutted the area east of it, subdividers, eager to capitalize on the

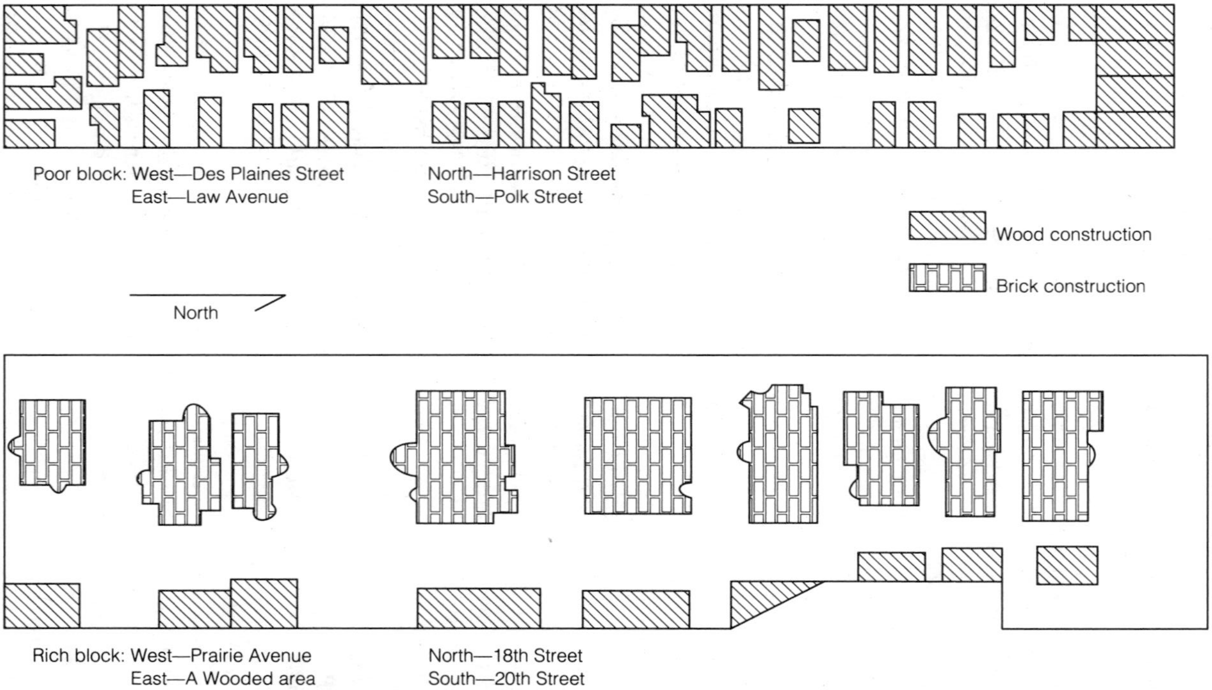
Poor block: West—Des Plaines Street
East—Law Avenue
North—Harrison Street
South—Polk Street
Wood construction
Brick construction
North
Rich block: West—Prairie Avenue
East—A Wooded area
North—18th Street
South—20th Street

FIGURE 1.1. Ground coverage on blocks occupied by poor families and rich families, 1886. (Source: Homer Hoyt, *One Hundred Years of Land Values in Chicago* [Chicago, 1933], p. 289.)

clearance, came in and re-cut the burned-over district into sliver-thin parcels. Although the flames had spared the block on Des Plaines, the real estate men did not. They sliced it lengthwise, making two "new" blocks where before there had been only one. Of the two, the *wider* one had lots only 100 feet deep. Hoyt picked the narrower one to illustrate overcrowding at its extreme.

The lots on this wretched block, which now covered barely two acres, ran an incredibly scant 56 feet from front to rear. Some of these lot stumps were only 20 feet wide. The block was within the "brick area" established in 1872, but either it was entirely built up before the fire limits were set or builders stuck in some additional structures in defiance of the statute. In any case, every one of the fifty-six crude buildings that honeycombed this block was frame. The blocks adjoining it to the north, west, and south were solidly packed with ramshackle wooden houses as well. The section to the east was part frame housing, part brick barracks, part factories, and part wilderness grown over with weeds.

The only frame structures on Prairie were the carriage houses, where the horses were stabled. The horses had considerably more room, and more pleasant surroundings, than did the average tenement dwellers on Des Plaines. The cottages of the poor were pinched onto lots less than half as big as the standard shoestring lot, whereas the rich men's grounds were nearly six times the standard size. Each mansion, Homer Hoyt commented, had "yard space enough to provide sites for from ten to twenty of these cottages of the poor."[17]

If Chicago's solid citizens were shocked by the glaring inequality that existed between Prairie Avenue at one end of the social scale and Des Plaines Street at the other, they gave no sign of it. Most families lived at a level between the two extremes. The middle class was well aware of the magnificence of Prairie Avenue. To ambitious Chicagoans, the mansions were proof of the promise of mobility. If they noticed the shacks, they accepted them as evidence of the depth from which a man could hope to rise. Ironically, Prairie Avenue and Des Plaines Street persuaded Chicagoans that democracy in Chicago was not failing, but was triumphant.

This was not the only irony. In the postfire decades, as the tenement came into its own as the common workman's house, Chicago became world-famous not for its cruel slums but rather for its mansions and office buildings. The men who designed the most tasteful residences and the towering skyscrapers—it was they who *invented* the skyscraper—were William Le Baron Jenney, John Wellborn Root, Daniel Hudson Burnham, Louis Sullivan, and Frank Lloyd Wright. They created modern architecture in the process. Collectively they came to be known, together with their disciples and imitators, as the Chicago School. What is ironic is the fact that this group of architects, especially Sullivan and Wright, won renown not only for the power of their imagination and the genius of their craft but also for some supposed ability to express *democracy* through building design. Whatever meaning democracy had for them, it did not include building homes for the people. The workers had no architects.[18]

The Chicago School built brilliantly. Their designs were modern, they were functional, but in practice they were not democratic. Downtown, the architects brought forth temples of commerce; elsewhere they built sacristies for the high priests of the temples. The finest residential work done by Louis Sullivan and Frank Lloyd Wright included the Charnley House, the Winslow House, Robie House—mansions all. Their commissions were almost exclusively confined to the suburbs and the plushest parts of the city. In the tenement areas, in the zone of skilled workingmen's homes, in ordinary middle-class apartment districts, they built practically nothing.

Wright designed just one complex—Francisco Terrace Apartments in the West Side's high-grade corridor—which was within the means of moderate-income renters. And he drew up the plans for a Unitarian social center conducted by his uncle, Rev. Jenkin Lloyd Jones. It was a massive, forbidding, factorylike building. Years later Wright said of his design for Abraham Lincoln Centre (the name was democratic enough), "I have always hated it." A few minor figures in the Chicago School also designed social settlements. These institutions were compounds where dwelt upper-class reformers bent on benefiting the poor. The buildings stood out starkly against the grim backdrop of the "horrid little houses" of the neighborhood people.[19]

"Chicago's most profound utterance in democratic art," one scholar has written, with no intended sarcasm, is a tomb that Louis Sullivan designed in 1890 for the interment of the wealthy Getty family. In the same year, John Wellborn Root produced one of his few notable plans for a noncommercial building: the First Infantry Armory at 16th and Michigan. These statements together make a fitting epitaph for the Chicago School's contribution to democracy and to an architecture for the masses.[20]

The most grandiloquent expression of Chicago architecture was the White City, the sprawling fairgrounds built for the World's Columbian Exposition of 1893. The work of the Chicago School's lesser lights, abetted by droves of conventional practitioners who melded their assorted styles into a confused pseudo-classical composite, it emerged from the drawing boards a monumental mishmash. The thing mortified Sullivan and Wright, but the multitudes went wild over it. In a base sort of way, the White City was democratic architecture. It was a big, gaudy, plaster-of-paris dreamland, full of pomp and splendor, where grime was whitewashed away and, as one visitor put it, there was no place for poverty. Twenty-one million people paid to mill around the grounds. Many Chicago tenement dwellers were undoubtedly among them. At the White City, set along the South Side lakefront amid lagoons and wooded lanes, a person could forget his troubles for a while, and the poor had much to forget.[21]

❧

It was while the whole world was watching the White City that a group of investigators tried to turn "the searchlight of inquiry" onto the gray city of the tenements. The investigators were agents of the U.S. Department of Labor, which was conducting a comparative survey of "slums" in New York City, Philadelphia, Baltimore, and Chicago. The department accepted the dictionary definition of slum—"an area of dirty back streets, especially when inhabited by a squalid and criminal population"—and asked the residents of Hull-House, a social settlement on the West Side, to select a representative study area. The settlement workers picked the area they knew best, the district east of Hull-House, from Halsted Street to State Street between Polk and 12th streets.[22]

Florence Kelley, a settlement resident, took charge of the investigation. Operating from their base at Hull-House, the canvassers spent ten weeks checking every room of every flat in the third-of-a-square-mile area. In 1894 the Department of Labor reported the survey results in tabular form in *The Slums of Great Cities.* A year later the settlement staff issued its own report, minus tables but with an elaborate series of color-coded maps. Together the volumes presented the most complete picture yet of America's urban housing problem.

The district was a jumble of land uses. Factories, warehouses, railroad yards, and stores took up much of the space; the 1,273 dwellings were jammed into the remaining blocks and parcels. Most of the people lived in thirty small blocks between Halsted and the river. East of the river the five occupied blocks were part of an "openly and flagrantly vicious" red-light district, where families rented rooms only when they had no place else to go. The population was largely "foreign," as the settlement workers put it. Of the 19,654 people, nearly 58 percent were first-generation immigrants, compared to 41 percent in the city as a whole. And the bulk of them were from the ethnic groups that were newest to the city and, in the opinion of the Hull-House staff, "least adaptable": Italians, Russian and Polish Jews, and Bohemians. Altogether, representatives of twenty-six different ethnic groups inhabited the area.[23]

Both the government and the Hull-House reports reinforced the tendency to treat "slum" and "foreign colony" as interchangeable terms. The Hull-House volume contained invaluable information on just what a foreign colony was, but no one absorbed it. While the government report aggregated data for the entire district, the Hull-House maps showed both the ethnicity and the income of families *lot-by-lot* for each block. The "nationality maps" give the most detailed breakdown of ethnic clustering ever done in any American city.

These maps were overlooked or dismissed at the time, and they have been ignored ever since. Knowing "whether a particular Russian Jew lives on the north or south side of Maxwell Street," one reviewer complained, was as pointless as knowing "just how thick is the dirt on the faces of the Italian children in a certain ward." "Such facts," he said, "are of no importance in solving the great questions involved in this study." The text of the report was not especially helpful in interpreting the maps; the authors did not seem to appreciate the significance of the evidence they had compiled so painstakingly.[24]

What the maps showed was tremendous ethnic mixture. The popular view was that a district with twenty-six ethnic groups must be broken up into twenty-six separate little "ghettos," each inhabited exclusively by a single ethnic group. Such ghettos do not appear on the nationality maps. Yet the Hull-House residents themselves spoke of immigrant "colonies" as if they were spatial entities that could be pinpointed on a map. The question of whether or not ethnic colonies were physical ghettos would turn out to be critically important. At the time, the only ethnic facts that seemed to matter were the basic ones: Slum dwellers were immigrants and, increasingly, they were Southern and Eastern European peasants. What the reformers wanted to document more than anything else was the kind of life the slum was offering to these poor simple people.

The information in the volumes was appalling. The laborers in the district worked, on the average, over sixty hours to earn ten dollars (a rate of sixteen cents per hour). They paid eight to ten dollars monthly in rent, and the housing they received in return was crowded, dark, and filthy.

The average building, though only one or two stories high, held three tenant families. While the families were large, averaging five members each, the flats were small. Over half had three rooms or fewer. Seventy-three percent of the rooms had insufficient light, and 74 percent had inadequate ventilation. There were 811 bedrooms without windows. Sixty percent of the tenants had less than 400 cubic feet of air in their sleeping quarters. That amount was supposed to be the bare minimum essential for health, but one out of five tenants had less than *half* of that.

The streets now had sewers, but only 26 percent of the families had access to a water closet. The rest had to rely on repulsive privy vaults, many of which were outside, in yards or under porches. Fewer than 3 percent of the families lived in a building with a bath. The condition of the yards, alleys, and streets was filthier in Chicago than even in New York, Philadelphia, and Baltimore, which were older, dirty, industrial cities. The authors of the federal report (who tried to take the "edge off" the findings, in the opinion of the Hull-House people) estimated that at least 162,000 Chicagoans, roughly 14 percent of the population, lived in areas as bad as the slum district.[25]

Dismal as the statistics were, a Hull-House resident noted, they conveyed only a partial idea of "the filthy and rotten tenements, the dingy courts and tumble-down sheds, the foul stables and dilapidated outhouses, the broken sewer-pipes, the piles of garbage fairly alive with diseased odors, and the numbers of children filling every nook, working and playing in every room, eating and sleeping in every window-sill, pouring in and out of every door, and seeming literally to pave every scrap of 'yard.' "[26]

The settlement workers divided the tenements into three main types, each of which cast its special curse on its occupants. The old "pioneer" shanties of one and two stories were slowly rotting away. In the advanced stages of deterioration, they were practically uninhabitable, but they were not abandoned until they were at the point of collapse. They were a menace, but their decrepitude seemed to guarantee their gradual disappearance.

The newer tenements of three, four, or even five stories were sturdier. Because the district was within the fire limits, these buildings were usually brick. Their "very permanence," the settlement staff feared, was "an evil." These large tenements looked better than the frame shacks, but inside them the crowding was more intense, the atmosphere more stifling, and the darkness more pervasive. They covered most of the lot, and their height blocked the light and air from adjacent buildings.

The last type was "the deadly rear tenement." This was a building that did not front on the street but occupied the yard space behind another building. The worst small houses could not compare in "hideousness" with the massive brick tenements, a Hull-House resident remarked, *unless* they were stuck in back of other houses—then they became the most wretched habitations of all.[27]

Sometimes, speculators built new tenements behind older ones, but more often someone picked up an old house that faced the street, plunked it down near the alley, and then put up a new structure in front. Because the old buildings were unencumbered with plumbing fixtures or foundations, pushing them back was not difficult. For many poor families, occupying a rear tenement was part of an elaborate and brutal home-buying strategy.

First, the family bought a cottage and paid for it by renting out as many of the rooms as possible. Then they moved it to the rear and, with a loan secured by the house and lot, built a more substantial dwelling in front of the old one. Now they rented out all the flats in the new building while remaining in the rear cottage until they had made considerable headway in paying off their debt. When they felt they could afford to forego the rent on one of the large flats, they moved into the front building themselves and continued to eke out a rental income from the old cottage until it practically fell apart. Finally, they dismantled the rear tenement and used the scraps for fuel.

At last the family had a yard, which they could leave vacant or rent out. Peddlers and shopkeepers with delivery wagons needed places to stable their horses, and homeowners whose land was overtaken by industry were glad to get a cheap spot on which to relocate their cottages. Industrial invasion was not reducing the area's population: The settlement workers observed, ". . . as factories are built people crowd more and more closely into the houses about them, and rear tenements fill up the few open spaces left."[28]

A family occupied a rear tenement at considerable risk to their well-being. The O'Learys had dwelt in a rear tenement, and the disaster that befell them was an extreme example of what could happen to anyone. If the houses caught fire—and they were extremely vulnerable—they were potential death traps. Congestion was extreme, and the front doors opened on the alleys, where outhouses and stables abounded and refuse and manure accumulated. Frequently, the tenement's lower floor was a stable or a compartment for privies.

Families had precious little room for "eating, sleeping, being born, and dying," and sometimes they used what space they had for working as well. Some families took in washing and ironing. Laborers in the garment trades were lucky to work as cutters in a factory or "inside shop"; the unlucky ones finished cut pieces in tenement flats. This was the infamous "sweating system." Jobbers ("sweaters") parceled out materials from clothing manufacturers to people who worked on them either in the sweater's house or in their own. The horrors of this homework inspired the term *sweatshop*.

Florence Kelley was the Illinois chief of factory inspection at the same time that she was supervising the federal government's slum investigation. She contributed two biting chapters on the sweatshops and child labor to *Hull-House Maps and Papers.* The settlement staff believed that the men in the slums put their wives and children to work for the same reason that they lived in such miserable houses and took in boarders. Wages for common labor were too low to support decent family life.[29]

When the federal canvassers asked the tenement dwellers if they were suffering from disease, the people overwhelmingly replied no. On the basis of these interview statistics, the Department of Labor reported that sickness was no more prevalent in the slums than elsewhere. The settlement staff disputed that finding. The district's inhabitants were "noticeably undersized and unhealthy," they claimed, and they suggested that the haggard appearance of the people was due less to "racial traits" than to housing and working conditions. It was the garment workers who looked especially "dwarfed and ill-fed"; their "stooping gait, and their narrow chests and cramped hands" were products of the sweatshop, not heredity. Tuberculosis and intestinal disorders were most common among occupants of rear tenements and the dark, gloomy tall tenements. City health statistics showed that mortality among children was great, and even though the ethnic groups from which the children came were noted for swarthy complexions, the babies looked "starved and wan."[30]

The gulf between the way "people of quality" lived and the way slum people were forced to live—indeed, the difference between the most minimal standards and slum conditions—scandalized the residents of Hull-House. They resolved to keep the searchlight trained on the poor districts until Chicago paid attention and took action. Florence Kelley kept issuing her scalding reports as long as she lasted as the state's factory inspector, and the city's health commissioner augmented her efforts with his bulletins. But the city seemed to dismiss all of the information (much as a reactionary governor dismissed Mrs. Kelley) until 1901, when an authoritative study entitled *Tenement Conditions in Chicago* appeared. A year after its publication, the City Council belatedly overhauled Chicago's primitive housing codes.

Robert Hunter, the author of the report, resided at Hull-House. He was a fugitive from a sleepy little Indiana town called Terre Haute, birthplace of two more famous migrants to the big city, Theodore Dreiser and Eugene V. Debs. Chicago did to Hunter what it did to many another small-town boy: It simultaneously exhilarated and appalled him. In 1896 he went to work for Chicago's Board of Charities, a private welfare organization. Three years later he became secretary of the City Homes Association, a new reform group founded by settlement workers and funded by well-meaning rich people. After failing to persuade the municipal authorities to conduct a citywide tenement census, the association made a survey of its own under Hunter's direction.[31]

The object of the inquiry was to secure an accurate picture of conditions prevailing in the great semicircular zone of tenements. This area, which had been at the outer edge of the municipality before annexations added a 154-square-mile residential rim around the periphery, was now the great "Inner Belt" of Chicago (see Map 1.1), with a population exceeding seven hundred thousand. Middle-class corridors cut through it, so not all of its inhabitants were tenement dwellers, but most were. Because a canvass of the whole tenement belt was beyond the resources of the City Homes Association, Hunter had to select "representative" study areas.[32]

Preliminary surveys revealed that some districts were too wretched to be representative. Both Back a' the Yards, near the slaughterhouses and city garbage dumps, and South Chicago, smothered in the smudge of the steel mills, suffered extremely from their industrial environments. South Chicago was a satellite slum, several miles outside the Inner Belt, but Hunter rejected it not for that reason but for its overwhelming filth. Its streets, like those Back a' the Yards, still lacked sewers and pavement. The houses in both areas stood in stagnant pools of sewage. No other parts of Chicago or, possibly, the world exhibited "such abominable outside conditions." Hunter also excluded the small but growing South Side Black Belt and Little Sicily on the Lower North Side, because the interiors of the houses were the worst in the city.

Finally, Hunter chose three typical districts from the "wilderness of bad housing and sanitary neglect." District 1, the largest, was a 44-block section just east of Hull-House (see Map 1.2, page 30).

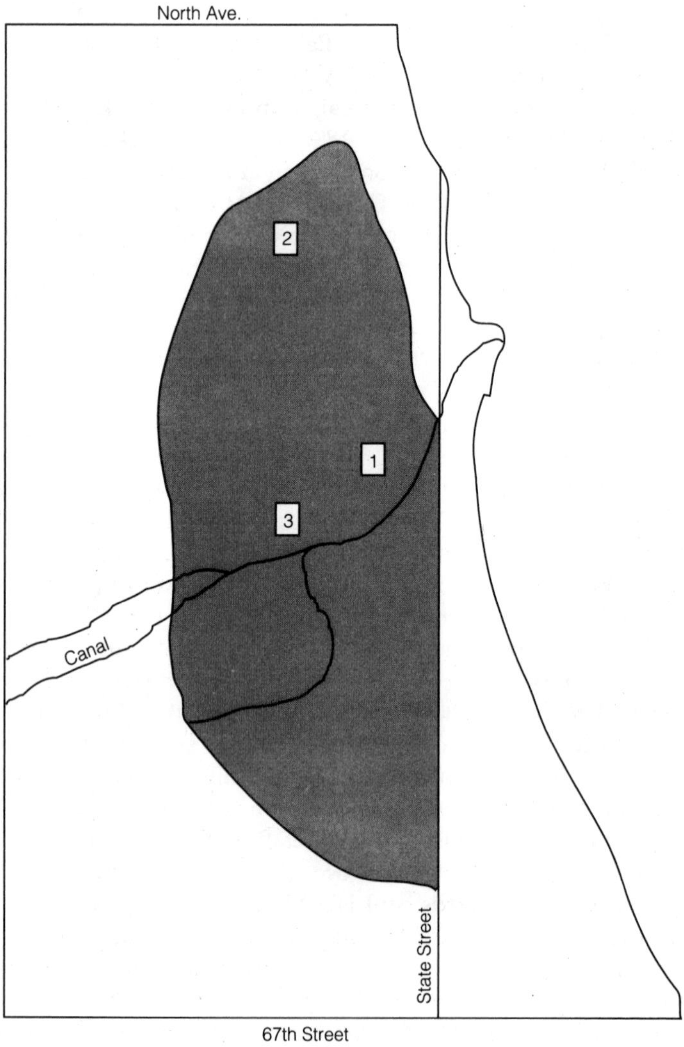

Chicago's "Inner Belt"

1. "Little Italy" and "The Ghetto"
2. "Polonia"
3. "Pilsen"

MAP 1.1. Chicago's "Inner Belt." Showing districts investigated by City Homes Association in 1900–1901. (Source: Robert Hunter, *Tenement Conditions in Chicago, Report by the Investigating Committee of the City Homes Association* [Chicago, 1901], p. 10.)

The 1893 survey had covered most of it. District 2 consisted of ten blocks opposite the Polish church St. Stanislaus Kostka. District 3, nine blocks in extent, was southwest of Hull-House.

All of the neighborhoods were immigrant enclaves, but Hunter, unlike the earlier Hull-House investigators, did not emphasize the fact that the tenement areas were "foreign colonies." Nor did he go into detail about their ethnic composition. So closely were the enclaves identified with individual ethnic groups that the area about 12th Street in District 1 was called Little Italy, while the area below it was the Jewish Ghetto. Similarly, District 2 belonged to Polonia, or Little Poland, and District 3 was part of Pilsen, or Little Bohemia (see Map 1.2). At one point, in an appendix, Hunter indicated that "many other nationalities" had representatives in each district, but elsewhere he adopted the common shorthand and referred to the "Italian quarter," "the Polish district," and so on, as if each enclave were ethnically homogeneous. He did not bother with fine distinctions about the populations. His main concern was to describe the physical environment in which the people lived.[33]

Above all, they were victims of oppressive overcrowding. The combined area of the three districts came to less than a third of a square mile, but the population was 45,643. Factories, stores, streets, and alleys sharply reduced the ground available for residences. Moreover, 70 percent of the buildings were only one or two stories high. The density of population on the *floor* space, as opposed to the ground space, Hunter argued, was equal to the worst in the world. And in the "Polish quarter" the ground density, which was only a fraction of "the real density," was "three times that of the most crowded portions of Tokyo, Calcutta, and many other Asiatic cities."

Nine of the ten blocks in Little Poland held over 1,000 people each, as did three of the nine blocks in Pilsen. In District 1 the blocks were smaller and the buildings were shorter (only one out of four exceeded two stories). Still, three blocks had over 1,000

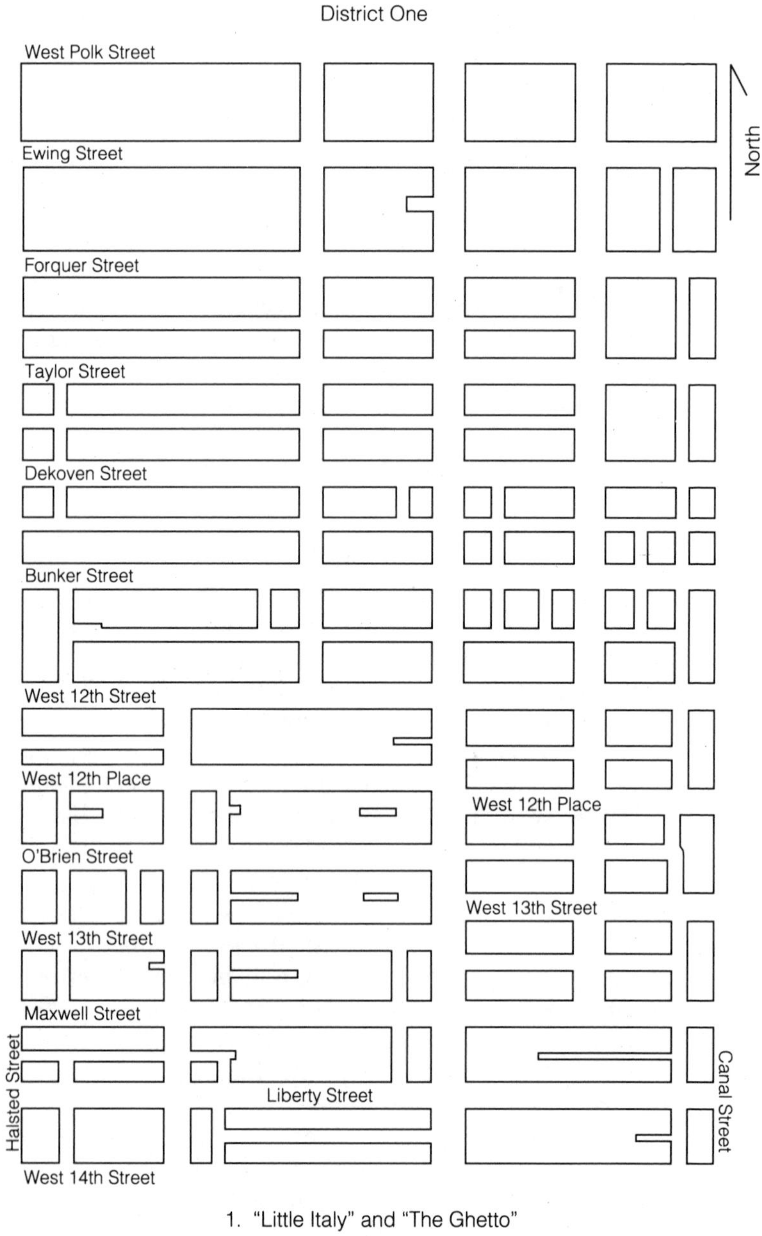

MAP 1.2. Tenement districts. (Source: Hunter, *Tenement Conditions*, pp. 13, 15.)

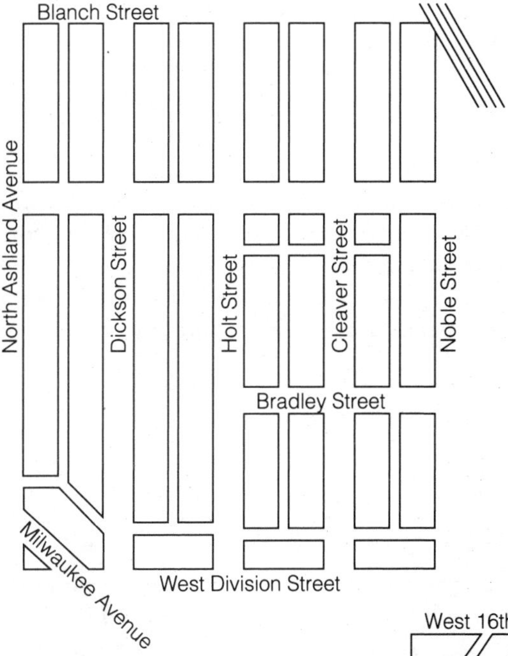
Blanch Street
North Ashland Avenue
Dickson Street
Holt Street
Cleaver Street
Noble Street
Bradley Street
Milwaukee Avenue
West Division Street

2. "Polonia"

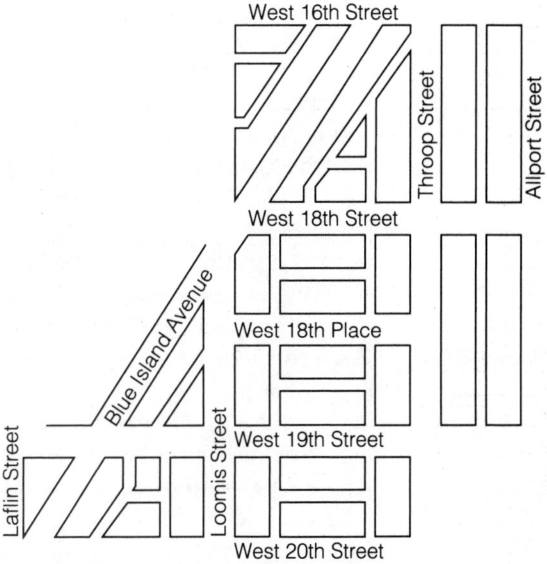
West 16th Street
Throop Street
Allport Street
West 18th Street
West 18th Place
Blue Island Avenue
West 19th Street
Laflin Street
Loomis Street
West 20th Street

3. "Pilsen"

inhabitants apiece. The most populous block of all was in Little Poland (block 50, Map 1.3, page 35). With 2,327 souls crammed onto 96 lots, 100 feet deep and 20 to 25 feet wide, it was nearly a city in itself.[34]

The way to fit so many people into so small a space was to build on every available inch and then stuff the buildings with tenants. There was nothing to prevent builders from covering lots completely except a statute demanding that 10 feet of space be left open. The provision was unenforced. The City Homes Association investigators reported back "somber and hideous" figures on ground coverage:

AMOUNT OF LOT COVERED	PERCENTAGE OF LOTS
More than 65%	39%
65% to 80	22
80 to 90	8
90 to 100	9

Massive buildings and smaller rear tenements both contributed to the congestion. Of the 3,117 buildings that jammed the sixty-six blocks surveyed, over 23 percent were obnoxious rear tenements. In Little Poland, the percentage of alley dwellings was nearly one-third. The large "dumb-bells" or "double-deckers" were still relatively rare, amounting to only 3 or 4 percent of all structures, but they often covered "the entire lot," they each harbored six to sixteen times as many people as did the average tenements, and they were spreading rapidly.

Robert Hunter used a ground plan (reproduced as Figure 1.2, page 36) to illustrate the conglomeration of structures on the lots. Buildings formed an almost solid wall around the block (block 36, Map 1.3, page 34), and sheds or tenements occupied the rear of every lot. On the lots marked "A" and "B," tenements were built back to back, with no space at all between them. At some points, the line of buildings extended unbroken from one side of the block to the other. And at the east end of the block, tall buildings of the double-decker type consumed every inch of ground.

The double-decker, Hunter wrote, was the most hopeless form of tenement. It was essentially a front and rear building joined by a narrow corridor. The rooms at the middle could not possibly be well lighted and ventilated, and despite brick construction the

MAP 1.3 *(pages 34 and 35)*. Density of population by blocks, Districts 1 and 2. (Source: Hunter, *Tenement Conditions,* pp. 56–57.) Hunter calculated *ground* density: the number of people per net acre of ground. By this measure, density in the Chicago tenements was not so great as that in New York City's worst districts. But the crowding of available *floor* space in Chicago was at least as bad as in New York City. There were more than two acres of ground for every acre of floor space in the Chicago tenement areas, where the buildings had an average height of two stories. In New York City, where the tenements stood five and six stories tall, the situation was just the opposite: There were over two acres of floor space for every one of ground space. The average ground density in the Chicago districts was 273 people per acre, but the *floor* density was upwards of 600 per acre. If, as Hunter implied, the average tenement flat had less than 300 square feet of floor space, the overall population density in the Chicago districts was over 700 per acre of floor. (For New York City's tenements, see Roy Lubove, *The Progressives and the Slums: Tenement House Reform in New York City,* 1890–1917 [Pittsburgh, 1962].)

buildings were not safe in case of fire. Hunter believed that the great problem in Chicago would be to prevent the spread of "this large tenement." A more immediate problem was the rear tenement. The old alley houses were doomed to extinction because of their ramshackle condition, Hunter thought, but while they lasted, they, not the double-deckers, made "the worst possible dwellings for human beings."[35]

It was the filth and stench of the alleyways that made life in the rear houses so horrible. Most of the 1,581 outdoor privy vaults were located in the alleys or in yards between the front and rear dwellings. People dumped their garbage in 1,203 alley garbage bins, mostly uncovered, and when these overflowed, the yards, gangways, and alleys filled up until the rear buildings were surrounded with rubbish. The smell from the toilets and the trash was enough to drive people indoors. Sometimes they had to shut the windows to ward off the odors. The cruelty of the situation was that the stench was most overwhelming on the hottest days, when the atmosphere of the crowded houses was stifling and people were desperate for air.

To make matters worse, there were almost as many stables in the three districts as rear tenements, and the 612 stables were in close proximity to the 730 rear dwellings. The horse population of the

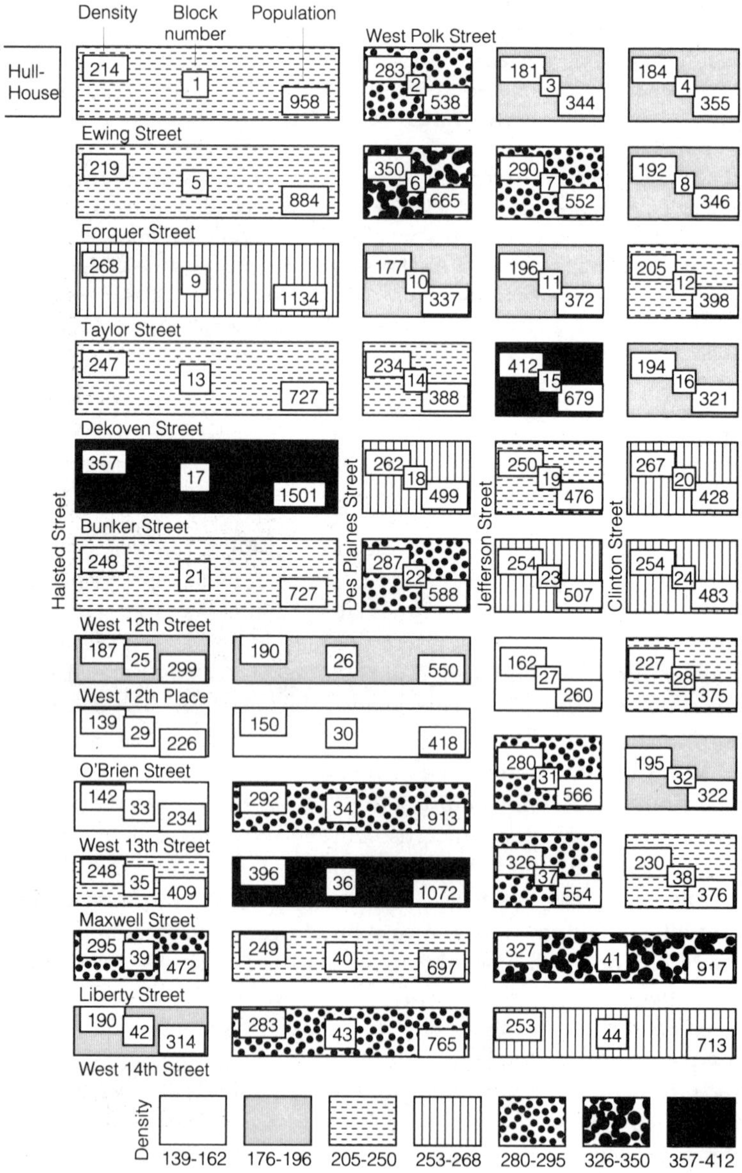
Density
Block number
Population
Hull-House
West Polk Street
Ewing Street
Forquer Street
Taylor Street
Dekoven Street
Bunker Street
West 12th Street
West 12th Place
O'Brien Street
West 13th Street
Maxwell Street
Liberty Street
West 14th Street
Halsted Street
Des Plaines Street
Jefferson Street
Clinton Street
Density
139-162
176-196
205-250
253-268
280-295
326-350
357-412

District One

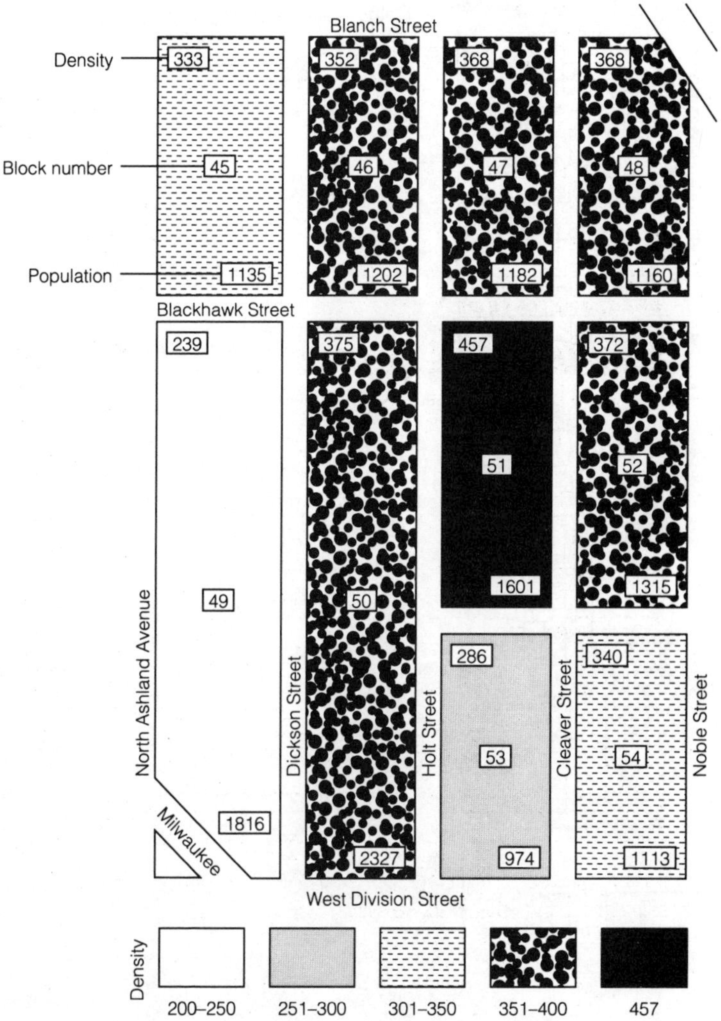

District Two

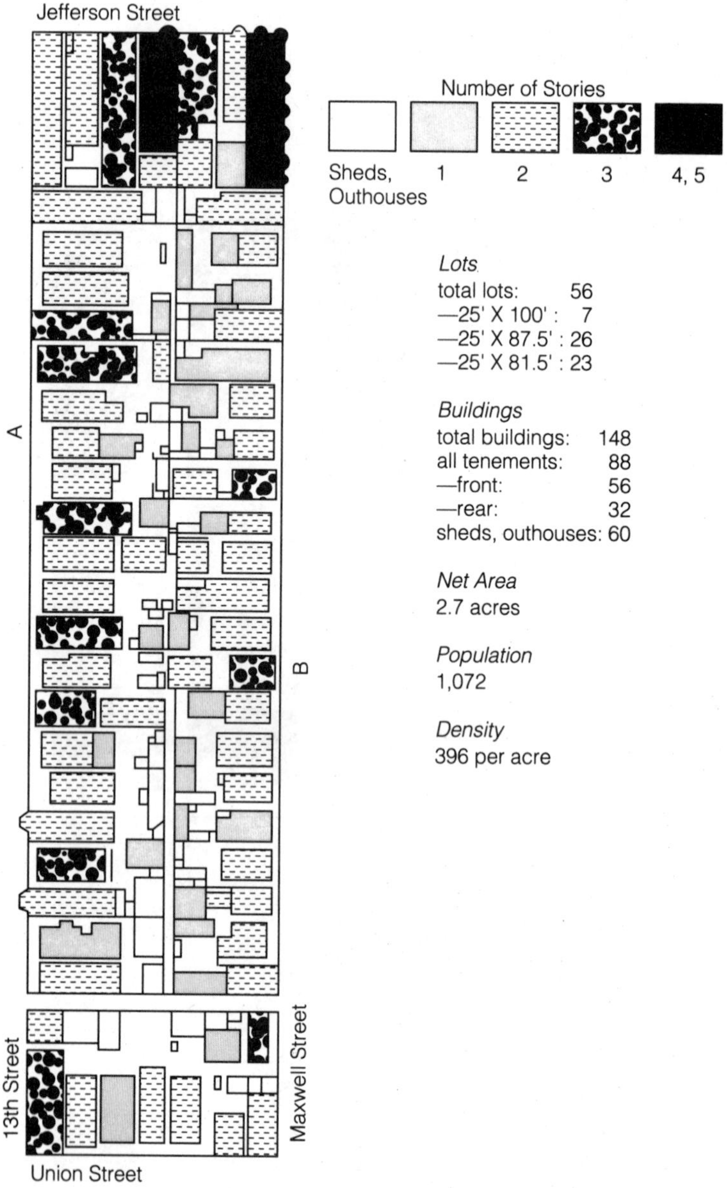

FIGURE 1.2. A block well covered by tenements. (Source: Hunter, *Tenement Conditions*, pp. 31, 195.)

districts was 1,443, or an average of 20 horses per block. Most of the stables had giant manure boxes attached; in the absence of such vaults, the manure simply piled up in the alleys. The enumerators encountered cows, goats, pigs, ducks, chickens, geese, and pigeons in sheds, coops, and pens, but they failed to keep track of the number. These creatures, too, were alley dwellers.

Figure 1.3 (page 38) shows how Robert Hunter outlined the arrangement of buildings on an ordinary alleyway. Nearly two hundred people depended for their air on this space polluted by twelve privies, four stables and manure boxes, and eight garbage boxes. The bins of trash and excrement were "uncovered and the contents strewn over the alley," Hunter wrote. "The alleys are unpaved and filth of all kinds has accumulated in large quantities. In one place a large pile of manure and trash has been thrown against a barn." The statistics and the diagram did not begin to show how "abominable" the situation was, so Hunter included photographs of children playing around massive heaps of manure. The photographs were shattering, but Hunter claimed that they, too, were inadequate. They seemed "to mellow or soften the disagreeable features, which when seen with the eye are extremely offensive." And they gave no inkling of the pounding heat, the stagnant, steaming air, and the stomach-turning smell.[36]

The crowding inside the dwellings corresponded to the crowding on the lots, with abysmal consequences for the inhabitants. The average family lived in three and a half rooms in a tenement occupied by two other families. When a family had a dwelling to itself, it was almost always a small hut, often facing the alley. At the other extreme, the double-deckers could hold as many as forty-eight families. Whatever the type of tenement, the flats were extremely small. Seventy-one percent had less than 400 square feet of floor space. Rooms rarely exceeded 10 feet by 10 feet; some were only 6 by 8. Half of these cubicles were "gloomy or dark," and three-fourths of the people had less than 400 cubic feet of air in the spaces where they slept. It was common for three or four people to sleep in one tiny room. Investigators came across cases of "five people sleeping in one bed." In such cramped quarters privacy was impossible, and a sense of modesty could be an unbearable psychological burden.

Except in a few double-deckers, there was no central heating. During Chicago's fiercely cold winters, a household was fortunate

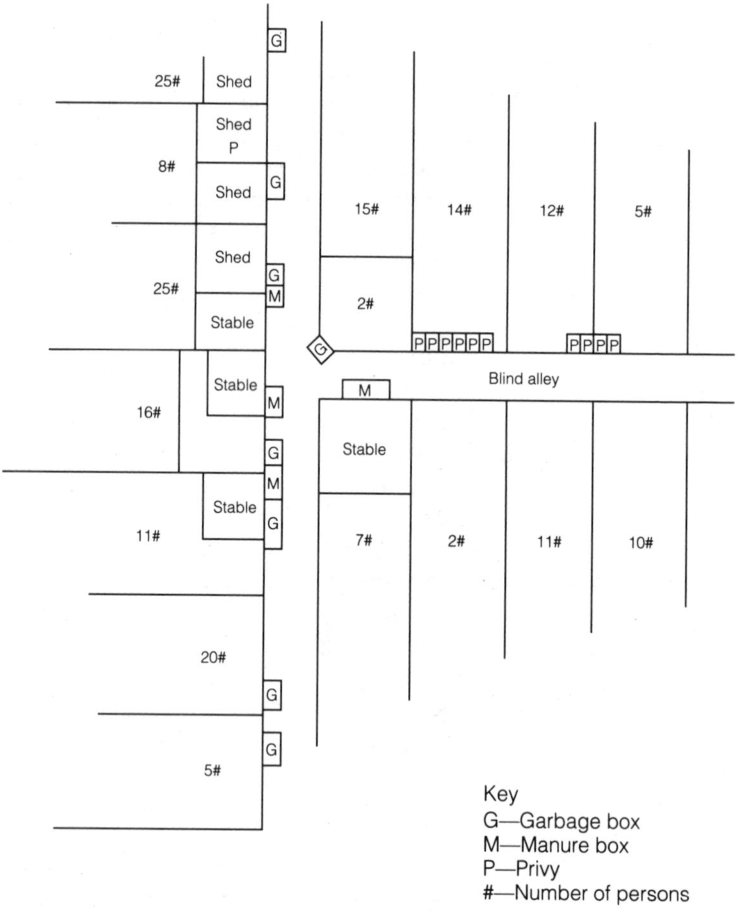

FIGURE 1.3. Insanitary arrangements on a tenement alleyway. (Source: Hunter, *Tenement Conditions*, p. 140.)

if it had "a basket of slate coal" for the stove. Lack of space was only one reason that people huddled together at night, Hunter believed. Another was "to economize the warmth which their bodies give out."[37]

Some flats had a sink as well as a stove, but bathtubs were practically nonexistent. Two to four families usually shared a toilet in a hallway, yard, or cellar. Privy vaults had been outlawed after the 1893 slum investigation, which showed three-fourths of the people using them. The later survey revealed that half of the families still had to use privies. The rest had water closets, but 90 percent of these had defects that made them disgusting and dangerous. They lacked traps and vents, and the pipes were exposed to the weather. They froze shut in winter, and they could clog, back up, or spew vapors at any time. The sinks were subject to the same hazards; 55 percent were defective.[38]

Intermixed with the residences in a haphazard pattern were 70 factories and over 1,200 stores and shops, an average of 20 industrial and commercial establishments per block. The most common shops were those that attracted vermin and threw off heat, odor, and noise: groceries, bakeries, laundries, meat markets, saloons, restaurants, candy shops, and cigar stores. Most people in the tenements lived above, behind, or beside a shop. One small block in District 1 (block 15, Map 1.3), for example, had two saloons, four stables (one with twenty horses), two butchers who did slaughtering on their premises, a barber shop, a laundry, three stores, and a Presbyterian church, which blotted out as much light and air as a dumb-bell tenement. All of this was jammed into thirty-one skimpy lots, where 679 people were trying to make homes. This block was the one where the O'Learys had lived; the O'Leary family continued to occupy that famous house. Its potential for tragedy was still tremendous.[39]

Almost 11 percent of the families lived below street level in cellars and basements. The streets, in effect, drained into their living quarters, and when sewers backed up, they spilled swill into the cellar residences. The offscourings of the privy vaults oozed into the soil, seeped through the thin walls and floorboards, and left a scum inside the flats.[40]

The buildings, half of them frame, all of them overcrowded, were badly battered. Seventeen percent were so dilapidated that they constituted "a menace" to their inhabitants and to all who lived nearby. Unbelievably, after the fearful example of the Great Chicago Fire, only 8 of the 927 buildings over two stories tall had fire escapes. Vermin, unlike humans, flourished in the tenements, adding to the menace. Hunter did not venture an estimate of the rat population, noting merely that they foraged all over the yards and alleys and overran the cellars. It is probably safe to say, however, that in the rear and basement dwellings, at least, rats outnumbered people.[41]

Complicating the whole question of overcrowding was the matter of boarders. Rental rates were low in the tenements, ranging from $5 to $12 a month, but they put a severe strain on family budgets. To help pay the costs, people subdivided their homes and took boarders into the fragments that once were family flats. Homeless families and unattached men and women needed someplace to go. For single men of meager means, the alternatives to boarding with a tenement family were the furnished rooming house and the lodging house. A furnished room was usually more expensive than bed space in a family's flat, and the lodging houses were cheap but horrible. For a single woman who could not afford a furnished room, there were a few "homes for working women." No other alternative was even semirespectable. Thus tenement families and boarders had powerful incentives for pooling their slim resources. But lodging arrangements aggravated all the frictions of living at close quarters. The presence of boarders further compromised the family's privacy and raised the ugly prospect of promiscuous sex and sexual conflict.[42]

To escape the atmosphere of the tenements, people took to the sidewalks and the streets, but these were not much more pleasant than the alleyways. On the sidewalks of the three districts there were over 550 garbage boxes and fewer than 150 trees. Almost all of the walks were planked with wood, not paved. Because most of them were graded several feet higher than the adjacent lots, they were essentially boardwalks or bridges. When a rotten plank gave way, a person could suffer serious injury. Hunter's surveyors reported that only 45 percent of the walks were in good condition. As for the streets, they were largely paved now, but paved very badly, and they were "always filthy."[43]

Robert Hunter did not pretend to understand the exact relation of bad housing to sickness, death, poverty, pauperism, intemperance, crime, and other "social diseases." He was confident that the investigation had proved that Chicago's housing was bad. And he was sure that bad home conditions handicapped people in "the competitive struggle" that was urban life in America. "No one who becomes a part of the life of these tenements," he wrote, "can escape their contaminated and corrupt atmosphere." [44]

Hunter's report was careful, thorough, and forceful. He illustrated it with more than forty photographs, equal in power, if not in artistry, to the better-known slum photographs by Lewis Hine and Jacob Riis. Like the best pictures of Hine and Riis, Hunter's focused on the children of the tenements. They were compelling documents. (And the emphasis on the children was not cheap sentimentality. Children were the chief victims of the slum. In some tenement wards, in some years, more than 60 percent of total deaths were among children under five years old. And this figure is on the low side, because the Health Department did not count in the mortality schedules the stillborn babies and the infants who died within twenty-four hours of birth. The chances of a child born in the tenements to survive three years were probably less than fifty-fifty.) But the most arresting thing about the report was the way Hunter combined his unassailable mass of evidence on the living conditions of 45,000 people in three small districts of the city with his estimate of how many Chicagoans had to live in a similar environment.[45]

On page after page he presented his data and then, with his credibility firmly established, he offered his considered opinion, which his readers were unwilling to accept but unable to disregard. It was a technique he would employ expertly a few years later in *Poverty*, the book in which he made the shocking claim that "no less than ten million persons in the United States are underfed, underclothed, and poorly housed." His assertions in *Tenement Conditions in Chicago* jolted the city's substantial citizens. Of the city's 1,700,000 people, "several hundred thousand" were ill-housed. Well over 300,000 people, possibly 400,000, lived under conditions as miserable as those in Little Poland, Pilsen, Little Italy, and the Jewish Ghetto. Another 300,000 to 400,000 lived in neighborhoods nearly as bad. The slum districts were getting worse and growing larger. And it was far less the fault of the poor foreigners who lived in the tenements than it was "the shame of Chicago." [46]

CHAPTER 2 ❧

Model Town and Model Tenement: Reform on a Business Basis

If city dwellers are to be better housed better housing must pay. There can be no question as to the remunerative character of housing operations conducted in the interests of the artisan and other well paid laborers. Money invested for this purpose brings a sure, safe, and stable return. There is, therefore, absolutely no reason why every workingman in receipt of a fair wage should not be able to command a favorable living environment.
—E. R. L. Gould, *The Housing of the Working People. Eighth Special Report of the Commissioner of Labor* (Washington, D.C., 1895), p. 419.

ROBERT HUNTER'S REPORT, LIKE OTHERS ISSUED AFTER THE DEPARTMENT OF Health first described tenement conditions in 1878, exposed glaring contradictions in the life of Chicago. Here was a city of magnificent distances, with its workers penned up like hogs and steers at the stockyards. In trade volume, in industrial output, in sheer wealth, Chicago was a colossus, yet the mass of laborers, those who did "the hardest and the most disagreeable kinds of work," could not provide decent shelter for their families. Their tenements, Hunter charged, did not deserve to be called homes. "Slaughterhouses" was a fairer description.[1]

Awareness of these contradictions moved thoughtful citizens to ask questions. They avoided asking outright how slums came to be and what society could do about them. They wanted to know if the tenement districts could endanger the well-being of people in the better residential areas. And they wondered if the slum population would rise up in revenge, as New York City's had once done, and what would happen if it did.

The Great Fire, of course, had proved that the exclusive sections were vulnerable to afflictions emanating from the slums. For years afterwards, the fear of a recurrence cast a pall over all parts of the city. Establishment of the fire limits in 1872, their gradual extension, and improvements in fireproofing finally assured residents of the brick districts that they would be safe even if the workers' enclaves burned down again. But the fear of contagious disease spreading outward from the slums persisted.

Scourges such as typhoid and tuberculosis were endemic to the poorest neighborhoods, and there was no way to quarantine every case or inoculate the rest of the city. A salesgirl at Field's could hand germs across the counter with the change; a house servant might carry sickness right to the employer's hearth. Middle-class householders could not secure complete immunity from working-class illnesses. They remained susceptible to appeals for sanitary regulation based on the scare-word contagion.

In the 1890s Florence Kelley of Hull-House became an expert at exploiting this fear. "I have myself found on Bunker Street a tenement house filled with Bohemian and Jewish tenants engaged in the tailoring trade and peddling," she said in a typical report. Five feet from the table where the tailor worked on a broadcloth dress coat of the finest quality, worth $70 to $100, lay a child wracked by typhoid fever. The boy died a day later; his father took the finished coat back to the shop of the merchant tailor, who delivered it to the customer "without fumigation or other precaution." The danger to purchasers of slum-manufactured goods, she declared, was "too palpable to need comment." But she would go on to cite case after case of cancerous old women and tubercular children working on garments, sewing disease into the fabric.[2]

The fear of lower-class disorder was somewhat harder to convert into an entering wedge for reform. The main victims of poor people's crimes were other poor people. So long as tenement dwellers confined their mischief to committing mayhem upon each other, the upper classes were not greatly disturbed. The specter of underclass insurrection was another matter. Except in periods of hysteria, few business leaders seriously believed that the workers were capable or desirous of waging all-out class war. Yet the increasingly turbulent character of labor relations in the period from the depression of 1873 through the industrial collapse of 1893 vexed the business class as a whole. Businessmen wanted a deterrent to violent upheaval. If someone could demonstrate that reforming conditions would forestall labor disturbances, businessmen might back reform. Otherwise, they would rely on a more obvious deterrent: repression.

In the summer of 1877, Chicago experienced its first labor uprising. The violence erupted after East Coast railroad owners slashed workingmen's wages in order to issue dividends to their stockholders. Workers retaliated by striking and disrupting rail traffic all over the country. When rioting broke out in a score of cities, the federal government dispatched troops to six states, including Illinois. While troop trains were en route to Chicago from Fort Laramie, Wyoming, and elsewhere, workers and police fought four pitched battles in the city in as many days. At least nineteen men died in the fighting, and hundreds more suffered wounds. Chicago's businessmen responded to the crisis vigorously. They armed themselves and formed patrols to protect business and residential areas. Marshall Field and other merchants turned over their delivery wagons to the police to move riot squads from one trouble spot to another quickly. And the businessmen collected funds to hire reinforcements from Allan Pinkerton's mercenary army.[3]

The leaders of commerce and industry had no doubt who was to blame for the "insurrection." It was the riffraff from Europe who must have agitated "the vicious and evil-disposed" elements of the working class with alien doctrines. To defend free enterprise from subversion, the business leadership mounted a drive to increase the manpower, firepower, and mobility of local, state, and federal police and military forces. The elite, normally bearish on government spending, lobbied for more National Guard armories and more federal forts (Fort Laramie was too far away). And the city's most prestigious "reform" group, the Citizens' Association, gave the police department money to procure a small but modern arsenal "for the City defense."[4]

On instructions from the Citizens' Association, which was composed entirely of prominent businessmen, the superintendent of police purchased a hundred handguns and rifles, four twelve-pounder Napoleon cannons with carriages and caissons, some lighter artillery pieces, one ten-barrel .50-caliber Gatling gun, and thousands of rounds of ammunition. The weapons, though entrusted to the authorities, remained "the property of the Citizens' Association." The department dutifully stamped each piece of equipment with the initials "C.A." and agreed to refrain from using the arsenal except in cases where "public order" was in danger, that is, during labor disturbances.[5]

Stockpiling lethal armaments seemed a sensible strategy to men who believed that capitalism had no defects, only enemies. If industrial warfare broke out again, the captains of industry would again conscript policemen as their foot soldiers, and the troops would be well armed.

As the riot hysteria waned, some business leaders began to suspect that repressive reaction in itself would not suffice. Foremost among these leaders was George M. Pullman, the sleeping-car tycoon. Pullman, who kept three plush homes besides his mansion at 18th and Prairie, keenly appreciated the value of pleasant surroundings. It occurred to him that workers, as well as millionaires, might have need of wholesome homes.

As an employer, Pullman wanted workers who were capable, dependable, and loyal to the company. For his workshops to operate at the peak of efficiency, he needed men who were "clean, contented, sober, educated and happy." He doubted that they could be if they went home from his factories to "crowded and unhealthy tenements, in miserable streets . . . subject to all the temptations and snares of a great city." [6]

Pullman believed that workmen frustrated at being unable to pay the cost of decent housing out of their hard-earned wages might blame their employers as well as their landlords for their predicament. His faith in capitalism was absolute, and he regarded unionization as anathema, but he suspected that union organizers would meet with more and more success unless capitalists countered them with something besides Napoleon cannons and Gatling guns.

It was an article of George Pullman's faith that private enterprise could master any problem. Beginning in 1880 he put into execution a bold experiment that, if it succeeded, would render unions, strikes, industrial warfare—and slums—obsolete. He built an entire town, a total community encompassing workshops and homes where his work force could reside free from the "baneful influences" of disorderly neighbors, slum landlords, saloon keepers, pawnbrokers, prostitutes, political bosses, and labor agitators.

Order prevailed throughout the environment. Pullman, as landlord, employer, and "city builder," saw that it did.[7]

Pullman's experiment was not completely without precedent. Pullman knew of planned industrial cities in England and Europe. The closest American analogues to these places were the company towns built by industrialists in the Northeast and the "model tenements" erected by philanthropists in New York City, Philadelphia, and Boston.

The theoretical foundation of the model tenement was this. Because the wage system was fundamentally fair, it followed that workingmen earned enough money to afford sanitary housing. If workers lived in hovels, the reason had to be that landlords were fleecing them. By building *sound* dwellings and charging reasonable rents, capitalists could net a respectable return and simultaneously set in motion a kind of reverse Gresham's law of housing: Good tenements would drive out the bad. To hold their tenants at the same rentals, slumlords would have no choice but to upgrade their properties to the level of the competing model tenements.

So went the theory. It had a tantalizing simplicity to it. All parties stood to profit. The workingman received adequate housing for his rental dollar, the philanthropist enjoyed a dividend on his investment, and the slumlord, now an honest businessman in spite of himself, continued to make money, but only as much as he was entitled to.[8]

The motivation behind the company town was less idealistic: exploitation. Company towns isolated the workers from unions and from alternative sources of employment and made them dependent on the company for income, shelter, credit, supplies, everything. The planners of some old New England mill towns, such as Lowell, Massachusetts, had tried, without success, to provide decent lodgings for workers, but most company plans aimed at achieving the barest minimum. In the typical company town the housing was anything but model.[9]

Pullman's innovation was to combine elements of the model-tenement and company-town ideas and then apply his "Pullman system" of manufacturing to the combination. The result was a novel American product: the model town.

Pullman viewed the squalor of ordinary company towns as a violation of capitalism, much as he viewed defective goods. And he scorned two features of the model tenement: its limited conception and the taint of philanthropy attached to it. While model-tenement promoters claimed that they adhered to "strict commercial principles," the public nicknamed their financial arrangements "philanthropy plus 5 per cent." Pullman wanted no such confusion about the model town. It was, he insisted, strictly a "business proposition." The Pullman Palace Car Company would be landlord to more tenants than all the model tenements in America. The houses would be model, but every dollar invested in them would yield the company a 6 percent return. And he would put the whole town together as ingeniously as he assembled his sleeping cars.[10]

In 1880 Pullman acquired four thousand acres outside the city limits, twelve miles southwest of downtown. The site was remote from settled areas but connected by multiple rail lines to the city and, for that matter, the rest of the country. Lake Calumet, a large body of water adjacent to the tract, was linked to Lake Michigan by a long, shallow river that Pullman ultimately hoped to make navigable by lake and even ocean vessels.

An architect and a landscape designer laid out the town site, designed the buildings, and supervised construction. Rather than rely on contractors, Pullman assembled his own construction crews. While some workmen were grading the streets and putting in lines for sewers, water, and gas, others were already at work on the first buildings. The drainage system emptied into Lake Calumet. A separate system of pipes carried sewage to vacant acreage three miles to the south. The first structures to go up were the car shops. As soon as they were completed, those departments that could contribute to construction, such as woodworking and painting, went into operation. Residences and public buildings went up next.

Every structure in the town was built of bricks manufactured by the crew from clay dredged out of Lake Calumet. As much of the material as possible was prefabricated. Carpenters made all of the sashes, windowsills, doors, paneling, and other wooden fixtures from timber that was bought green and then cut and dried at the site. Nothing went to waste. Exhaust from a giant engine that powered the shop machinery was used to fill an artificial lake on the broad boulevard separating the factories from the residential community. Leftover clay went back into Lake Calumet as landfill for an artificial pleasure island. Even the sewage was put to use. Pullman installed a model vegetable farm on the dump site and marketed the produce at a profit.[11]

The first employees took up residence in 1881. A little over two years later the town was substantially completed. The cost had been about $8 million. With a population of approximately eight thousand, it was no mean city. Pullman wanted the place to be more than functional. Beauty, he believed, had commercial value, and he sought to capitalize on it.

The factories that dominated the north end of town were tall, stately, and impressive. Inside they were as bright, airy, comfortable, and visually appealing as workplaces could be. The streets and alleys were well paved, and the sidewalks, though wooden, were solid and safe. The red and yellow brick row houses that lined the streets looked attractive as well as durable. Each building had a small front lawn, and on the parkways trees were planted at intervals of twenty feet. Flowers ringed the base of every tree. The arrangement of public buildings—a hotel, a huge arcade-style shopping center, and a market house, among others—relieved the monotony of the gridiron street plan. A playground, a park, a ball field, and a six-acre greenhouse and tree nursery heightened the impression that the whole setting was "a park studded with buildings."[12]

The town was a showplace of private enterprise. Its founder named it after himself: Pullman. He called the front street running parallel to the Illinois Central commuter tracks Pullman, too, and he named both the boulevard that ran east from Pullman Avenue to Lake Calumet and the town hotel for his daughter Florence. Pullman regarded himself as an industrial innovator, and he named the remaining north-south streets in the town after other pioneer inventors: Morse, Watt, Stephenson, and Fulton. The street names, he hoped, would inspire his employees.

The whole town occupied less than an eighth of the land Pullman had acquired (see Map 2.1). Railroad tracks bordered it on three sides, the car works on the other side. Across the tracks to the east was Lake Calumet. All around the town, to the north, west, and south, was a cordon *sanitaire* controlled by George M. Pullman and his company. Inside the town as well, the industrialist attempted to dictate every detail of life. His factories turned out matchless products. He saw no reason why his houses and community facilities could not produce matchless workmen.

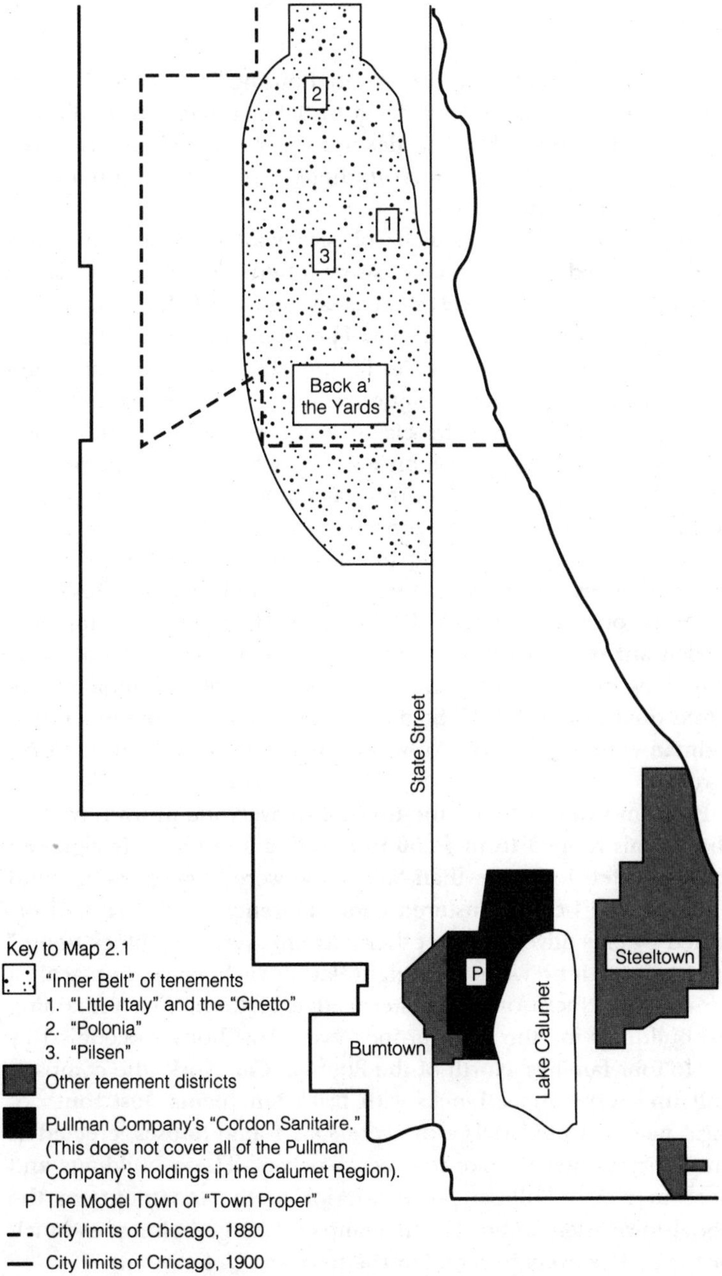

MAP 2.1. **Location of Pullman in relation to tenement areas.**

Pullman believed that "improved housing" was crucial to his scheme for elevating and pacifying his labor force, but he did not think that it could effect the desired transformation by *itself.* For that reason he stressed "surroundings" and supervision in the community's organization.[13]

The streets were immaculate, physically and morally. Sanitation crews collected garbage daily, swept often, and kept the lawns trimmed. All evil influences, such as saloons, bordellos, pawnshops, and cheap theaters, were banned. The company provided a broad range of edifying institutions "to fill the gap." The town had abundant outdoor recreation facilities, community meeting rooms, a library, billiard rooms, a first-class theater, a kindergarten, an outstanding elementary school, an evening school, a savings bank, a band, choirs, and clubs. All of this was supposed to help the people "forget all about drink" and improve themselves.[14]

Pullman included housing for managers and foremen in the plan so that his upper-echelon employees could exert an exemplary influence on the rank and file. A corps of inspectors compelled recalcitrant residents to conform to acceptable standards of decorum. This moral maintenance, like the sanitary maintenance, involved financial overhead. So did all of the facilities and amenities. Pullman charged the cost to his workers. They paid it in the form of rent.[15]

Pullman would not sell the houses, so everyone in town rented. The rentals ranged from $4.50 to $77.25 a month. Only eighteen houses rented for more than $50; these were large detached and semidetached homes clustered about Florence Boulevard and occupied by executives. At the other extreme were ten "block-house" tenements with twelve to forty-eight flats in each, backed up against the railroad tracks on the eastern edge of town. The remaining 170 buildings in "the town proper" were row houses occupied by one to four families. North of the Pullman Car Works the company built up several more blocks with brick tenements. Just south of town, near the old brickyards, were sixty frame houses, erected as temporary shelter for construction workers. These buildings and those in North Pullman were inferior to the tenements in the model town itself, although the company charged almost as much for them. The average rental in the town was $14 a month.[16]

In return for their rental payments, Pullman's tenants received housing that was superior to tenement housing in Chicago, but they did not get a dollar's worth of shelter for a dollar of rent. That was because Pullman imposed a surcharge on beauty, order, and uplift.

The lots were extremely small, or, to use Pullman's word, "cozy." As many as sixty-three parcels were cut into a block 260 by 600 feet. Some of the lots were only 14 feet wide. A single-family row house on a lot 17 by 100 feet had three bedrooms, one of which was just 7 by 8 feet. It had an indoor toilet, and on each of the two floors there was a water tap, but it lacked a bath. The rent was $18 a month, not including the charge for gas.[17]

The four-family row houses were cheaper to live in, but they were "inferior in every way to the rows of one-family dwellings." Three of the flats had three rooms, the other one had four. Each family had its own toilet, but not inside the apartment. Four toilet compartments were grouped underneath the steps of the front entrance hall. And these arrangements, severe as they were, compared favorably with those in the blockhouses.[18]

In the blockhouses, flats of three and four rooms rented for $8 to $9 per month. There were usually six flats to a floor, three on either side of a long, dark hallway. In the smaller block houses, each family had a toilet to itself; in the larger ones, two families shared each compartment. Either way, all water closets were outside the apartments, at the end of the hallway. Next to them was a single sink, which had the only running water on the floor. The flats had no sinks, taps, or tubs inside them, and there were no laundry facilities anywhere in the building. Thus six families had to carry all of their water for cooking, washing, bathing (if they could contrive a way to bathe), and laundering from one hall sink, which also supplied their drinking water. None of these buildings, even those with forty-eight apartments, had fire escapes. The only means of egress were wooden staircases. Gas for lighting was available to each flat, but it was optional and cost extra. Ordinary stoves furnished the heat.[19]

Company inspectors were free to enter the flats at any time to see if tenants were complying with the terms of their very detailed leases. A large percentage of families paid a third or more of their income in rent, even when the shops were operating at full capacity and paychecks were fat. In slack periods incomes plunged, but the rent levels stayed the same. Once fixed in 1882, they never changed. To help their tenants make their rental payments, the company allowed them to take in boarders. In hard times, especially, families shared their snug quarters with lodgers.[20]

Even if the town was not the industrial Utopia its founder envisioned, it shone by comparison with workers' neighborhoods in the city. One early resident compared his $15-a-month brick dwelling with the cottage he had come from on the West Side. "There was mud on all sides of us, two beer saloons within a block, clouds of soft coal, poor sewerage, villainous water, and everything else that was bad and disagreeable." It was impossible to keep things clean; every day, it seemed, some child died of diphtheria or scarlet fever. He was glad to have his children living healthfully in "a clean and comfortable house" in Pullman. As caustic a critic of capitalism as Henry Demarest Lloyd gave George M. Pullman credit for a concept of self-interest that was broader than "selfishness of the ordinary type." Lloyd believed that the Pullman experiment might succeed in making laborers placid. In 1883 Pullman was confident that the town's "handsome surroundings" would becalm even "the hardest" men.[21]

Some of Pullman's executives doubted that the men would be so tractable. The town seemed to attract men who were "hard." From the beginning most of the workers were immigrants. A census taken in 1885 revealed that Swedes, Germans, and Irishmen made up nearly a third of the population. People of nineteen or more nationalities lived and worked in the town. According to the traditions of many of these people, there was no harm in a glass of beer or a bit of whiskey, and a man who would deny those pleasures to other men was a crank or worse. And the manager of the Pullman bank thought that the foreigners had such extravagant expectations that nothing would satisfy them.[22]

Actually, the ethnic profile of the model town closely resembled that of Chicago, with one glaring difference. There were no Negroes in Pullman. This was peculiar, because George M. Pullman was famed for his paternal solicitude for black people. He hired them to serve the passengers on his sumptuous sleeping cars. He thought they made ideal porters. Then why were the tenements and the workshops in the town lily-white? Pullman never stated his reason for excluding blacks. None of the histories of the town or of black Chicago has discussed the question. The answer here is conjectural, though obvious. The porters, uniformed, well mannered, dripping with decorum, gave a flavor of the old plantation

South to the palace cars. Pullman could not picture blacks in any role but that of menials. The elevated working force of his town had no place for "darkies." [23]

For a time the workers at Pullman were quiescent enough. The experiment seemed to be proving that reform was as effective, in its way, as repression. Heartened by the Pullman example, other Chicago businessmen now considered the merits of a two-pronged approach to the problem of disorder.

In 1882 the Department of Health reported on the seriousness of housing conditions and appealed to capitalists to build model tenements. The repression-minded Citizens' Association responded by appointing a committee on "Tenements for Working Classes." A year later the committee affirmed that there was indeed a housing crisis. It reported that workmen were forced to pay an "extravagantly high" proportion of their wages to live in "crowded and unwholesome dens." The committee claimed to have found avaricious landlords who squeezed profits of 25 to 40 percent per year out of their properties. Those figures seem astronomical, and they were undocumented, but there were at least some cases of such extortionate rents. In fact, the $8 monthly that George Pullman charged the tenants of the frame houses near the brickyards south of his town netted him a 40 percent return. The association, the report in hand, acted once again. It appointed another committee to develop plans for model tenements in Chicago.[24]

After twelve months of preparation, the new committee on tenements came forward with its report. The time, the committeemen believed, was opportune. It was the autumn of 1884. The nation appeared to be entering "a long period of mercantile depression." In Illinois unemployment was climbing, wages were dropping, and discontent was spreading among workers. "Popular outbreaks" were inevitable unless "capitalists, manufacturers and merchants" organized to "apply the proper remedies." Labor was already organizing to force through "an advance in wages." This would be disastrous. The committee subscribed unquestioningly to the business credo that the wage system was fundamentally fair. The only way to relieve the distress of the workingmen was to let wages seek their own level and *then* engineer a reduction in the cost of living.[25]

When labor complained of wage cuts, it was customary for businessmen to fulminate about the improvidence and profligacy of workingmen. In 1883, for example, Joseph Medill, owner of the

Chicago *Tribune* and ex-mayor of Chicago, claimed that workers had no savings to tide them over hard times because they squandered their earnings on "intoxicating drinks, cigars, and amusements." But the committee, instead of exhorting workers to cut living costs by abstaining from vices, argued that the item that broke their budgets was rent. What drove so many men to "indulgence in strong drink" was the desperation of living in "crowded tenement houses and dark, foul slums." They had to pay excessive rents, and they knew that they could not possibly overcome their condition "by their own efforts." Men who did not turn to the bottle might look to the Knights of Labor for deliverance. It was up to "the rich men of Chicago" to see that the poor were not led astray.[26]

Of course, the committeemen did not expect the rich men to perform this service for nothing. The committee assumed that most common laborers, if they practiced stringent economy, could afford to pay $10 a month for housing, but not much more. After establishing that a tenement at that rental could meet minimum standards of decency, the committee moved on to what it termed "the momentous question," which was "Will it pay?"

The committee took the position that accepting a return of less than 6 percent on a tenement was bad business. Yet profits much in excess of 8 percent, when the commodity was shelter for the poor, seemed rapacious. To avoid the perils of philanthropy on the one hand and robbery on the other, the committee set the proper rate of return at 6 to 8 percent. If a tenement could not pay its investors that much, it was not worth building, no matter how badly the poor needed it.[27]

In 1883 Joseph Medill had made the startling, and for him somewhat incongruous, statement: "If private capital is unwilling in this country to provide decent and healthy abodes at moderate rents for the industrial classes of our cities, it may become necessary for municipal corporations to do it." The committee thought that talk of that sort was socialistic bilge. "Our system of business needs no governmental aid or advice," it said. The committeemen spoke with confidence. They had worked out designs for four model tenements that would elevate the poor and pay the required return.[28]

Ideally, all four plans would have incorporated three features: comfort for the tenant, low rent, and the sine qua non—solid profit. Practically, this was impossible. In each plan the committee sacrificed something. The only feature present in all four was the profit of 6 to 8 percent.

Two designs allowed for a measure of comfort. One was a single-family house of two stories. It had a kitchen, a living room, and four bedrooms. The fourth bedroom was a travesty—with about 40 square feet, it was a glorified closet—but the other rooms were adequate. The design included a luxurious bonus: a bathroom with a tub as well as a toilet. The other plan combining profit with some amenity was a three-story tenement with one flat to a floor. Each unit had a kitchen, parlor, living room, and two bedrooms. Both bedrooms were so small—about 6 feet by 6 feet—that either the parlor or the living room would have to serve as a sleeping room. There was one compensation for the tightness of the quarters: Each family would have its own toilet inside the flat, and with it a tub.

To provide even such meager comforts as these designs included and still guarantee the profit, the committee cut down drastically on yard space and set the rents prohibitively high. Both buildings covered the width of the lots. The single-family dwelling was on a plot only 16 feet 8 inches wide and 75 feet deep, which was small even by slum standards. The lot for the three-flat tenement was longer by 59 feet but just as narrow. Because the smaller building was only two rooms deep, every room had direct light and air, even though there were no windows on the sides. But each floor of the three-flat had three interior rooms that depended on a shaft for light and ventilation. The monthly rentals in the three-flat were to be $15, $17, and $18; the one-family house would rent for $15 to $18 a month and sell for upwards of $1,500.

Only better-paid workmen could afford such rentals. When they moved into the model dwellings, the flats they vacated would swell the supply of cheaper housing. Thus the benefit of the expensive tenements would trickle down to the poor. The businessmen designed the other two model tenements to help the poor directly. The designs substituted cheapness for comfort without violating the committee's minimum standards of decency. With these plans the upper-class committeemen showed how low they thought the minimum could be "for that class who can afford to pay but about $10 per month" (and this was the tenement population).

One of the projected cheap tenements was a boxlike structure of two stories with a front and rear flat on each floor. The stairwell was at the center of the building, not at the front, and the only entrance was on the side. This arrangement made it simpler to build square-shaped, relatively spacious rooms. The flats all had four rooms and an inside water closet. The drawback was that the building plus the sheltered entryway extended to the limits of the 24-foot-wide lot. Half of the bedrooms in the building, one in each flat, were interior rooms with their only windows on the lot line. There was no air shaft. The occupants of those rooms would be at the mercy of whoever owned the lot next door. If he built to *his* lot line, they would have no light and air. With this hazard, the rent of just over $10 a month could hardly be called low.

The fourth model-tenement plan was truly an innovation. The like of it was "nowhere to be found," not in Chicago, nor the rest of America, nor, so far as anyone knew, the whole wide world. It was a combined tenement and one-night lodging house, designed to "reach down to the necessities of the poorest class of families and of the unmarried workingmen." Such people, because they were irregularly employed and needed to be near the downtown hiring exchanges, required "quarters in some central locality." The other tenements were planned for areas a few miles from downtown where land was cheap. This tenement had to be in a rooming-house district in or near downtown, where the lots were extremely expensive. Instead of buying a lot, the committee hit on the expedient of buying up the unused space at the *back* of five or six adjoining lots, "the front of which" was "already occupied by stores or other buildings." For a street the tenants would have "the present alley." In other words, the proposed model dwelling was a lateral *rear* tenement.

The space between the alley and the backs of the stores was 70 feet by 125 feet. This was the "lot." The building, five stories tall, stood right at the alley line. It was 50 feet wide and ran the entire length of the lot, covering everything but a 20-foot-wide strip that separated it from the stores. Residents entered from the alley or through porticoes at either end that connected with "the street proper" by means of "narrow passages," that is, gangways. The two upper stories were "for the lodgment of single men." The other three stories were for families to occupy.

The top floor or "loft" was one huge dormitory with beds "set up, as closely as possible . . . about 150 of them." There were no sinks or toilets in the loft, only the beds. A man would be able to spend the night there for twelve or thirteen cents. The floor below was divided into eighteen "sleeping apartments" with "from two to six beds in each." The charge for a bed in one of these cubicles would be a quarter a night. There was a reading room and also a lavatory equipped with five washbasins and six urinals. All of the lodgers from both floors, which had a combined capacity of 220 or more, would share these facilities. There were no dining rooms in the plan.

On each of the three lower stories there were "quarters" for twelve families. These quarters consisted of a living room, a bedroom, and two small closets. Four of the compartments were somewhat larger than the rest, and they had "real partitions reaching to the ceiling." In the eight smaller compartments, the partitions were only seven feet high. The average floor area in the quarters was about 350 square feet. To ensure "decency and morality," the committee planned to forbid boys beyond a certain age to sleep with their families in the tiny two-room units. The manager would require parents to lodge their adolescent sons upstairs with the single men "at a certain especially low rate." If they were unwilling to split up their families in this way, they would have to seek shelter elsewhere.

As planned, the compartments had no fixtures of any kind—no sinks, no water taps, no stoves, no gas jets, nothing. Tenants who wanted light would have to get kerosene lamps. If they wanted to heat their rooms and to cook, they would have to buy stoves and install them on their own. The hallways had light and heat provided by the management, and each hall contained "a slop sink and an iron bowl for water." The nature of these fixtures is uncertain, but they were probably receptacles into which people could dump the contents of "thunder mugs" (chamber pots); excrement and other solid slop would go into the "sink," urine and waste liquids into the "bowl." Perhaps both containers could be flushed. At any rate, they could not be used directly, in the manner of a toilet or urinal, because they were not enclosed.

There were real "water closets" in the building plan, but they were all in the basement, where there were also laundry rooms and baths. A nickel would entitle any tenant to take a bath in one of the sixteen tubs. Use of the other facilities would be free. The two "women's rooms" had a total of ten toilet stalls. The two "men's rooms" had, altogether, twenty toilets and three banks of urinals. The male lodgers as well as the married men would enjoy toilet rights, which accounted for the preponderance of fixtures for males. The entire managerial and maintenance staff of the building, as budgeted by the committee, would consist of one "competent, honest, and sober janitor." A family could have a unit for as little as $7 a month. The larger compartments would go for $10.[29]

If this kind of thing was good enough to build for low-paid workers, what was too bad? The answer, as Robert Hunter would show, was "nothing." This is the ultimate indictment of Chicago's slums: They were even worse than this model-tenement design.[30]

Incredibly, the Citizens' Association committee took the greatest pride in this blueprint for slums. The committeemen believed that tenements built on this ghastly pattern were "an urgent necessity." The combination flophouse and tenement house "would be the means of raising the lower grades of society to a higher level and of implanting in their minds, especially those of the rising generation, a higher degree of self-esteem and morality," they claimed. The committee urged the city's "rich men" to invest in building these monstrosities on a grand scale. "They are much more needed than the modest apartment and other houses. They are *the* want of the present age and generation."[31]

The Citizens' Association published the report, circulated it widely, and noted afterwards that it met with "general public approval." The organization vowed "to bring forward the project," but it moved cautiously. By this time the labor scene was storming over. The association watched and waited. Early in 1885, *Harper's Monthly* printed an article that raised serious questions about the Pullman experiment and all constructive reform.

The author of the piece was a young, as yet little-known economics professor named Richard T. Ely. He had visited the town in the autumn, just after the tenement committee's report came out. The physical layout of Pullman impressed Ely, but he concluded that the overall atmosphere was un-American. The company controlled everything in the town. The resident had "everything done for him, nothing by him." Despite the superiority of their surroundings, the townspeople were not contented. Far from it. They felt that the company subjected them to intolerable "restraint and restriction."

Pullman's vaunted system, Ely charged, was inapplicable to community life. Pullmanism was "benevolent, well-meaning feudalism." To businessmen the disturbing thing about Ely's article was the evidence that the workingmen were dissatisfied. If labor did not appreciate reform, then what was the use of reform?[32]

As 1885 wore on, labor unrest mounted, and there were signs that businessmen were giving up on reform and gearing up for repression. The powerful Commercial Club, which two years before had founded a manual-training school to teach poor youngsters skilled crafts, donated a tract of choice suburban land to the federal government. The condition: The government must put a military base there. The site became Fort Sheridan. Another business group, the Merchants' Club, gave the government a comparable piece of property on the same condition. This became Great Lakes Naval Training Station. At Pullman the company slashed wages in several departments. Instead of accepting the cuts, the men began to organize, which was forbidden. And the Citizens' Association announced that it would hold the tenement project "in abeyance" until disturbances died down.[33]

The following year, 1886, was "the year of the great uprisings." Chicago became the center of a national movement for the eight-hour day. By May 1 nearly eighty thousand workers in the city were on strike to force the demand. On May 3 police killed two workmen during a scuffle between strikers and scabs. The following night a protest rally led by anarchists ended in tragedy when police attacked the crowd and someone hurled a bomb that killed seven policemen. This was the notorious Haymarket Riot, which horrified respectable Chicagoans. While hysteria was gripping the city, the workers at Pullman went out on strike. They wanted the eight-hour day as well as restoration of the wages they had lost. Within ten days the plants reopened under armed guard. The strike and the union crumpled, but George M. Pullman was no longer confident that benevolent autocracy could subdue the "excesses of our turbulent population."[34]

A Chicago railroad executive said that the Pullman walkout proved that "the more you do for your men . . . the more they want." The Citizens' Association now abandoned its program to build model tenements and a related plan to establish a pawner's bank for "the deserving poor." The implication was clear: The poor were not deserving. For the next two years the association lobbied strenuously to secure a new headquarters for Illinois's First Infantry. The effort was successful. By 1890 the guardsmen had a formidable new home, designed by John Wellborn Root. Instead of aiding Chicago's workers with model housing, the Citizens' Association awed them with a model armory.[35]

A surface calm prevailed at Pullman for several years after the abortive strike, but bitterness seethed underneath. The company had never required its employees to reside inside the town. In the early years there were few alternatives, but nearby settlements slowly developed, and as they did, more and more Pullman workers elected to move from the model town. The streets in Kensington and Roseland, two communities west of the Illinois Central tracks, were badly graded, badly paved, badly lit, and practically unsewered. The houses were cheap frame dwellings. But the rents were 10 to 25 percent lower than in Pullman, and the lots were 20 to 60 percent larger. A man could buy his house if he wanted to, he could quench his thirst at the tavern of his choice, and he could be free of Pullman's surveillance.

In 1889 the City of Chicago annexed the model town, thus breaking the completeness of Pullman's hold, but workers did not feel any less intimidated. By 1893 more than one-third of the work force lived outside the community in neighborhoods that were far from model. And one man who still lived in Pullman complained, "We are born in a Pullman house, fed from the Pullman shop, taught in the Pullman school, catechized in the Pullman church, and when we die we shall be buried in the Pullman cemetery and go to the Pullman hell."[36]

In 1894 the experiment ended in disaster. Hard times had come again, the worst in a decade. George Pullman, determined to keep paying stockholders their dividends as proof of the company's soundness, retrenched ruthlessly. He laid off 40 percent of the workers, and he reduced the hours of the rest, who suffered an average 25 percent cut in wages. But he would not reduce rents. The workers were in agony. They did not ask for restoration of their pay levels, but they demanded a reduction in rents. When Pullman refused to consider their position, they went out on strike. Railway workers all over the country struck in sympathy with them, and before it was all over National Guardsmen and federal troops (the latter dispatched from the new Fort Sheridan) intervened. Thirteen men were slain in street skirmishes, and the workers were utterly crushed.[37]

The Pullman uprising shocked business leaders. As they saw it, the town had "no close stuffy tenements . . . no overcrowding, no bad air, no poorly clad half-famished men." Of course the town *did* have congested tenements, but they were so far above the average that the businessmen's point was hardly worth debating. The strikers themselves had proclaimed their love for their "beautiful town." They were fighting to liberate it from Pullman's paternalism. People like Professor Richard Ely thought that the lesson of the Pullman experience was that paternalism could not substitute for self-government and self-respect. Businessmen in Chicago saw it differently. The debacle at Pullman persuaded them that reform, not iron-fisted rule, had soured the workers. For them the moral of the story was that reform did not pay.[38]

A year after the smoke settled at Pullman a Protestant clergyman named D. E. McLennan reviewed the newly published volumes on Chicago's West Side slums by the U.S. Department of Labor and the residents of Hull-House. He felt that the books confirmed his own belief that *"the chief cause of the slums is the abandonment of the poor by the well-to-do."*

The poor could not overcome their surroundings without "influential neighbors to aid them," McLennan argued. The Railroad Riots of 1877, the Haymarket Riot, and the Pullman Strike had opened the chasm between the classes disastrously wide. "The only salvation for the city lies in bringing the rich and poor together," Reverend McLennan declared. "The poor cannot go to the rich; the rich must go to the poor." For proof he pointed to Hull-House. The settlement had been at work a little over five years. Its efforts to improve the material circumstances of the people were largely unsuccessful: to all appearances the Nineteenth Ward was still a slum. But the settlement workers were transforming the "spirit" of the people, converting a "moral jungle" into a neighborhood. "With powerful neighbors to sympathize with and plead for them," the minister concluded, "the poor take heart."[39]

CHAPTER 3 ❧

Settlement House and Tenement House: "With, Not for"

The settlement house is really an addition to every little tenement home. Its books and pictures, the nursery and play spaces, the lobby and the living room, the music and flowers, the cheery fireplaces and lamps, the auditorium for assemblies or social occasions and dancing, are an extension of the all too scant home equipment of most of the neighbors.
—Graham Taylor, *Chicago Commons through Forty Years* (Chicago, 1936), pp. 41–42.

The motive of our whole movement is in being "with," not merely "for," others.
—Ibid., p. 21.

IN 1889, A TIME WHEN CHICAGO WAS NEITHER RECOVERED FROM THE SHOCK of Haymarket nor braced for the coming collision at Pullman, two resolute young women of the upper class took up residence at Polk and Halsted streets on the Near West Side. This was "the poorest, and probably the most crowded section of Chicago," a district that middle-class people feared and avoided. Jane Addams and her friend Ellen Gates Starr, college-trained and independently wealthy, hoped to soothe class conflict by sharing, instead of shunning, the life of the poor in the slums. They also expected (exactly how, they were not sure) to transform that life for the better. These were Chicago's first settlement workers, and the building they moved into was Hull-House, the city's pioneer social settlement.[1]

Hull-House was a huge residential relic of the days when South Halsted Street was at the outskirts of the city. Urban sprawl overtook the one-time suburb, stranding the stately manor between an undertaker's parlor and a saloon. By 1889 the old building was badly faded, but it stuck out sharply from the dreary rows of tenements that lined the surrounding streets and alleys. At this imposing headquarters, the Misses Addams and Starr proposed to reconcile the alien worlds of the mansion and the tenement.

They took it for granted that the poor needed the help of emissaries from the ranks of education and privilege. And for their part, they sorely needed to feel helpful. From their studies they knew something of "the social maladjustment" afflicting the industrial city. They felt "smothered and sickened with advantages." The thought of "the bitter poverty" of the masses haunted them at tea. They longed to break out of their sheltered leisure-class lives and see how the other half lived. Jane Addams and her friend did not care to sit out the urban crisis of their time in some drawing room. They were determined to play an active part in solving it.[2]

Unlike George M. Pullman, they had no master plan, only a devotion to the principles of class conciliation and democracy, which they believed to be complementary. For a long time their new neighbors wondered why ladies would stay at such an unfashionable address when they could obviously afford to live somewhere else. Some people thought that they were setting up a high-toned whorehouse. Others suspected "that Hull-House was a spy in the service of the capitalists." Gradually, however, the workers' families came to accept their upper-crust intruders as permanent fixtures of neighborhood life.[3]

The settlement women began by walking around the area, observing things and asking women and children they met to come to Hull-House for a visit and maybe bring along the menfolk. Julia Lathrop, another college graduate who joined them in residence, secured appointment as charity visitor to all Cook County relief "cases" within a ten-block radius of the settlement. "This gave her a legitimate opportunity for knowing the poorest people." The Hull-House residents used these early contacts to get the feel, as well as the acceptance, of the neighborhood. They tried to learn what their neighbors were up against, and they looked for ways to help out.[4]

What struck them first was the condition of the housing. Never had they seen houses so "horrid." The dearth of conveniences condemned the tenement women to life at hard labor. To scrub a floor, cook a meal, wash dishes, or bathe children was no simple task in a flat with no sink or tap or tub. The Hull-House residents, who hired other women to do their housework, marveled at the heroism of housewives who lugged water by the bucketload up two or three flights of stairs in the battle to keep things clean. Everything in the tenements conspired against doing the wash. The inadequacy and inaccessibility of water was only one obstacle. Yards were mere gaps between buildings, devoid of space and sunlight. Smoke and dirt from railroads, factories, streets, and unpaved alleys clogged the air. Tramps and gangs of boys sometimes made off with unwatched garments. There were plenty of people who quit fighting, who let the wash go and pitched garbage out of windows or down air shafts. The wonder was that so many refused to give up. Defying all the odds, tenement mothers persisted in stringing up clotheslines. And they kept on wrapping the garbage neatly in newspaper and taking it outside to deposit in garbage boxes that they knew very well the sanitation crews would not empty.[5]

Listening to the tenement dwellers, the women of Hull-House heard about things like "hot beds" and "can-rushing." When a family rented out space in one bed to two or more lodgers who took turns sleeping in it, the bed had no time to cool off between shifts, hence the name. Can-rushing was the stampede of people to use shared toilets during the day's rush hours and during the frequent outbreaks of dysentery. The residents of the fine big house on Halsted Street learned that tenement flats were places that the inhabitants tried to avoid except for sleeping and eating. In the dead heat of summer, the flats were not even good for sleeping. People commonly spent the night sprawled out in yards, stoops, roofs, or any place that offered escape from the hell of their rooms.[6]

"The dreary tenement" was the only kind of house the working people could afford. The great majority of the laborers had no marketable skills. The work they did was hard, stultifyingly dull, and often dangerous. They swept and shoveled streets, dug ditches, sweated over garments, peddled from pushcarts, tended machines. Employment was irregular because of market fluctuations and weather conditions. Laborers went long stretches without work, and then when they got jobs they worked "incredibly long hours." And always, the pay was pitifully small.[7]

Settlement residents found out that "the theory that 'every man supports his own family' is as idle in a district like this as the fiction that 'every one can get work if he wants it.' " Men trying to build up some savings or make payments on a home often had to put their wives and children to work. Many families resorted to child labor less from ambition to get ahead than from sheer inability to make ends meet otherwise. Children hustled newspapers, blacked boots, and did many other kinds of work that did not require the physical strength of a full-grown man. Yet they worked as hard as adults, and the adults toiled like brutes.[8]

Garment workers, for instance, were idle several months of the year, but in the rush season they sometimes stayed on the job forty-five to fifty hours. "You don't mean at one sitting, do you?" a settlement investigator asked a man who had done it many times. "Yes," he replied, "it is a common thing." Because it was vital to finish as many pieces as possible in the shortest period of time, the workers would make their children help by pulling threads until their fingers stiffened. The Hull-House residents knew fourteen-year-olds who packed candy, wrapped soap, or "ran cash" fourteen hours a day (minus twenty minutes for lunch), six days a week, eighty-two hours in all (exclusive of lunchtime), for four dollars or less. A pay rate below a nickel an hour made streetcar fare a luxury, so many children walked to and from work, regardless of the distance, the hour, or the weather.[9]

Industrialists claimed that child labor gave boys and girls the chance to learn a trade. Settlement workers saw that dead-end jobs, such as labeling cans, taught the children nothing but "a dull distaste for work." Men and women who had been working since their early teens were often old by thirty-five, broken down from overwork, no longer fit for heavy labor. To support themselves they sent their children into the workshops, thus continuing the cycle.[10]

The earnings of fathers, mothers, and children did not add up to a living wage. In 1892–1893, the last year of "prosperity" before the great depression of the nineties, the families in the section east of Hull-House had an average annual income of less than $500. Many families had to get by on less than $260 a year. A family would be fortunate to have thirty weeks in which some member was working and bringing home pay. In those weeks income might total $10 to $25, but for the rest of the year there would be no income at all. On the other hand, the pressure to pay bills never let up. For Near West Siders, even good times were hard.[11]

The people lived all the time in want or in "the fear and dread of want." No amount of labor could guarantee economic security. Compared to their neighbors, the settlement "workers" had never done a day's work in their lives. Nor had they ever experienced the terrible insecurity that always stalked the poor. They came from comfortable backgrounds, and Hull-House, with its nicely appointed, spacious parlors, contrasted sharply with the cramped quarters of the working people. The settlement residents were different from the people living all around them, and there was more to the difference than the fact that they were better-off. Jane Addams, Miss Starr, and most of the residents who came after them were Protestants of old native stock. The neighborhood, in their word, was "foreign," teeming with Catholic and Jewish immigrants. The social distance between Hull-House and the nearby tenements was enormous.[12]

As they got to know the area, the settlement workers discovered that the people were divided not only from the city outside and from its upper-class representatives but from each other as well. Jane Addams believed that these internal divisions cut deep into the social fabric of the community.

To begin with, the four-square-mile Near West Side was not a neighborhood but rather a congeries of neighborhoods, delimited vaguely, and named, if at all, for streets, churches, or landmarks such as railroad tracks. If somebody asked a Near West Sider where he lived, he would answer with something like "Taylor'n Halsted," "Saint Wenceslaus," or "The Valley" (a stretch of tenements overshadowed by a steep train embankment). If the questioner then said, "Where's that?" the person might say, "the West Side." Only a fraction of the larger district was within easy walking distance of Hull-House. Yet what Jane Addams called "the neighborhood of the settlement" straddled the boundaries of a dozen different neighborhoods. To some extent, heavy-traffic streets, train tracks, and other breaks in residential usage barricaded the neighborhoods from each other. What made the physical barriers difficult to cross, however, was the existence of *social* barriers. The people "were separated," Miss Addams observed, "by every possible social distinction."[13]

The Near West Side was a workers' district, but neither it nor any section of it was a homogeneous unit. West of Halsted the neighborhoods were progressively less run-down. And even among inhabitants of the poorest areas there were differences of income, background, outlook, and "mode of life."[14]

Incipient capitalists such as the "sweater" and the small shopkeeper occupied high rungs on the working-class occupational ladder. Skilled workmen ranked high above ordinary laborers. Strivers who kept straining to pull themselves up to the level of the labor aristocracy or beyond to the great middle class looked down on those who were "too battered and oppressed" to cling to such ambitions. It was all that many people could do to keep from slipping lower. Tenants of front flats enjoyed a status advantage over occupants in the rear, unless the latter happened to be landlords. At the bottom of the social scale, below the working class, were those who lived by begging, stealing, pimping, whoring. Even here there were differences: Paupers and crooks had little in common.[15]

Ethnic cleavages complicated class and cultural differences. The area around Hull-House was a "labyrinth" of nationalities and creeds. Catholics predominated on three sides of the settlement, and the Jewish "ghetto" was to the south. Protestants were scattered through the district, and there were adherents of oriental religions as well. Most Jews were either Russians or Poles (though some of the Poles were not Jewish), but there were "thirteen nationalities of Jews" altogether. The Catholics, too, came from more than a dozen different countries. The ethnic mixture of the area was constantly changing, like the patterns of a kaleidoscope. The most numerous foreigners at the beginning were Irishmen, Bohemians, and Germans. They gradually gave way to Italians, Russians, Poles, and Greeks. But at any given time in the 1890s people of twenty-six or more nationalities could be found living within three blocks of Hull-House.[16]

Despite their inclination to cluster in colonies, members of the various ethnic groups were "more or less intermingled" in the housing, the workshops, and the public accommodations of the district. The average block had residents of eight ethnicities. No block, nor even one side of a block, was ethnically homogeneous. Sometimes an ethnic tenement was exclusively Jewish or Italian, but these buildings often shared a lot with another tenement. Only one lot out of five had residents of a single ethnic stock.[17]

It was impossible for people to confine all of their face-to-face contacts within their ethnic group. They could ignore people of other nationalities, but they were bumping up against them all the time, not just on the streets, on the job, and at the markets but also on stairways, in gangways, backyards, and halls, on the way to the water tap, and in line to use "the can." Contact across ethnic lines was unavoidable, and it was often abrasive. "The lofty disdain with which the *Dago* regards the *Sheeny* cannot be measured except by the scornful contempt with which the *Sheeny* scans the *Dago,*" a settlement worker commented. The names the immigrants called each other were as cruel as any that the settlement women had ever heard nativists use. Sheeny, Kike, Shonniker, Hebe, Mockie, Yid: There were a dozen dirty ways to label a Jew. The Jews categorized everybody else as Goyim. Non-Jews, mostly Catholics, looked on each other less as coreligionists than as Micks, Dagos (also Wops, Guineas), Krauts, Canucks, Bohunks, Hunkies, Lugans, and Polacks.[18]

Divisions within the ethnic "colonies" were marked as well. Not only did Jews from Eastern Europe resent the condescension and contempt that the Deutschniks (German Jews) directed at them. "Ghetto" Jews of whatever nationality were split into Orthodox and Conservative camps, wary of each other and on their guard against bourgeois Jews from outside—alrightniks—who might lure them into Reformism or some form of infidelity (Ethical Culture, Christian Science, Protestantism, or atheism). Similarly, most North Italians looked down on "Southerners," whose mutual loyalties were minimal except among *compari* (kinsmen) and *paesani* (people from the same village or province in the old country). Every ethnic group had its contending factions and sects.[19]

Finally, differences of sex and age formed barriers between people of the same ethnicity and members of the same family. Most group activities were exclusively male or female, adult or youth. To the emancipated settlement residents the immigrant women and girls looked like victims, not only of American industry, which exploited them ruthlessly, but of their own rigid peasant traditions as well, which tied them to household drudgery when they were not in the factory. The settlement saw beauty in many of the folkways too. For that reason the conflict between the generations struck them as especially tragic.

Immigrants demanded the same deference from their American-born children as they had shown their elders back home. The Americanized young people, who often knew the ways of the New World better than their parents did, resented and resisted the control of mothers and fathers who seemed "old-fashioned." Parental harshness could crush the spirit of youngsters or goad them into rebellion. If the young rejected their ethnic heritage altogether, they would wound their parents and deprive themselves—and America—of something rich and irreplaceable. The young women who had bent bourgeois conventionality by moving into the slums knew the bitterness of generational clash from experience. Compared to the gap between them and their parents, however, the "chasm" dividing immigrants and their children appeared "cruel and impassable."[20]

A community crisscrossed by so many lines of cleavage seemed to lack all coherence. Nothing the settlement workers encountered in the tenement districts distressed them more than the disorganization and disorder they saw all around them. To Jane Addams it looked as if the entire "social organism," from the family level on up, had "broken down" on the Near West Side.[21]

The struggle for subsistence drained the energy of the workers. In the anxieties of day-to-day living, wives nagged their husbands, who turned on the women and children, at times violently, and took to the streets and saloons for respite. Sometimes, "in the face of non-employment or domestic complexity or both," they deserted their families temporarily. "Paradoxically enough," wrote Julia Lathrop, the charity visitor, "the intermittent husband is a constant factor in the economic problem of many a household."[22]

Shifting from job to job and from "one wretched lodging to another," the workingmen had little opportunity to develop lasting relationships and establish community solidarity. People who worked in the same factory and lived in the same tenement hardly knew each other. For those who came out ahead in the competitive struggle, the surest way to demonstrate their triumph was "to move away as rapidly as they can afford it." It was every man for himself and for his own family. With the successful people always leaving, "newly arrived immigrants," whom Jane Addams described as "densely ignorant of civic duties," kept crowding in to replace them. Politicians would do nothing to improve local conditions without persistent prodding. But the people showed "no initiative." The streets, the sweatshops, the schools, the houses—everything suffered. "The idea underlying our self-government," Miss Addams lamented, "breaks down in such a ward."[23]

The question for the settlement workers was, What could they do about it? Jane Addams thought she knew the answer. The workers lacked many things, but what they seemed to lack most of all was social organization. "Men of executive ability" regimented them into industrial armies, but no one saw to it that they were "organized socially." No one, that is, except the "local demagogue." The "chaos" that resulted, she said, was "as great as it would be were they working in huge factories without foreman or superintendent." The settlement's task was cut out for it. Hull-House would superintend the working class. Only people "of ability and refinement, of social power and university cultivation" could bring order to the chaos of the slums. Miss Addams disclaimed any intention of imposing an artificial structure on the workers. She was sure that they had latent "social energies" capable of being tapped and trained for good or ill. Hull-House aimed "to bring into [the neighborhood] and develop from it those lines of thought and action which make for the higher life."[24]

To rally the neighborhood folk it was first necessary to get them to the settlement. Jane Addams was shrewd enough to realize that the "higher life," as such, would have limited allure. Recitals, concerts, art exhibits, and lectures drew a predictably small segment of the population. Over time the settlement devised a variety of services and activities as so many "hooks" to "grapple" the rest of the neighborhood into attendance.

Within a few years of its opening, Hull-House had an extensive educational program. Jane Addams believed in the democratization of beauty and culture, which to her meant that any subject which well-to-do children learned ought to be available to the children of the poor. So the settlement offered instruction in art, drama, dancing, and music. The classes were as much like clubs as the teachers could make them. One subtle purpose of the classes was to teach the children respect for the European heritages of their parents and of other ethnic groups. The settlement wanted to Americanize the children without blotting out their ethnic identity. The emphasis was on *folk* music, *folk* art, *folk* drama, *folk* dancing.[25]

The bulk of the Hull-House curriculum was more mundane. The public schools, like everything else the city provided the neighborhood, were inadequate. Even though truancy rates were high and most children dropped out of school long before they reached fourteen, the buildings were overcrowded. In the "barren and repellent" classrooms, teachers concentrated on disciplining the unruly pupils, who did their best to "torture the teacher." The best-equipped Catholic high school in the area, St. Ignatius, was a kind of parochial boys' prep school, serving ambitious Catholic families from a wide geographical area. It had little to do with the neighborhood boys, except for the relative handful whose parents could afford the tuition. The settlement tried to plug the gaps that the public schools and St. Ignatius left in education. It conducted classes in homemaking and handicrafts as well as conventional subjects from the elementary level up through university extension. And it held classes in English and citizenship for adult immigrants.[26]

The neighborhood had no nurseries, no day-care centers, and no kindergarten. Hull-House provided them. That was Jane Addams's basic approach: Investigate to see what needs to be done, then do it. The area was notoriously unhealthy, but there was little money to be made in healing sick people who were so poor. The main medical practitioners were not doctors but rather drugstore clerks and midwives. Hull-House set up an infant clinic, a free medical dispensary, and a pure-milk station, and it became an outpost of the Visiting Nurses' Association. Because the tenement houses lacked bathtubs, the settlement installed showers in a basement and finally built a bathhouse for the neighborhood. In the absence of a local library, the staff opened a reading room.

The settlement also ran a cooperative coal yard, an employment bureau, and a low-priced coffee shop and restaurant. It supervised a playground, equipped a gym, furnished a men's club room with billiard tables, and made several rooms available for the meetings of local groups. To mitigate the "lodger evil," the settlement acquired buildings and rented them to cooperative boarding clubs, one for men, one for women. It was a tribute to Miss Addams's local standing that the young workingwomen named their cooperative the Jane Club.[27]

As the programs proliferated, Hull-House expanded its physical plant, annexing several nearby buildings. The old saloon and the undertaking establishment both gave way to the settlement. To administer all of the activities, Miss Addams and Miss Starr required the aid of sixteen other residents and a staff of one hundred part-time volunteers, mostly commuters from more "favored" communities. Hull-House offered something, its residents felt, for everybody. Jane Addams wanted it to serve as the very center of the community's intellectual, social, and civic life.

By 1894 Hull-House was attracting nearly 1,900 visitors a week, but that number represented a tiny fraction of the 70,000 people who lived within six blocks of Polk and Halsted. There were competing centers in the neighborhood, and Hull-House was no match for them.[28]

The action was never at the settlement but rather on "the sordid streets" outside. Except on cold or rainy days the streets and sidewalks swarmed with people. When it was warm, the ovenlike atmosphere of the flats drove tenement dwellers outdoors. They camped on porches and stairways, huddled in doorways, and sat on sidewalk benches improvised from crates. People clustered on the corners and along the curbs. Every lamppost, fireplug, hitching post, and garbage box was a forum. On the business streets, the stores and vendors' stalls served as meeting places as well as markets. People also gathered at the small shops that abounded in the basements and ground floors of the side streets. Men held forth in cigar stores and barber shops, the women in bakeries and groceries, the youngsters in candy shops. Vendors pushed their carts up the side streets, cajoling pedestrians to buy their wares and hollering for anyone who was still inside to come on out.[29]

The size and composition of the street crowd varied with the weather, the time of day, and the business cycle. When work was slack, the number of men increased. The children were most evident after school hours. At sundown in the heat of the summer, everybody seemed to be outside.[30]

Children played on the sidewalks and, when the traffic was not too heavy, in the streets. The adults, off by themselves, nevertheless kept an eye on the children. Older girls had difficulty evading the supervision of their elders. Often they were saddled with the job of looking after the little ones. The adults tended to keep the girls close enough to be seen, if not overheard. The boys were more successful in contriving some seclusion. They played stickball, shinny, buck-buck, and pom-pom-pullaway out in the open, just as the girls jumped rope and played jacks. And they prowled the sidewalks in packs, lagging buttons or pennies, pestering the vendors and sometimes swiping their goods, and roughhousing. Each pack tried to establish a corner or a stretch of street as its turf. To keep rival gangs at bay, the boys had to spend a good deal of time patrolling the sidewalks. But when too many adults were around, the boys headed elsewhere.

Alleys, gangways, backyards, cellars, and open spaces underneath stairways and boardwalks were among their favorite haunts. Flat rooftops and vacant lots made good hangouts too. So did the railroad overpasses that cordoned off the Near West Side. Free from the oversight of older people, the boys could swear, smoke, drink beer, shoot craps, tell obscene stories, and look at "indecent postal cards." It took money to support some of these activities. If the boys didn't work, or if their parents commandeered their pay, they had ways of getting cash. They stole bottles from back porches, raided clotheslines and window iceboxes, foraged for junk in garbage heaps, robbed coal yards, looted freight cars, ripped the cedar paving blocks out of the streets, and stripped pipes from vacant buildings. Obliging junkmen exchanged their plunder for pennies and nickels.[31]

The hangouts served as hiding places when the boys were on the run. Stealing was not the only form of mischief the gangs practiced. Jane Addams listed some of the things boys did, as she thought, for lack of something "constructive" to do. They "flipped" wagons and trains, turned in false fire alarms, broke streetlights, threw rocks at moving trains, knocked down signs, pelted stage actors with slingshots, overturned pushcarts, threw switches to derail streetcars, and cut Western Union cable. Even when constructive play was available under the supervision of Hull-House, most boys preferred to fool around outside.[32]

Of course, the streets, for all their color, were crowded, noisy, hectic, and dirty. People who got tired of the sidewalk routine could repair to one of the district's numerous commercial establishments. "Destructive agencies" the settlement workers called them, "vicious amusements" that preyed on the popular craving for relaxation and recreation. In return for their hard-earned money, Jane Addams lamented, the people received "illicit and soul-destroying pleasures." Poolrooms, "vulgar" dance halls, and cheap theaters enjoyed a thriving trade. The first time Miss Addams ever saw Halsted Street she noticed a long line of men and boys. It was a Sunday, but they were not queued up for a church service.

The crowd was waiting to get into the 2:00 P.M. show at the Bijou, although it was only noon. The hold of the cheap shows on "the entire population" never ceased to amaze and depress her. Far worse than the local vaudeville and dance palaces were the burlesque halls, arcades, massage parlors, and whorehouses downtown. The vice district, less than a mile from Hull-House, lured customers from all over.[33]

Of all the strictly local institutions, the most heavily patronized was the ubiquitous saloon. In 1890 there were 255 of these places within the square-mile limits of the Nineteenth Ward, and there were hundreds more just beyond the boundary lines. Miss Addams acknowledged ruefully that the saloon, not the settlement, was "the center of the liveliest political and social life of the ward.[34]

Hull-House commanded so small and select a following that Jane Addams referred to the faithful as the "transfigured few." It was no wonder. A workingman who happened into the Coffee House one—and only one—time put it very well on his way out: "This would be a nice place to sit in all day if one could only have beer." The settlement, of course, would not condone the fatal glass of beer. Nor swearing, nor spitting, nor playing cards for money. The staff tolerated tobacco (for smoking only, not chewing). This grudging concession was not enough to satisfy most workingmen. As a resident observed, it was not "the man in overalls" who visited regularly, "but the teacher, the clerk, and the smaller employer."[35]

The Men's Club was made up of 150 of "the abler citizens and more enterprising young men of the vicinity." On these men the staff bestowed the ultimate accolade: "They are in sympathy with the aims of Hull-House, and are prompt to assist and promote any of its undertakings." Similarly, "ninety of the most able women in the ward" constituted the Women's Club. The "most successful clubs" were "entirely composed of English-speaking and American-born young people." Members of the boys' clubs had to "behave in a quiet and orderly manner," as defined by the staff. Outside, the boys could follow their own code of conduct.[36]

For those who did avail themselves of the settlement's offerings, Hull-House was hardly the common center that Jane Addams contemplated. People who came daily, such as the mothers who left their babies at the nursery, spent little time there. Those who took part in some activity usually attended only once or twice a week. And the regular participants segmented themselves much as they did in everyday life: by age, sex, territory, and ethnicity.

Eventually, Hull-House provided separate buildings for men, women, boys, and girls. In clubs formed around "natural groupings," that is, preexisting gangs and cliques, there was no more ethnic mixture than in the ordinary street group. Many of the children's clubs were multiethnic, but that was due to the influence of the street, not of the staff. The people who came most often were those who lived nearby. For everyone else, attendance involved leaving home turf. At any given time, Hull-House probably held residents of more different pieces of territory than did any other single spot in the district, but that did not mean that the people interacted much. For adults from the immediate environs, Hull-House found itself hosting "German evenings," "Italian evenings," and so on.[37]

Nevertheless, in classes and in clubs formed around interests (such as debating), ethnic and territorial insularity did break down significantly. Sometimes, people who met in these interethnic activities formed new "natural groupings." And the staff sponsored regular "House-wide" events to gather together everyone who used the place. While these formalistic galas were something less than howling successes, they provided a sheltered setting in which amicable contacts could occur across, and despite, social barriers.[38]

This heterogeneity was both a weakness and a strength. To function as a melting pot, the settlement had to establish its ground as neutral turf. Because the buildings stood in heavily Italian territory, the Italians, even though they did not flock to the settlement themselves, regarded other visitors as interlopers. The staff relentlessly resisted identification of Hull-House as "an Italian institution." By 1895 an Italian-language newspaper conceded that the "neighborhood-house" was there "to help not only Italians but other nationalities." Everyone was welcome. On the other hand, no group could regard the settlement as its own. Because it belonged equally to everybody, it belonged to nobody—except the settlement residents themselves.[39]

Despite the narrowness of their clientele, the Hull-House residents believed that they were helping the entire West Side and the whole poverty belt of Chicago as well. Anyone could call on the staff for help. The settlement acted both as an aid station, dispensing some services directly, and as a clearinghouse, channeling people in need to the appropriate charitable agency. In mediating between the poor and the remote, callous welfare institutions, the settlement assumed the role of "the big brother whose mere presence on the playground protects the little one from bullies." For a long time, Jane Addams thought that acting as "big brother" was the settlement's main neighborhood function. It had other functions, however, which reached beyond the local area's boundaries.[40]

One of the stated objectives of Hull-House was "to investigate and improve the conditions in the industrial districts of Chicago." First the staff investigated, and then, armed with facts, they agitated for reform. In 1892, for instance, the settlement pressured the State of Illinois Bureau of Labor Statistics to make an investigation of the sweating system in Chicago. The bureau named a Hull-House resident, Florence Kelley, to conduct the survey. There was already a lurid literature of exposés on the subject, and the Chicago Trades and Labor Assembly had published a competent report of its own, but none of this moved legislators. Miss Kelley issued her report, the staff lobbied strenuously for outright abolition of the sweating system, and within a year the Illinois legislature passed a bill regulating workshops and factories. The law was a disappointment, but it was a beginning. The governor of Illinois at the time was the liberal John Peter Altgeld, who appointed Miss Kelley state factory inspector. In 1893 Miss Kelley directed the federal government survey of Chicago's slums. She kept up her agitation for abolition of sweatshops throughout her tenure as state inspector, and when Altgeld's successor fired her, she continued to gather "facts, facts, and more facts" and to publicize the need for reform.[41]

Hull-House tried to improve the lot of the workers without alienating "the power-holding classes." Its aim was conciliation, not confrontation. If the settlement could "interpret" the have-nots to the haves, Jane Addams believed, the elite would enlist in the movement to help the poor. And the response of the rich seemed to justify her faith. Between 1890 and the spring of 1894, ten other groups of upper-class uplifters established compounds in the tenement districts in imitation of Hull-House. All of the settlements owed their existence to the financial support of the rich. In her fifth year at Hull-House, Miss Addams could feel the strength of the settlement impulse growing. She looked forward confidently to the unification of "all good citizens, capitalist and proletarian" in a single, solidary society.[42]

It took a "great social disaster," the Pullman Strike, to jolt Jane Addams into awareness of the abiding conflict between the classes. She served on a committee that tried unsuccessfully to arbitrate the strike. At the model town, she saw men irreconcilably divided. Managers, straw bosses, and other company men wore miniature American flags on their lapels; the strikers wore white ribbons. There were no neutrals in sight. Coming back to Hull-House, she noticed "almost everyone on Halsted Street wearing a white ribbon, the emblem of the strikers' side." The neighborhood was unanimous in its support of the workers. The residents of Hull-House, on the other hand, were "divided in opinion."[43]

Florence Kelley felt that it was time for the settlement to decide whose side it was on, that of "the oppressed" or "the oppressing." Two other residents, Ellen Gates Starr and Alzina Stevens, agreed. Miss Kelley was a socialist, and Miss Starr was fast becoming one. Mrs. Stevens was one of the very few settlement workers who had ever worked at common labor. She lost two fingers in a textile mill accident when she was a child. These women wanted Hull-House to come out for the workers. The rest of the staff, split in sympathies, agreed with Jane Addams that the settlement should stand above the struggle. If Hull-House took sides, Miss Addams insisted, it would fail in its responsibility to reconcile capital and labor.[44]

Jane Addams sympathized with the workers. She considered George M. Pullman a benevolent despot who turned on his men once they asserted themselves. She had sympathy for Pullman also. He reminded her of King Lear, a victim of self-inflicted tragedy. His flaw was that he tried to be " 'good to people,' rather than be 'with them.' " The workingmen reacted like Lear's daughters. If labor could content itself with winning just terms from capital, then it would correspond to Cordelia, Lear's good daughter. If it went beyond the demand for justice and sought vengeance, then it would take on the character of Lear's evil daughters. In Shakespeare's play, the old king and his good child reconciled too late. To prevent the Pullman strike from developing into a general tragedy of industrial relations, workers and employers would have to work out a democratic accommodation before time ran out. The settlements, from their vantage point between the contending parties, had to hasten the process of conciliation.[45]

Jane Addams realized that the Pullman revolt contained a lesson for settlement workers as well as industrialists: "One does good, if at all, *with* people, not *to* people." The model community had "comfortable homes" and "beautiful surroundings," both of which the poverty belt lacked, but without democracy these meant little. Similarly, if the settlements transformed the tenement districts without the participation of the people, the effort would be meaningless.[46]

Shortly after the Pullman strike was smashed, a Hull-House resident named Mary McDowell moved to Packingtown to take charge of a new settlement house. This was one of the grimiest, roughest areas of Back a' the Yards. The city's most-fearsome gangs came from there. During the Pullman strike, packinghouse laborers who struck in sympathy with the car workers rioted for days. The new settlement was half a mile from the spot where state troopers gunned down twenty-four members of a massive mob, killing four. The heaviest concentration of saloons in the city, a strip on Ashland Avenue called Whiskey Row, was just around the corner from the settlement. The main municipal garbage dump was nearby. The whole neighborhood reeked with the stench of the dump, the great slaughterhouses, and Bubbly Creek, a branch of the Chicago River that the packinghouses filled with blood and animal waste. The streets were unpaved, the houses had no sewer connections, and as Mary McDowell discovered to her disgust, "the ditches were covered with a green scum from standing water."[47]

Packingtown was one of the districts that Robert Hunter excluded from his 1900 tenement survey because it was too bad to be representative. A few years later, Upton Sinclair selected it as the setting for *The Jungle.* Mary McDowell wanted to do settlement work in this neighborhood, she said, because it would give her "a chance to work with the least skilled workers in our industry; not *for* them as a missionary, but *with* them as a neighbor and seeker after truth; not to proselytize Jews or Catholics but to express my ideas of right social relationships."[48]

"*With,* not *for*" became a central tenet of the settlement creed. The challenge to settlement workers after 1894 was to put their creed into practice.

❧

Between 1895 and 1917, reformers in Chicago founded sixty-eight settlements. Twenty of these would-be neighborhood centers floundered and folded. Those that survived credited their success to strong community support.[49]

Hull-House, the pioneer settlement, continued to expand. Jane Addams maintained that the local people shaped the settlement's program. Hull-House kept growing because of popular demand, she said. But this was true only in the most indirect sense. From the start Jane Addams, not the neighborhood folk, made the decisions. At first she shared her policy-making power with other members of the staff. Later she set up a formal panel to guide the settlement and sustain it. The Hull-House Board of Trustees, incorporated in 1894, was made up of wealthy residents of Chicago's lakefront communities and the suburbs. These were Jane Addams's real peers. The board eventually included one philosopher who believed in the power of the people—Professor John Dewey of the University of Chicago—but it never included any local people. The only trustee who lived on the Near West Side was Jane Addams.[50]

Supposedly, the board set policy to suit the "demands of the neighborhood." Yet the activities that the trustees approved—kindergarten, clubs, playgrounds, and the like—were the very activities that George Pullman made available to his tenants. Hull-House had its Men's Club and Women's Club; Pullman had its Men's Society and Woman's Union. The Pullman organizations were not representative, but neither were those at Hull-House. The company town had a population only a fraction of the size of the district around the settlement, but the Pullman clubs had more members than the Hull-House clubs. The settlement staff stood for the right of workers to organize in industry, and, of course, Pullman was an enemy of unionism. Still, the neighborhood people had no more representation on the settlement's Board of Trustees than the Pullman employees had on the company's Board of Directors.[51]

Only one settlement permitted any measure of "neighborhood control" over policy. In 1895 members of the Universalist Church in Englewood opened a day nursery and kindergarten for the benefit of the poorer workingwomen of the neighborhood. As the program expanded, the church relaxed its surveillance over the work instead of tightening it. In 1900 the church relinquished all control. Three years later the settlement incorporated under the name Neighborhood House.

The directors of Neighborhood House and the clientele were "people of different classes and conditions." But most of the twenty-five board members lived in Englewood. Thus the small wage earners who used the place and the more well-to-do people who ran it were in fact neighbors. When the settlement needed a new building, the board financed it (at least in part) by selling certificates at five dollars each to people "of the locality." Individuals or families could buy shares. All shareholders became members of the Neighborhood House Association. The board was self-perpetuating, not elective, and it made all of the decisions, but "in important matters" its actions were "subject to a referendum vote by the entire membership of the Association."

Perhaps Neighborhood House did not "really belong to the whole people," as its staff claimed. But its organization was the closest approximation to "democratic control of neighborhood social efforts" in the history of Chicago settlements.[52]

In other neighborhoods the impetus for settlement work came from outside, and institutional control remained in the hands of outsiders. Mary McDowell won acceptance in Packingtown, but she owed her appointment and her tenure as head resident of the settlement to the Philanthropic Committee of the Christian Union of the University of Chicago. She was loyal to the people in Back a' the Yards, but she was accountable to the university community. The university group that founded and maintained the settlement did not intend to "introduce a foreign element" into Packingtown. The Christian Union crowd simply wished to "fertilize and cultivate the springing elements of good already found in the neighborhood." Even Packingtown, the university uplifters believed, had "some aspiring souls. The settlement aims to discover these and help them in moral leadership." This was Mary McDowell's mandate when she established the University of Chicago Settlement. No one had consulted the people in Back a' the Yards to see if they cared for this sort of benefaction. Her initial welcome in Packingtown was a very cold one.[53]

The usual neighborhood response to the establishment of a settlement house was aloofness, if not overt hostility. A resident of

Little Bohemia expressed a common feeling when a group of Protestant college graduates set up a day nursery near his home. He protested that "strangers of a different part of town and another nationality had no business to come into the neighborhood and start something the people had not asked for."[54]

Two Protestant clergymen who founded settlements on the Northwest Side tried to avoid offending local pride by selecting neighborhoods where Protestants and North Europeans were still dominant. Graham Taylor and Charles Zeublin hoped that people who were "akin" to them in "heritage, traits, speech, and faith" would be receptive. In fact, many neighborhood people were "suspicious" of them. And almost as soon as Taylor opened Chicago Commons and Zeublin started work at Northwestern University Settlement, the whole district around them underwent "a rapid and radical racial transformation."

The Scandinavians, Germans, and Irish people who were the mainstay of the club activity at Chicago Commons moved on, to be replaced by people who were more "alien" and less "assimilable"—Italians, Greeks, Poles, and Armenians. Around Northwestern University Settlement too, the North Europeans lost the upper hand in "the struggle of the nations." The settlement staff noted sadly that the area had changed from a "self-respecting German and Scandinavian neighborhood, to one made up almost wholly of Poles and Russian Jews." The task of "Americanizing and socializing and Christianizing" the neighborhood became harder year by year.[55]

The Poles who lived around Northwestern University Settlement stayed away in droves. Thousands of children lived in the blocks adjoining the settlement, but only a handful had any contacts with it. The Jews, whose homes were farther away, were willing to walk the extra blocks to take advantage of the staff's educational and recreational programs, but they had no desire to be Christianized.[56]

Two-thirds of the settlements established before 1917 had some Protestant affiliation. Most of these settlements claimed that they did not proselytize, but half of them included religious services among their activities, and as many offered "religious instruction." One settlement worker in a heavily Polish area responded to a charge that her staff was trying to convert Catholics with the statement: "If inviting people of all and no denominations to join Bible classes and attend religious meetings might be termed proselyting, then we do it. We do not make any distinction in our invitations." To Catholics and Jews, this was missionary work, and they wanted no part of it. Catholic and Jewish leaders established settlements of their own in self-defense.[57]

Immigrants resisted proselytizers, and they resented "Americanizers" from outside their own ethnic group as well. While they did not reject Americanization, they wanted to control the process themselves. Jews, Poles, and Italians aspired to be something more than *just* Americans: They wanted to be Jewish-Americans, Polish-Americans, and Italian-Americans. Reformers who thought that a settlement was a "factory" for mass production of a "good, law-respecting type of American citizen" had to learn to respect self-Americanization. This was a difficult lesson for settlement workers. Those who learned it learned very slowly. Most of them never quite caught on.[58]

Even the Catholics and Jews who set up settlements for their coreligionists had trouble tailoring their programs to fit the aspirations of the immigrants. At the beginning, especially, the Irish who dominated the Catholic settlements and the Germans who controlled the Jewish settlements alienated the East European aliens they were trying to assimilate.

In 1893 German Jews established "a Jewish Social Settlement like the Hull-House" for the benefit of the Russians and Poles who were pouring into the Ghetto. The settlement on Maxwell Street was never popular among the newcomers. The neighborhood people had "no voice" in managing the enterprise, and they "resented the philanthropic interest of the South Side Germans" even more than they resented Hull-House. A later group of Jewish reformers, mindful of the failure of Maxwell Street Settlement, concluded that they could never succeed in the Ghetto unless they cast off the appearance of "patronage." In 1906 they opened Chicago Hebrew Institute as "a People's Palace maintained for the people, used and governed by the people."[59]

The founders claimed that the new settlement was a creation of the local community, entirely independent of the South Side Deutschniks. In fact, the main contributors were South Side German Jews. The institute was more candid about its Americanizing role. An early circular stated that the institute was to be "the rallying place of the immigrant in search of true American citizenship." The staff's aim was to help the Ghetto's inhabitants "to become American Jews." The institute promised to foster both "a deeper Judaism and better Americanism."[60]

Few settlements learned to appeal to the immigrants' sense of self-respect as astutely as the Chicago Hebrew Institute did. Most settlements mastered the language of class brotherhood, however. A few of them, notably Mary McDowell's University of Chicago Settlement, came out squarely on the side of the working people during industrial disputes. Nevertheless, paternalism ran strong in the veins of settlement workers, despite the creed of *"with,* not *for."* In some settlements, the Pullman spirit was rampant. Most of the settlement houses served God, a God who was a Protestant. There were those that served Mammon as well.

One settlement, South Deering Neighborhood Center, admitted to being the creation of the Wisconsin Steel Mills and its affiliate, the Byproducts Coke Corporation. The staff was surprised at how "difficult" it was "to get hold of" the foreigners who lived and worked in the neighborhood. Late in the 1890s a Methodist church and the WCTU (Women's Christian Temperance Union) joined forces to promote temperance and uplift among the beer-drinking Bohemians, Poles, and Lithuanians of the "Lumberyards" district. According to the uplifters, the working people of the area were "filled with false ideas of American freedom, with hatred of all social order," as well as with spirituous liquors. The evangelists founded Gads Hill Center to counteract the "baleful influences" that were debasing the people. The main support for their work came from International Harvester Company and other manufacturing concerns in the district.[61]

Gads Hill Center drummed up contributions from businessmen with appeals to their sense of self-interest. A prominent Bohemian-American businessman named Frederick A. Lorenz wrote a fund-appeal letter for the settlement in 1911. "You have business interests in the vicinity where Gad's Hill Center is located," Lorenz reminded local merchants and industrialists. "The influence that it exerts on those living and working in that neighborhood will be felt directly or indirectly in your own business. Men without ideals, without hope, and with no outlook into the future become Anarchists, and at best make but indifferent and poor workers and unfaithful employees." As for the children of "the poor illiterate, foreign element," Gads Hill provided them with a clean, bright place "where, for the hour at least, poverty, squalor and lack of comfort are forgotten."[62]

Probably the most unpopular settlement to survive for any length of time was a Methodist Parish House that attempted to look after stockyard employees "morally, mentally and religiously." The area where the settlement did its work was overwhelmingly Catholic. One of the great meat-packing dynasties endowed the little settlement. It was called Gustavus F. Swift Memorial. To packinghouse workers the ministrations of Methodists were unwelcome, and the memory of old man Swift was hateful. The neighborhood avoided the place like the plague.[63]

The settlement workers who were genuinely committed to the ideal of "*with*, not *for*" originally hoped that they could stimulate local people to "develop their own guilds." Once established, these neighborhood guilds would get along "without further guidance," and the settlement workers would move on to new localities. But the guilds never developed. "Such neighborhoods," Graham Taylor wrote, depended on "the more continuous initiative" that a permanently fixed settlement house could provide. Chicago Commons and other settlements continued to set up neighborhood guilds and community clubs, but the membership always remained small. Sometimes, the roster of such an organization consisted entirely of settlement staff members and people who had moved away from the neighborhood. In 1894 Northwestern University Settlement organized a Civic Federation. A year later the federation "died," as the staff put it, "for lack of interest and energy on the part of the people." This happened over and over again.[64]

The political bosses were more successful in maintaining organizations in the settlement neighborhoods. Some settlement workers tried to work "with" their neighbors to take power from the hands of the bosses. For the most part these efforts failed resoundingly.

Charles W. Espey founded Archer Road Settlement "to furnish Christian example" to the "Germans, Italians, Greeks, Croatians, Bohemians and Irish" in a run-down section of the old Fourth Ward. Nowhere did the people of that "river ward" need example so much as in the area of civics, Espey decided. Accordingly, he offered himself as a candidate for alderman two times. Both of his campaigns were "unsuccessful but educational." What moral the neighborhood drew from the settlement worker's civics lesson is uncertain. Espey learned not to bother running again.[65]

Mary McDowell also tried running for office. She knew she had no hope of winning an aldermanic contest in the Twenty-ninth Ward, so she sought a wider constituency. In 1914 she ran with a slate of reform candidates for a place on the Cook County Board of Commissioners. She lost overwhelmingly. Harriet Vittum of Northwestern University Settlement was one of Mary McDowell's running mates in the county board election. They went down to defeat together. The same year Miss Vittum lost her race for county commissioner, she also ran for alderman of the Seventeenth Ward. She distributed campaign literature in Polish and English and stumped the precincts tirelessly. Miss Vittum, a trained nurse, was a towering figure of a woman. Her invariable attire was a severe brown suit and dark stockings, a uniform that made her look like a man to the adults. The children of the neighborhood called her "the police lady in brown." She lost the election badly. This was five years after she referred to her neighbors as "ignorant foreigners, who live in an atmosphere of low morals . . . surrounded by anarchy and crime."[66]

Jane Addams never ran for office, but she did direct four highly publicized aldermanic campaigns in the old Nineteenth Ward. The candidates she put up against Alderman Johnny Powers, the Prince of the Boodlers, were Irish Catholics from the neighborhood, not outsiders. They lost anyway. As Miss Addams recognized, the neighborhood sensed that "the movement for reform came from an alien source," namely Hull-House. After Big Johnny's victory in the 1898 election, Jane Addams decided to withdraw from ward politics. Powers was "notoriously corrupt," but he dealt in jobs and favors among people who were desperately dependent on both. That made him practically unbeatable. At any rate, no opponent running under the auspices of Hull-House could beat him. The settlement brand of politics appealed mainly to "the more substantial citizens in the ward," and there were not enough of them to swing an election. It might have been possible for Hull-House to forge a winning coalition with an anti-Powers Italian bloc that was emerging in the ward, but Jane Addams never even considered a political partnership with the Italians. The four futile campaigns, and the decision to abandon politics rather than cooperate with Italian precinct organizers, exposed the settlement's shallow neighborhood roots.[67]

One settlement did score significant successes in ward politics. Candidates backed by Chicago Commons won aldermanic seats in 1896 and 1897, and from 1901 to 1917 no man endorsed by the settlement failed to win election to the city council. Graham Taylor boasted that the Commons held the balance of power in the Seventeenth Ward, and it was true. The settlement endorsed men of both parties and of four nationalities: Irish, Norwegian, German, and Polish. Whoever ran with the blessings of the Commons won. The record of the Commons would seem to prove that at least one Chicago settlement had solid grass-roots support. However, this was not the case.[68]

The Seventeenth Ward Community Club was Graham Taylor's political organization. Like any political machine, it was built as much on *nonvoting* as on voting. Ward bosses did not win elections by getting out the vote but rather by getting *the right people* to vote. In the Seventeenth Ward, the Republican and Democratic machines were about evenly matched. Like a shrewd political boss, Taylor had "seen his opportunities and he took 'em." He organized the "decent voters" of the ward into a third political force. Taylor concentrated on getting *his* people to vote. The fewer of the rest who voted, the better.[69]

From the 1890s to 1915, Taylor's allies had an advantage over other people in the ward that gave them voting power out of all proportion to their numbers. They were citizens; they could vote. The newcomers who were swarming into the ward from Poland and Italy were aliens. Until they were naturalized, they could not register to vote. Poles and Italians constituted a majority in the ward by 1905; nevertheless, Scandinavians, Germans, Irishmen, and "Americans" of other ethnic backgrounds maintained their numerical superiority at the ballot box. Between 1904 and 1911 the population of the ward increased from 60,000 to 71,000, but the number of registered voters fell from 11,644 to 6,899. There were years when immigrant men of voting age—but ineligible to vote—outnumbered registered voters by more than two to one.[70]

Graham Taylor's power in the Seventeenth Ward lasted until naturalized Poles and Italians and their children who came of age started voting in appreciable numbers. When they overtook the dwindling older-stock voters, the Commons organization stopped winning elections. From 1902 to 1910 the Seventeenth Ward aldermen, one an Irish Democrat, the other a German Republican, were both steadfast "Commons aldermen." Each year one of them came up for reelection; usually they won by large margins, with the support of their respective party organizations as well as that of the Commons. But in 1910 a renegade Democrat named Stanley Walkowiak challenged the Democratic incumbent, William E. Dever. According to Graham Taylor, the challenger was "a dangerous demagogue" who appealed straight to "the race prejudice of the Poles to elect one of their own number." Dever won, but Walkowiak made a strong showing. A year later, when Dever vacated his post to take a judgeship, Walkowiak announced his candidacy to serve out Dever's unexpired term. This was the beginning of the end of the settlement's Community Club.[71]

Instead of opposing Walkowiak, the Commons endorsed him. The alternatives were to support an Italian Republican whom the Commons had turned out of office in 1897 or to launch an independent race. Taylor was unwilling to back the Italian, Stephen Revere, and unable to find a candidate of his own. Besides, it did not look as if either Revere or any independent could win. So Taylor and the club went along with Walkowiak. The "dangerous demagogue" won, and, for the record, the Commons did not *lose*, because it backed him.[72]

In the regular aldermanic contest of 1911 the veteran "Commons alderman," Republican Lewis Sitts, beat back a challenge from an Italian Democrat, Stephen Malato. This was a real victory for the Commons, but a costly one. While the Poles had become the leading nationality in the ward as a whole, the Italians predominated in the precincts all around the Commons. Whenever an Italian had run for city council in the past, Graham Taylor had opposed him. Now two prominent neighborhood Italians had tried to win office, and the settlement spurned them both, the Democrat and the Republican alike. In 1912 Stanley Walkowiak ran for his first full term; again, the Commons endorsed Walkowiak, who won. The politics of the Community Club still seemed to be successful. In fact, the

Commons had lost its old leverage at the ward level. And the ward politics of the Community Club had become an affront to people at the precinct level, that is, to the local community.[73]

Alderman Walkowiak won reelection in 1914 and 1916, both times with the backing of the Seventeenth Ward Community Club. But by 1916 the club's endorsement did not count for much. In 1915 Alderman Sitts had been challenged by a Pole named Stanley Kielczynski. With an all-out effort by the regular Republican organization and the Commons, Sitts squeaked through with 50.6 percent of the vote. For Graham Taylor and his Community Club, this was the last hurrah. In 1917 Sitts lost his bid for an eighth term to a Pole named Stanley Adamkiewicz.[74]

Graham Taylor had an explanation for the collapse of his club. His most dependable members had all moved away, and "the rapid influx of foreign-speaking immigrants" left him with "too few English-speaking men." The result, as he saw it, was twofold: "the Polish ascendancy," and "a sharp decline of political independence and public spirit." Actually, it was the participation of people long excluded from the franchise that brought the Poles to power and finished off the Commons as a force in politics.[75]

The Community Club at Chicago Commons never was a grassroots organization. Its members were a kind of local elite, and they were not truly independent. The club was under Reverend Taylor's thumb. He made the rules, and the men adhered to them or out they went. In his high starched collar, with his pince-nez and his thin straight-combed hair, he looked every inch the minister, and he acted like one. He had one vice: smoking. So he let the men smoke, sometimes joining them. But he neither drank, nor swore, nor gambled, and he made a rule that no one could drink, swear, or gamble in the club room. In 1911, when he discovered that "card playing for stakes [had] been going on," he ordered the membership to put an end to it. Otherwise, he said, he would close the club room down.[76]

Reverend Taylor was one of the settlement workers who tried to be "*with,* not *for*" his neighbors. He never succeeded. A remark that Jane Addams made reveals something of the reason. She said that Hull-House employed "every possible device to make operative on the life around it, *the conception of life which the settlement group holds* [italics added]." That was what she and Taylor and the others were doing all the time. Miss Addams also declared that she had no intention of making Hull-House "the largest institution on the West-Side," but that is just what it became. "What we wanted," she confided in her autobiography, was "to be swallowed up and digested, to disappear into the bulk of the people." The neighborhoods could never swallow the settlement or the settlement workers' conception of life.[77]

The people of the tenements had their own views on life, and even though their neighborhoods looked disorderly to the settlement workers, they had a social order of their own as well. Neighborhood society was segmented, but it was still organized. Family relationships, peer groups, and adaptations to work and living conditions formed the bases of that society. Street corners, saloons, cheap shops, and "vicious amusements" were all part of its institutional network. The settlements could not supplant that network, and they only partially succeeded in establishing a place for themselves within it.[78]

Still, the very effort that the settlements made to be "with" the workers made a difference in some people's lives. "It was that word *with* from Jane Addams that took the bitterness out of my life," said Mary Kenny, a workingwoman who joined the Hull-House staff as a labor organizer. Others, who did not swallow the settlement viewpoint whole, nevertheless went to the settlement to take advantage of what was available there. And there they got a taste of what life could be like away from the sweatshops, the streets, and the tenements.[79]

CHAPTER 4 ❧

The Housing Movement, 1893–1917: The Limits of Restrictive Reform

The inhabitants and their housing must be improved together.
—E. R. L. Gould, *The Housing of the Working People. Eighth Special Report of the Commissioner of Labor* (Washington, D.C., 1895), p. 161.

The business of housing the poor, if it is to amount to anything, must be business . . . .
—Jacob Riis, *How the Other Half Lives: Studies among the Tenements of New York* (New York, 1890; reprint ed., New York, 1957), p. 205.

THE SETTLEMENTS NEVER BECAME GENUINE COMMUNITY CENTERS IN THE tenement districts, but they did become the centers of the movement to reform the tenements. As neighbors to the poor, settlement residents learned—better than any other members of the favored classes—how the other half lived. From 1893, when Hull-House made its pioneering neighborhood survey, to World War I, settlement workers led the year-in, year-out battle against Chicago's slums. Their investigations and agitation cleared the path for tenement ordinances in 1902 and 1910, which were as important for Chicago's housing history as the more famous Tenement House Act of 1901 was for New York City's. Settlement workers put intense pressure on politicians and inspectors to make them enforce the legislation, and they beat down repeated attempts to cripple the laws by amendment.

These were significant achievements, and the reformers scored other successes along the way. Yet in 1921 Mary McDowell, looking back on nearly three decades of struggle, admitted, "There has been very little real improvement in housing." And Jane Addams noted sorrowfully that the settlement workers' efforts on behalf of better housing "strained their relations" with the neighborhood people instead of cementing them.[1]

Given the reformers' hopes and the limits within which they worked, the results were bound to be disappointing. The settlement residents wanted to see their neighbors housed decently, but the cruel fact was that the poor could not afford decent homes. If the housing stock improved but the incomes of poor families did not, then the poor would pay dearly for reform, because the cost of their accommodations would rise. On this basis the tenement dwellers did not want reform, but it was the only basis there was. Regulating incomes or rents was unthinkable to all but a handful of settlement workers like Florence Kelley and Ellen Gates Starr, who were socialists. Regulating sanitary conditions, on the other hand, was acceptable even to conservatives. Government had no right to "build homes for the poor," acknowledged Frances Buckley Embree, an upper-class ally of the settlement workers. But it did have a duty, she argued, "to make the way clear for the independent action of the law of supply and demand. This can be done by refusal to allow false and injurious products to be offered in the housing market."[2]

Regulating tenement conditions when the poor lacked the wherewithal to pay for improvements amounted to regulating the poor themselves. As Jacob Riis, the nationally famous New York reformer, wrote in *How the Other Half Lives*, "Those who would fight for the poor must fight the poor to do it." The biggest obstacles to housing betterment, Riis contended, were the tenants. "They are shiftless, destructive, and stupid; in a word, they are what the tenements have made them." Jane Addams agreed: "One of the most discouraging features" about the Chicago tenement situation was that tenants and landlords alike tended to be "sordid and ignorant immigrants."[3]

Miss Addams did not expect better housing to turn immigrants into model citizens automatically. She thought that "the pathetic stupidity of agricultural people" was practically insurmountable. South Italian peasants could never adjust to crowded city conditions, she feared. The place for them was in the Southern states, where they could live in rural colonies. For years she promoted a colonization scheme, but few of her neighbors were interested.[4]

An incident in 1893 illustrates Jane Addams's skepticism about the regenerative powers of good housing. Florence Kelley of Hull-House publicly attacked the owner of a large block of tenements near the settlement for his failure to install plumbing and sewer connections. The absentee landlord, a young reform-minded man named William Kent, denied that he was profiteering off the poor. After inspecting the flats with Miss Addams, he offered to turn them over to Hull-House rent-free, to see if the settlement staff could turn them into model tenements. If she took up his challenge, he predicted, she would fail miserably. Miss Addams declined. "Supplying South Italian peasants with sanitary appliances," she conceded to Kent, "would be throwing our money away." She asked him to tear down the buildings instead and build a playground on the site. He complied. Eventually, this became Chicago's first municipal playground. Seventeen years after the demolition of the old houses, Miss Addams noted that "the dispossessed tenants, a group of whom had to be evicted by legal process before their houses could be torn down, have never ceased to mourn their former estates."[5]

Obviously, Jane Addams did not look on improved dwellings as a panacea. As one of her Hull-House colleagues, George Hooker, put it, housing was "only a part" of the larger "community organization problem." Settlement workers advocated a wide range of reforms in education, recreation, industry, and government. They pushed so hard for housing reform because tenement conditions were intolerable and because they believed that without better housing all other reform would prove futile.[6]

"I don't see how a child can grow normally in an abnormal house," Graham Taylor said, and he spoke for the settlement movement. What good did it do, asked a Hull-House resident, to put children into "good schools, with good teachers" in the morning if they had to go home in the afternoon to dark, unventilated, overcrowded rooms? Sophonisba Breckenridge answered her own question: None. Bad housing "handicapped" children, and schools, reformatories, and playgrounds could not undo the damage. Tenement dwellers would not benefit from housing improvements unless neighborhood workers "trained and disciplined and informed" them, Graham Taylor argued. Conversely, neighborhood work would not have a chance of succeeding unless the homes of the people improved. Housing reform and neighborhood work had to go together. "The stability of the community depends upon this question of better housing," Taylor insisted:

> . . . for if the house deteriorates, the better type of families will not remain there, those who constitute the nucleus around which the new citizenship must be gathered and trained and more or less assimilated. That is one of the trials in working in these social settlement districts. The people who have come together at that common center to mingle and exchange values depart, and then new, crude, untrained people flock around with far too few to train them, and down goes the neighborhood. . . .[7]

To accomplish reform in housing, the settlement workers had to win the support of those whom Jane Addams called "the power-holding classes." They stressed the "economic waste" that bad housing involved. Reform, they argued, would cost society less than neglect when the final balance was tallied. Regulation of tenement conditions would simultaneously satisfy the demand for "social righteousness" and the need for "social order." Settlement workers depicted tenement dwellers as "the steerage passengers" of the "municipal ship" and promised to sanitize the steerage accommodations for the good of the whole vessel without, so to speak, rocking the boat. The essential strategy of reform was twofold. Settlement workers rallied "enlightened public citizens" behind municipal inspection of tenements and such related measures as provision of parks and playgrounds for the poor. And they tried to teach "the immigrants," as Jane Addams wrote in *Twenty Years at Hull-House,* that they must "not only keep their own houses clean, but must also help the authorities to keep the city clean."[8]

❧

Early in 1897 a group of settlement workers, charity visitors, and wealthy contributors to charitable causes gathered at Northwestern University Settlement to consider Chicago's housing problem. After several days of conferences, the participants concluded that the most pressing needs were an official city census of tenements and enforcement of building codes, which only the city government could provide, and model tenements, which the city's "capitalists" alone could build. Jane Addams argued that it would be better to build small cottages rather than large tenements as models, but, while everyone agreed that the ideal home for a workingman was an individual house, the consensus was that land costs rendered the ideal a practical impossibility. Before disbanding, the reformers established a permanent committee to "obtain" the "needed reforms" and, in addition, to explore ways to help workers "secure their own homes."[9]

Over the next three years the housing committee, led by Jane Addams, Graham Taylor, and Mrs. Henry Wade Rogers (the financial patron of Northwestern University Settlement) put together a large organization with a solid base of business support. In 1900, after a week-long conference featuring speeches by Jacob Riis and Lawrence Veiller of New York City, the nation's best-known tenement reformers, the organization reconstituted itself as the City Homes Association. While the association patterned its program on lines laid out by older housing groups in other cities, it was original in one respect: It coordinated a variety of reform activities that separate organizations undertook elsewhere. Other cities had investigative committees, model-tenement societies, and model-lodging-house associations. The City Homes Association attempted to direct the entire housing reform effort in Chicago through five "working bodies" made up of social workers, architects and engineers, doctors, and "civic leaders," that is, "society" women and businessmen.

The Investigating Committee, like the original housing committee, made a futile effort to induce the city to conduct a tenement census. Then it carried out a first-rate survey on its own, published in 1901 as *Tenement Conditions in Chicago* with the text by Robert Hunter. The Small Parks and Playgrounds Committee worked to provide the tenement districts with "breathing spaces." The Model Tenement Committee planned to build large-scale housing projects for workingmen "on sound business principles." The Committee on Law Enforcement had the responsibility of drawing up a tenement code for Chicago and seeing that the City Council passed it. The Lodging-House Committee looked for ways to eliminate the "lodger evil" and the "tramp menace."[10]

The City Homes Association, directed and bankrolled by Cyrus McCormick's daughter Anita McCormick Blaine, one of the financial mainstays of organized "good works" in Chicago, was capable, energetic, and determined. The people who contributed their time, talent, and treasure to the organization were the sort who were used to getting things done, and done their way. Of the association's working bodies, there was only one whose efforts produced no tangible results.

The Model Tenement Committee made plans, but it did not see any of them through to completion. Ever since the Pullman episode in 1894, Chicago's capitalists had viewed model housing projects of any kind with deep suspicion. Some members of the City Homes Association shared their feeling that philanthropy, even "philanthropy that pays," had no place in the housing market. "There is not only no need for philanthropic enterprises in this line," insisted one member, Frances Buckley Embree, "but such enterprises are positively harmful." If other City Homes Association committees were successful, tenements that were dangerously decrepit or located on sites suitable for play facilities would be torn down. The Model Tenement Committee planned only to replenish the diminished housing supply—not add to it—by building model projects on vacant, relatively cheap land in the zone just beyond the "Inner Belt." The proposed tenants were better-paid workmen, not displaced occupants of demolished slum buildings. The committeemen expected people whose homes were razed to find shelter in the units vacated by the workers who moved into the model housing. The committee's proposals, though consistent with "business principles," did not win the backing of the whole association, which never built the projects.[11]

Failure to provide new housing did not deter the association from urging extensive demolition of occupied dwellings. The committees on investigation and legislation put pressure on the commissioner of health to use the authority granted to him in an 1897 ordinance to destroy dwellings "unfit for human habitation." In the spring of 1900, the Health Department declared "war on bad tenements." Health officials demolished only a handful of inhabited houses in this and subsequent spring campaigns. They gave owners sixty days in which to remove nuisances before sending the wreckers in, and they usually won the owner's consent before razing his building. No owner went to court to contest a demolition order. Probably most owners benefited from the removal of buildings that brought them no more profit and raised their real estate assessments. The Chicago Fire Department did the wrecking and hauled away the debris. This method of clearance was cheaper for owners than hiring a commercial wrecker. Few people suffered from the Health Department's demolition program. But the condemnation of whole blocks of congested tenements to clear the way for parks and playgrounds displaced thousands of families. This is where the suffering came in.[12]

Between 1900 and 1917, Chicago established more than ninety new parks and over a hundred municipal playgrounds. Aided by settlement residents who lobbied to get new facilities for their neighborhoods, the City Homes Association's Committee on Parks and Playgrounds saw to it that about one-third of these "breathing spaces" were located in the tenement districts. In outlying areas, where open land was available for development, the recreation facilities were an unqualified boon. But in the poor neighborhoods vacant space was scarce. There was an undeniable need for parks in the poverty belt, but before the parks could go in, acres of crowded buildings had to be destroyed. Apparently, nobody bothered to keep a count of all the people who lost their homes to make room for these neighborhood improvements, but the number was large. And nobody took the responsibility for relocating displaced families.[13]

Of all the advocates of playgrounds and parks for poor neighborhoods, settlement workers were in the best position to witness the suffering that their policies caused. They showed little concern. It was the story of Jane Addams and that first playground all over again, reenacted time after time with a cast of thousands. To cite only one example: Northwestern University Settlement and Chicago Commons worked very hard and won two parks for their ward. The population of the blocks that were leveled to clear the sites was *over 3,500*, possibly as high as 4,200. The settlements, like the park officials, ignored the protests of the uprooted families. Graham Taylor, in fact, was a member of the park board.[14]

The callousness of the reformers shows through clearly in the following account of an incident that occurred in 1913. The tenement involved was on Plymouth Court, one of the streets surveyed in the 1893 slum investigation. The building faced the Dearborn Street railroad station, the arrival point of two-thirds of the immigrants entering Chicago. The narrator is Edith Abbott of Hull-House, writing years after the event, and expressing no regrets:

> . . . the railroad authorities offered to give the use of one of the tenements to the Immigrants' Protective League as a distributing center to care for the large numbers of immigrants who poured out of the immigrant trains that arrived almost daily. The tenement, of course, was solidly Italian, and when notice was given to the Italian families to vacate the house, the order was received as a calamitous blow. Great excitement followed, and the little street was full of gesticulating people bewailing their fate. How and where could they move? They complained that they had "nowhere to go," and it was true that housing accommodations in this particular area were limited. . . . The evicted families finally refused to move, and the railroad authorities gave orders that their household goods were to be carried out and put on the sidewalk. This was actually done, and the confusion of the noisy street, with women and children crying, and sympathetic neighbors trying to offer consolation, was a scene of great disorder. It was strange to find people so attached to homes that were so lacking in all the attributes of comfort and decency.

It is revealing that this scene, which filled "sympathetic neighbors" with sorrow and grief, struck the neighborhood worker as strange and disorderly.[15]

Miss Abbott added that "it was possible to find tenements for the evicted families in the West Side Italian colony." Whether these tenements were an improvement on the old one she did not say. The families were "very destitute"; they could hardly have afforded anything better. "They looked upon the journey one mile west and across the river as a journey into a far country," the bemused reformer recalled, "and felt that they were being harshly dealt with because they were compelled to leave."[16]

There was nothing sentimental about the reformers' approach to slum clearance, however much they rhapsodized about the parks they built over the ruins. The City Homes Association's solution to the problem of "the homeless man" was uncompromisingly severe and businesslike as well. The solution was multifaceted. The Committee on Legislation planned to deal with the excessive boarders in tenement flats by limiting the number of people who could inhabit a given amount of sleeping space. Enacting a minimum space standard and enforcing it would cut down the overcrowding in cramped family quarters. It would also leave many families without a much-needed source of income, and it would deprive the evicted boarders of a place to stay. The City Homes Association did not consider the plight of the families whose source of rent money would be cut off, but it had a committee that devised ways to furnish the homeless men with suitable shelter.

Chicago's lodging accommodations for unattached poor men were notorious. The best of the "cheap hotels" provided bath and toilet facilities and a bed in an enclosed cubicle or "cage" for fifteen to twenty-five cents a night. The cheaper lodging houses had no baths and little plumbing equipment. In the ten- and fifteen-cent establishments, a man could get a wire cot with a mattress on it. Some of these places put the cots in separate cages; others arranged them along the walls of large dormitory rooms. The five-cent lodging houses were equipped with "double-deckers," metal bunk beds with quilts instead of mattresses, or "board bunks," wooden shelves three feet wide built out from the walls, "generally three deep." Sometimes these shelves were made of stretched canvas instead of wood. For two cents a night, a man could buy a space on the floor of a "flop house" with no bedding except perhaps a newspaper, which he would have to supply himself. Some saloons, called "barrel houses," would let a man drink until he dropped and then leave him undisturbed on the floor all night for no extra charge. Men who had no money at all slept outside or in such makeshift shelters as outhouses and stables. On cold nights many of them trudged to police stations, which let them sleep in the corridors between the rows of jail cells, fed them soup and coffee, and turned them out in the morning.[17]

Even at its best, lodging-house life lacked "the wholesome restraints of the home," Robert Hunter wrote. At its worst it stacked the men like sardines in conditions of "despicable foulness and filth" and cut them loose "from every restraint." The Committee on Lodging Houses worked to provide better accommodations than these for men who could not rent beds in tenement flats.[18]

Two types of men required lodging, the committee found: "the clean, the well-dressed, the gentlemanly, who are endeavoring to live economically and lay away something for a rainy day," and "the deserving poor who are temporarily out of employment." The business of housing the first group decently "could be made to pay," as a New York banker named D. O. Mills had proved with his model men's hotels. There was no direct profit to be had from quartering the other group, but it was wrong to pile them up in jail corridors with "tramps" and "bums." They deserved to be sorted out from the vagrants and provided for; the vagrants should be incarcerated in correctional asylums or driven from the city.[19]

The committee proposed that capitalists in Chicago invest in the building of "Mills hotels" to house "the better class" of men for twenty to thirty cents a night. With good management it would be possible to give "men of very moderate means" clean rooms and still realize "a safe 6 to 8 per cent" on the investment. For the indigent but upright men, the committee recommended a lodging house to be maintained by the City of Chicago.[20]

The proposals found wide acceptance. Even critics of model tenements responded warmly to the idea of model workingmen's hotels and a municipal lodging house. Reformers expected political bosses to oppose lodging-house reform because the politicians supposedly used the barrelhouses and flophouses for "the colonization of voters" at election time. Yet the two most corrupt politicos operating in the lodging-house district, "Bathhouse John" Coughlan and Michael J. ("Hinky Dink") Kenna, endorsed the committee's recommendations. The clientele of the projected Mills hotels were not the sort of characters the Hink and the Bath dealt with anyway, so they were not afraid of competition. And if the city were to run a lodging house, that would be all right, too. Hinky Dink and Bathhouse John liked to think of themselves as men who ran the city.[21]

The Mills hotel appealed to business-minded reformers because it appeared to be a straightforward "paying" enterprise. The municipal lodging house struck them as the "one line" in which the municipality could act in housing the poor because the police stations were already doing the job, and doing it badly. The municipal lodging house as depicted by the City Homes Association was a semicorrective institution, no more socialistic than a jail house.[22]

The committee claimed that a municipal lodging house would cost no more to run than the odious police-station method of quartering "bums." Moreover, with the new institution in operation it would be possible to shut down the nightly police operation. Thus the lodging house would entail no new expense to the taxpayer. The lodging-house caretakers would fumigate and examine the men. Incorrigible idlers would be committed to state work farms; the sick would be sent to dispensaries. The police could crack down on panhandlers, who would no longer have an excuse to beg nickels for a "flop." The lodging house would free Chicago of "the pest of beggars" and "the tramp problem." The name of Chicago, instead of being a synonym for Mecca among bums, would inspire "dread." The benefits of the lodging house would far outweigh the expense:

> Streets without beggars; a greatly diminished number of petty thieves and hold-up men (which means less work for the police); clean men with clean clothing in your streets instead of vagrants spreading contagion. The saving to the city in the way of prevention of crime would many times exceed the cost. It would be of the highest importance to the health department by facilitating examination where disease would most naturally be found, and in case of epidemic the concentration of such a large proportion of the floating population would greatly simplify the department's work.[23]

In the fall of 1900, the city of Chicago announced its intention to establish a municipal lodging house. The next year, when the city ran short of funds and declared its inability to carry out the plan for the time being, the City Homes Association raised five thousand dollars, rented a building, equipped it, and in late December began operation on the understanding that the city would assume control as soon as possible. The city was unable to take over for nearly two years; until then, a private citizens' group ran Chicago's Municipal Lodging House. The first superintendent was Raymond Robins of Chicago Commons, who kept his post after the city took charge and held it for four years.[24]

The regimen for the men was severe. After registering they had to "give a concise but searching account of themselves." If they lied and were detected they were put under arrest. After a supper of coffee and bread they surrendered their clothes to be fumigated, took baths, donned uniform nightshirts, relaxed under supervision, and then, at lights out, retired to individual iron beds. In the morning they breakfasted on coffee and bread. Afterwards the supervisor put them out and locked the doors until evening. If they returned and could convince the management that they had been "honestly endeavoring to secure employment," they could stay another night. No man could have lodging more than four nights in a row. The management ran a small employment bureau and assigned men to jobs. Once the bureau assigned a man to a job, his stay at the lodging house was over, whether he accepted the position or not.[25]

At the end of the first year's operation, Superintendent Raymond Robins reported that "corrupt loafers and vagabonds" were no longer exploiting the city. In 1901, before the lodging house opened, the police stations provided 92,591 lodgings. In 1902 the lodging house gave men 11,097 lodgings, and the police stations gave only 5,740. Thus the lodging house *reduced* the amount of municipal service to homeless men by 82 percent. As long as the Municipal Lodging House could prove that it was a bargain, it enjoyed high repute.[26]

The first Mills hotel opened for business in 1903. It proved to be a model for other lodging enterprises, many of them semireligious. For years the Salvation Army had run a mission lodging house. In 1899 a State Board of Health inspector declared that this place was "as unsanitary and noisome as any other tramp resorts in Chicago." By 1905 the Salvation Army redeemed itself. Its Reliance Hotel was a sanitary, well-run establishment ("Rooms 15–20–25¢, Bed and Bath–10¢"). A Presbyterian organization, the Christian Industrial League, sponsored a lodging house and "sheltered workshop" called the Popular Hotel. Men who could not pay for their lodging in cash worked off their obligation in shops on the premises. The league reported that its process of "remaking men and material" was "financially successful" and "spiritually fruitful." Millionaire Charles G. Dawes established two workers' hotels, one for men (named for his father), one for women (named for his mother). By 1917 there were two Mills hotels and more than three dozen other model lodging houses for men and women of small means.[27]

Most of these establishments turned away no one who could pay except "inebriated" applicants—and Negroes. Even the hotels that tolerated quiet, orderly drunkards denied admission to sober blacks. The manager of the New York Mills hotels had told a group of Chicago businessmen, "We will not admit colored men, not because we have any prejudice against the colored laborer, but because the hotel is managed upon a business principle, and we cannot afford to do anything which would interfere with its business." The Chicago hotels adopted the same policy without announcing any justification. A few of the establishments were sectarian, but most had a clientele that was ethnically and denominationally mixed. Not one was racially mixed. The only model hotels that accepted Negroes were three establishments for "colored women." Black males were excluded not only from the model enterprises but from the cheapest tramp lodgings as well. Black men could get accommodations nowhere but at "colored man's" lodging houses and flophouses. Whether or not the municipal lodging house was segregated is not clear. It almost certainly was. Everywhere else the evidence of the color line is unmistakable.[28]

The opening of the Municipal Lodging House in December 1901 was a triumph for the City Homes Association. The enactment of a "New Tenement" ordinance a year later was an even greater victory. Robert Hunter's report, *Tenement Conditions in Chicago*, created a demand—among influential citizens, not the poor themselves—for legislation to ensure "light, air, and a sufficient amount of space to every human being." The City Council could not avoid taking action on the bill drafted by the association's Committee on Legislation. When the stately Mrs. Anita McCormick Blaine finished speaking on behalf of the bill at a council hearing, the aldermen had the choice of voting for reform or standing up in public as enemies "of an effective motherhood, of a happy childhood, of the integrity and the promise and happiness of family life." The bill, modified but still very much intact, passed 47 to 7.[29]

The "New Tenement" ordinance took its nickname from the fact that it applied mainly to future construction. Tenements built after December 17, 1902, came under all of the provisions; "old tenements" were largely exempt as a concession to owners of existing buildings, for whom compliance would have entailed undeniable hardships. There were some concessions to the builders of new tenements as well. The lot-coverage provision was almost a surrender. Instead of the 65 percent standard that Hunter had advocated, the bill allowed 90 percent coverage on corner lots in blocks with alleys, 85 percent on corners in blocks without alleys, and 75 percent on other lots. The minimum floor area prescribed for rooms was a scant 70 square feet. The sleeping space requirement was a bare 400 cubic feet for each adult and 200 cubic feet for each child under twelve years of age. Most of the other major provisions were satisfactorily stringent.

The law banned further construction of the rear tenements, which Hunter's study had made notorious. Ceilings had to be 8½ feet high. Every room had to have at least one window with an area equal to 10 percent of the floor space, and the window had to open directly on the outer air. The law defined a story that was more than one-half below the level of the sidewalk as a "cellar"; a "basement" was *less* than one-half submerged. Cellars could not be occupied at all, and basement occupancy was severely limited. Every apartment had to be equipped with a kitchen sink and a private toilet. In buildings with apartments of one and two rooms, however, one hall toilet for every two apartments was sufficient. In addition, the ordinance discriminated against buildings more than three stories high: They had to have fire escapes, more fireproof materials, more court space, and so on. These provisions, the reformers hoped, would check the spread of the tall tenement of the New York City type and "set forever in Chicago the standard of height at three stories and basement."[30]

The provisions on sleeping space applied to "old" as well as "new" tenements. Moreover, owners of old tenements had to provide a few minimal conveniences. Every *floor*, not every apartment, of their buildings had to have a sink. They had to supply one water closet for every *two* tenant families. The toilet did not have to be inside the building, however. A yard closet was sufficient, provided it was not under a staircase or on a sidewalk or porch and not too close to the occupied premises. The toilet had to be connected to a sewer, *if* the adjoining street had a sewer. Rooms with less than sixty square feet could not be occupied, but cellars and basements, under certain conditions, could be. As long as the old tenements lasted, they would contain features that were far below minimal standards, and they would do so legally. Dilapidated as they were, they endured for decades.

The most "remarkable" feature of the ordinance was its definition of a tenement. "Any house or building or portion thereof which is intended or designed to be occupied or leased for occupation as a home or residence of two or more families, living in separate apartments," was a tenement. Including two-family units in the tenement category greatly expanded the coverage of the law. By definition, the typical working-class homeowner, paying for his house by renting part of it out, became a tenement landlord, subject to the regulation of sanitary inspectors. The widened coverage put a premium on enforcement.[31]

In 1902, with their law enacted, the housing reformers were at the peak of their prestige and power. In the next fifteen years, they would learn that it was one thing to legislate reform and quite another thing to enforce it.

❧

One reason the 1902 ordinance passed so easily was that the biggest boodlers in the City Council backed it. Their motives became clear as soon as the law went into effect; it was made-to-order "four-flush" legislation. A four-flush law was one that politicians passed for the purpose of soliciting graft in return for *not* enforcing it. A certain amount of enforcement was necessary, of course; otherwise, no one would be willing to pay to violate the law. In the first four months of 1903, the City Council issued twenty-eight orders exempting builders from the new provisions. Reformers suspected, not unreasonably, that the exemptions were for sale. The bosses had "seen the opportunities" in tenement regulation, and they "took 'em." And the council actions were only the tip of the iceberg.[32]

The ordinance did not create an independent Tenement House Department like the one in New York City. Two old-line departments split the responsibility for inspection. The Building Department examined buildings for structural conformity to the ordinance; the Sanitary Bureau of the Health Department inspected the sanitary condition of buildings. Neither organization had tenement inspection as its sole function. Before an owner could put up a building, alter one, or move one, he had to secure a permit from the Building Department, which was supposed to make sure that the plans conformed to the law. The building could not be occupied until two inspectors, one each from the Health and Building departments, certified it. The Building Department had authority to examine any building if a citizen complained of a defect. The Health Department had police power; it could inspect any tenement at any time without waiting for a complaint. The volume of inspections was so great that inspectors in both departments worked singly, not in pairs. They operated, in other words, with no witness to their transactions with the builders and owners, who had a vested interest in indulgent enforcement, except God Almighty. For a God-fearing man, the job of inspector was a nightmare of temptation. For anybody else it was a dream.[33]

The summer before the law went into effect, Chicago experienced a typhoid epidemic that struck with special ferocity in the tenement districts. The area around Hull-House was hit hardest of all. When the epidemic was over, residents of the settlement, led by Dr. Alice Hamilton, tried to track the spread of the disease to its source. In their survey of 2,002 houses occupied by typhoid victims, they found 460 uncovered privy vaults. Dr. Hamilton concluded that flies had carried the disease from privy to privy. She also concluded that the sanitary inspectors were either on the take or incompetent, for the privies had been outlawed as far back as 1894. Most of the men who had been on duty during the epidemic were still with the Sanitary Bureau in 1903. Hull-House raised a terrific clamor for their removal. Ultimately, eleven of the entire force of twenty-four inspectors were discharged. Five of them, including the head of the Sanitary Bureau, were indicted for accepting bribes. The others were judged merely negligent.[34]

One of the dismissed inspectors, Jane Addams wrote, was "a kindly old man" who had not taken a dime in bribes. He simply did not have the heart to enforce the law on poor homeowners. If a tenant complained that the pipes were leaking gas or that the toilet bowl was clogged, that was one thing. But it was another thing to make a man throw out his boarders because the rooms lacked a few cubic feet of air, to fine a family without closets or cupboards for putting food or clothing on a fire escape, or even to force a poor owner to install a decent water closet when his house was sure to be "torn down to make room for a factory." Simple kindness could obstruct regulation as surely as avarice could.[35]

The settlement workers saw rampant violations of the law. There were loopholes in the ordinance, too, which could be exploited with impunity. The ban on *building* rear tenements, for instance, did not stop people from *moving* old tenements to the rear of other ones. That was the way most rear tenements had come into existence, and they continued to crop up. The City Homes Association launched a struggle to establish a centralized administrative authority with impartial inspectors who would enforce the requirements and plug up the loopholes. It turned out to be a hopeless fight.[36]

In 1903 the association hired a permanent secretary to direct its campaign. The man who took the job was Charles B. Ball, the chief inspector of New York City's Tenement Department. Ball, an engineer, had long experience in sanitary inspection. Lawrence Veiller, the great New York City reformer, hailed him as "the Dean of the Housing Workers" in America. Ball came to Chicago with the aim of establishing a New York City–style Tenement House Department with himself at its head. There was nothing vainglorious in his ambition: Chicago needed such a department, and no man in America, including Veiller, was better qualified to direct it.[37]

When Ball accepted the position with the City Homes Association, the chief of the scandal-ridden Sanitary Bureau had already been ousted. Ball moved from New York City with the intention of filling the vacancy at the top of the bureau. Once in office, he planned to serve as secretary of the City Homes Association without compensation and work toward the goal of a new department from his double position as public official and citizen-reformer. The Sanitary Bureau position was not appointive. Because the job was supposed to be awarded on the basis of a competitive examination, it was a foregone conclusion that all Ball had to do to get in office was take the test. He took the examination and easily scored first. But he did not get the post. In March 1904, the Civil Service Commission certified the man who scored *tenth* on the test as chief sanitary inspector. For the next three years, the main activity of the housing movement in Chicago was the fight to install Charles Ball as head of the Sanitary Bureau.[38]

Hull-House led the fight. The Civil Service Commission had named C. L. Clarke to the post reluctantly because of a clause in the Civil Service law guaranteeing preference to military veterans, and Clarke was an ex-soldier. He was also one of the sanitary inspectors who had been assigned to the Hull-House district during the 1902 epidemic. Clarke's conduct had not been demonstrably derelict, only dubious, but Hull-House demanded his removal. Less than a month after Clarke took office, the Civil Service Commission removed him for incompetence. Then Charles Ball became chief sanitary inspector—for one month. He lost the post because someone complained that he had not established residency in Illinois at the time he took the examination. The Civil Service Commission sustained the complaint. The issue moved into the courts, and a year later the Illinois Supreme Court upheld Ball's claim to the office. Finally, in 1907, this bizarre episode ended with Ball's reinstatement as head of the Sanitary Bureau. Ball stayed in the post for the rest of his life. He died at his desk in the Health Department in 1928.[39]

Charles Ball never succeeded in uniting all tenement inspectors within a single, independent department; division in regulation was too valuable a source of graft for the politicians to give up. But within the Sanitary Bureau he worked wonders. When he took command the staff of eighteen inspectors was demoralized and inept. By 1915 he had eighty-one inspectors who were well trained, closely supervised, and as honest, probably, as tenement inspectors could be. In the same period, the Building Department grew larger, too, but it also became more inefficient and more corrupt.[40]

The Sanitary Bureau never had enough resources for inspection, research, and reporting, so Ball enlisted the aid of social workers as unofficial inspectors and research associates. Settlement workers and charity visitors noted conditions in the homes and reported them to the Building Department and to the Sanitary Bureau. The difference between the two organizations, of course, was that Ball's subordinates could be relied on to take some action. On the part of the social workers, informing the authorities was a violation of the client's confidence, although the social workers did not regard it as such. Ball, the sanitary engineer, was not to blame for the way social workers interpreted their code of ethics. He needed information, and they helped to provide it.[41]

In 1908, when the Chicago School of Civics and Philanthropy opened, Ball approached the faculty to incorporate sustained housing research in the curriculum. The guiding spirits behind the school, which later became the University of Chicago's School of Social Service Administration, were Graham Taylor and several of the women at Hull-House. Edith Abbott and Sophonisba Breckenridge, faculty members who resided at Hull-House, agreed to direct the studies. Between 1908 and 1917, they and their students surveyed seventeen tenement areas. The results of the research, published in *The American Journal of Sociology* and reissued in pamphlet form, were invaluable to Ball in assessing the operation of the tenement ordinance and in building up support for housing reform.

Ball's adept administration of the Sanitary Bureau and his tireless efforts at explaining the need for regulation made reform seem increasingly respectable to businessmen as well. By 1911 the City

Club and the Chicago Association of Commerce both had active housing committees. The Association of Commerce issued a pamphlet in 1912 urging higher appropriations for inspection. The pamphlet, titled *The Housing Problem in Chicago,* listed four reasons why the importance of housing "cannot be over-emphasized":

> Bad housing means death and disease. . . .
> Bad housing means inefficient workers. . . .
> Bad housing makes bad citizens. . . .
> Bad housing gives the city a bad appearance and a bad reputation. Both for our own satisfaction and for the reputation of the city, tumble-down shacks and unsightly tenements must go.

It was a simplistic litany, but it was an advance over what businessmen had been saying in 1900. The City Club sponsored an important Housing Exhibition in 1913. By that time opposition to restrictive reform had become a breach of good taste. Every gentlemen's and ladies' organization was showing interest in good housing. Among business leaders, only the realtors and builders continued to show hostility to reform, and even their resistance was softening.[42]

The Commercial Club's Plan of Chicago, officially presented to the city in 1910, showed both the expansiveness and the limits of business thinking. The plan, developed over several years, called for stupendous improvements in streets, parks, and public buildings. Planning, one backer said, was "simply good business." Another declared, "Businessmen now know that these things pay." The plan left out any consideration of housing for the reason that the building of houses, unlike the widening of streets and boulevards, was business in the *strict* sense and therefore not a proper matter for public endeavor. Settlement workers, led by Mary McDowell, protested to no avail the omission of housing from the plan.[43]

At the same time, the settlement workers were pushing for passage of new tenement provisions. The very businessmen who refused to include housing in the Plan of Chicago supported the proposed legislation. With the sustained backing of the settlement houses and the businessmen's civic organizations, Charles Ball was able to persuade the City Council to make some changes in the tenement regulations. The important provisions of this 1910 ordinance increased the minimum area of rooms to eighty square feet and widened the spaces to be left vacant on the sides of a lot. The net effect of these changes was to make it almost impossible to build a multifamily building on a shoestring lot. The ordinance practically outlawed the 25-foot lot for large tenement buildings.[44]

To the extent that the laws of 1902 and 1910 were enforced—and they were not enforced the way they would have been if Charles Ball had been in charge of all inspection—they did have an effect on new tenements. But the laws left the old buildings "practically unchanged." Housing that conformed to the codes was beyond the financial reach of poor workingmen either to buy or to rent. And although the "new-law tenements" were too expensive for the poor, they were still far from desirable. In 1910 housing investigators photographed an enormous frame tenement built in accordance with the minimum requirements of the Act of 1902. The building, in the Back a' the Yards district, contained "a saloon, a bakery, a butcher-shop, a milk depot, a stable, and nine families." The rubbish and manure heap in the alley behind it was as tall as the men lounging about the sidewalk. The City Club Exhibition of 1913 had two displays showing "how bad a tenement can be and still comply with the ordinances." Enforcement of the meager requirements for the "old tenements" raised the rents of the poor. The costs of graft, when the laws were not enforced, came out of the pockets of the poor as well. And the relatively high standards in new tenements made the poor cling all the more desperately to their cheap accommodations. One reason for exempting the old tenements from strict regulation was that they were doomed to extinction anyway. But now the poor could not afford to leave them. Thus the laws *prolonged* the life of the old substandard buildings. Charles Ball announced in 1917 that there were still thirteen thousand occupied rear tenements in the city. These wretched dwellings stood for generations.[45]

Restrictive reform had limits even when it worked properly. And in 1915 its chances of working properly suffered a severe setback with the election of Big Bill Thompson as mayor. No sooner had Thompson assumed office than "the raid on the Civil Service began." Big Bill took over the Building Department and plunged it to a new low in competence. He purged the members of the year-old Department of Public Welfare, which had worked closely with Ball.

The new welfare commissioner auctioned off staff appointments and then levied assessments on the purchasers: Employees had to pay to get the jobs and then pay to keep them. Thompson closed the Municipal Lodging House in 1917, on the ground that it failed in its function of keeping poor, homeless men out of Chicago. The lodging house was vulnerable on this score. In 1914 it had provided 452,361 lodgings, *forty-one times* as many as in 1902. Instead of chasing drifters from Chicago, the institution seemed to be attracting them. When the place shut down, it had no businessmen to defend it. It no longer looked like a bargain.[46]

Big Bill Thompson did not spare the Health Department. He forced out Ball's superior, the commissioner of health, and replaced him with a hack, who in turn appointed a flunky to serve as Ball's chief assistant. "I got that appointment from Mayor Thompson," Ball's new assistant admitted cheerfully, "in recognition of the work I did in the 50th precinct of the 33rd Ward." Sandwiched in between a chief and an aide who were stooges, Ball struggled on as best he could. Then Thompson tried to squeeze him out. Big Bill cut the number of inspectors on the beleaguered reformer's staff from eighty-one to thirty-one and slashed away one-third of his budget. Ball would not quit, but he could barely function.[47]

In 1917 the housing movement in Chicago was in tatters. A despondent Charles Ball, unable to enforce the laws properly, lamented, "In the crowded sections we are producing a degenerate race." Miss Abbott and Miss Breckenridge suspended the School of Civics and Philanthropy housing investigations because they seemed to produce "only further illustrations of the futility of such investigations." And George Hooker of Hull-House asked what would happen if inspectors were somehow able to bring all houses up to standard and neighborhood workers were able to teach people how to take care of their property—"How are you going to bring it about that people shall have means to pay for decent homes?" That was a question which reformers had failed to face up to since 1895, when Hull-House printed its maps of wages along with its grim descriptions of slum housing.[48]

There was, however, no immediate prospect of making all houses physically decent. By the end of 1917, residential construction was slowing down drastically. After twenty-five years of more or less sustained and partly successful reform effort, Chicago was entering a period of "famine" in housing. Robert Hunter had written in 1901 that Chicago was both "uninformed and unprepared for the future." In 1917, thanks to Hunter's survey and others that followed, Chicago was not nearly so uninformed as it had been. But reformers had no idea what to do about the housing shortage. And they were woefully ignorant about the Black Belt that had been building up in their midst for decades. It was the worst slum in the city. During the war its population doubled, and the demand of its inhabitants for more room brought on a racial crisis. For there was no more room. The reformers were utterly unready for the tragedy that was shaping up in 1917.[49]

PART II

The Ghetto

The color line, as it appears in the problem of Chicago and of every other northern city, is too important to be overlooked.

—Edith Abbott, *The Tenements of Chicago, 1908–1935* (Chicago, 1936), p. 118.

For as long as black people had lived in Chicago, most of them had known only hovels for homes, and blacks had been in the city from the very beginning. Yet housing reformers and neighborhood workers paid little attention to the grim Black Belt that was developing on the South Side. They were dimly aware of the miserable slum conditions that dogged the Black Belt's inhabitants, but they were more familiar, and more concerned, with the intractable "tenement evils" that plagued the great immigrant districts. Not until the World War I housing crisis, when whites—native and immigrant alike—fought ferociously to keep Negroes out of their neighborhoods, did reformers take special notice of the plight of the blacks.

Before the war, reformers occasionally voiced some apprehension about the squalid surroundings in which black people had to live, but they took it for granted that "the colored" would live in colonies of their own. All ethnic groups lived in colonies—or so the reformers supposed—and the housing in every district occupied by poor people was wretched. "The mass of people in tenements," Robert Hunter wrote in 1901, "have not what people commonly call a home," and the Negroes were no exception to that bitter truth. Hunter found the housing of the "colored people" so "exceedingly bad" that he omitted the Black Belt from his detailed tenement survey; he wanted to explore typical conditions, not "the worst." But he also excluded some immigrant districts for the same reason.[1]

No white observer noticed any "peculiarities of living conditions in the colored sections of the city" until 1912, when a social-work student named Alzada P. Comstock made an intensive study of Negro housing. Sophonisba P. Breckenridge, who supervised Comstock's investigation, summarized the central finding: "The problem of the Negro" was "quite different from that of immigrants."

Foreign workingmen and their children had to stay in the shabbiest neighborhoods only so long as they remained poor. When they could afford better housing, they were free to move away. But "every man who is black, whether rich or poor" was "compelled to live in a segregated black district." Negroes had a "special" predicament because whites drew "the color line."[2]

Even though Miss Breckenridge was able to see the difference between "the great black belt" and "the Bohemian, Polish, and Lithuanian districts," she did not really grasp the profound consequences of the fact that the Negro ghetto was no ordinary ethnic enclave. Neither did other white reformers. The racial violence that accompanied the wartime influx of Southern blacks caught them completely unprepared.[3]

The struggle between whites and blacks over living space culminated in a brief but awesome race war in the summer of 1919. The bloodshed forced the reformers to face the fact that the Black Belt was a separate city within Chicago. Now they viewed the housing of "the colored man" as a separate part of the housing problem, "of equal importance" to the housing of the whites. White tenement dwellers of foreign stock greatly outnumbered ill-housed blacks before the riots and they continued to do so for many years thereafter, but reformers no longer felt that they could safely defer the question of what to do about sheltering the blacks. With only a fraction of the city's population, blacks had come to constitute Chicago's most pressing housing problem.[4]

Subsequent sections of this book trace the color line as it worked its way through housing reform and neighborhood work. The subject here is how and where whites drew the line in housing itself, what they did to hold it, and, to a limited extent, what shape it gave to the lives of those it circumscribed.

CHAPTER 5 ❧

The Outlines of the Ghetto

The real problem of the social life of the colored people in Chicago, as in all northern cities, lies in the fact of their segregation.
—Fannie Barrier Williams, "Social Bonds in the 'Black Belt' of Chicago," *Charities*, 15 (7 October 1905), p. 40.

THE "GREAT MIGRATION" OF BLACK PEOPLE TO CHICAGO DATES BACK ONLY to 1915. Most Chicagoans looked upon the blacks as late arrivals and expected them to step to the end of the line for advancement without complaint. But Negroes bridled at the suggestion that they had come to the city too late to reap its rewards. "We came here first," they protested. It was not *they* who were the latecomers, but the Poles, Jews, Italians, and other "foreigners" from Southern and Eastern Europe.[1]

The black population of Chicago was almost negligibly small through most of the nineteenth century—the whites were right about that. Nevertheless, Negroes had a solid claim to the title of Chicago's oldest ethnic group. The first permanent resident on the city's site—besides the Indians—was a Negro named Du Saible, who set up a trading post there in 1779. Chicago did not begin to develop until Du Saible had pulled up stakes and moved on. But when the town incorporated in 1833, a few of its residents were

TABLE 5.1. BLACK POPULATION OF CHICAGO, 1840–1930

Year	*Total Population*	*Black Population*	*Percent Black*
1840	4,470	53	1.2
1850	29,963	323	1.1
1860	109,260	955	0.9
1870	298,977	3,691	1.2
1880	503,185	6,480	1.3
1890	1,099,850	14,271	1.3
1900	1,698,575	30,150	1.8
1910	2,185,283	44,103	2.0
1920	2,701,705	109,458	4.1
1930	3,376,438	233,803	6.9

Source: U.S. Census Reports.

black, and from then on there was a continuous Negro presence in Chicago. Compared to the mushrooming white population, the size of the black community was insignificant. Still, the number of Negroes in the city increased decade by decade, tripling in the 1850s, nearly quadrupling in the 1860s, then roughly doubling in each of the following three decades.[2] (See Table 5.1.)

The blacks who came to Chicago before the Great Migration entered the city's life under conditions that scholars of ethnicity regard as optimum for the assimilation of a group and its members. The only factor affecting assimilation that they did not have working in their favor was their color. That proved to be the factor that mattered.[3]

To begin with, they arrived early in the city's history, when the burgeoning urban economy had need of the unskilled labor they had to offer. Long before the Poles, Italians, Greeks, and other fugitives from Southeastern Europe established footholds in Chicago, there was a black community struggling to make its way. If Negroes occupied the lowest rung of the socioeconomic ladder, then the groups that came after them should have replaced them at the bottom and pushed them up a notch.

Moreover, the blacks came in moderate numbers, unlike the Irish and Germans of the 1850s and the Poles and Jews of the 1890s, who came in droves. From the start the number of Negroes was small, and their proportion in the total population showed remarkable stability, advancing a mere eight-tenths of a percentage point over a period of seventy years. Their comparative fewness should have eased their efforts to move at will within the larger society around them. Small numbers supposedly enable members of a minority group to slip through whatever nets the host society might weave to exclude the unwanted. At no time did the blacks threaten to upset the city's ethnic balance. The immigrants, on the other hand, overwhelmed Chicago.

In 1850 the foreigners already constituted a majority in the city. In 1900, with Negroes still amounting to less than 2 percent of the population, 77 percent of the city's inhabitants were of foreign stock. Over four hundred thousand of them belonged to the new wave of immigration that came flooding in upon the city from Southeastern Europe after 1880.[4]

Among the "older" immigrants, that is, Northwestern Europeans, some could speak English and some worshipped the God of the Anglo-Saxon Protestants. Some, like the Scots, had done both, but the great mass of immigrants failed to conform with the Anglo-Saxons in one way or the other, or both. The "new" immigrants were overwhelmingly Catholic or Jewish, and they spoke a babel of foreign tongues. To the older immigrants and to old-stock natives alike, these newcomers seemed utterly alien. The blacks, by contrast, were not foreign in either language or religion. They were native sons. "The only difference" between them and the native stock, as a black editor put it during the nativist resurgence of the 1920s, was "the color of our skins."[5]

The advantages of early arrival, modest numbers, gradual growth, native birth, common language, and common religion did not give blacks the edge on the alien groups that inundated the city. Alone among Chicago's ethnic groups, blacks encountered official discrimination. A state law of 1858 forbade free Negroes to enter Illinois. Negroes who already resided there or who slipped in undetected by the authorities were subject to "black codes." They had no civil rights. They could not vote, serve on juries, testify against whites, or intermarry with them. Repeal of the discriminatory statutes came piecemeal and slowly. It was 1870 before Negroes could vote. The State of Illinois did not ban school segregation until 1874, and it waited another ten years to prohibit racial discrimination in public accommodations. No longer "Jim-crowed by law" after the 1880s, blacks found that they still had to stay on their own side of "a line" that was "drawn by usage."[6]

The process of arrival and adjustment was harsh and bitter for everyone who came to Chicago, but only blacks suffered the special strains of contending with the color line. In employment the line meant that certain menial jobs were "nigger jobs." Where the real opportunities were—in construction, transportation, industry, and commerce—blacks were "the last hired and the first fired," a phrase that was already a cliché a generation before the Great Migration. They seldom got a chance for better jobs unless white men went on strike; then employers would take them on as scabs, only to throw them out when the beaten strikers came back to work. Even the model community of Pullman, where foreigners filled the tenements and workshops, excluded blacks. Pullman was no more a paradise for immigrants than Chicago was, but it was a white man's town. So was the great city itself. Chicago did not keep blacks out altogether, as the model community did, but it kept them in their place. Every foreign newcomer to Chicago, no matter how late he arrived or how fast his kinsmen were crowding into the city, had the advantage over the black migrant who got there ahead of him.[7]

Immigrants experienced nativist hostility, to be sure, and Eastern and Southern Europeans sometimes encountered a kind of racial prejudice. In 1890, for instance, a railroad construction boss told a congressional committee that "a Dago" was not "a white man." During the Pullman Strike a trooper with the U.S. Seventh Cavalry scanned the faces of the "Hunkies" and "Polacks" in the mob near the Union Stockyards, turned to a fellow soldier and snarled, "Them things ain't human." Later, sometime before 1900, a skilled workman quit his job at the Pullman Works because—with the shops full of Italians, Greeks, and Poles—car construction no longer seemed to him to be "white man's" work. But there were still no Negroes employed at Pullman, and that was the point. Foreigners had low status, but they got the jobs—on the railroads, at the stockyards, in Pullman—which black men could not get.[8]

Negroes were the objects of virulent race prejudice, and they were the victims of discrimination as well. Discrimination is prejudice carried over from the realm of attitude to the area of action.

In practice, the bigots quoted earlier probably redrew their color line to separate the blacks from all the rest, once they encountered blacks. Certainly that was what the mass of white Chicagoans did. Next to a Pullman porter, even the darkest immigrants looked white. The presence of the blacks permitted all of the ethnics to pass for white, to be white. Italians, Greeks, Hungarians, and Poles drew the line as sharply as anyone else. On one side, "niggers"; on the other, everybody else. The blacks were *others*. Because of them, all whites could "think of themselves, at least at some times, for some purposes," as brothers.[9]

In social relations, whites drew the color line even more decisively, and more indelibly, than they drew it in employment. The State of Illinois, along with most states outside the South, eventually recognized the civil equality of Negroes. Down South the system of segregation and subordination was practically total. There was no question as to the Negro's "place." Even if blacks and whites in Southern cities lived side by side or, as was more often the case, back to back (whites overlooking the avenue, Negroes facing the alley), the blacks could not possibly mistake themselves for the white people's peers. Southerners knew how to keep "darkies" at the proper social distance, no matter how small the spatial distance between the races. But Northerners were not masters of the etiquette of race relations.[10]

White people in the North feared that the Negroes, who were their civil equals in principle, would attempt to make themselves social equals in fact. If a black man moved next door to a white family, he would be more than just the occupant of a house, he would be a neighbor, an ostensible equal. His children might win their way into the play groups of the white children, as equals. The self-esteem of a white man with a "nigger" for a neighbor was sure to fall, and with it, his social standing, and also the value of his property. For no self-respecting white family would move into "a nigger neighborhood," and residents who prized their reputations would have to move away. To keep blacks at a distance socially, white Chicagoans segregated them spatially.

Until the 1890s no large, solidly Negro concentration existed. Blacks clustered in a number of small colonies, usually close by, but separate from, the white residential districts where so many of them worked as domestics. The influx of thousands of Southern migrants in the nineties swelled the size of these enclaves. By 1900 several of the old colonies had merged to form a long, narrow Black Belt on the South Side. This concentration and two satellite districts contained the great majority of black Chicagoans. "No large Northern city," observed Richard R. Wright, Jr., a black student from the University of Chicago, "shows a greater degree of segregation."[11]

The black population, only 30,000 in 1900, soared in the following decades, passing 100,000 by 1920 and approaching 250,000 ten years later. As their numbers climbed and they strained to spread out from their old sections, they met ever-stiffening white resistance. Year by year the degree of segregation increased, and the black population piled up in a ghetto circumscribed as no immigrant enclave had ever been.

The census tabulations for the period 1900–1930 give the impression that the constriction of the blacks intensified drastically in these years. The frequently used maps drawn from the census data heighten that impression (Maps 5.1 through 5.6). The 1900 map shows blacks scattered over all of the Southwest Side, most of the South Side, and much of the West Side as well. No Black Belt is visible. On the 1930 map, one can see a sharply delimited Black Belt and several satellite districts. Segregation did increase appreciably from 1900 to 1930, but not nearly so much as the census tables and the maps indicate. The data do not overstate the extent of segregation at the end of the period (in fact, they understate it), but they greatly exaggerate the rise in segregation. The reason is that the early data underestimate the degree to which blacks were already segregated in 1900.

The residential confinement of the blacks was nearly complete at the turn of the century. The maps make it look as if a widely dispersed population was pushed out of a large territory into a comparatively small, restricted strip. Actually, the blacks were hemmed in tightly from the start. In 1930 they occupied *more*, not less, territory than they had thirty years earlier. The ghetto was five times as large as before, but now whole districts were virtually all-black, whereas only buildings and some streets and blocks had been black earlier. And the chances of a black family's living outside of the enlarged territory were less than ever.

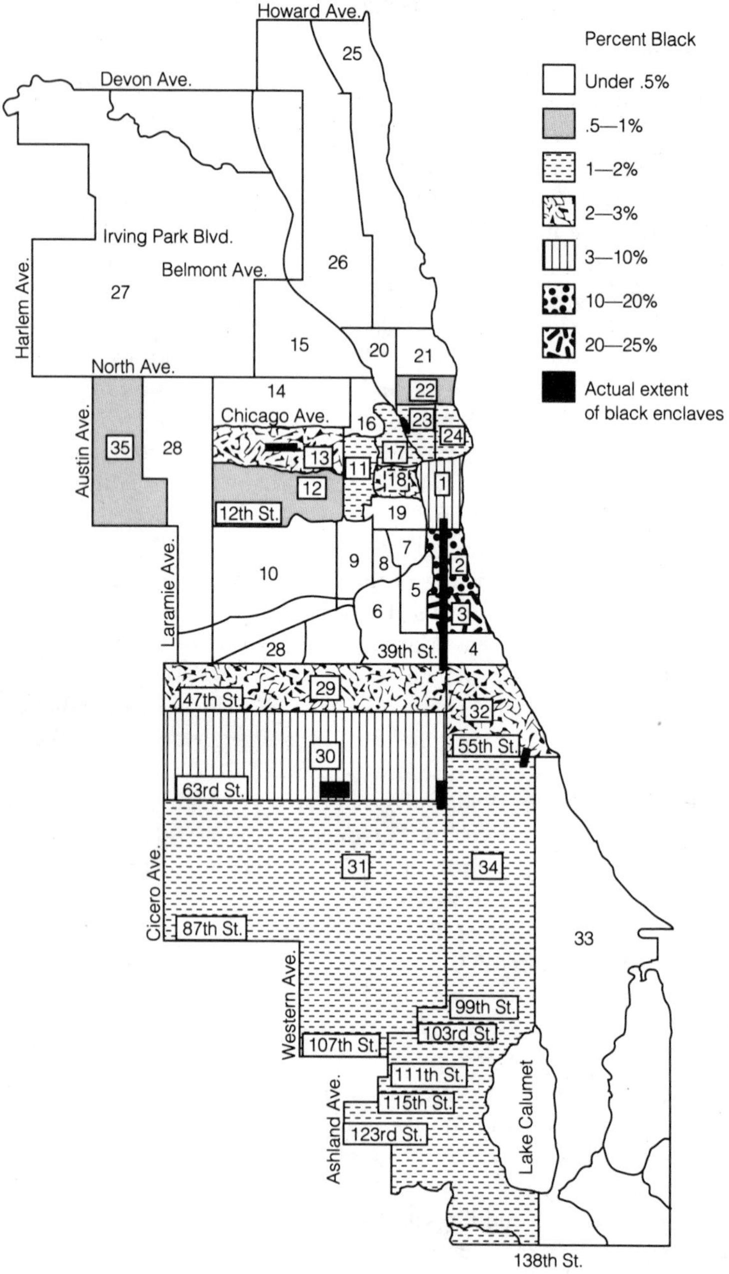

MAP 5.1. Black population by wards, 1900. (Source: *U.S. Twelfth Census,* 1900.)

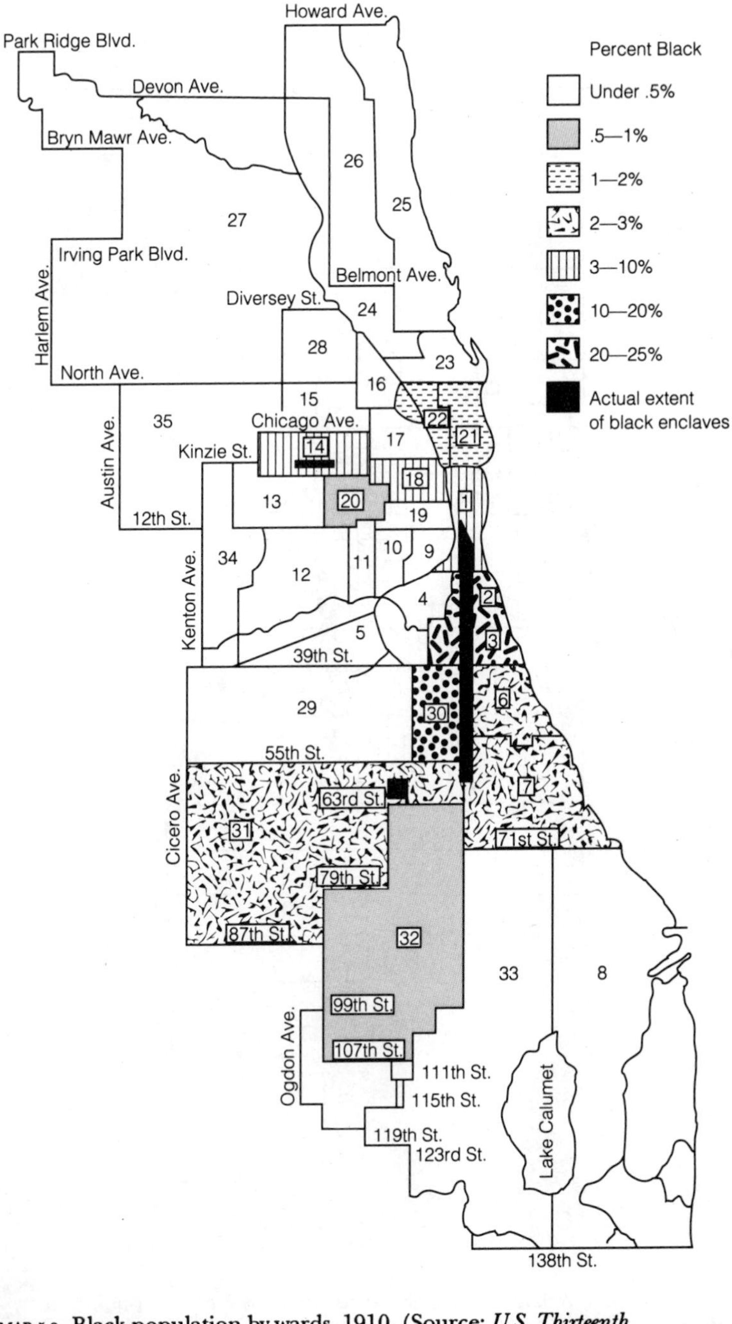

MAP 5.2. Black population by wards, 1910. (Source: *U.S. Thirteenth Census*, 1910.)

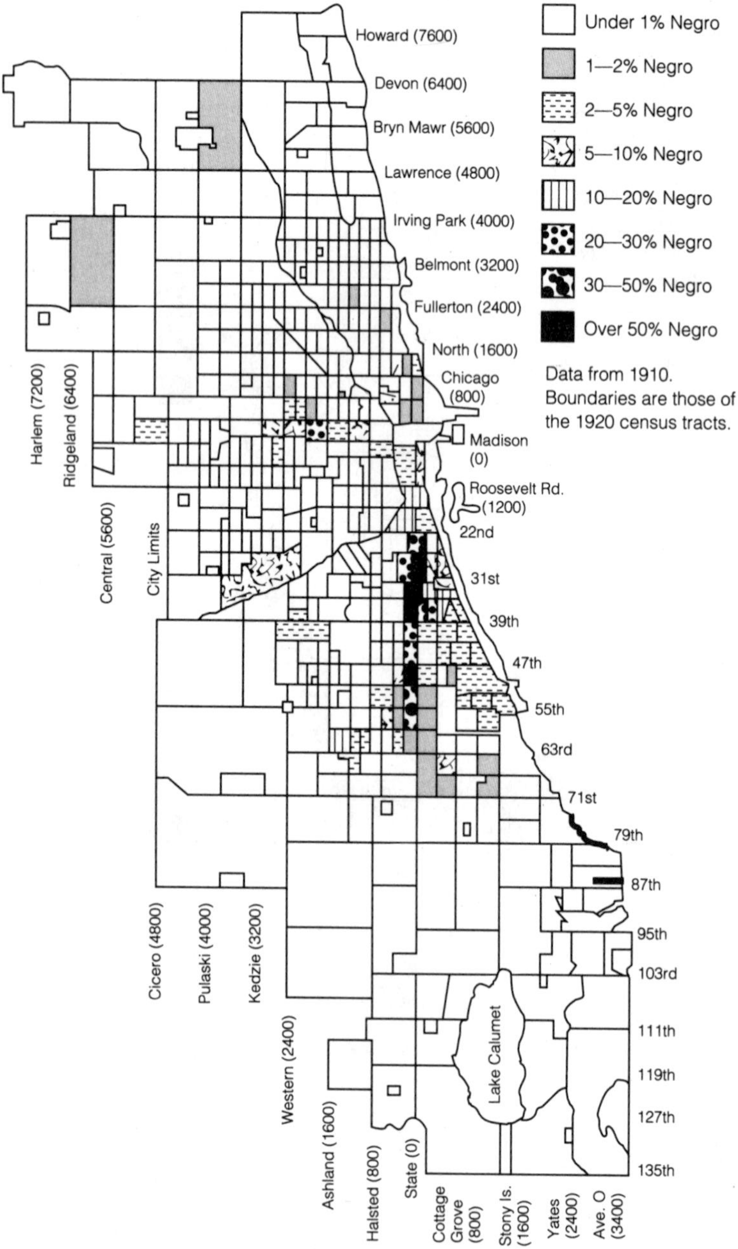

MAP 5.3. Black population by census tracts, 1910. (Source: Unpublished census data for 1910, compiled by Otis and Beverly Duncan, Population Studies Center, University of Michigan.)

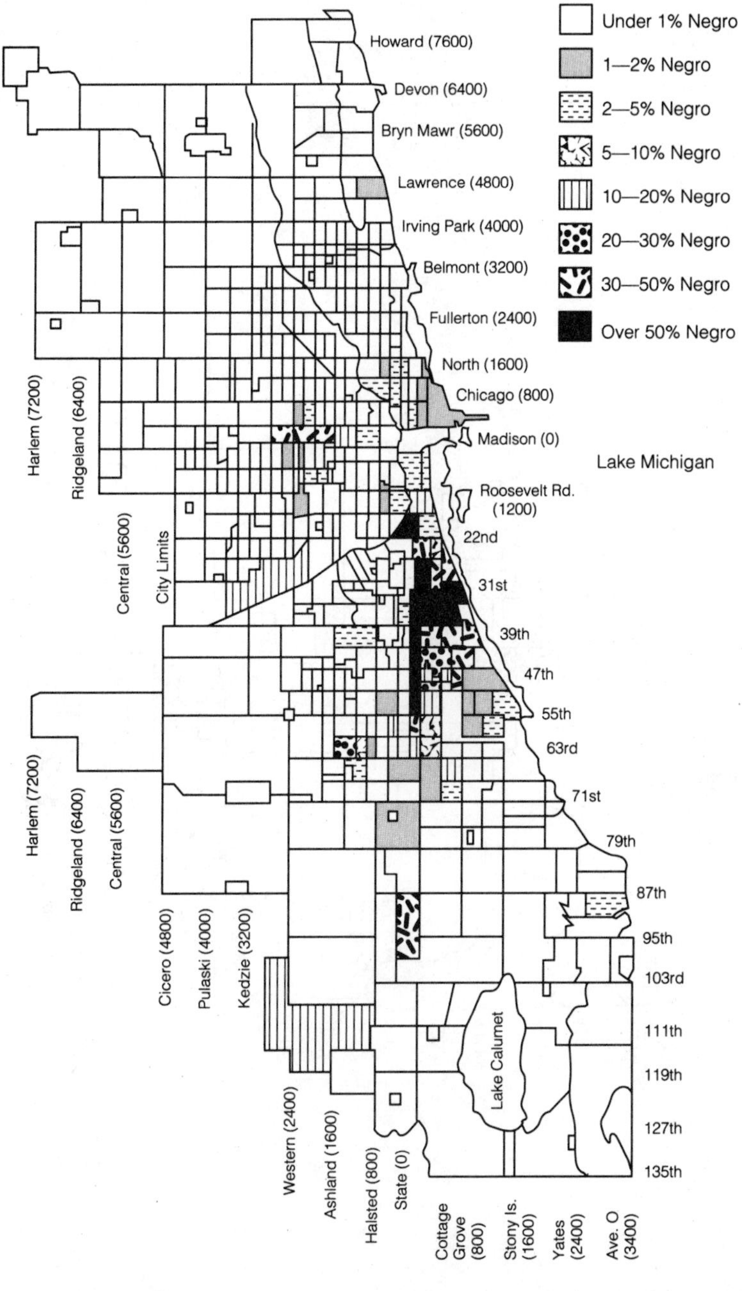

MAP 5.4. Black population by census tracts, 1920. (Source: Ernest W. Burgess and Charles Newcomb, eds., *Census Data of the City of Chicago, 1920* [Chicago, 1931].)

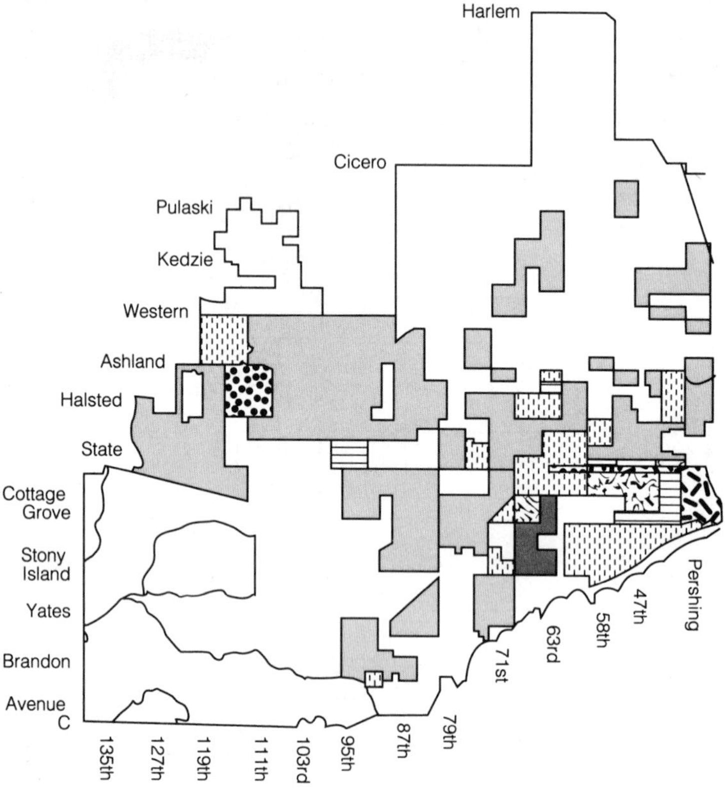

MAP 5.5. Black population by redrawn census tracts, 1920. (Source: Data compiled by Otis and Beverly Duncan.)

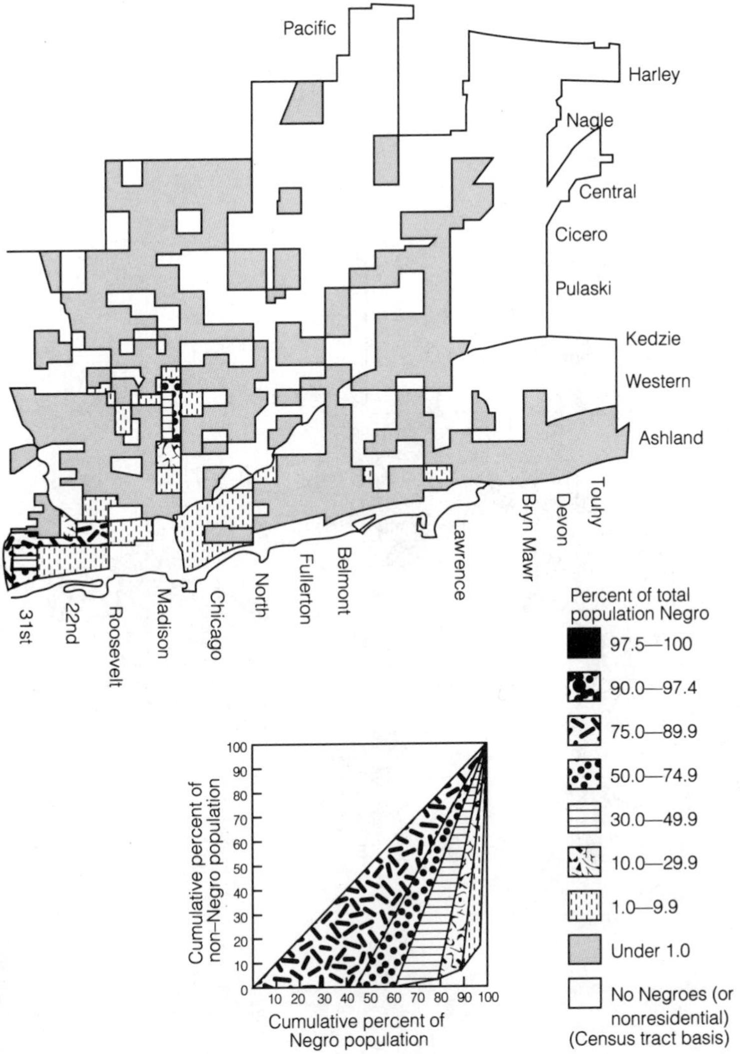

Pacific
Harley
Nagle
Central
Cicero
Pulaski
Kedzie
Western
Ashland
Touhy
Devon
Bryn Mawr
Lawrence
Belmont
Fullerton
North
Chicago
Madison
Roosevelt
22nd
31st
Percent of total population Negro
97.5—100
90.0—97.4
75.0—89.9
50.0—74.9
30.0—49.9
10.0—29.9
1.0—9.9
Under 1.0
No Negroes (or nonresidential)
(Census tract basis)
Cumulative percent of non–Negro population
0
10
20
30
40
50
60
70
80
90
100
Cumulative percent of Negro population

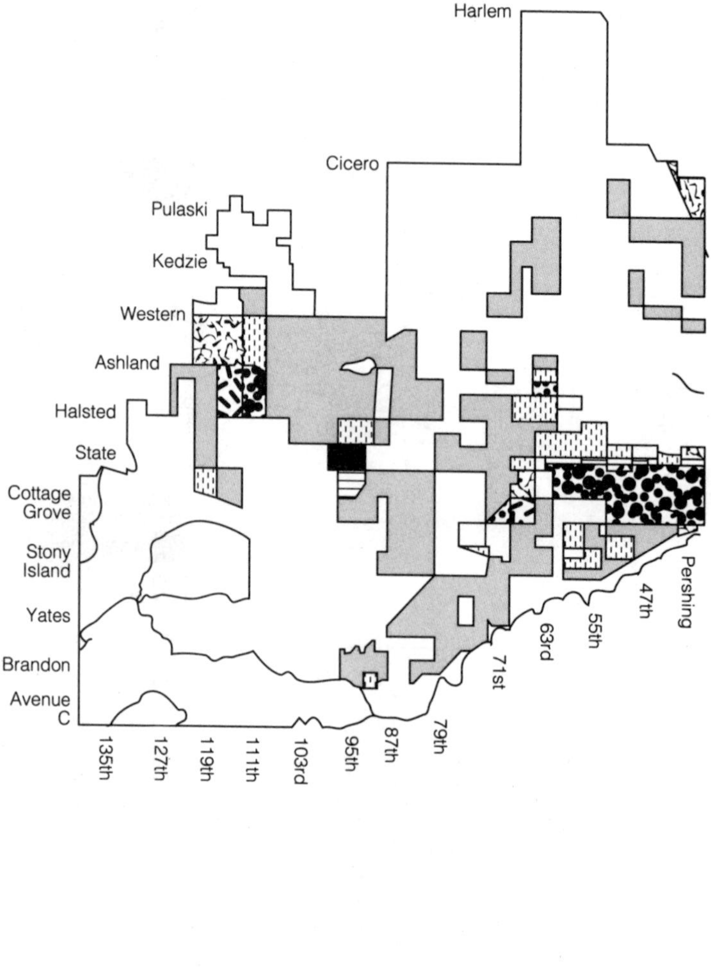

MAP 5.6. Black population by census tracts, 1930. (Source: Ernest W. Burgess and Charles Newcomb, eds., *Census Data of the City of Chicago, 1930* [Chicago, 1933].)

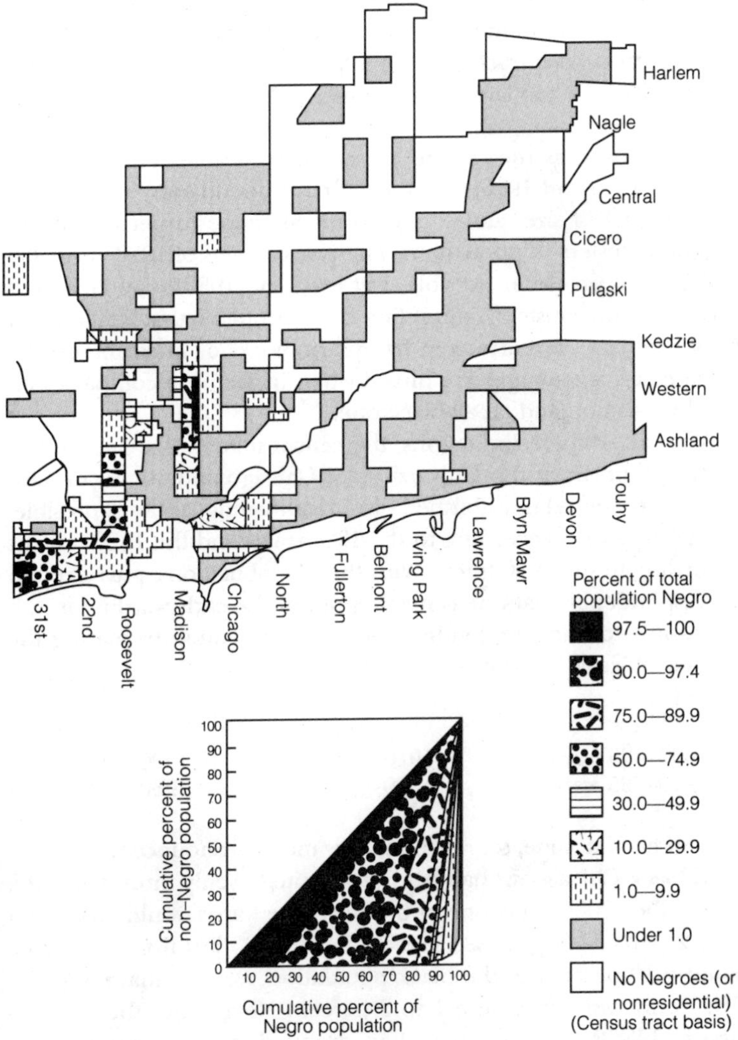

Harlem
Nagle
Central
Cicero
Pulaski
Kedzie
Western
Ashland
Touhy
Devon
Bryn Mawr
Lawrence
Irving Park
Belmont
Fullerton
North
Chicago
Madison
Roosevelt
22nd
31st
Percent of total population Negro
97.5—100
90.0—97.4
75.0—89.9
50.0—74.9
30.0—49.9
10.0—29.9
1.0—9.9
Under 1.0
No Negroes (or nonresidential)
(Census tract basis)
Cumulative percent of non-Negro population
0
10
20
30
40
50
60
70
80
90
100
Cumulative percent of Negro population

The main trouble with the figures from the four federal censuses is that they are arranged by four different sets of enumeration districts. The returns for 1900 and 1910 are listed by thirty-five wards whose boundaries were redrawn between canvasses (to suit political, not statistical, requirements). The census takers divided the city into 431 special census tracts for the 1920 enumeration. After finding these units to be too large, they redivided the city into 935 tracts for the 1930 census.

The figures, as they stand, are not comparable. The thirty-five wards of 1900 and 1910, with their variant boundaries, are too few, too unequal in size, and too aberrant in shape to permit one to pinpoint clusters of population. The census tracts of 1920 and 1930 make some precision possible, but even the 1930 boundaries cut through some clusters, concealing concentrations that would show up if the data were arranged by square blocks or linear blocks. In some cases, a tract appears mixed when in fact it encompasses an all-white section and an all-black one.

With all of these limitations, the census materials are still informative. Scholars at the Universities of Chicago and Michigan have partially reworked unpublished data, retabulating, as far as possible, the 1910 returns according to the 1920 tracts and the 1920 returns according to the 1930 tracts. With these retabulations, plus a rough correspondence that one can wring out of the early ward figures, it is possible to trace the tendency toward segregation by pairing the census tables as follows:

1900S	1910S	1920S
1900—35 wards	1910—431 tracts	1920—935 tracts
1910—35 wards	1920—431 tracts	1930—935 tracts

Within each decade, segregation grew more pronounced.

If black Chicagoans had been distributed evenly throughout the city in the 1900s, every one of the thirty-five wards would have been 1 to 2 percent Negro (see Table 5.2). In 1900 just five wards, containing 10 percent of the black population, were in that range. By 1910 only two wards were 1 to 2 percent Negro, and the percentage of blacks living in them had dropped below three. In 1900 sixteen wards were 99.5 to 100 percent white. Over half of the city's blacks lived in three contiguous South Side wards which, taken to-

TABLE 5.2. SEGREGATION OF BLACKS IN CHICAGO, 1900-1910

	1900			*1910*		
Percent of Ward Population Black	*Number of Wards*	*Black Population*	*Percent of Total Black Population*	*Number of Wards*	*Black Population*	*Percent of Total Black Population*
Under .5	16	1,300	4.3	22	2,273	5.1
.5–1	5	1,376	4.5	2	883	2.0
1–2	5	3,020	10.1	2	1,245	2.8
2–3	4	4,040	13.4	3	5,671	12.9
3–10	3	8,144	27.0	3	5,810	13.2
10–20	1	4,752	15.7	1	6,431	14.6
20–25	1	7,518	25.0	2	21,790	49.4

Sources: U.S. Twelfth Census, 1900, Bulletin no. 72, July 13, 1901, p. 8; *U.S. Thirteenth Census*, 1910, *Statistics for Illinois*, pp. 644–46; Allan Spear, *Black Chicago* (Chicago, 1967), Table 3, p. 15.

gether, were 16 percent black. Ten years later three different adjoining wards covering much the same area had a combined population 20 percent black; nearly two-thirds of the city's blacks lived within the limits of these wards, and the number of wards over 99.5 percent white had risen to twenty-two. In the course of the decade, the percentage of blacks in areas more than 20 percent Negro had jumped from one-fourth to one-half.

The black population of Chicago grew more slowly between 1900 and 1910 than it had in any previous decade. Still, blacks experienced mounting segregation. In the next ten years, their growth rate shot up from 46 to 148 percent, and alarmed Chicagoans succeeded in segregating them still more. Table 5.3 re-sorts the 1910 data to make them comparable to the census tract enumeration for 1920. The first thing to notice is how much segregation the 1910 ward tabulation concealed. While Table 5.2 shows no Negroes living in areas (i.e., wards) more than 25 percent black in 1910, Table 5.3 indicates that almost a third of the city's blacks lived in areas more than 50 percent black.

Segregation, though great in 1910, grew worse in the next decade. In 1920 nearly 36 percent of black Chicagoans lived in tracts more than 75 percent Negro; ten years before, no blacks had inhabited such a tract. Fully one-half of all blacks lived in a tract

TABLE 5.3. SEGREGATION OF BLACKS IN CHICAGO, 1910–1920

Percent of Tract Population Black	Percent of Total Black Population	
	1910 (N = 44,103)	*1920 (N = 109,458)*
Less than 5	24.1	7.4
5–9	8.2	2.6
10–19	4.4	6.9
20–49	32.5	32.6
50–74	30.8	14.8
75–100	. . .	35.7

Sources: Ernest W. Burgess and Charles Newcomb, eds., *Census Data of the City of Chicago, 1920* (Chicago, 1931); estimates for 1910 by Otis and Beverly Duncan, Population Studies Center, University of Michigan, as cited by Spear, Table 4, p. 16.

more than 50 percent Negro in 1920; a decade earlier, fewer than a third of them had lived in tracts that were half-black.

In the twenties, as in the preceding decade, the number of blacks more than doubled, and by 1930 their residential separation from white Chicagoans was practically total. Table 5.4, based on the 935 census tracts of 1930, retabulates the 1920 data to make the two censuses comparable. The use of smaller units uncovers a degree of segregation for 1920 that remained hidden in Table 5.3. The percentage of blacks living in areas more than 50 percent Negro turns out to be not 51 but 60, and the percentage of those in tracts more than 75 percent black goes up from 36 to 45. Ten years later, 90 percent of the black population lived in tracts more than 50 percent black; nearly 80 percent lived in tracts over 75 percent black. In 1920 no black people had lived in tracts that were 90 percent Negro. In 1930 *two out of three* black Chicagoans were packed into tracts where the population was 90 percent black, or more. One black person in five lived in a tract where 97.5 percent or more of the people around him were also black.

These tables, and more particularly the maps based on them, have misled some scholars into believing that the black population, "still relatively well distributed in 1900," encountered extreme resi-

TABLE 5.4. SEGREGATION OF BLACKS IN CHICAGO, 1920–1930

Percent of Tract Population Black	*Percent of Total Black Population*	
	1920 (N = 109,458)	*1930 (N = 233,903)*
Less than 1	3.0	1.3
1.0–9.9	8.3	2.8
10–29.9	10.1	3.8
30–49.0	18.4	2.5
50–74.9	15.4	10.2
75–89.9	44.8	15.8
90–97.4	. . .	44.6
97.5–100	. . .	19.0

Source: Otis Dudley Duncan and Beverly Duncan, *The Negro Population of Chicago: A Study of Residential Succession* (Chicago, 1957), pp. 93–97.

dential segregation only afterwards. In fact, the extent of black segregation was already extraordinary in 1900, despite the appearance of Map 5.1. The part of each ward that black people actually occupied was very small. A number of sources besides these census data make it possible to trace the growth of the Black Belt and its satellites. For example, the columns of the Negro newspapers furnish the addresses of people who were making "news" in the enclaves as well as realtors' listings of houses available to blacks. Plotting these addresses is a reasonably accurate way to locate clusters and determine boundary lines. In 1917 the Chicago Urban League made a study that showed when black people first moved south of 31st Street on each of the fourteen north-south streets from Wabash Avenue to Cottage. The shaded area in Maps 5.1 and 5.2 indicates the approximate limits of the actual Negro concentrations, as determined by use of these materials. Map 5.7 shows the extent of the Black Belt and its satellites decade by decade.[12]

Sociologist David A. Wallace employed some of these materials as a check when he combined ward, precinct, census tract, and block data to construct a roughly consistent series of black-white segregation indexes by small units. On Wallace's scale, 0 represents completely even residential dispersion, and 100 indicates complete

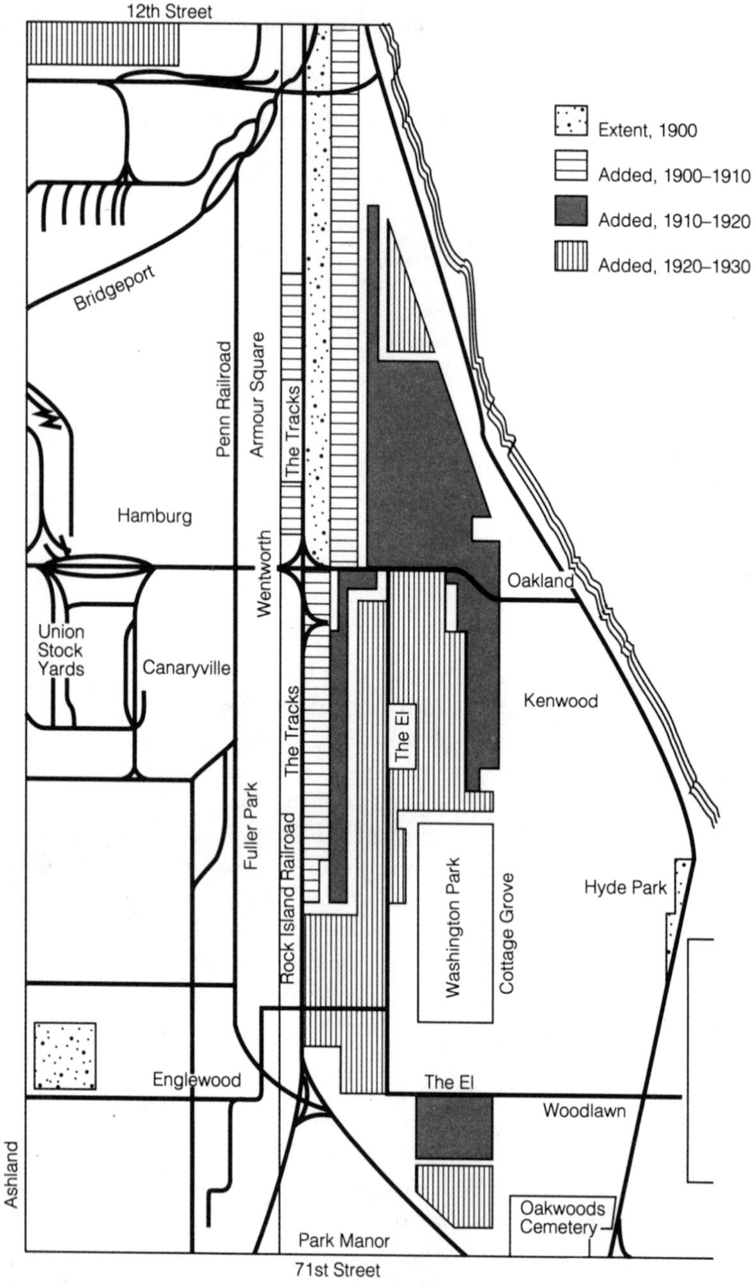

MAP 5.7. **South Side Black Belt and satellites.**

unevenness, or total segregation. He found segregation consistently high from 1898 through 1930:

YEAR	1898	1910	1920	1930
Index	91.8	92.4	94.0	98.4

The astonishing thing is that segregation so severe could have sharpened steadily for thirty years.[13]

No white ethnic group had experienced anything comparable. Immigrants had "a decided tendency to drift into little colonies," as one of Jane Addams's associates at Hull-House observed in 1894, and the hostility of outsiders may well have reinforced their inclination to huddle with their countrymen. Nevertheless, many immigrants managed to make their homes outside of the neighborhoods identified with their own groups. And the "foreign districts," such as the area around Hull-House, agglomerated people of many nationalities at the same time. An ethnic enclave was not a district in which all of the inhabitants were of the same ethnic stock and in which all of the people of that ethnic group lived. It was a place where the members of one nationality set the tone, because they outnumbered everybody else, or had been there the longest, or were simply the most visible and voluble. Settlement workers used the term *colony* in three different ways. A colony could be an ethnic enclave; a catchall name, such as "community," for all people of a nationality living in the same city, whether or not they lived together in the same enclave; or a geographical point where an ethnic group's institutions clustered. The residents of Hull-House spoke of the "Greek colony" on Blue Island Avenue at a time when Greeks amounted to no more than 7 percent of the district's population. The Greek newspapers, stores, restaurants, and poolrooms on Blue Island catered to all of the Greeks in the metropolitan area. Geographically, this colony was practically coterminous with the Italian colony and several other colonies.[14]

An outsider who came into a district would detect the dominant tone if he had a sharp eye and a keen ear, but he could easily miss it if all Italians, Hungarians, Greeks, Bohemians, Poles, Lithuanians, and Yugoslavs looked alike and sounded alike to him. For some reason, the area west of Wentworth Avenue between 22nd and 63rd streets was known for decades as "Polish" or "Irish" or "Irish and

Polish" territory. But it was always a patchwork of nationalities. Of the twenty-seven ethnicities represented in the area in 1920, the Irish ranked third, the Polish fifteenth. Italians, the leading ethnic group, had 25 percent of the foreign-born population.[15]

Even a longtime resident could be fooled about the composition of a neighborhood. A woman raised in the South Side neighborhood Park Manor in the twenties and thirties recalled decades later: "It was an Irish neighborhood; everybody was Irish." When she was growing up, if anybody asked her where she was from, she did not answer "Park Manor" but rather "Saint Columbanus." As she remembered it, "everybody" was Catholic too, so naturally "everybody" belonged to Columbanus parish. The neighborhood's most celebrated resident, the gangster Al Capone, was not Irish, she explained, but because his wife was, "everybody" regarded the Capones as Irish. The fond reminiscences of this woman conflict with the cold figures of the U.S. Census, which reports that twenty-six to thirty-three ethnic groups occupied Park Manor between 1920 and 1940. In 1930 two residents out of five were old-stock "Americans." Among the nationality groups, the Irish ranked not first but second—behind the Swedes. Only 13 percent of the area's 21,000 people were Irish-stock. And Park Manor was predominantly Protestant: In a 1920 religious survey St. Columbanus parish, whose boundaries exactly coincided with those of the area's four census tracts, claimed only "5,000 souls."

When an interviewer showed this woman the census tables, she said, "I really don't remember anything but Irish." Unlike the empirical world that the census tabulated, the social world she experienced and kept alive in her memories was peopled with relatives, friends, and public characters—nuns and priests, the mailman and the trolley flagman, storekeepers, policemen, and politicians—who were mostly Irish-Catholic or at least part-Irish, like the Capones. So for her it was an Irish neighborhood. Statistically, however, it was a melting pot.[16]

Usually the students and reformers who walked the streets and alleys of the ethnic neighborhoods to inspect the housing were canny enough to catch the flavor of the areas they canvassed, but their very ability to identify the neighborhood's predominant ethnic group could mislead people who read their reports. For they did not always pause to explain that a "Lithuanian district" or an "Italian district" was not the exclusive preserve of a single nationality, and even when they did, it was easy for the reader to disregard the qualification.

In his 1901 study, *The Tenements of Chicago*, Robert Hunter called the districts he surveyed "Italian," "Jewish," "Polish," and "Bohemian." Only at the end of his lengthy report, in an appendix, did he mention that "many other nationalities" lived in each of the districts. In the same manner, housing investigators in 1924 noted that twenty-two ethnic groups had representatives in the twenty-two blocks of industrial Burnside and then went on to label it "a Magyar district." At the time of their house-to-house survey, 37 percent of the family heads were Magyar. The 1930 census showed that Hungarians (Magyar and otherwise) and Poles (mostly Ukrainians) each accounted for 26 percent of Burnside's population; twenty-three other nationalities, plus old-stock Americans, were also present. Yet housing reformers kept on calling the district "Magyar."[17]

In the 1890s Jane Addams, making an attempt at precision, spoke of "three or four more or less distinct foreign colonies" that together dominated the vicinity of Hull-House. At the same time, another Hull-House resident reported that the immigrants in the neighborhood lived "more or less intermingled." Miss Addams and her coresident were not in conflict: The colonies *were* more or less distinct, and the immigrants in them *were* more or less intermixed. To show "just how members of various nationalities" were "grouped" near the settlement, the residents made a series of maps, based on the 1893 Department of Labor investigation of the West Side "slums." These maps give the ethnic breakdown, lot by lot, of the thirty-five occupied blocks between Hull-House and State Street, from Polk down to 12th Street. The maps spanned two quite different areas, separated by the Chicago River and a belt of factories, warehouses, and railyards: a 29-block neighborhood next to Hull-House, composed of working families, and, east of the river, a section that families shunned, which was occupied by rooming houses, saloons, and whorehouses.[18]

The entire district contained more than 18,000 people, nearly 60 percent of whom were foreign-born. Of these immigrants, 17 percent were Italians. Another 17 percent were Russians and Poles whom the Hull-House staff believed to be "uniformly Jewish." In fact, not all of the Poles were Jews. The number of Polish Catholics was increasing so greatly that they took over the Bohemian church, St. Wenceslaus. The area had a pronounced Italian and Jewish flavor, but two out of three immigrants living there were neither Italians nor Jews.[19]

The remaining immigrants came from twenty-two different countries or ethnic stocks, which the map-makers reduced to fourteen "nations" to avoid "confusing the mind by a separate recognition of every country." On the maps, Swedes, Norwegians, and Danes show up as "Scandinavians." Anyone from Austria-Hungary appears as a "German" or a "Bohemian." The "English-speaking" category excludes American Negroes and the Irish but includes Englishmen, English-Canadians, Scots, Americans of native parentage, and "such children born in this country of foreign parents as are over ten years of age, or if younger, are in attendance upon any public school."

The eighteen colors, which represent twenty-six or more ethnic groups, produce a rainbow effect all over the maps. Italians clearly predominate in some sections, Bohemians or Russians or Poles in others, but the clusters are not exclusive or contiguous, and they overlap. One does not see eighteen separate enclaves. No block, nor even a single side of a block, is solidly one color. The average number of "nations" to a block is eight. Incredibly, four out of five *lots* are mixed. Fully half of the lots show three or more "nations" in possession. The maximum mixture occurs in the respectable working-class family district: There the average block harbors nine ethnic groups, nearly 90 percent of the lots are mixed, and over 70 percent of the lots have residents from three or more countries. One building on a shoestring lot has occupants of ten different ethnicities.

According to the commentary accompaning the maps, the Irish are "pretty well sprinkled" through the area. They could be found in twenty-eight of the twenty-nine blocks west of the river. The Irish were not the only ones who were scattered, however. The Germans and the Russians also inhabited twenty-eight of the "respectable" blocks. The Poles could find countrymen living in twenty-seven of these blocks. The Bohemians had homes in twenty-six, the Italians in twenty-one. Only one group of any size was confined to a small section. Of the 1,125 "colored people" in the area, all but *two* lived in the "criminal district" east of the river. All of the ninety-five known brothels in the area were located in the five blocks where the black people roomed.[20]

The area around Hull-House was called Little Italy, but as the maps showed, and as a later investigator observed in 1910, it was "by no means exclusively Italian . . . for families of almost every other nationality may be found within it." The same thing was true of the city's other Italian districts, and of the Jewish Ghetto, Pilsen, Polonia, and the other "foreign colonies." In none of the Little Italys was there an all-Italian block; in fact, in the whole period 1890–1930, not even one side of a single square block was ever 100 percent Italian. Of all of Chicago's white ethnic groups, Italians were the most "segregated," but as historian Humbert Nelli has shown, "the population density of Italians in the city's various Italian districts fell considerably below 50 percent." At the core of the Lower North Side's Little Sicily, Italians barely outnumbered the other immigrants in 1912. A harrowing survey of a wretched four-block district that was 80 percent Italian in 1914 revealed that "only the comparatively *recent* immigrants," who could not speak English, lived there. "The Italians, when they grew more prosperous, do move out of the Italian district," the investigators reported.[21]

Similarly, Jews could move from the so-called Ghetto if their incomes permitted. Many chose to move. In 1903 Clarence Darrow observed, "There are different kinds of Jews. There are Jews who live on Grand Boulevard and Jews who live on Maxwell Street. For the most part, the Jews on Grand Boulevard own wholesale clothing stores, and for the most part, the Jews on Maxwell Street work in the stores." Professor Louis Wirth of the University of Chicago echoed the observation twenty-four years later. "If you would know what kind of Jew a man is," Wirth said, "ask him where he lives." Wirth, a German-born Jew, resided near the university in exclusive Hyde Park. Some Jews lived uncomfortably close together in the Ghetto's back streets, but others had fashionable addresses. The Jewish community of Chicago was always a diaspora.[22]

As early as 1874 a rabbi lamented the dispersion of the Jews. With its members "scattered over a space of nearly thirty miles, in hundreds of streets," he cried, the community was "dissolved in the mass" of Chicago's population. Two decades later, as Eastern European Jews poured into the city, the old Ghetto, an area less than one-quarter of a square mile, filled up until 90 percent of its inhabitants were Jewish. But only 14,000 of Chicago's 75,000 Jews lived inside. The "overflow" reached every community in the city. As Louis Wirth observed, the Ghetto contained only "the first generation of immigrants." Other Jews "scattered over [ever] wider areas" until, in the 1920s, the Jewish community again seemed to be disintegrating.[23]

In the peak period of immigration, before World War I, there was a part of Pilsen that was nearly 90 percent Bohemian, and there was a ten-block section "by St. Stanislaus" that was 95 percent Polish. But at no time did more than 6 to 12 percent of the city's Bohemians and Poles live in such concentrations. In the larger "Polish" districts surrounding the densest clusters, an investigator reported in 1920, there were Bohemians, Bulgarians, Croatians, Serbians, Lithuanians, "other Slavic nationalities," and people of "many other nationalities." The Poles were usually so "intermingled with other Slavic groups" that it was "difficult to distinguish one group from another." Seasoned workers in the Immigrants Protective League believed that some Slavs simply identified themselves as Poles to avoid confusing census takers and other social investigators. At the peripheries of Slavic concentrations, the populations meshed with non-Slavic peoples. However intense the clustering was in a given district, individuals were "continually moving to better localities" as they improved their "economic status."[24]

Housing reformers and neighborhood workers tended to talk, and even think, of immigrants as residents of separate foreign colonies. Actually, immigrants lived in so-called native neighborhoods as well as "foreign" enclaves, and as a rule the enclaves were ethnically mixed. Great immigrant neighborhoods grew up in the city's industrial districts because, as Edith Abbott put it, "workmen needed to live near their work." Industrial neighborhoods housed "representatives of the various nationalities" who labored in the nearby mills and plants. Eventually, Negroes secured jobs in the gut shanties of Packingtown, the furnace rooms of Steeltown, and the factories of Burnside and Pullman, but unlike the immigrants, they could not obtain housing nearby. The housing investigators and settlement staffers seldom mentioned this exception, and when they did, they did not explain it. Berenice Davis's simple statement on Burnside in 1924 was typical: "The negroes employed are all residents of the negro district of Chicago." The fact which the observers never put into focus was that the ethnic enclaves, those in the better residential communities as well as those in the industrial sections, were essentially mixed *white* neighborhoods, closed to Negroes. The converse of this fact was also true, and also obscured by

TABLE 5.5. "GHETTOIZATION" OF ETHNIC GROUPS, 1930

*Group**	*Group's City Population*	*Group's "Ghetto" Population*	*Total "Ghetto" Population*	*% of Group "Ghettoized"*	*Group's % of "Ghetto" Population*
Irish	169,568	4,933	14,595	2.9	33.8
German	377,975	53,821	169,649	14.2	31.7
Swedish	140,913	21,581	88,749	15.3	24.3
Russian	169,736	63,416	149,208	37.4	42.5
Czech	122,089	53,301	169,550	43.7	31.4
Italian	181,861	90,407	195,736	49.7	46.2
Polish	401,316	248,024	457,146	61.0	54.3
Negro	233,903	216,846	266,051	92.7	81.5

* "Group" includes foreign-born and their children, that is, "foreign stock."
Sources: Map, "Nationality and Racial Groups," 1930; Burgess and Newcomb, eds., *Census Data of the City of Chicago, 1930* (Chicago, 1933).

the reports of reformers. White neighborhoods, whether they were dominated by natives or foreigners, were polyethnic and uniracial.[25]

Sociologists at the University of Chicago (in exclusive Hyde Park, opposite the Black Belt) constructed a map based on the 1930 census to show the spatial distribution of the city's major ethnic groups. Robert Park, Ernest Burgess, and Louis Wirth, the pillars of the Chicago school of sociology, believed and taught their students to believe that all ethnic neighborhoods were—or once had been—ghettos, like the Black Belt. They viewed Negroes as just another ethnic group, whose segregation was largely voluntary and would prove to be only temporary. They subjected Chicago's social life to "blinding scrutiny," but they never saw the difference between the ethnic enclave and the black ghetto.[26]

The visual evidence of the map they made seems to support their thesis (see Map 5.8). Eight ghettos and more than forty ghetto satellites stand out. They all look alike, but examination of the census data on which the map was based reveals that they were not. The Black Belt and its offshoots were unique. Table 5.5 gives the population of the "ghetto" districts, the percentage of each ethnic group "ghettoized," and each group's percentage of its own "ghetto's" population.

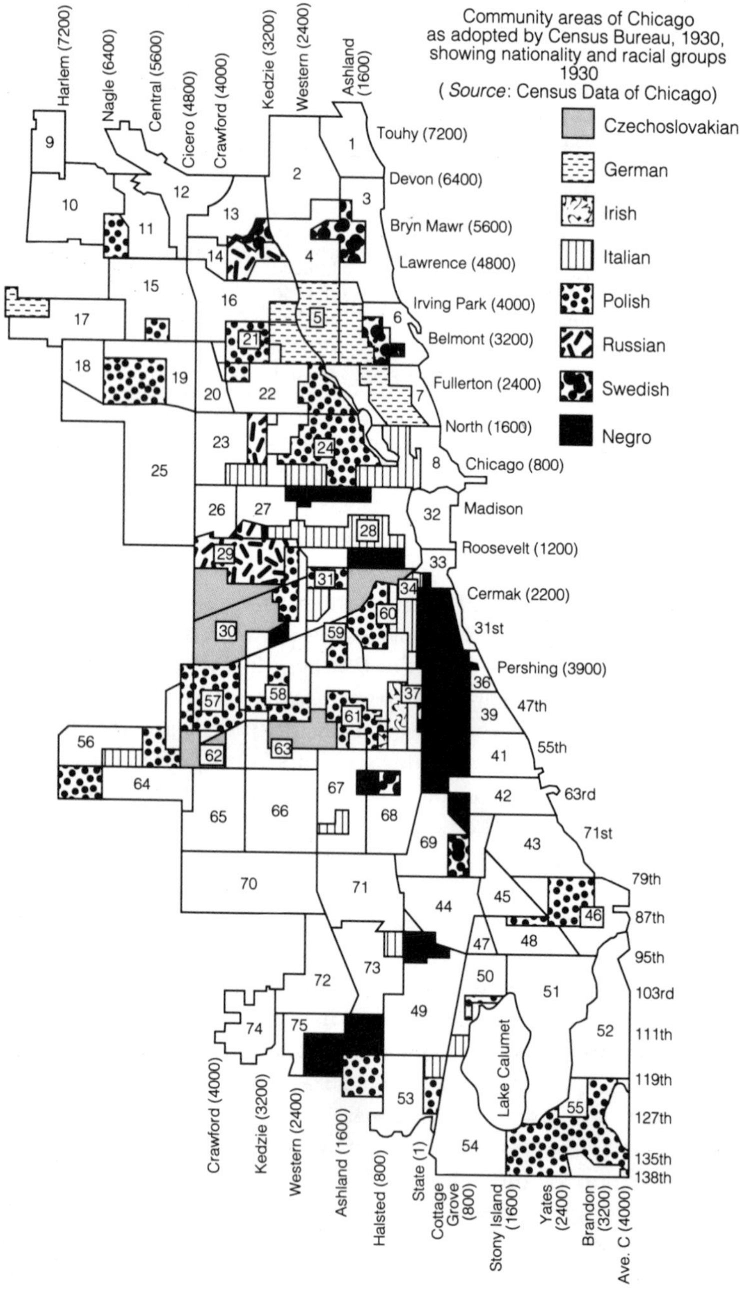
Community areas of Chicago
as adopted by Census Bureau, 1930,
showing nationality and racial groups
1930
(*Source*: Census Data of Chicago)
Czechoslovakian
German
Irish
Italian
Polish
Russian
Swedish
Negro
Harlem (7200)
Nagle (6400)
Central (5600)
Cicero (4800)
Crawford (4000)
Kedzie (3200)
Western (2400)
Ashland (1600)
Touhy (7200)
Devon (6400)
Bryn Mawr (5600)
Lawrence (4800)
Irving Park (4000)
Belmont (3200)
Fullerton (2400)
North (1600)
Chicago (800)
Madison
Roosevelt (1200)
Cermak (2200)
31st
Pershing (3900)
47th
55th
63rd
71st
79th
87th
95th
103rd
111th
119th
127th
135th
138th
Crawford (4000)
Kedzie (3200)
Western (2400)
Ashland (1600)
Halsted (800)
State (1)
Cottage Grove (800)
Stony Island (1600)
Yates (2400)
Brandon (3200)
Ave. C (4000)
Lake Calumet
1
2
3
4
5
6
7
8
9
10
11
12
13
14
15
16
17
18
19
20
21
22
23
24
25
26
27
28
29
30
31
32
33
34
36
37
39
41
42
43
44
45
46
47
48
49
50
51
52
53
54
55
56
57
58
59
60
61
62
63
64
65
66
67
68
69
70
71
72
73
74
75

MAP 5.8. Ethnic "Ghettos," 1930 (Map: "Nationality and Racial Groups," University of Chicago, 1930). *Note:* There were ethnic majorities almost everywhere that white people lived. "Native Americans" predominated in only six of the areas not shaded in this map—those numbered 9, 36, 39, 42, 72, and 75. Even in the supposedly "native neighborhoods," immigrants and their children were just barely in the minority.

The Negro ghetto, it turns out, was Chicago's only real ghetto. To begin with, the white "colonies" were anything but homogeneous. All twenty-five nationalities listed in the tables of the census for Chicago were represented in each of the ethnic "ghettos." The seven white "ghettos" and their satellites together covered 308 census tracts, most of which were less than one-eighth of a square mile in extent. The average number of nationalities recorded for these tracts was twenty-two, ranging from twenty in the Italian and Czech tracts to twenty-five in the Irish, German, and Swedish tracts. Thus the typical neighborhood that shows up on the map as the exclusive domain of a single "nationality group" was in fact an ethnic hodgepodge.

For the most part, the territories identified with a nationality did not contain the mass of that group's population, and within these territories the group did not constitute a solid majority. Little Ireland was only one-third Irish, and only 3 percent of the city's Irish-stock population lived there. A higher percentage of Germans, Swedes, and Czechs resided within "their own" colonies, but their pluralities inside those areas were only 24 to 32 percent. Little Russia had three sites. These heavily Jewish neighborhoods were 43 percent Russian, but they contained only 37 percent of the Russian population. Half of Chicago's Italians lived in the city's eleven Little Italys, but most of the inhabitants of those places were not Italian. Polonia was scattered over nineteen locations. Three out of five Poles lived in one or another of the little Polands, but almost half of Polonia's residents were not Polish.[27]

By contrast, more than nine out of ten black Chicagoans lived in areas over 80 percent Negro. No immigrant group was, or ever had been, so impacted. The most all-encompassing ethnic enclave was Stanislawowa, on the northwest side "by St. Stanislaus." This was the Little Poland of the 1901 tenement survey. In 1930 it was still "the center of Polish life in Chicago." The area was three-fifths Polish, but it held only 24 percent of Polish Chicagoans. The Black Belt on the South Side contained four out of five Chicago Negroes, and it was 89 percent black. Half of the blacks (51 percent) whose homes were not inside the main ghetto lived in pocket ghettos which, aggregated, were more than three-fourths Negro.[28]

Ethnic clustering did occur, but unlike Negro segregation, it was never complete, it was not basically compulsory, and it was not permanent. The polyglot ethnic communities in such industrial slums as Packingtown and Steeltown were places where a man could live cheaply near his work. To be stuck in Back a' the Yards forever with no hope of escape might have been a grim fate, but to be locked out of the neighborhood, when that was where the jobs and cheap houses were, would have been worse. Neighborhoods such as Packingtown, wretched as they were physically, represented opportunity to poor laboring men. As Charles Zeublin, the settlement worker, said in 1894, "Opportunity is what the foreigner in our cities needs." The immigrant was free to enter, free to stay, and free to leave. If he worked his way up the economic scale, he could move out of the tenement district to a place with better homes and gardens.[29]

The ethnic neighborhoods that form a rim around Map 5.8 were full of people who had moved up and out of the old areas. Beyond the city limits there were more enclaves. In the suburbs, as in the city, immigrants and their children outnumbered native whites of native parentage in 1930; a few suburbs exceeded the city in the proportion of residents who were of foreign stock. And scattered all over the city and the suburbs were neighborhoods that were not noticeably "ethnic." Nearly all of them contained a sizable ethnic component. Usually this component was highly mixed: The average "native American" census tract harbored twenty-four nationalities, more than the average ethnic tract. Surprisingly, *these* were the communities—the unshaded portions of Map 5.8 and corresponding sections in the suburbs—where the majority of first- and second-generation immigrants made their homes.

The old neighborhoods in the inner belt harbored a succession of newcomers, and they continued to serve a function for those who had emerged from the tenements as well. Despite the slum surroundings, such places as Stanislawowa had a rich array of ethnic institutions. The old enclaves were concentrations to which ex-residents could constantly return, to shop, to dine, to worship, to celebrate holidays, to visit family and friends, to reminisce—in short, to maintain ties and be "ethnic." They were centrally located, easily accessible from outlying neighborhoods and suburbs. Milwaukee Avenue and Archer Avenue, for instance, were Polish corridors, leading to "Polish downtown" in Stanislawowa. The triangle formed by Halsted Street, 12th Street, and Blue Island—three major thoroughfares—was the location of "Italian downtown," "Greek downtown," "Bulgarian downtown," and many another ethnic groups' downtown.[30]

Observing the dispersion of the immigrants and their children in the twenties, Louis Wirth and others predicted that ethnic "communities" would disintegrate. They assumed that ghetto conditions had created the old community consciousness and sustained group life. If the ghetto passed away, they thought, solidarity would vanish with it. They were mistaken. The immigrant ghettos never existed. In essence, the "Jewish community" and the other ethnic communities were webs of social relationships and "states of mind," not geographic concentrations. They came into being, and were capable of enduring, with almost no fixed residential base.[31]

During the twenties a new ethnic community established itself in Chicago. If such observers as Louis Wirth had looked carefully at its development, they could have seen the ethnic residential pattern in the making. In 1910 there were not enough Mexicans in Chicago "to warrant a separate classification of them in the Census." The total Mexican population of the State of Illinois was only 672. The wartime boom brought some Mexicans to Chicago, but their number in the city was a scant 1,224 in 1920. Then, in the twenties, the Mexican population increased fifteenfold, to almost 20,000. Most of these were Mexican aliens, not Mexican-Americans. These people came to the city late, they arrived all in a rush and in comparatively large numbers from a foreign land, they were dirt-poor peasants who knew almost nothing of city life, they spoke a foreign tongue, and their complexion was dark. By all the working rules of ethnic and urban studies except one— about half of white Chicagoans were Catholics, and so were most of them—the Mexicans were prime candidates for ghettoization.[32]

Yet when a University of Chicago sociology student, Manuel Bueno, a Mexican migrant himself, went to study the Mexicans in the mid-twenties he found that they were "scattered" in "different and separated sections of the city." By 1930 there were four main Mexican "colonies," but Mexicans were not the dominant ethnic group in any of them. In 1934 their share of the population in these Little Mexicos ranged from 10 to 23 percent. For every three Mexicans who lived inside one of these districts, there were two who resided somewhere else. Wherever Mexicans found jobs, they were able to make homes. Because many of them worked in the slaughterhouses, in the steel mills, and in railyards and warehouses, they made their main "colonies" in Packingtown, South Chicago, and South Deering, and on the white West Side. They had access to the housing in Burnside, Pullman, and other industrial communities as well. These were all areas that Negroes entered, in Edith Abbott's circumspect phrase, "only during working hours," because housing was denied them even when jobs were not.[33]

A member of the Chicago Chamber of Commerce stated in 1929 that "people would like to segregate the Mexicans as well as the Negroes," but it did not happen. Mexicans found that despite the prejudice of some Chicagoans, they could move wherever they could afford to live. Employers and landlords preferred them to Negroes. And light-skinned Mexicans enjoyed more freedom of movement than those with darker skin. Ironically, the 1930 U.S. Census classified Mexicans as "nonwhites," but their residential pattern was basically the same as that of the European immigrants.[34]

The Black Belt and its satellites were different. They were great physical entities, sharply outlined, and the border all around them was the color line. Whites drew it—not the blacks. Perhaps if Negroes had enjoyed the option of living in "white" neighborhoods, "mixed" neighborhoods, or Negro neighborhoods, nine out of ten would have elected to live in all-black enclaves. But it is not likely. All groups that had the choice—and every white group had it—opted for a combination of mild clustering and wide dispersion. And in doing so, they did not have to surrender ethnic identity and abandon ethnic associations. Theoretically, then, blacks also could have been soul brothers without being ghetto inmates. The point is moot, for Negroes never had the choice.

Bluesman Big Bill Broonzy saw the pattern much more clearly than did the reformers and the university's sociologists, and Big Bill told it like it was:

> They say if you's white, you's all right.
> If you's brown, stick around.
> But if you're black,
> Mmm, mmm, Brother, git back, git back, git back.[35]

CHAPTER 6 ❧

Drawing the Color Line

A writer once summed up the Negro question by saying, "the North has the principles and the South has the Negroes." We are coming to have the Negroes, and we want to keep the principles so far as they are applicable.
—"White and Black in Chicago," Chicago *Tribune*, editorial, 3 August 1919.

"Goddamit, look! We live here and they live there. We black and they white. They got things and we ain't. They do things and we can't. It's just like living in jail. . . . Can't you see?"
—Bigger Thomas, in Richard Wright's novel *Native Son* (New York, 1940; reprint ed., New York, 1966), pp. 23 and 27.

AT THE TURN OF THE CENTURY, THE MAIN GHETTO WAS A CORRIDOR OVER three miles long but barely a quarter-mile wide, bounded on all sides by rail lines. The Black Belt, as people were already calling it, stretched southward from the downtown railroad yards to another tremendous block of railway property just below 39th Street. The broad embankment of the Rock Island Railroad sealed it from the working-class immigrant communities to the west, and the South Side Elevated Railroad walled it off from "the white belt of aristocracy and wealth" to the east.[1]

The narrow slot between the Rock Island and the "alley el" contained about half of the city's 30,000 Negroes. Almost all of the rest resided in other segregated pockets. On the West Side an enclave was growing up in the gap between the Northwestern Railroad's freight lines and the new, noisy Lake Street El, and there was a sizable colony in Englewood, two and a half miles southwest of the Black Belt. The Pittsburgh, Cincinnati, Chicago, St. Louis

Railroad tracks ridged the colony on the north; the Englewood El ran along its southern rim. There were smaller clusters in rooming-house strips in Hyde Park, along the Illinois Central tracks, and on the Lower North Side, near the el. Wherever blacks lived in Chicago, it seemed, train tracks hemmed them in.[2]

The tracks were racial barricades, but only because there were white people on the other side to man them. It was the color line, not any railroad line, that checked the free movement of Negroes. A train track was simply a convenient place to draw the line. The railways were merely instruments of folkways.

A black person who wanted to move out of the Black Belt could not slip inconspicuously into a white neighborhood and wait to blend into the surroundings. He was bound to stick out and create a stir. "As soon as he is discovered," *The Economist,* a realty publication, noted in 1908, "it is with difficulty that any one is secured to occupy adjoining flats or houses." If vacancies could not be filled with whites, other blacks would come in. Then all of the whites who could go would go, leaving behind those who were too old, too poor, or just too tired to make the move. In this way, whole streets "went black." Even before 1900, when the total black population was not large enough to pose a real "threat" to large residential districts, the presence of a single Negro householder could throw a neighborhood into panic. Concerned property owners learned that if they acted quickly enough, they could arrest the panic and cement the neighborhood's universal fear of Negro neighbors into a solid block of resistance.[3]

Property owners in Woodlawn were pioneers of community containment. In 1897 they "declared war" on the managers of some cheap hotels near the 63rd Street El and the Illinois Central tracks. These hotels had grown like weeds in Woodlawn during the great World's Fair. With the dismantling of the White City, the hotel managers had trouble finding tenants. They tried to solve their problem by renting rooms (probably the worst rooms, those looking out on the train platforms) to Negroes. When the neighborhood rose up in wrath against them, the hotel managers gave in, and the blacks had to move out. Five years later a hotel owner tried to break the ban against black tenants. "The Society of Woodlawn," that is, the most influential personages in the community, warned that they would make "war" on him unless he abandoned his plan to convert hotel suites into apartments "for colored people." When the owner attempted to proceed with alterations, policemen "under instructions from the building department" ordered his workmen to leave the job site. With that the hotel man capitulated. As a result of the "victory" of Woodlawn's whites, only a few rooming houses harbored any blacks by 1910. Within another decade Woodlawn proper, the area east of Cottage Grove, was practically all-white. The Negro percentage was down to 0.2.[4]

Real estate speculators were as anxious to trigger panic as resident owners were to spike it. There were profits to be made in buying cheap from whites and reselling dear to blacks. "A colored man has bought next door": These words induced many a white family to sell at a loss for fear that staying on would result in even greater loss.[5]

Despite the job ceiling in employment, there were blacks who rose to the middle class—economically. Like other Americans who strived and "made it," they wanted social status equivalent to their economic standing. That meant that they coveted more than just good housing; a self-made man felt entitled to a good *address*. In the Black Belt there was precious little good housing, and by the white majority's definition, there were no good addresses. Moreover, middle-class Negroes, like others of that class, wished to put some distance between themselves and those who stood beneath them on the ladder of success. After all, for people of ability to seek their own level was the American way. They wished to surround themselves with neighbors whose level of achievement and style of living matched their own.

Most black Chicagoans were poor, very poor. And as old as the city's Negro community was, the overwhelming majority of blacks at the turn of the century were newcomers from outside of Illinois. They hailed "chiefly from the small towns and country districts of the South." Like the immigrants who thronged to Chicago from the fields of Europe, they were unaccustomed to big-city ways. "They know but little concerning sanitation, ventilation, filtered water, the effects of overcrowding, or the use of the bath tub," wrote Richard R. Wright, Jr., in 1908. Wright, a middle-class black scholar, added, "They know but little of the theory of rents." Inexperience was a handicap to migrants of all ethnicities. But the color of these newcomers left them open to a special kind of exploitation. Consequently, Wright stated, "they generally have to pay whatever rent the landlord or his agent asks."[6]

Middle-class blacks wanted badly to live apart from the newcomers, but because poor Negroes paid exorbitant rents, and because better-off blacks could not cross the color line, Negroes of all conditions contested for the same housing supply. Thus, as the status-conscious Wright put it, "the good and bad" lived in "close proximity," not only in the same district or in the same block but "indeed in the same house, often in the same room." Some aspiring black families occupied a single building or a small section at the fringe of the ghetto, where they tried to make a middle-class island for themselves. Others ventured alone or with a few like-minded families to put up housing in isolated, unoccupied prairie land. (That was how the Englewood enclave originated: The blacks got there ahead of the developers, who, instead of dislodging them, built white Englewood around them.) But most bourgeois Negroes lived amid their poorer brethren. Established communities and new developments, open to everyone else of their class, were closed to them.[7]

The discontent of the Negro middle class and the Negrophobia of the whites gave rise to the practice of blockbusting. White agents began placing black families in previously all-white neighborhoods. The Negroes invariably paid more for the housing than the former residents had paid, enabling the realtor to boost his commission by 5 to 50 percent, or even more. For a time the new tenant would be able to say, "We don't live in a colored neighborhood," or "We live in a white neighborhood," or "We are the only colored people living in our block." But the appearance of a solitary black family would send tremors through the neighborhood. Then the blockbuster would double-cross his Negro customer. The trick was to scare all of the whites into selling out. If it worked, the "mixed" middle-class block would become an annex of the Black Belt. Poorer families would flock in, double up or take in boarders to "make" the rent, and the original black resident would be back where he started.[8]

The blockbusters operated largely through black subagents. Some were carefully attired, decorous Negroes who dealt with middle-class customers in storefront offices. Other employees hustled real estate on the sidewalks. These "colored runners and curbstone brokers" had two functions: They signed up tenants for low-grade ghetto properties, and they recruited the most rustic-looking people they could find for the purpose of parading them through, and thus panicking, white neighborhoods. The following incident illustrates one method realtors contrived to stampede the whites from one street.[9]

One day in the summer of 1900, "a colored man" appeared on a "select and exclusive" block of Vernon Avenue. He went from door to door announcing that he was authorized to sell the property at No. 3342, which had been vacant for a year. The agent offered the residents of the block one last chance to buy the building before Negroes moved in. Predictably, the white people were appalled. Next he appeared leading a procession of prospective "customers" who ostentatiously stopped and gaped at every house on the street. Soon he had workmen remodeling the building at 3342. They cut each apartment in two and tacked on a stairway in back to facilitate access to the new rear flats. With the repairs completed, the agent moved in three "colored families" who spent their evenings camped in chairs on the porch, taking "the breezes that blow through the streets so carefully nurtured on Vernon Avenue." Every morning a black "sandwich man" shuffled out of the basement apartment. The clanking boards he wore to work proclaimed, fore and aft, WEAR NEVER-RIP PANTS.[10]

The conversion of the building, the placing of the black tenants, and their minstrel-show behavior drove the white residents into a state of "nervous prostration" for a while, but the scheme failed to drive them off Vernon Avenue. They rallied round and agreed to stay where they were. For another seven years, they protected their block from further encroachments.[11]

This was one instance where the blockbusters failed. But as the black population grew, the profits in blockbusting grew with it. And Negro families who paid dearly to escape the Black Belt soon found themselves engulfed in the expanding ghetto. Some black men who started out working for white agencies went into the real estate business for themselves. The firms of Neighbors and Johnson, Jesse Binga, Oscar De Priest, and others did not resort to all of the crude tactics of the white operators. But they did handle slum properties, where they charged all the traffic would bear, and they leased large buildings in transitional areas and rented the flats to Negroes. They charged their "own people $10 to $15 more than the white renters had been paying." Their excuse was that the money was there to be made in Negro housing, and black businessmen should get some of the profit. As realtor William D. Neighbors said in self-defense, "If the Colored real estate dealers did not charge the rent required by the owner, there would be found plenty of white agents who would." And that was true. Before 1910 "colored real estate men" transacted less than 5 percent of Negro real estate dealings. Seven years later white agencies still controlled 75 percent of the market.[12]

As a rule, blockbusters were successful only in neighborhoods immediately adjacent to the Black Belt. White resistance in districts at a distance from the ghetto was practically insurmountable. But white people who lived hard by the Negro area could not always stop the transformation of their neighborhoods from white to black, even when they overcame their initial panic. Business and light industry were pushing south from downtown, driving blacks out of the area above 22nd Street. While the old Black Belt was losing territory after 1900, the black population was growing. The blacks had to go somewhere.

West of the Rock Island tracks the houses were almost as decrepit as those in the Black Belt. Not only was the housing stock uninviting, but the immigrants who occupied it held on to it tenaciously. Often the poor workingmen had poured everything they had into their modest homes. They frequently bought on the "contract" system, putting a small amount down and paying the balance 'like rent." They sometimes spent their whole lives making the payments. Until all of the principal and interest were paid off, the "owner" acquired no title and built up no equity. It was all or nothing; if a buyer missed a single payment, the seller could make him forfeit the house. A contract buyer stood to lose everything. Fending off foreclosure was a hard struggle for these people. They viewed the prospect of Negro neighbors as a catastrophe equal to loss of their homes. They drew a line at the railroad tracks and used force to keep blacks from crossing it. Negroes who tried moving across the tracks toward Wentworth Avenue met such violent opposition that most people in the Black Belt gave up hope of expanding to the west.[13]

Expansion to the east and south was easier. The land in the slot between the Rock Island tracks and State Street was filled with cheap houses, many of which never were intended to be permanent. The owners of the land were mostly speculators who had expected factories and warehouses to bid for the space near the tracks. They built rental housing on their property to produce enough income to cover taxes while they marked time. But the industrial development never happened. Eventually, owners let the buildings fall to ruin. A new kind of speculator then appeared. One white realty firm alone—Watson and Bartlett's—bought up thousands of parcels. "They paid about twenty-two hundred dollars on the average for these dwellings," a competing realtor recalled, "and then they would sell them to the negroes for about four thousand dollars, a hundred dollars down and about forty dollars a month. The hundred dollars secured them against nonpayment, and forty dollars a month netted them a good profit." So blacks pushed slowly southward down the corridor by the tracks. By 1910 the Black Belt had stretched along Federal Street as far down as Garfield Boulevard.[14]

East of State Street and the "alley el" were large districts of town houses and apartment buildings occupied by middle-class whites. These people did not want to give up any territory to blacks, but they seemed to accept the gradual expansion of the Black Belt as an unfortunate but unpreventable process. As their buildings aged, they moved, reluctantly giving up first Wabash Avenue, then parts of Michigan Boulevard and the intersecting east-west streets down to 39th Street. Just south of 39th the tall steel stilts of the Kenwood El stood like so many sentinels along the new boundary. The retreating whites did not concede blacks the right to live wherever they could afford to; they simply withdrew from boundaries that were no longer tenable and drew new ones that they were determined to hold until the time came again to move back and redraw the lines.[15]

Expansion was something that the whites could not always stop. What they had to prevent was dispersion. By and large their efforts succeeded. Between 1900 and 1910, blacks secured a toehold in only one established neighborhood removed from the Black Belt: West Woodlawn, across Cottage Grove from Woodlawn proper. The whites of West Woodlawn did not yield to the "invasion" of their neighborhood without a struggle.

In 1907 four black families moved into West Woodlawn, which was then more than a mile from the Black Belt. Indignant whites gathered at a mass meeting to demand race loyalty from area realtors and to pledge to one another that they would not run from the neighborhood. The organization that emerged from the gathering soon launched an ambitious program to "raise land values and force the Negroes out." Committees set busily to work. One was responsible for prodding city officials and local businessmen into making major improvements, including a new el station at 63rd and St. Lawrence. Another committee called on grocers and storekeepers, soliciting their promises to trade only with whites. Despite the whirling activity of the property owners, however, the improvements did not materialize, and more black families came in.[16]

Now the challenge to the property owners was to influence opinion not only in their *own* area but everywhere else that whites lived as well. The best they could hope to do was to keep turnover down to ordinary levels and then, as vacancies occurred, find other whites to fill them. It was "the whites who weren't there yet" who had to be convinced that the area was not a "nigger neighborhood." Residents went to great lengths to preserve West Woodlawn's name as a "white man's neighborhood." Schoolboys threw stones at the homes of Negroes, and adults sent notes to the newcomers warning them to move out or be burned out. It was all to no avail. Blacks kept coming in, and soon a small panic was on. Within three years over three hundred blacks were living in West Woodlawn, mostly in a two-block strip on Rhodes Avenue. By 1920 they numbered thirteen hundred. The whites, who had failed to keep them out, nevertheless succeeded in keeping them confined to a "rather definitely segregated" section. Still, the "little neighborhood" of blacks continued to press outward, threatening to eclipse the whole area.[17]

Elsewhere, whites managed to repulse black incursions. A white man bought a home in Englewood in 1913; when he tried to move in and his neighbors saw that his wife was black they quickly pooled their money and forced the couple to resell the house. It was dangerous to defy the demands of white property owners. In 1910 a black woman secretly bought a vacant lot several blocks beyond the boundaries of the Lake Street enclave and built a cottage on it. Only after she moved in did the neighborhood discover that "a colored family had acquired property there." Immediately, her neighbors went into action. When a steady campaign of "insults and threats" failed to budge her, a masked band broke into the house under cover of dark, "told the family to be quiet or they would be murdered" and then, with the terrified family looking on, "they tore down the newly built house, destroying everything in it." This was "an extreme instance," as the Juvenile Protective Association pointed out in 1913, but "in the past three years" there had been "many similar to it."[18]

No Chicagoans were more conscientious about keeping their communities closed to blacks than the white elite who occupied the lush lakefront. They tried to be more fastidious about their methods than were the residents of less fashionable communities but, above all, they were efficient. Along the exclusive North Shore, in suburban Wilmette, a committee requested any families unable to domicile their maids, servants, gardeners, and handymen on their own premises to dismiss "all negroes" in their employ. The committee recommended the firing of black janitors who lived in the basements of apartment buildings as well. The presence of unsupervised blacks, the committee felt, had "depressed real estate values" in the village. There was no machinery to enforce the edict; still, it accomplished its purpose. Few blacks who did not have quarters in their white employers' homes remained in Wilmette. Other domestics had to commute to their jobs from the small ghetto in the adjoining suburb, Evanston, or all the way from Chicago. In 1970, sixty years after the "anti-Negro committee" made its decree, there were only 81 blacks among the 32,134 villagers of Wilmette: 59 were females, primarily domestic servants.[19]

Far south of Wilmette, in the lakeshore community of Hyde Park, status-conscious whites took steps to control the growing black population in their midst. For the most part, the Negroes were domestics employed in neighborhood homes, apartments, and hotels. They lived in several small rooming-house districts that together served as a sort of off-premises servants' quarters for all Hyde Park and neighboring Kenwood. The community barred the blacks from its churches, restaurants, and entertainment centers. Gradually, separate social resorts and specialty shops sprang up to cater to the blacks. By 1906 Hyde Parkers had come to feel that their servants' leisure places were casting a blight over the whole community. Rumors circulated that the hotels were going to replace their black help with whites. In 1908 prominent residents organized the Hyde Park Improvement Protective Club to clarify the property owners' objectives and to implement them.[20]

The club had no desire to rob black people of their "vocation" of waiting on whites. Black people who stayed inside the black districts and behaved themselves did not need to worry about losing their jobs.

But whites were going to crack down on disorderly saloons and gambling houses. The club wanted to clean up the black districts. Even more, it wanted to make sure that no blacks resided outside those districts. The sporting life of the servant class disturbed the whites far less than the effort of middle-class Negroes to break out of the rooming-house areas. "The districts which are now white," the club's director announced in 1909, "must remain white."[21]

The club's program focused on forcing middle-class blacks out of white streets and keeping them out. A committee pressured black owners in white blocks to sell their property. It also offered black renters bonuses for moving before their leases ran out. The club threatened to blacklist any realtor who placed a black family on a white street or any landlord who kept a black resident janitor in a white building. If merchants, especially grocers, butchers, and druggists, did business with Negroes who lived outside the prescribed boundaries, the club urged whites to boycott them.[22]

The Hyde Park campaign, backed by "some of the wealthiest dwellers of the South Side," succeeded spectacularly. Blacks withdrew to the small sections allotted to them, leaving the bulk of the community lily-white, and the black districts all lost population. The largest rooming-house strip, on Lake Park Avenue in the shadow of the I.C. tracks, had 438 black residents in 1910 but only 238 ten years later. Blacks believed that the Negro population in all of the strips combined was in excess of 2,500 before 1908. By 1920 the number had dwindled to 800, and it continued to decline after that. Elegant Hyde Park, home of many of the city's most influential people and locale of the renowned University of Chicago, set a kind of standard in race relations as it did in fashionability.[23]

At the height of the Hyde Park agitation, one middle-class black woman complained bitterly about the example that the community's "public spirited citizens" were giving Chicago. Fannie Barrier Williams had lived in the area for fifteen years. She was sure her presence had not inflicted anything "very dreadful" on her neighbors, and she resented being harried from her home. She could understand why refined people would fight to rid their neighborhoods of gambling dens and unlicensed saloons ("blind pigs"). But the Hyde Parkers were searching out "Negroes of the better class" and "pushing these people into the dark corners, alleys, and back streets." In this respect, the South Side seemed more cruel to her than the South, where race prejudice was supposed to be "so dominant." At least in the South, Mrs. Williams charged, "the best people do not band themselves together to keep negroes in the alleys and in unsanitary and unhealthy streets."[24]

If the genteel residents of Wilmette and Hyde Park had nothing else in common with the working-class whites who lived west of the Rock Island tracks, they had this: They would not tolerate black neighbors. When white people excluded Negroes from their neighborhoods, they were not simply maintaining class lines. They were drawing the color line. No white neighborhood, rich or poor, was open to blacks. "A decent, well-behaved, industrious, intelligent black man," even if he was wealthy, as a few Hyde Park Negroes were, could not cross the line. If he tried, whites would resist. Collisions kept occurring between aspirant blacks and adamant whites because black people, like other people, demanded "good homes on desirable streets" for their families, and there were never enough decent accommodations in the districts consigned to the blacks. By 1912, when a housing investigator finally made a close study of conditions in the Black Belt, it was easily the most "conspicuously dilapidated" section in the city.[25]

In 1912 Miss Breckenridge's student, Alzada P. Comstock, made a house-by-house survey of two black districts, one in the Black Belt, the other on the West Side near Lake Street. The buildings that she and a team of aides inspected were low, one- or two-story frame houses thrown together long before the tenement house code of 1902. What struck Comstock at once was the overwhelming dilapidation of both sections. Everywhere she looked on the narrow "shoestring" lots she saw crumbling walls, broken railings, boardwalks that sagged, and porches and stairways that seemed to be "almost falling apart." She found "Window panes . . . out, doors hanging on single hinges or entirely fallen off, and roofs rotting and leaking." Inside, the houses were gloomy, dark, and damp.

More than a third of the toilets were in hallways, basements, or yards. The lots were not so crowded as those in some of the white ethnic districts—the buildings were smaller and there were fewer rear tenements—but the additional yard space was "almost always" heaped with trash.[26]

The buildings in which most black families lived had only one or two flats, and unlike the cramped quarters in the larger tenements where so many immigrants lived, these flats usually contained four to six rooms. But larger apartments were a mixed blessing for poor people. To pay the rent black families, more than any other ethnic group in the city, had to resort to taking in lodgers. On the South Side, where one-third of the black people were lodging in someone else's apartment, the lodgers outnumbered children by more than two to one. Comstock came across the extreme case of a South Side housewife in a large apartment with its own toilet and an even rarer amenity, a private bath: The woman rented out all of her rooms, put her ironing board across the bathtub at night, and slept on it.[27]

Compared to the housing in "the foreign districts" that Comstock's fellow students had canvassed, what the black people inhabited was worse, "inside and out." The surveyors reported that the percentage of dwellings in good repair was 71 percent in a "Polish" area, 57 percent among "Bohemians," 54 percent in the stockyards district, and an appalling 28 percent in South Chicago and in the Jewish Ghetto. In the South Side "colored district," the percentage was lowest of all: only 26 percent. On the West Side, 35 percent of the buildings were in good repair, but another 31 percent were "absolutely dilapidated." The reason the West Side houses were not quite so "broken-down" as those in the Black Belt, Comstock believed, was that the population of the three West Side blocks was still two-thirds white. On the South Side the transition from black to white was complete: The four blocks were "almost solid Negro." The whites who were left on the West Side blocks could still secure some "advantages or improvements," whereas "colored tenants . . . found it impossible to persuade their landlords to make the necessary repairs." As buildings in the West Side blocks were "given over to colored tenants," landlords commonly raised rents and discontinued upkeep; in some instances, they actually doubled the rents.[28]

High rent was a feature of Negro housing almost as conspicuous as dilapidation. The median rental for a four-room apartment in the Black Belt was $2 to $4 higher than it was for an apartment the same size in any of the surveyed immigrant neighborhoods. Yet the houses in which "the colored people" had to live were in the worst condition. Half of the families in the "Polish" district, where nearly three houses out of four were in good repair, paid less than $8.50 a month for four-room apartments. Blacks on the South Side, where three houses out of four were in disrepair, paid a median rental of $12 to $12.50 a month for their miserable four-room flats. It was obvious, as Comstock noted, that "the immigrant, for a smaller amount of money, may live in a better house than the Negro." If Chicago gave the hard-pressed immigrant no other solace, it at least offered him that.[29]

Black families that tried to make decent homes in the midst of their depressing physical surroundings faced a difficult enough task. What made the difficulty close to insurmountable was the wide-open vice district that city authorities allowed to flourish in the Black Belt. No white people, not even the sort who patronized whores and gaming tables, cared to live next door to bordellos and casinos, any more than they wanted to live near Negroes. Because it was not possible, or at least not politic, to suppress vice, the police segregated it. Black people were helpless to prevent the authorities from locating the red-light district where they lived, just as they were unable to stop whites from segregating them. When white Hyde Parkers closed down some of the more lurid dives in the black enclave along Lake Park, the operators simply relocated in the Black Belt, whose residents lacked the power to keep them out. Blacks as well as whites operated Black Belt dives, and the clientele was mixed, but most of the profits went to whites, who also provided the bulk of the trade.[30]

Alzada Comstock's survey showed that the housing problem of the blacks differed from that of the immigrants in several ways. The accommodations available to the blacks were the worst in the city. Black people had to pay more to live in rotting shacks than other groups paid for housing that was, if not quite good, at least better. And "colored people of all positions in life," not just the poor, found it practically impossible to escape the "relatively small and well-defined areas" to which Chicago relegated all black people, along with gamblers, prostitutes, and pimps. "The explanation for this condition of affairs among the colored people," Comstock concluded, was "comparatively simple." Negroes did not live in solid black districts because they preferred to stay among their own people. The prejudice of the whites, not the preference of the blacks, was what mattered. White people could not stand having "colored people living on white residence streets, colored children attending schools with white children, or entering into other semi-social relations with them." Sophonisba Breckenridge, commenting on Comstock's study, used blunter language. There was a "color line," she said. Blacks were "segregated." And "the segregation of the Negro quarter" made it "a black 'ghetto.' "[31]

In 1910 four out of ten immigrants in the city had been in America less than ten years; half were not citizens; one in four could not speak English. An unknown but presumably large percentage were poor. Still, immigrants of all ethnicities, aliens as well as naturalized citizens, Catholics and Jews alike, had access to neighborhoods where black native Americans could not go. Because of the color line, blacks were the most ill-housed group of Chicagoans several years before the Great Migration. Usually, the territories that the Black Belt absorbed were badly run-down before the first Negroes moved in. Yet banks, savings and loan associations, and insurance companies blamed housing deterioration in the black areas on the black people. To buy a home a Negro had to put down a larger down payment, pay higher interest on the balance, and pay higher insurance premiums than anyone else. Families who would have been able to afford a conventional purchase arrangement if they were white often had to buy on contract or not at all. And the burdensome obligations that the Negro home buyers assumed made it impossible for them to keep up repairs. White owners who rented flats to blacks were lax about upkeep. Municipal authorities neglected all poor areas and all districts with Negro residents, poor or otherwise. So deterioration in Negro-occupied property continued, whether the owners were absentee slumlords or residents struggling to meet payment deadlines. The Black Belt was a ghetto-slum, and there was no way out of it.[32]

Between 1915 and 1920, Chicago's black population more than doubled. The international crisis simultaneously increased the need for industrial workers and reduced the number of immigrants coming to America to work. The resultant vacuum in manpower pulled several hundred thousand rural Negroes northward. White Chicagoans were not happy to have thousands of "DARKIES FROM DIXIE"—as a *Tribune* headline put it—"SWARM" to their city. "Black man, Stay South!" the *Tribune* implored, but Negroes headed for the city anyway, and they came to stay. A *Tribune* offer to help pay the way for blacks who would go back South got no takers.[33]

While black Chicagoans had misgivings of their own about the migration, the reaction of the whites infuriated them. "I have noticed train load upon train load of Italian, Hungarian, Irish, Polish, Bohemian, German and in fact, almost every nationality upon the globe migrating to Chicago," one longtime black resident complained in 1917. These people, he said, were no more familiar with big-city life than were the Southern migrants, and they came "from a foreign country, unaccustomed to our way of living or to our language." Still, the press raised no outcry against the immigrants. On the contrary, at the same time that the newspapers attacked Negroes, they implored whites of all national origins to unite as Americans in support of the war effort. The *Tribune*, the paper most outspoken in its demands for racial segregation, ran an editorial called "Damn the Hyphen," denouncing *ethnic* prejudice.[34]

One of the first American words the foreigners learned to say, blacks believed, was "nigger." And the immigrants quickly picked up new words to strengthen their vocabulary: coon, spook, jigg, smoke, dinge, spade, eight-ball, shine. The European newcomers readily acquired American racial attitudes. As the Negro influx accelerated, Chicagoans pondered ways to keep the races separated. In 1918 a member of the Chicago Board of Education raised the question of segregating the schools. This man, Max Loeb, belonged to the Real Estate Board, which excluded Negroes. He lived in Hyde Park, which also barred them, and as the *Defender* pointed out, he was a Jew of foreign descent. "Would a proposition of this kind be entertained or considered for one moment," the *Defender* asked, "if it had for its object the segregation of Polish, Jewish, Italian or even the children of those with whom we are now at war?"[35]

Despite the pressures for segregation, these were flush years for blacks. Economic opportunities remained restricted. The telephone company, department stores, most business offices, construction firms, and the mass transit and taxicab companies still hired only whites except in the most menial capacities. Yet more blacks worked in the steel mills and packing plants than ever. A number of Negroes secured employment in factories such as the Pullman Works, where no black person had ever held a job before. Never had black workers been so well paid. Never had so many Negro families been able to afford adequate shelter. At the same time, the Black Belt and its satellites had never been so overcrowded, with twice as many people in need of accommodations as the available space could hold.[36]

As the South Side ghetto filled to overflowing, whites resisted the black demand for living space more ruthlessly than ever. Gangs of young men patrolled the border of the "foreign" district to the west and terrorized black trespassers. Black people learned, sometimes the hard way, that "they didn't allow niggers in that neighborhood." The Black Belt expanded slowly along its eastern and southern edges, absorbing the aged but not yet decrepit buildings west of Hyde Park and Kenwood. From 1917 on, as wartime industrial needs cut down residential construction, white people found it increasingly difficult to abandon whole streets to the advancing blacks, for there were fewer and fewer places to run to. The blacks had no choice but to keep pressing for additional territory. The property owners in genteel Hyde Park–Kenwood mobilized to keep their neighborhoods pure-white. Often the most vociferous leaders of the local improvement associations were Catholics and Jews of foreign stock who joined with their native neighbors to hold the line. In 1918 they stretched an enormous banner across Grand Boulevard (now Dr. Martin Luther King, Jr., Drive) at 43rd Street. Emblazoned across the canvas was their battle cry, borrowed from the trench warfare in Europe: THEY SHALL NOT PASS![37]

CHAPTER 7 ❧

Holding the Line: Violence

We are going to BLOW these FLATS TO HELL and if you don't want to go with them you had better move at once.
—Message delivered to Negroes who moved into the 4500 block of Vincennes Avenue in 1918, cited in the *Defender*, 18 September 1918.

Every owner has the right to defend his property to the utmost of his ability with every means at his disposal. . . . Protect your property! Property conservatively valued at $50,000,000 owned by some 10,000 individuals is menaced by a possible Negro invasion of Hyde Park. The thing is simply impossible and must not occur.
—*Property Owner's Journal*, 13 December 1919, cited in Chicago Commission on Race Relations, *The Negro in Chicago* (Chicago, 1922), p. 121.

IN THE SPRING OF 1917 THE CHICAGO REAL ESTATE BOARD, ALARMED BY "the invasion of white residence districts by the negros," appointed a committee to devise a segregation plan. Amid reports that the committee was drafting a racial zoning ordinance to present to the city council, committee members sounded out "influential colored citizens," hoping that the blacks would volunteer to segregate themselves. One black realtor suggested that Negroes living in the same block with whites would be glad to turn over their quarters if a large enough section of the city could be "given exclusively to colored people." Another black businessman, noting that half of the white realtors at the meeting were Catholics and Jews, suggested that blacks might submit to segregation if the realtors segregated "the other nationalities" as well, "especially the Jew." When the white realtors told newsmen that the black leaders had offered to cooperate in a program of segregation, the blacks denounced the committee for misrepresenting their views. The one Negro who had spoken favorably of segregation retracted his statement after the black newspaper the *Defender* recommended that he be "run out of town."[1]

In its report to the Real Estate Board, the committee acknowledged that "the old districts" were packed beyond capacity and that "more territory must be provided." However, the realtors claimed that property values plunged 30 to 60 percent "the moment the first colored family moves into a block." The committee recommended a "block method" to stop "promiscuous" destruction of property values and confine the damage as much as possible. Realtors would agree not to sell or lease to Negroes in "scattered blocks"; once every block in the Black Belt was "filled solidly," realtors could place blacks in "contiguous blocks." Any agent who introduced a black family into a section "more than 75 percent white" would not only forfeit his good standing with his colleagues, but also would have his membership revoked. The board approved the proposal.[2]

In practice the Real Estate Board's scheme to control the expansion of the Black Belt became an effort to stop it from expanding at all. Because the board denied membership to black realtors, it had no way of disciplining them. To get their cooperation, the board offered to make loans available for new building and remodeling in the Black Belt. The black realtors rejected the offer, which was an empty gesture, anyway, coming as it did when funds for residential construction were drying up. White dealers who did not care about reputation simply disregarded the board's code. Speculators now made a specialty of opening up all-white blocks. Because reputable dealers refused to place Negroes on streets that were all-white or nearly so, the blockbusters would enjoy a free field at the beginning. But as the black percentage in a block mounted, more and more realtors could compete without compunction for the profits of the lucrative "turnover" period. Once a block became 25 percent Negro, even the most scrupulous agent could join the scramble for the spoils. At least one major firm, R. M. O'Brien's, specialized in following in the immediate wake of the blockbusters and cashing in on the panic of the whites.[3]

The board's provision for allowing the Black Belt to annex adjacent areas depended on a continued supply of new housing to which whites who were vacating the border areas could flee. The construction slump locked whites in where they were, at least temporarily. For the board's segregation plan to function smoothly, some new territory had to be provided, but there was no way the board could provide it. By October 1917 the board acknowledged that conditions were beyond its control. It petitioned the city council to pass an ordinance prohibiting the further migration of "colored families" to Chicago until "such reasonable restriction of leasing or selling be enforced as to prevent lawlessness, destruction of values and property and loss of life." Such a law, as even the *Tribune* acknowledged, would have been unconstitutional. A month later, after the U.S. Supreme Court overturned a Louisville ordinance dividing that city into racial zones, the board announced a campaign to organize "owners societies in every white block for the purpose of mutual defense."[4]

Beginning in the summer of 1917, whites in the threatened districts east of the Black Belt banded together in organizations that became the middle-class equivalent of the ethnic gangs protecting the workingmen's bungalow belt. Like the gangs, the property owners' associations were intent on "keeping 'undesirables' out," and they classed all blacks as undesirables. The Hyde Park–Kenwood Property Owners' Association, which formed in 1918 to "make Hyde Park white," took the lead in establishing a "united front" along Grand Boulevard from 29th to 39th streets and then along Michigan Boulevard from 39th south to 63rd Street. The object of the alliance, which soon claimed over a thousand paying members, was to reestablish the entire area behind the front lines as "an exclusively white neighborhood" and then "prevent further incursion by undesirables." "You cannot mix oil and water," one member said at an association mass meeting. "You cannot assimilate races of a different color as neighbors along social lines. Remember this: That order is heaven's first law."[5]

Middle-class blacks did not object to the formation of community organizations to set standards and exclude "undesirables." What stung them was the white assumption that all Negroes were "undesirables." They went to great lengths to prove that they were capable of living in "respectable" communities without depreciating property. When they took over the once elegant but greatly faded residential streets east of the "alley el," they organized associations of their own to make sure that everyone in the neighborhood kept his "front porch and back yard respectable." And as migrants fresh from the cottonfields down South crowded into their neighborhoods, they imposed their standards on the newcomers.[6]

Established blacks kept insisting that Southerners had as much right to come to Chicago as "the Poles, Italians, Greeks, Lithuanians and Hebrews," and the *Defender* actually encouraged migration. But they expected the newcomers to abandon their "obnoxious" country habits and adopt "the customs of their new homes." The new arrivals wore aprons and caps on streetcars and said "Man, give us a transfer" instead of "Transfer, please." Women walked the boulevards in nearly transparent calico dresses without "the least semblance of an underskirt." "Half-clad, unkempt" men and women lounged on doorsteps, sipping "suds" and hollering to "equally boisterous" people who passed by, often in their bare feet. Persons of both sexes arranged "their toilets" in front of open windows. And they let hucksters stick signs in their windows advertising "some particular system of hair culture." This kind of behavior, middle-class blacks feared, was "a detriment to the Race." The *Defender* urged its subscribers to "pull together" and "break up these evils."[7]

Middle-class Negroes joined with white sympathizers in forming a new organization, the Urban League. Like the National Urban League, the Chicago branch concentrated on getting the migrants to adjust to the regimen of big-city life. In cooperation with the league, the *Defender* sponsored neighborhood clean-up campaigns and barraged the newcomers with lists of "Dos and Don'ts." A *Defender* editorial urged neighborhood clubs to make the lot of recalcitrant migrants "a hard one" until they forsook "habits of life little better than [those of] hottentots." The Negro "uplift organizations" may have had some impact on the newcomers, but they did not impress many whites.[8]

To most residents of white neighborhoods, all blacks still looked like "low grade 'plantation-niggers.' " White men did not like to think of their wives and daughters riding on streetcars "breast to breast with Negroes," as one man put it, whether the blacks said "Transfer, please" to the conductor or not. A prominent mechanical engineer, Charles L. Samson, declined to buy a house his wife had picked out in an all-white neighborhood because State Street, three blocks away, was a "nigger line." He did not want to be dependent on streetcars "jammed with niggers."[9]

White people did not want "niggers living next door," even if the blacks seemed to be their social equals. The "effrontery and impudence" that impelled a Negro to choose a white neighbor, if not discouraged, would inflame his desire for "a white as a marriage mate," the Hyde Park–Kenwood Association maintained. The demand of blacks for access to housing in Hyde Park was "a corollary to their ambition on sex equality." A white woman who lived just south of the West Woodlawn enclave closed the windows on the north side of her house when "a colored family" moved next door and kept them shut for more than three years. The black family seemed "pretty nice," the woman thought, but she stopped sitting on her front porch after they moved in. "What white person," she said, "will sit on a porch next door to a porch with black ones on it?" Even a white man who claimed to have "nothing against the black man as a black man" said he would "not live with niggers." His explanation was straightforward: "Niggers are different from whites and always will be, and that is why white people don't want them around." [10]

Blacks who viewed themselves as "the better element" resented being lumped together with "riff-raff" in the minds of whites and, as a consequence, in living accommodations. Some Black Belt landlords began discriminating between so-called "shadies" and "high class tenants," but whites in general refused to make distinctions. The white organizations did not categorize all members of other ethnic groups as undesirables. As the *Defender* complained, they "single out our group alone." Whites, ignoring the excessive rents, the minimal upkeep, and the overcrowding in the Black Belt, put the blame for depreciation on the black population as a whole. "What of other neighborhoods of Chicago?" asked the *Defender*'s editor. Who was responsible for depreciating property in Little Italy, in the Polish area on the Northwest Side, in the Jewish "ghetto," and in Back a' the Yards? No blacks lived in those areas; "thousands of foreigners" inhabited "tumbledown, disease-breeding shacks," but no one was holding all immigrants responsible for making slums. "The alien," the *Defender* pointed out, "can now live where he pleases." [11]

In fact, the *Defender* claimed, Jewish refugees from the old "ghetto" were making a "New Palestine" out of Hyde Park. Jews and Catholics were prominent in the leadership of the Hyde Park–Kenwood Association. The president was a Catholic born in Canada, the treasurer was an Irish Catholic, the secretary was a Jew, and the executive committee was heavily Jewish and Catholic. Ulysses S. ("U.S.") Schwartz, alderman of the ward that included Kenwood, was Jewish; he avidly supported the association.[12]

One night in 1919 the light-skinned Reverend Archibald Carey, a clergyman and political leader whose parents had been house slaves, infiltrated a meeting of the Hyde Park–Kenwood Association. Afterwards he described the gathering for the *Defender* in furious old-time "indignation" style. It was "a strange convocation" for a country "supposed to be a democracy," Reverend Carey said. Men "of various nationalities" conspired there "to draw the color line."

There were many Jews, who at the same time were raising millions to aid Russian pogrom victims "segregated in the Jewish quarter." Germans were there—Kaiser Wilhelm would have been proud of them, Carey claimed. "Yes! Irishmen were there," taking time off from their fund-raising campaign "to free Ireland." And "Italians too": "Perhaps," Carey speculated, "some of them had just laid aside their sawed-off guns with which they kill each other in the North Side murder zone." Also present were "five Poles," whose brothers in Poland had just celebrated their restored nationhood with a massacre "almost as fiendish as the mob murders down in Mississippi and Texas"; some "Czechoslovaks," who were taking the side of oppression now that they had a new state of their own in Europe; "a few Russians," undoubtedly advocates of "soviet rule"; "an honorable Japanese gentleman"; and "even a Turk," whose hands might have "dripped with the blood of murdered Armenians." The largest group appeared to be white Southerners. To a man, the speakers at the meeting talked of protecting their communities from "undesirables," "coons," and "darkies." It was unendurable, Carey declared, to hear these "alleged Americans" talking that way about black people, who were proven "SUPER-AMERICANS."[13]

The property owners' associations, organized down to the block level and covering an extensive territory, employed all of the tactics that the old Hyde Park Club had used so effectively before 1910: newspaper publicity, mass rallies, blacklisting of realtors, boycotting of merchants, and intimidation of black residents. When these methods failed to produce the desired results, they resorted to violence on a scale unknown before.

Now it became commonplace for mobs of fifty to two hundred chanting people armed with bricks, bats, and lengths of pipe to surround the home of a black "invader," deface the exteriors, and smash all of the windows. Occasionally, when a house under siege was not too far away from the Black Belt, blacks standing around on street corners would get the word that a brother was being attacked and would arm themselves and race to the scene to meet the white mob head-on. But whites introduced a new, more frightening terror device against which there was no defense: the homemade bomb. In the summer of 1917, a bomb blew away the front part of a black couple's house in Hyde Park. It was not clear until the next year that bombing had become a conventional weapon in the housing struggle. Between March 1918 and August 1919, twenty-five bombs exploded at the homes of blacks and at the homes or offices of blockbusting realtors.[14]

Several black families in "strategic" blocks suffered more than one attack when a single explosion was not enough to dislodge them. One victim of repeated bombings was a postal employee named Charles H. Davis, who moved into the 4500 block on Vincennes Avenue in the spring of 1918. Three years earlier he had tried to occupy a house on the same square block, on the Forrestville side. That time his neighbors had forced him out. In 1915, even before Davis had moved in, the white residents of the block, led by two Republican officeholders (one an assistant corporation counsel, the other a Sanitary District trustee) collected money to buy him out. Davis vowed that he would not submit to "blackmail," but in a few days, fearful that the two Republicans would pull strings at the post office and get him demoted or dismissed, he gave in. Davis went back to the Black Belt, put up with the deteriorating conditions there for three years, then decided to try again to buy a decent house and live in it. This time he was determined to stand his ground.[15]

As before, the property owners pressured Davis to sell and leave. When he held firm, someone bombed his home. He continued to reject offers for his house, and the bombers struck again. His nerves shattered, Davis left the city to try to regain his health. On May 25, 1918, while he was in Michigan convalescing, a third bomb intended for his home exploded a few doors away. The next day he died, and the *Defender* claimed it was the relentless bombardment of his home that killed him. Three years earlier, after expelling him from the neighborhood, Sanitary District trustee Wallace G. Clark had pronounced a kind of epitaph for Charles H. Davis—premature but still appropriate:

> I could tell the minute I saw him that Davis was an honorable man. The residents of the block never had any hard feelings against him personally, we assured him. We feared the presence of Negroes on the block would lower real estate values.[16]

Charles Davis was not the only bombing fatality. Two black people, one a six-year-old girl, died in the explosions that ripped apart their homes. Still, the bombers were not out to maim and kill blacks, and although their bombs did extensive property damage, their real aim was not to blow up buildings. Even if they had no respect for Negro life, they valued property. What they were trying to blast away was the resolve of the people who lived in those buildings to defy the color line.[17]

By the spring of 1919, bombs were going off at the rate of two per month, and the rate was rising. Servicemen were returning home, intensifying demand for housing that was already scarce. By summer, the number of families in need of housing exceeded the stock of available units by fifty thousand. Racial clashes, in recreation, transportation, and employment, as well as in housing, were becoming daily occurrences. West of the Rock Island tracks the ethnic gangs mauled blacks who tried to use public parks and swimming pools on the white side of "the gang line." Fights broke out on crowded streetcars. In the stockyards, mills, and factories, wherever blacks were employed, white and black workers were frequently at each other's throats. White workers saw the blacks as a threat not only to their jobs but to their neighborhoods as well: Blacks who worked in South Chicago, Pullman, and Back a' the Yards might demand to live within walking distance of their jobs. When policemen intervened in racial disputes, they often took the side of the whites. The police, who overwhelmingly resided in a broad crescent adjacent to and "threatened" by the Black Belt, may well have seen themselves as defenders of their neighborhoods. To blacks, the force looked like a thin blue line, lethally fortified, around the ghetto.[18]

In late June white gangs murdered two black men, and a small race riot on the West Side left one man dead and six wounded. By then there was a bombing every week, and any hope of a construction boom to ease the housing shortage vanished in mid-July when building contractors locked out their workmen. Chicagoans, black and white, braced themselves for a race riot on the Fourth of July. The holiday came and went without incident, but the bombs continued to explode weekly, and finally, at the end of the month, the anticipated riot came. It exceeded everyone's expectations, and the rioting, like the bombings that led up to it, demonstrated how dangerous it was for black people to try living in white neighborhoods.[19]

❧

The rioting broke out on Sunday, July 27, when a black youngster swam across an invisible line that whites had "drawn" in Lake Michigan to separate black and white swimming areas. A white youngster stoned the boy, drowning him. Within hours blacks and whites were clashing in many parts of the city. The violence did not subside for a week, until the combination of police, state militia, a downpour of rain, and mob exhaustion ended the bloodbath. In the meantime, Chicago policemen fatally gunned down seven rioters, all black men; rioters killed one policeman, also black; and thirty other people—fifteen black, fifteen white—died in street fighting. Chicagoans feared that the casualty list ran into the thousands. A biracial Commission on Race Relations, appointed by the governor of Illinois to study the riot and its causes, tallied the riot's victims much more conservatively than the public did and still arrived at awesome totals: "Thirty-eight persons killed, 537 injured, and about 1,000 rendered homeless and destitute."[20]

White mobs seized on the opportunities that the riot situation created to terrorize blacks whose homes were outside of "the colored districts." Residents of the Black Belt and its satellites had a torturous time getting to and from their jobs in white areas, but if they could make it home they were relatively safe. Within solidly black enclaves they were numerous enough to band together and resist the mobs. Moreover, they were concentrated enough for police to cordon them off. For the most part, the mobs were content to bypass Negro concentrations. The favorite targets of the mobs were individual households or small clusters in otherwise white neighborhoods. For blacks scattered outside the Negro enclaves, there was no protection.

Marauding bands wrecked and burned dozens of houses and forced black families to abandon many others. "Premeditated depredations," as the Riot Commission put it, "were the order of the night." Where roving gangs did not appear, they were expected: No black household in white territory could feel safe. Many families who had pioneered in opening new districts to Negro occupancy, fearful of what the night would bring, left their homes in daylight under police guard. Those who stayed in their houses felt, night after night, the full loneliness, the total peril, of their position.[21]

Mr. and Mrs. Ernest Clarke bought two properties in the 4400 block of Grand Boulevard in 1919, when few blacks had penetrated south of 37th Street. The buildings had stood vacant for a full year before the sale, and before that the occupants were prostitutes. The Clarkes rented out one dwelling—to family groups, not prostitutes, and the tenants were white—and occupied the other one themselves. Before moving in, they renovated both buildings, but their neighbors did not appreciate their efforts to upgrade their property. They were "colored," so they were "undesirables." Although they were snubbed, they were not bombed, but when the riots came they found themselves besieged.

An old man on the street outside started yelling that "the niggers" were arming and coming to get the whites. He attracted a sizable crowd, and soon the cry went up, "Hang the niggers! The niggers in the house are firing at every white man that passes!" With no one else to turn to, the Clarkes called the police, who eventually showed up, surveyed the scene, and after consulting with the attackers, battered down the door and put Mr. and Mrs. Clarke under arrest. The charge was sniping. As evidence the officers confiscated a vintage 1894 rifle that had not been fired, some bullets that did not fit the piece, and a ceremonial sword.[22]

The Clarkes' home was in the contested area east of the Black Belt, where the bombers had been active for two years. Assaulting parties prowled the streets of this territory, "searching for niggers," singing, yelling, and throwing bricks at buildings "where they thought niggers lived." On the other side of the Black Belt, where no black households had been bombed, mobs now moved to settle old scores.[23]

Events in Englewood gave black Chicagoans a powerful lesson in the advantages of staying inside the ghetto. White gangs made repeated forays into the Englewood enclave, but without success. Negroes shot it out with their attackers, driving them back. In one clash, the black defenders killed a white gang leader. When huge retaliatory mobs were reported to be massing on Ashland Avenue and along 63rd Street for an all-out attack on black Englewood, the residents, aided by prominent whites who lived nearby, were able to secure the protection of police and militiamen. The assault did not materialize, and families inside the district's boundaries came out of the riots unscathed. But Negroes whose homes were scattered outside were at the mercy of raiding parties.[24]

The pastor of a Baptist church in black Englewood lived half a mile west of the ghetto. He had built his house in 1899, when the area around it was "vacant prairie." As the neighborhood filled up, the minister's family remained the sole Negro inhabitants. On the night of July 30, a mob forced its way into their home and drove them out. Other "highly respectable and law-abiding colored people" who had bought a run-down house over a mile south of black Englewood and worked on it until it was "beautiful" had to flee while a mob "completely wrecked" the place. A gang led by three Irish youngsters (and a lad named Henry Rachman) broke into another home a mile south of the Englewood enclave, grabbed Owen Harris ("colored, has a white wife," the *Tribune* noted), beat him, turned a fire extinguisher filled with gasoline on his house, and then put a match to it.[25]

White people living on a short stretch of 60th Street in the narrow corridor between the Pennsylvania Railroad tracks and the Rock Island tracks tried to assure the lone Negro family on their block that nothing would happen to them, but the Archibald Motleys were apprehensive just the same. The block was three-quarters of a mile east of black Englewood and only a few blocks west of the Black Belt. The Motleys had lived there since 1907 without any trouble, a solitary Negro household in white territory "threatened" from two sides by blacks. The Motley house was right next to the Pennsylvania embankment, which cut the street off from the rest of Englewood. The Motleys were not afraid of their own neighbors.

They feared that some mob of whites would come howling through the Pennsylvania underpass, headed for the Black Belt borderline, but hunting for "niggers" along the way.

The Motleys barricaded their front door with furniture. The younger members of the family carried in rocks from the outside and piled them in the doorway, where Mr. Motley stood with a loaded rifle. Prepared for the worst, they sweated it out. When "the mob came—perhaps 50 or more," a white woman who lived across the street ran from her house, imploring the marauders to leave the Motleys alone. She claimed to be speaking for everyone on the block. The mob moved on, muttering that they would go elsewhere "to get some niggers."[26]

The Motleys were lucky, even luckier than they knew. For ten blocks directly north of them, in a little row of houses shadowed by the Pennsylvania Railroad embankment, lived nine Negro families who were not spared. Their homes were deep in the turf, on the very home street, of the gang called the Shielders, whose reputation rested on their prowess at keeping blacks on their own side of Wentworth. Much to the Shielders's embarrassment, these families had occupied their homes west of Wentworth for several years without being molested. Now the gang's foremost rivals, Ragen's Colts, announced that they were coming into Shielder territory to show the other lads how to "run all the niggers out."[27]

Blacks who heard that the Colts were coming called frantically for police protection. Ten policemen came by, took a look around, said there was no danger, and left. Two hours later, two to three hundred of Ragen's finest descended upon the 5000 block of Shields Avenue. They peppered the houses with rocks and bricks, fired handguns into them, ousted the inhabitants, smashed the household belongings, and finished up by setting the homes on fire. They sent the blacks away and told them that the penalty for returning would be death. The Colts warned a white man who had rented one of the ruined houses to Negroes not to let blacks in again. Otherwise, they assured him, they would burn his house down and kill him. It was nearly thirty years before anyone sold or rented a house on that block to Negroes again. (On October 3, 1947, a black couple moved into 5003 Shields, one of the houses damaged in the riot. Late on the night of October 11, someone set fire to their garage.)[28]

Not to be dishonored nor outdone, the Shielders did some evicting of their own. They lost no time. That very night, several hundred strong, they rampaged up and down Wentworth and Wells Street, one block to the west, between 47th Street and 48th Place, where "there were houses with colored people dotted in among the whites." "Whites pull up shades and turn on all lights," they yelled, "Niggers keep their houses dark." They shot into dark houses, smashed windows, and battered down doors. After inspecting all buildings to be sure that they had found every black household, they ransacked the Negro homes for valuables, demolished furniture or pitched it through windows, and burned the houses down. Police did not interfere with the mob. In fact, policemen responding to an alarm from "William O'Deneal, Negro," of 4742 Wells "took O'Deneal to the station and left the mob to sack and burn his house."[29]

To top the evening off, the crowd staged a raucous street dance on Wells. In the glow of a dozen burning Negro houses, with musical accompaniment provided by a player piano stolen from a black family, the mob sang, danced, drank, fired their pistols, and picked over the belongings strewn about the sidewalk. As the music subsided they carried off some of the goods, burned the rest, and for a finale smashed the piano and pitched hunks of it onto the fire. In that one night, a white resident said later, the gang "put the Negroes out of the Wells Street neighborhood." It was no exaggeration: The Riot Commission verified that "all Negro families" on that square block were "driven out."[30]

July 30 was a night to remember in the small nine-block section west of Wentworth between 47th and 51st streets. In addition to the blazes they set on Shields and Wells, the gangs put at least sixteen other houses to the torch. A militia captain who reached "the burned district" after 10:30 counted forty buildings on fire. It is impossible to tell how many black families the Colts and Shielders burned or frightened out that night, because there is no way to calculate how many blacks were living there at the onset of the riot. At any rate, when census enumerators canvassed the area in 1920, they found only six black families left.[31]

Even black families who lived *inside* the supposed boundary lines drawn around black districts were exposed to mobbing if their houses were along an enclave's edge, for the boundaries were irregular and not always absolutely distinct. In particular, it was folly for a black person to assume that he was secure so long as he stayed on the east, or so-called Negro, side of Wentworth. Whites west of the Black Belt regarded Wentworth as their last line of defense, not their first. The Rock Island embankment constituted a physical barricade that whites believed no Negro had the right to disregard. (Why? Because it was there. If God in His infinite wisdom had ever intended that blacks should live outside the Black Belt, then why did He put the Rock Island there, right alongside it?) Despite Providence, Negroes did break through the barricade above 39th Street after 1905, occupying first the east side of LaSalle Street, which ran between the tracks and Wentworth, then gradually overtaking the west side as well. That was as far as the blacks got. Whites held on to both sides of Wentworth, angry that blacks had pushed across the tracks, adamant that they would not get past the alley dividing LaSalle from the white street. All along Wentworth, whites were itching to get even with blacks who had moved to the white side of the tracks.

Six black families who lived on the "Negro" side of Wentworth between 43rd and 44th streets fared no better than those whose homes were on the white side. Warned by white neighbors that something was going to happen, they took what belongings they could carry and fled. An "aged darkey and his wife" who were regarded as "good Negroes" got white friends to help them move and give them safe conduct as far as the Rock Island underpass. Later, a mob burned down their home and the homes of "the five 'bad Negroes' in the neighborhood." Just south of 59th Street, on the "Negro side" of Wentworth, a subgroup of the Shielders zeroed in on a building occupied by two black couples. The gang, appropriately named the Sparklers, set fire to the place. After firemen squelched the blaze, the boys returned and set the building on fire again. Firemen put out the second fire as well, but the Sparklers struck a third time. After looting the Negro flats, they attempted one last torch job. This one was successful.[32]

To Chicago's blacks the moral of the story was brutally obvious. A Negro's life and property were not worth much unless he kept close within the confines of "his own" community. Throughout the rioting the main force of the police was deployed around the rim of the Black Belt, both to keep white mobs out and to contain vengeful blacks inside. Few policemen were available to assist endangered blacks who lived elsewhere, and as the Clarkes and others found out, those who were available were not necessarily reliable. Policemen who rushed to the defense of a Black Belt building occupied by *whites* gave Negroes a vivid demonstration of how formidable police protection *could* be and how cheap black life was.

The Angelus, an enormous apartment house at the intersection of 35th Street and Wabash, was "for white people" when the surrounding area was white, and it remained so even after Negroes occupied all of the adjoining property. The whites would probably have been all too glad to leave the building and let the blacks have it, but with the logjam in housing there were few places they could go. So most of them stayed on. Because there were enough whites hard-pressed for housing to fill the vacancies of those who did move, Negro applicants were turned away, although their need for shelter was desperate. As the housing crisis deepened, the Angelus became more and more of a sore point with blacks. So it was big news when a Negro banker announced, six weeks before the riot, that he had bought the Angelus with the aim of making it the grandest "Race institution" on the South Side, employing "Race people" in the lower floor offices and housing them in the flats above. When the riot came, the whites were still in the Angelus, waiting for their leases to lapse, fearful that the new management would throw them en masse onto the real estate market during a critical housing shortage. The neighborhood, for its part, was waiting for the whites to clear out and make way for the "Race people."[33]

On the second day of rioting, word spread through the area that whites were mobilizing west on 35th Street to come in and "clean up the 'Black Belt.'" Blacks massed on 35th Street from State to Wabash in response to this rumor. As they awaited the onslaught from the west, they heard that whites in the Angelus were preparing to gun them down from behind. By the time the story had made the rounds through the crowd, many people were convinced that shots had actually been fired. Before long a Negro was reported dead, shot through the head by a sniper concealed in the Angelus. Now the crowd moved for the building, whose tenants, terrified, summoned the police. In short order, a hundred policemen appeared and positioned themselves between the building and the mob, now grown to fifteen hundred.

To mollify the crowd, the police made a quick sweep through the Angelus. They found no sniper and reported that they had been unable to locate a single weapon in the whole building. The "search" did anything but placate the crowd, which was already angry with the police for guarding the white folks on Wabash when they were needed farther west to protect the Black Belt. Now the people felt that the cops were telling a lie so bald that nobody could believe it, throwing the lie at them like a taunt. Someone in the crowd lofted a brick toward the policemen, who responded with a volley leveled straight at the people. The blacks fell back, leaving behind four men shot dead or dying and "many" others wounded.[34]

The contrast with the police action in the cases of the Clarkes, the O'Deneals, and the families on Shields Avenue was total. The facts were appalling enough; the rumors were even more grisly, and people believed the rumors. Word spread through the Black Belt that hundreds of black families had been hounded from their homes. "The homes of blacks isolated in white neighborhoods were burned to the ground," the *Defender* reported, and that was true enough, but the paper reinforced the widespread impression that almost all such houses had been destroyed. And the *Defender*, honestly but inaccurately, went on to confirm its readers' worst fears: "The owners and occupants were beaten and thrown unconscious into the smoldering embers."[35]

Whites took pains to see that blacks did not miss the message. No sooner had quiet been restored than they started sending "colored people" who lived outside black districts "a new series of threatening letters." On August 4, Mrs. Hanna James, one of a half-dozen "colored residents" on either side of Wentworth in the 7200 block, found this note at her door:

> *Warning—*
> All colored people in this block will be given two days to move. If they are not gone at the end of that time we will burn and bomb out and hunt them down through the streets and alleys.

The next day Charles Fox, president of the Hyde Park–Kenwood Association, addressed a lengthy public letter to Mayor William H. Thompson, demanding official support for the property owners' segregation campaign. And Alderman Terence E. Moran of the

Thirty-first Ward, which contained black Englewood and bordered the Black Belt on the west, stood up in the city council to urge the establishment of separate "residential zones for white people and colored people." Both Fox and Moran were Catholics, and Fox was an immigrant as well. Nothing came of Moran's resolution, but the written threats, the breaking of windows, and arson continued, and soon the bombers went back to work.[36]

Within days of the rioting, Jesse Binga, the city's leading Negro realtor, a blockbuster whose own home was in the otherwise white 5900 block of South Park, received this message:

> HEADQUARTERS OF THE WHITE HANDS
> TERRITORY MICHIGAN AVE. TO LAKE FRONT
>
> You are the one who helped cause this riot by encouraging Negroes to move into good white neighborhoods and you know the results of your work. This trouble has only begun and we advise you to use your influence to get Negroes to move out of these neighborhoods to *Black Belt* where they belong and in conclusion we advise you to get off South Park Ave. yourself. Just take this as a warning. You know what comes next.

Binga knew quite well—his office had been bombed in March.[37]

In November a second bomb left his office "in ruins." The next month the bombers hit his house twice, with only minor damage the first time and none the second. After another bomb "tore up the porch" in January 1920, Binga demanded police protection. He was granted an all-night guard—one policeman from dusk to midnight, another from midnight to dawn. "On the night of February 28, the policeman on duty until twelve o'clock left a few minutes early," the Riot Commission discovered, "and the policeman relieving him was just a few minutes late." In the "unguarded interval," a man leaned out from a passing automobile and pitched a black powder bomb at the house. The bomb missed its mark, plunked into a puddle, and sputtered out. Police authorities, somewhat embarrassed, doubled the guard, but neither man on duty was anywhere in sight when the car reappeared in June.[38]

This time the car pulled up to the curb, stopped, and waited while a man darted up to the building and carefully placed a bomb. As the automobile sped away, a thundering boom jolted the neighborhood from its sleep. The explosion "demolished the front of the house and smashed windows throughout the block." Whites hastily clad in bathrobes and raincoats gathered near the two policemen standing guard before the rubble and debated whether this was the fourth or fifth time "that the jigg had been bombed." (It was the fifth, counting both duds but not counting the two explosions at his office.) Binga swore that he would not "run," and in November he was bombed again.[39]

The bombers had never been so active. In the two years before the riots, they had touched off more than two dozen explosions, but in the following year and a half they notched up thirty-four. They ushered in the new year, 1920, with eight bombings in the first eight weeks. Blockbusters remained prime targets. In one period of ten days, the bombers struck at the homes of Jesse Binga and two white blockbusters, one of whom had arranged the sale of the South Park properties to the Clarkes. But most of the bombs exploded at the homes of black people who had "invaded" white neighborhoods, people like the Clarkes.[40]

When Mr. and Mrs. Clarke returned to their home after the rioting was over and the charges against them had been dismissed, they found the neighborhood dead set on driving them out. Late in 1919 a bomb went off outside the building they rented out. Their insurance company paid the $500 damages but canceled their policy. In January 1920, one of the white newspapers printed a brief item about the bombing of a residence "said to have been a Negro 'sniping post' during the riot." This second bomb did $3,360 damage to the house the Clarkes lived in; the insurers withdrew their coverage without settling the claim. To collect, the Clarkes would have had to retain legal counsel and sue. Nor could the Clarkes get new coverage on their properties. They were a hopelessly bad risk, and the Hyde Park–Kenwood Property Owners' Association warned insurance companies "that it is dangerous to insure some people."[41]

In February a dynamite bomb tossed from a passing car crashed through the plate-glass hallway door of the Clarkes' home, blew away the staircase, and tore gaping holes in the walls. Warning notes and phone calls followed, and the Property Owners' Association sent word that they had someone ready to buy whenever the Clarkes were ready to sell. Two policemen detailed to guard the house were on duty on April 13 when someone threw another bomb from the white-occupied building next door. This time the police nabbed a suspect near the house, but when they identified him as the "nephew of a prominent businessman living in the neighborhood," they let him go. The morning after the last explosion, Mrs. Clarke received a note that said:

> Move out or sell, there is nothing else for you to do. We missed you last night but we will get you the next time. We are determined.[42]

Now the company that was financing the Clarkes' purchase of the properties put pressure on them to sell. The buildings were being ruined, and the couple could hardly continue to make repairs and keep up with their payments at the same time. The Clarkes were buying on contract, so if they fell in arrears on their payments even ten days they could lose everything through foreclosure. There was nothing to do but sell, the company insisted, reminding them that "the Hyde Park–Kenwood Association people" had already lined up a buyer. The Clarkes said that they were going to stay as long as they could meet their payments. Within a year they were gone, unable to hold out any longer, and white people were living at their address.[43]

The Hyde Park–Kenwood Association's drive to bomb or buy black residents out of the territory under its "jurisdiction" proved successful. If people like the Clarkes couldn't withstand the onslaught, the question went, who could? And the answer was no one. The association purchased a few homes from black owners "amicably," and it goaded landlords and mortgage holders into canceling leases and making foreclosures. By such methods the Hyde Parkers "renovated" more than one hundred buildings "polluted by Negro tenancy" in the year following the riots. The campaign of bombing and intimidation did not let up until the large-scale resumption of building in 1920–1921 made it possible for whites in the zone bordering the Black Belt to move elsewhere. By that time white opposition had put an end to "the promiscuous scattering of negroes."[44]

The white campaign of intimidation and violence tightened "the iron circle" around the bulging Black Belt, "making it practically impossible for Negroes to move out." The Riot Commission's staff made a housing investigation to document some of the consequences. The on-the-spot notations of the investigators speak eloquently of the cost Negroes paid for being "colored":

> No gas, bath, or toilet.
>
> Plumbing very bad; toilet leaks; bowl broken; leak in kitchen sink; water stands in kitchen; leak in bath makes ceiling soggy and wet all the time.
>
> Had to get city behind owner to put in windows, clean, and repair plumbing.
>
> Sanitary conditions poor; dilapidated condition; toilet won't flush; carries water to bathtub.
>
> Plastering off from water that leaks from flat above; toilet leaks; does not flush; washbowl and bath leak very badly; repairs needed on back porch; room needs calcimining.
>
> No water in hydrant in hall; no toilet, bath, or gas; general repair needed.
>
> Water not turned on for sink in kitchen; water for drinking and cooking purposes must be carried in; toilet used by four families; asked landlord to turn on water in kitchen; told them to move; roof leaks; stairs and back porch in bad order.
>
> Sewer gas escapes from basement pipes; water stands in basement.
>
> No heat and no hot water; no repairing done; no screens; gas leaks all over house; stationary tubs leak.
>
> Water pipes rotted out; gas pipes leak.
>
> Toilet leaks; plastering off; windowpanes out.
>
> Plastering off; large rat holes all over; paper hanging from ceiling.

These conditions, the staff reported, were "common" in the kind of housing in which 85 percent of black Chicagoans lived—and were being forced to live.[45]

CHAPTER 8

Holding the Line: Restriction

Before I built a wall I'd ask to know
What I was walling in or walling out,
And to whom I was like to give offence.
Something there is that doesn't love a wall,
That wants it down. . . .
—Robert Frost, "Mending Wall."

For it is only with regard to the negroes that race segregation has heretofore been seriously suggested in any American city. We are yet to learn of the American city that suggests the establishment of separate districts for Russians, or Irish, or Poles, or French, or English or any other race.
—"Racial Zoning," *Housing*, 17 (December 1928): 297.

DURING THE ERA OF MASSIVE MIGRATION AND VIOLENT CONTAINMENT, WHEN housing was in short supply, Negroes managed to move into three areas far from the Black Belt: Morgan Park, Lilydale, and suburban Robbins. All three locations were remote, uninhabited, and ill-suited for residential development. They became satellites of the Black Belt, exclusively Negro, unwanted by whites, and hemmed in on all sides by nonresidential land and subdivisions developed "exclusively for whites."[1]

Morgan Park was the first of the pocket ghettos to develop. Blacks employed as menials in the institutions and residences of white Morgan Park had long had exclusive occupancy of the cheap, low-lying, flood-prone prairie concealed behind the embankment of the commuter railroad that served the white community. Chicago annexed Morgan Park in 1914. Soon blacks in search of breathing space came upon the swampy no-man's-land east of the tracks. There, at the edge of the old Negro shantytown, they built homes for themselves. Many of the government employees and industrial workers who settled the enclave built their houses with their own hands. Others hired carpenters by the day to do some or all of the work. By 1920 nearly seven hundred people lived in the frame houses along the area's unpaved, largely unlit streets. White contractors were planning to build bungalows "for Negro occupancy" on adjacent swampland. The white people of Morgan Park were "not unfriendly" to the blacks across the tracks; they simply insisted "that Negroes must not live west of Vincennes Road."[2]

Lilydale, on the west side of State Street near 95th Street, was a white realtor's answer to the hunger of black people for homes of their own. The site was a desolate marsh surrounded by railroad tracks, industrial property, and empty acreage. Blacks paid "fairly high prices" for their lots, even though the subdivision had no lighting, no water, no sewers, no sidewalks, and no paving. The developer provided nothing but "the shells" of the houses. He left it up to the purchasers to finish the interiors and to arrange with the city for installation of utilities. The city laid water and sewer lines in some of the streets by 1920, but for many years there was "no paving and no lighting." The Board of Education "conveniently located" a portable school unit in Lilydale and assigned a black teacher to administer it. That way the black children did not have to leave their enclave. In 1920 the "Negro colony" consisted of only sixty families, but white contractors intended to build additional dwellings "especially for Negroes" in the area.[3]

Robbins was the dream community of black developer Eugene Robbins. In 1917 he subdivided a barren tract of unincorporated land southwest of the city limits and invited settlers to buy lots and build their own houses. Three years later the "exclusively Negro community" incorporated as a village. The homes in Robbins were makeshift at best, there was "no pretense of paved streets, or even sidewalks," and the nearest streetcar line was a mile away. But the four hundred inhabitants seemed "proud of their village and certain of its future." Nonresidents marveled alike at the homesteaders' morale and the palpable squalor of their surroundings.[4]

Unpromising as these places were, they represented hope to people trapped in the Black Belt. If Negroes could not aspire to break out of the main ghetto individually, at least they could look forward to escaping in groups. Segregation in scattered sites was still segregation, but it had advantages over confinement in one massive concentration. In the outlying areas, a family could buy a new home instead of a cast-off tenement. And for a long time industry had been moving toward the periphery of the metropolitan area. The outskirts of the city was the place to go for jobs as well as homes. Robbins, Morgan Park, and Lilydale were in the industrial South End, along one of the three main corridors of industrial development. Blacks hoped that the resumption of building would enable them to establish additional satellites, not only in the South End but in the west and northwest sectors as well. It was a very modest dream, but even so, it eluded them.

Beginning in 1921, a seven-year construction boom produced 50,000 new houses and 30,000 apartment buildings. Even though the black population doubled during the decade, whites denied blacks access to practically all of the new units. Subdividers restricted their developments to white occupancy. Negroes were unable to establish additional enclaves. There was no way, of course, to cram twice as many people into the old ghetto limits. Whites met the undeniable need for additional Negro living space by allowing the Black Belt and its existing satellites to expand into contiguous territory. Just as the building boom was getting under way, in the spring of 1921, the Chicago Real Estate Board voted unanimously to expel any member who rented or sold property on a white block to black people. There was a tacit understanding that the rule did not apply in the transitional blocks bordering the ghetto. It was all right for a realtor to "turn a building over" if whites were fleeing the neighborhood and Negroes were the only ones available to fill vacancies. So the ghetto grew along its edges.[5]

As new dwelling units opened up, whites in "threatened" territory flocked to fill them. The strip between the "alley el" and Cottage Grove, so savagely defended during the housing shortage, lost 76,000 white residents during the building bonanza. Over 92,500 Negroes crowded into the properties the whites left behind. There was only sporadic resistance to the newcomers. White diehards burned two churches (one Catholic, one Protestant) after blacks took them over in 1924, and a year later assailants bombed a synagogue three times to prevent the black Baptists who bought it from holding services. The white rearguard action was futile. Parishioners of Washington Park Congregational Church placed a placard over their portal with THIS IS A WHITE CHURCH painted on it in letters three feet high. Blacks bought the church in 1927. They posed beneath the sign for the *Defender*'s photographer, then they tore it down. In the same year, a syndicate of Jewish businessmen demolished the building where the Grand Boulevard branch of the Hyde Park–Kenwood Association had staged its anti-Negro rallies. In its place they built a million-dollar theater and ballroom "for Negroes." Almost instantly the corner of 47th and South Park became the new cultural center of the enlarged Black Belt.[6]

As long as the building boom lasted, neighborhoods continued to change from white to black, and there was no full-scale campaign to stop the Black Belt from spreading. By the time the areas west of Kenwood and Hyde Park had become "nigger neighborhoods," however, the boom was past its peak. Now whites redrew their line at Cottage Grove and resolved that blacks would never cross it. Residents of Hyde Park–Kenwood, east of the line, believed that their area had won "a reputation too splendid as a neighborhood of white culture to allow Negroes to use it as their door mat." The Chicago Real Estate Board took the initiative in fashioning a new weapon for property owners to employ against "undesirables": the restrictive covenant. Unlike bombs and brickbats, the covenant was both legal and respectable, and its designers claimed it would be even more effective in holding the line against black invasion than explosives and mob assaults.[7]

For nearly six years before the realtors introduced restrictive covenants into the arsenals of white communities, anti-Negro activity flared up only occasionally. Briefly, in 1922 and 1923, immigrants came under the attack of disgruntled natives and diverted attention from the blacks. The nativist effort was abortive, utterly failing to hold white ethnics in check. This is significant because of the contrast it provides to the subsequent campaign to control the movement of blacks. The latter effort, in which ethnic and native whites collaborated, was successful (see Map 8.1).

Immigrants and their children took advantage of the housing boom. In unprecedented numbers they poured out of the old areas of "first immigrant settlement" and scattered throughout the metropolis. The ethnic enclaves, such as they were, largely broke up or relocated. Those that held their ground and retained the old ethnic mix underwent a great churning of population, too, as thousands of

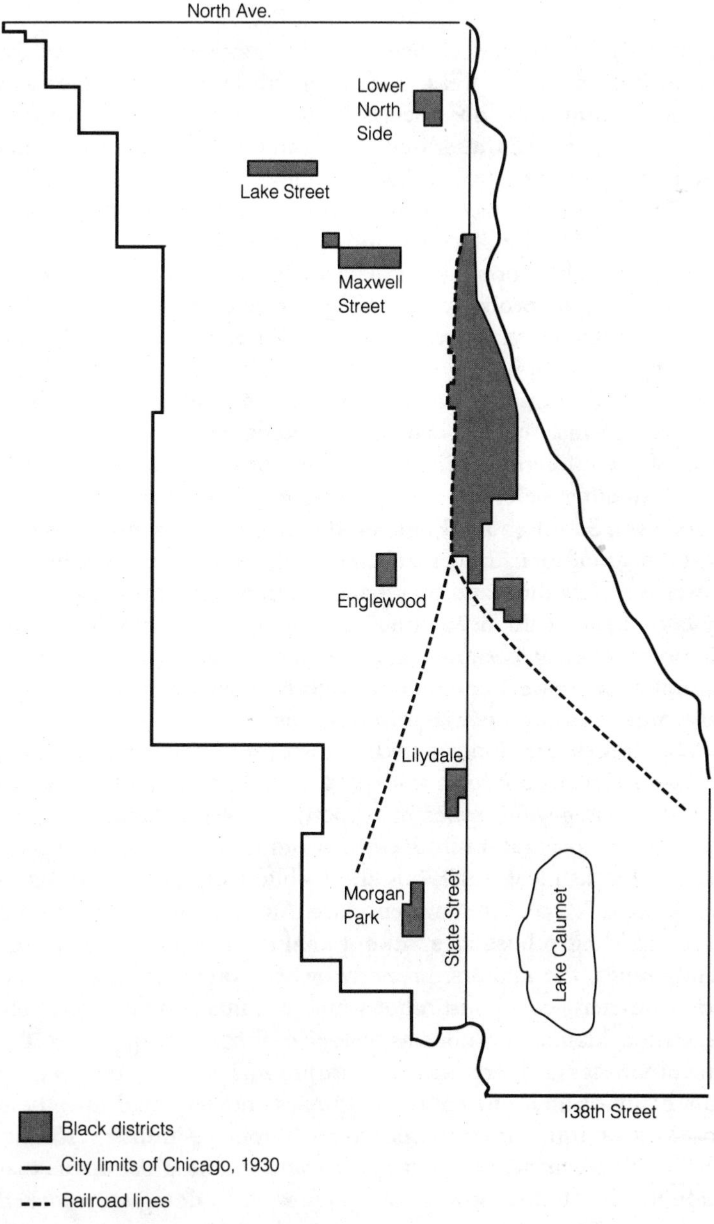

MAP 8.1. **Black Chicago, 1930.**

individuals filtered out to new neighborhoods, leaving room for new arrivals in the old areas. The magnitude and the suddenness of the population shifts unsettled a good many Chicagoans, who resented the surge of the ethnics. Six contiguous middle-class communities to the east and southwest of the changing zone bordering the Black Belt had to make room for an additional 89,000 white residents in the twenties. Many of these newcomers were fugitives from the neighborhoods overtaken by blacks, and a considerable number of them, probably the majority, were Catholics and Jews.[8]

Organizers for the revived national Ku Klux Klan, sensing an opportunity to capitalize on the sentiment for a more serene and stable society, came to Chicago in 1921 to establish an Invisible Empire of white, native-born adult Protestants. Their most fertile field of recruitment was in the communities inundated with refugees retreating before the black advance: Hyde Park, Kenwood, Woodlawn, South Shore, Englewood, and Greater Grand Crossing. At the peak of their influence, Chicago's twenty Klan klaverns had upwards of fifty thousand members, but their vogue was very brief. By late 1924 the Klan was not functioning in the city. It lost its members when it became clear that there was nothing the Klan (or any other power) could do to restore Chicago to what the Klan called "one hundred per cent Americanism."[9]

The "lower echelon white-collar workers, small businessmen, and semi-skilled laborers" who paid their hard-earned dollars to don the Klan's white robes had a long list of enemies: Catholics, Jews, all aliens, naturalized citizens, and nonwhites. Klansmen loathed blacks most of all, but all of white Chicago was united in the effort to keep blacks in their place. Anyone could give full vent to his anti-Negro hostilities without joining the Ku Klux Klan. The youth gangs, the realtors, property owners' organizations, and an extensive network of institutions and voluntary associations rendered the Klan superfluous as a vehicle of black suppression. On the other hand, there was no institutional system for keeping ethnics subordinate to natives. Catholics and Jews had long held positions of influence in Chicago's commerce, industry, society, and politics. The Klan rallied natives who resented the status that Catholics and Jews of foreign stock enjoyed. In doing so, it locked itself in combat with a segment of society that was every bit as powerful as the blacks were powerless. It was a fight the Klan had no chance of winning.[10]

There was no bastion of power and prestige in Chicago that Catholics and Jews had not breached. It was this fact that so embittered thousands of lower middle-class native Protestants and furnished the Klan its constituency of malcontents. And it was this fact that guaranteed the Klan's defeat. Catholics and Jews held commanding positions in management as well as labor. They had what Chicagoans call "clout" not only in politics and civil service but in trade, the professions, and in social circles as well. The Illinois Manufacturers' Association, the Chicago Bar Association, the Association of Commerce, the Board of Trade, the Real Estate Board, Chicago Title and Trust Co., all had Catholic and Jewish officers. At the pinnacle of society, Protestants were still predominant, but the best private societies and country clubs admitted well-to-do Catholics and Jews to their ranks. There were Jewish Masons and even Jewish Shriners. In "native" neighborhoods, such as Hyde Park, Woodlawn, and Englewood, Catholics and Jews controlled the largest banks and realty firms. People of foreign stock constituted a majority of the white population in all but six of the city's seventy-five community areas. And even in those six areas the "Americans" barely outnumbered the ethnics. There was no such thing as an exclusively native white Protestant community, either in the city proper or its suburban perimeter.[11]

The Klan pitted itself against formidable adversaries, and its campaign coalesced its enemies into a vengeful counteralliance. The Klan could not exploit interethnic rivalries because it denounced all ethnics. Anti-Jewish sentiment was strong in the city, partly because so many blockbusters were "Jewish speculators." "Once the kikes get in a neighborhood," people grumbled, "it's all over": like Judas, "those kike real-estate bastards" would betray their neighbors and "sell to niggers" to make a dollar. The Klan could not take full advantage of anti-Semitism, however, because it denied membership to the Chicagoans who detested Jews the most: namely, Catholics, particularly Irish Catholics. The Klan could not even assume the leadership of the city's Negro haters, because it alienated the ethnics who played so crucial a rôle in keeping the blacks in place. The Catholics and Jews whom the Klan chose to attack united to destroy the Klan, much as they had cooperated to hold the line against blacks. They used the same weapons they employed against the Negroes, but now they had even the blacks on their side.[12]

The anti-Klan crusade began in the fall of 1921, when Ragen's Colts, famed for their exploits during the race riot, hanged a sheeted Klansman in effigy before a roaring crowd of three thousand. The city council condemned the Klan and, led by Ulysses S. ("U.S.") Schwartz and a band of zealous aldermen, the council later voted to dismiss all Klansmen from the public payroll. Court action blocked the purge of the public employees, but a Catholic-dominated organization called the American Unity League launched a successful program to ruin privately employed Klansmen. The league pressured employers to fire Klansmen, and it circulated an effective blacklist of those fired. League-directed boycotts forced Klan merchants out of business. And Chicago Klansmen, instead of inflicting punishment as Klansmen elsewhere did, found themselves the victims of violent attacks. Several homemade bombs, of the type that had terrorized blacks and blockbusters before, now exploded at the homes and offices of reputed Klan members. The league intimidated the Klan out of existence by the end of 1924.[13]

Some black Chicagoans mistook the rout of the Klan for a repudiation of racism, but the fact was that the people who killed the Klan had no more respect for the rights of blacks than the Klansmen had. The Ku Klux Klan failed, not because it wanted to segregate blacks but because it tried to segregate white ethnics along with them. What the Klan episode proved was the futility of efforts to treat immigrants, Catholics, and Jews like nonwhites.

A few years after the demise of the Chicago Klan, the declining national organization made a last-ditch effort to deny Alfred E. Smith the Democratic party's presidential nomination. The Klansmen could not stop Smith, a Catholic, from being nominated, but they had the consolation of seeing the handful of Negro alternates (there were no black delegates) segregated from the rest of the conventioneers by means of a specially built chicken-wire fence. A Catholic could win the Democratic nomination in 1928, but a black Democrat had to settle for a Jim Crow seat at the rear of Houston's convention hall. And in that year white Chicagoans of all nationalities and creeds were busy building an "invisible barbed-wire fence of restrictive covenants" around the Black Belt.[14]

A restrictive covenant was a contractual agreement among property owners that none of them would permit a "colored person" to occupy, lease, or buy his property. The signators to the covenant bound not only themselves and each other but all "their heirs and assigns" to exclude nonwhites from the restricted area for a stated period of years. In case of violation, any party to the pact could call on the courts to enforce it. Moreover, "injured parties" could sue transgressors for damages.[15]

In some cities, restrictive covenants were in effect before the 1920s, but in Chicago they were rare. However, deed restrictions, covering a single parcel or a whole subdivision, were common. Individual owners placed restrictions on their properties to bar subsequent owners from renting or selling to Negroes. Developers stated in their tract prospectuses that all occupants and owners must be white. Increasingly they strengthened these statements by recording race restrictions with the subdivision deeds. After 1923 the initial plats that subdividers filed with the county recorder commonly carried restrictions against persons "not of the Caucasian race." The trouble with deed restrictions was that they could be applied only to new territory or isolated lots. Restrictive covenants were made to order for established neighborhoods. A covenant was a social compact. It symbolized and guaranteed community solidarity. It vested a large group with an interest in maintaining racial boundaries vigilantly, and it gave them the means to do it.[16]

After the U.S. Supreme Court struck down residential segregation ordinances in 1917, real estate boards and property owners' groups turned increasingly to the use of restrictive covenants. In 1926 the Court dismissed the case of *Corrigan* v. *Buckley* for want of jurisdiction, thereby giving tacit approval to lower-court rulings that held covenants valid and enforceable in the courts. Later that year, as Chicago's building boom began to subside and competition for shelter started to sharpen, the Chicago Real Estate Board initiated a drive to cover the city's "desirable" communities with covenants. Board members believed that restriction was the most important mission they had ever undertaken.[17]

The board's first step was to devise a model covenant that property owners' organizations in threatened districts could adopt. To supervise the drafting of a standard agreement the realtors called on Nathan William MacChesney, a lawyer of national reputation and a commanding figure in Chicago society. A Republican of avowedly "progressive" leanings, MacChesney had held appointive posts at all levels of government, and he was an officer of the state and national bar. For years he worked as counsel for the National Child Labor Committee. Locally he served on the boards of the United Charities, the Salvation Army, and the YMCA, and along with his wife he actively supported settlement work. What made MacChesney so useful to the realtors, besides his prestige, was his expertise in realty and planning. He was a trustee of Northwestern University's Institute for the Study of Land and Public Utility Economics and author of the standard text on real estate law. His knowledge was not merely academic: He was general counsel to the National Association of Real Estate Boards. And not least among his qualifications was his membership on the executive committee of the Chicago Plan Commission. Having MacChesney prepare the covenant made it seem almost official.[18]

MacChesney's home was on the North Side Gold Coast, but he had formerly lived in Hyde Park–Kenwood. From 1908 to 1910, during the district's anti-Negro drive, he was president of the Men's Club of Hyde Park. Whether or not he took part in the campaign, he had an abiding interest in what he called "race development." As general counsel to the National Association of Real Estate Boards, MacChesney drew up Article 34, which the association added to its Code of Ethics in 1924. This amendment forbade realtors to introduce "members of any race or nationality" into neighborhoods where their presence would damage property values. To give Article 34 credibility, MacChesney drafted a model real-estate licensing act, which thirty-two states eventually adopted. The act empowered state commissions to revoke all licenses of agents who violated the National Real Estate Board's Code of Ethics. The MacChesney Act, as it was called, upgraded the ethical level of real estate transactions, but it also authorized state commissions to enforce Article 34. And in his book *The Principles of Real Estate Law*, published in 1927, MacChesney designated only one ethnic group as undesirable: blacks.[19]

The standard form that MacChesney fashioned was ready for use in the fall of 1927. Predictably, it restricted the movement of no race or nationality except the "negro," defined as "every person having one-eighth part or more of negro blood or having any appreciable admixture of negro blood, and every person who is what is commonly known as a colored person." The agreement barred "negroes" from renting, buying, or otherwise acquiring covenanted property. No "negro" could use or occupy any part of the covered premises, unless that person was employed as a janitor, chauffeur, or house servant. A white resident could quarter his black domestic help "in the basement or in a barn or garage in the rear" or in special "servants' quarters."[20]

The model covenant was a complicated instrument (see Appendix A). It took effect only when the owners of a specified percentage of the property frontage in a given area signed. Because the agreement applied only to the property of signators and not to the entire district, it was desirable to get all of the owners in an area to sign. However, if the agreement called for 100 percent coverage and a few owners declined to sign, it was inoperative. Therefore, the Real Estate Board recommended that property owners' groups divide their districts into sections of six to eight blocks with separate covenants for each section; set the agreements to go into effect once 75 percent of the property was signed for; and *then* drive for total coverage throughout the entire district. The recommended time limit on the covenants was twenty-one years. If, because of changed conditions—such as decline of property values to the point where selling to blacks would be profitable— the signators or their successors wished to abrogate the agreement, they could do so with the written consent of the owners of a stated percentage of the covenanted property (the board recommended 60 percent).[21]

With the model covenant perfected, the Real Estate Board sent speakers across the city to stir up interest in restriction. "The colored people of Chicago are bent on invasion," board spokesmen claimed. They made the rounds of YMCAs, churches, women's clubs, PTAs, Kiwanis clubs, chambers of commerce, and property owners' associations, sounding the alarm: Black organizations were conspiring "to settle a negro family in every block in the city" and make Chicago a "mecca" of racial mongrelization.[22]

Homeowners and businessmen were anxious to ward off the threat to their communities. "Should the negro come amongst us and acquire property," one merchant said to his local chamber of commerce, "the next move would be ours, and out." Restriction was peaceful and defensive, not aggressive, and as a board spokesman who called himself "Judge" Henry Lunt (although he was never a judge in Chicago) reiterated endlessly, it was "constitution-proof," unlike racial zoning ordinances. Restricted districts had "almost positive insurance of stability," one local editor argued: "Protection keeps homeowners" in the covered territory and attracts "new residents" and "new business." Within a matter of months there was widespread support for the Real Estate Board's "progressive movement" to safeguard neighborhoods of "good standing" from "the influx of negroes."[23]

Restricting a large area was "a tremendous undertaking." A residential square mile encompassed one hundred or more square blocks with as many as four thousand parcels of property. Compiling legal descriptions of the properties, calculating the extent of coverage, tracking down the individual owners, and persuading them to limit their freedom to convey their property, then properly filing the signed documents with the recorder of deeds, took time, talent, and money. Staff salary, filing fees, and other expenses involved in covering Central Uptown on the Far North Side to keep the square-mile district "99$^{44}/_{100}$% Pure (White)"—a phrase taken from the ads for Ivory Soap—exceeded $7,200. The cost would have been much greater if large numbers of people had not given freely of their time and services.[24]

For many years one block of Central Uptown had been occupied by Negroes who worked in the hotels, restaurants, and private residences nearby. Because the street on which the blacks lived was up against the noisy Northwest El and "almost inaccessible, no one was concerned about them." But in 1928 businessmen and property owners "became alarmed" when they discovered that "on some streets negroes lived in the basements in buildings of which they were not janitors." Community leaders formed the Central Uptown Chicago Association to restrict the neighborhood. They divided the area into sixteen districts, each with its own covenant, and set the coverage requirement at 90 percent, instead of settling for the 75 percent recommended by the Real Estate Board. To pay the costs of the restriction drive, individual signers made contributions, banks and businesses assessed themselves five to ten dollars for each employee, and neighborhood institutions made donations.

There were ten churches and synagogues in the area, and every one of them helped pay for the restriction. One church "sent in $10.00 from its cemetery fund." It took two years to get sufficient signatures to put all sixteen covenants into effect.[25]

Despite the difficulties restriction entailed, covenants proliferated. By the spring of 1928, the *Hyde Park Herald* was pleased to announce that a "fine network of contracts" extended "like a marvelous delicately woven chain of armor" from "the northern gates of Hyde Park at 35th and Drexel Boulevard to Woodlawn, Park Manor, South Shore, Windsor Park and all the far-flung white communities of the South Side."[26]

When outlying communities discovered that the neighborhoods between themselves and the Black Belt were protected from "undesirables," they hastened to erect "restricting fences" of their own. Central Uptown was one of the first to act. Late in 1928 white residents of the Industrial South End mobilized as well. They formed the Greater Pullman Property Restriction Association with the intention of protecting all of the white neighborhoods in the district south of the Lilydale ghetto and west of black Morgan Park against "invasion from 'undesirables.'" The area was huge. It covered the old town of Pullman, almost all of Roseland, and parts of some adjoining communities. Over forty thousand parcels of property were involved. The Pullman restrictionists scored a feat in blocking the southwestern industrial corridor to blacks. Their counterparts on the Far West Side and the Far Northwest Side sealed off the other major lanes of growth. By the end of 1930 more than 175 white property owners' associations were standing watch over the Black Belt's boundaries. Tremendous tracts of territory in middle-class and working-class communities, covering mile upon square mile, were closed to "any negro or negroes."[27]

For the suburbs, which formed an almost lily-white ring around the city, restriction was a status symbol as much as a safety measure. But a few suburbs did have a "negro problem." Evanston and Waukegan on the North Shore and Maywood, west of the city, had significant Negro populations. Whites in these communities used covenants to contain their black minorities. The restriction campaign in Maywood was especially thorough. The village's six hundred Negroes lived in a small section blocked on two sides by railroad tracks. In the summer of 1928, property owners covered the areas on the other two sides to "check the spread of the black belt." Later, at a meeting in St. John's Lutheran Church, the Maywood Real Estate Board announced a plan for "making the black belt . . . smaller and smaller." A syndicate would "buy up property now held by Negroes." With a shrinking black population, one realtor explained, Maywood would be "the coming town west of Chicago."[28]

Blacks were incensed that programs to protect property values always turned out to be anti-Negro. "Foreigners," the *Defender* observed, could move anywhere "unmolested" by the covenants. Some real estate manuals of the 1920s classed "unassimilated aliens" along with blacks as undesirables, but the *Defender* was correct: No one advocated the all-out segregation of any group except "colored people," in Chicago or anywhere else. "It is only with regard to the negro population that race segregation is suggested," *Housing* magazine observed in 1928. *Housing* was not a realty publication, it was the journal of American housing reform, published by the National Housing Association. Far from attacking segregation, the association recommended it as the only solution for the "Negro problem." Because racial zoning ordinances were unconstitutional, *Housing* endorsed the "private covenant" as a "perfectly legitimate method" for establishing separate districts for "the negro element."[29]

"The foreigners get better treatment than we do," the *Defender* complained. Not only were they exempt from restriction; what was more, they were "apt students of segregation." They did not want blacks living next door any more than native whites did. The immigrant communities west of the Rock Island tracks remained uncovered by covenants, for the most part, but that did not mean that Negroes were free to move in. Residents of those communities lacked the skills and resources required to conduct a restriction campaign, so they relied on their traditional methods of keeping blacks out, and those violent methods continued to be effective. Other predominantly ethnic areas adopted the use of covenants.[30]

The territory of the Greater Pullman Property Restriction Association was inhabited largely by ethnic workingmen who could "ill afford to face the big depreciation in property values" that would follow "encroachment by undesirables." Italians, Swedes, Netherlanders, Poles, Lithuanians, Germans, and twenty other nationality groups shared the area. The leaders of the association included

Catholics, Protestants, and Jews. They had names like Perlman, Zimmerman, Korzeniecki, Birkhoff, Larocco, Hockstra, Teninga, Novak, and Bezdek, as well as Hillstrom, Brandt, Johnson, Gibbons, Devine, and Richards. Ethnically diverse, the people of Greater Pullman were sticklers for *racial* purity.[31]

Most of the restricted communities were self-styled "American" districts, but they were by no means exclusively native. In 1930, 70 percent of white Chicagoans—and 54 percent of white suburbanites—were foreign stock; thus any community that was "only" 40 or 50 or even 60 percent ethnic could qualify as American. Ethnics were a substantial element in every "native" community, and they played an important part in keeping the "undesirables" out.[32]

The whites of staid, suburban Evanston were 45 percent foreign stock. In the other suburbs with Negro ghettos of their own, Maywood and Waukegan, the ethnics outnumbered the native stock. The area that the *Hyde Park Herald* liked to call "Yankeeland" —the lakefront communities from Oakland to South Shore, where the Klan had briefly flourished—was more than 50 percent foreign stock. Catholics and Jews were active in all of the area's restriction associations. Mark Levy, a Jewish realtor who lived in the exclusive Madison Park section of Kenwood, was vice-president of his neighborhood association. In 1923 he was vice-president of the Chicago Real Estate Board; eight years later he became president. In the meantime he helped organize the citywide restriction campaign. The president of the Woodlawn Property Owners' Association was Neil J. O'Hanley (almost certainly an Irish Catholic), and the secretary was Fred Helman (probably Jewish). Helman doubled as secretary of the South Shore Property Owners' Association. Englewood, another former Klan stronghold, was nearly 60 percent foreign stock. Among the officers of the Englewood Property Restriction Association were men named Rathje, Kussman, Lenz, Eidmann, Anderson, Hughes, and Rosen. The president was William G. Donne, a banker who belonged to the Knights of Columbus.[33]

The realtor who launched the Real Estate Board's restriction drive was Oscar Boenicke, a German-born immigrant who lived in Hyde Park. Boenicke's successor as coordinator of restriction was an Italian named Peter Curto. Curto's brother Victor was chairman of the association that restricted Central Uptown. More than half of the residents of fashionable Uptown, which bordered the lake on the Far North Side, were of foreign stock. One-third or so of the financial sponsors of the Uptown covenant were Catholics and Jews. Of the speculators and subdividers who filed plats in the twenties excluding non-Caucasians, eleven identified themselves as owners instead of listing a corporate trustee. A few of the names might be old native stock, but the rest are almost surely ethnic: Branigar, De Lugach, Dunas, Buckley, Eckwald, Finitzo, Gubbins and McDonnell, Luulz and Shapiro. Frank De Lugach was one of the leading subdividers operating southwest of the city. In less than three years he covered over thirteen hundred acres in and around what is now Evergreen Park with this proviso: "This property shall not be sold or leased to nor occupied by any other than a Caucasian."[34]

"We are no alley rats or vermin," protested a black doctor who lived in Maywood's "black belt"; "we are men and women, respectable, and demanding respect." Yet whites claimed that they could not see how an "intelligent" black person could object to being restricted. After all, they said, "the motive was not one of antagonism but rather to protect property values." And what was more, as Nathan William MacChesney argued, "the power of the whites to exclude the blacks . . . implies the power of the blacks to exercise the same prerogative over property which they may own. There is, therefore, no discrimination. . . ." A white realtor claimed that the covenants would promote racial harmony and "foster individual pride in the members of both races."[35]

When Archibald Motley, the black man who lived on a white street in Englewood, received a mail request to cover his property in the Englewood covenant, he thought it was a mistake. But one of his white neighbors, "a German," urged him to sign the agreement, promising that the other signers would never enforce it against him. They would wait until he moved or died and then use the covenant to keep other blacks from occupying the house. Motley declined. His neighbor had no idea that Mr. Motley had any hard feelings about the conversation, but as Willard Motley recalled, his father was "storming." "Why, Mae!" Mr. Motley said to his wife. "I wouldn't be able to sell or leave our home to my own brother!" Nor to his children. Ironically, Willard Motley remembered the document that his father refused to sign as a pact "not to rent or sell to Negroes or Jews." In fact the covenant excluded no one but "negroes," and Jews were prominent among its sponsors.[36]

Large companies that did business citywide, including Illinois Bell Telephone, Commonwealth Edison, People's Gas, Light & Coke, and the Chicago Rapid Transit and Motor Coach companies, endorsed the covenant campaign. The Salvation Army restricted noninstitutional property to which it held title. There were even public officials who did not respect or fear the black electorate enough to conceal their connivance with restriction associations. Among the sponsors of the Uptown covenant were the chairman of the Illinois Commerce Commission, two aldermen, a judge, and ex-Mayor William E. Dever. Dever, an Irish-Catholic Democrat, was not an ordinary machine politician. He owed his start in politics to the settlement workers at Chicago Commons, who backed him for five terms in the city council and supported his election as judge. He received his party's nomination for mayor in 1923 because the Democrats wanted the reform vote that year, and he lost his bid for reelection in 1927 because his administration was too thoroughly identified with reform. Though defeated, Dever remained the city's foremost political reformer when he gave his support to the restriction campaign.[37]

"The whites have not played fair," the *Defender* charged. They laid down discriminatory rules and then broke even those. They denied blacks the right to scatter "promiscuously" throughout the city but promised to permit the Black Belt to expand at its edges. Yet when blacks needed more room the most, when housing was in short supply, whites blocked their efforts to move, first by force, then by means of covenants. Even part of the area inside the Black Belt was off limits to blacks. The whites, having drawn the boundaries, did not relinquish all of the territory on the "black" side of the line. They maintained a "white island" one-quarter of a square mile in size as a buffer between the blacks and the white communities east of Cottage Grove. Businessmen and property owners in Woodlawn, aided secretly by the University of Chicago, took the lead in covering the Washington Park Subdivision in West Woodlawn with a restrictive covenant. For the whites to deny blacks this area after denying them access to all of the territory beyond the boundary lines was "particularly offensive to the Negro community."[38]

Restriction left Negroes of all classes and income levels at the mercy of landlords whose specialty was to "rent to niggers." In the oldest parts of the Black Belt, along Federal Street, the buildings were barely habitable. Rents were low (though not so low as they were for better housing outside the Black Belt), but people still had trouble making their payments. "These niggers are the most irresponsible cusses in the world," one landlord grumbled. The reason they fell behind in their rent, another slum owner explained, was not that they were poor or exploited but that they were shiftless and lazy. "The hardest work they do is shoot craps," he said, "and they all can't win."[39]

On the better streets inside the eastern boundary of the Black Belt, middle-class families paid exorbitant rents. "When we had white tenants in there we weren't realizing enough return on our investment," a building agent admitted. "So we decided to turn the buildings over. . . . Now we are getting more." Converting flats into "kitchenettes" was another way for realtors to get more. Instead of renting a four-room flat to a middle-class family, a landlord could cut it into four one-room "apartments" and rent them to four poor families on a weekly basis. Installation of a gas burner in each room gave every one-room flat its own "kitchen." The option to convert apartments into kitchenettes increased the landlord's advantage over middle-class renters. No matter how high he jacked up the rents, he could always claim that he could get more by making the conversion. "If we are cheating the people why don't they move?" a Black Belt realtor asked. "We don't worry about tenants! We've got a waiting list for our flats." That was just it. There was no place else to go.[40]

The fact that many Black Belt landlords and realtors were ethnics aggravated the animosity which Negroes felt for "foreigners," especially Jews. "Whenever and wherever you get this kind of property you'll find Jews own it and rent to niggers at exorbitant prices," a gentile realtor claimed. "Of course Jews aren't the only ones that do this," he added, "but they are in the majority." True or not, blacks believed it, and it embittered them.[41]

❧

There was no city in America with a population more diverse than Chicago's. It became a byword that the city's many ethnic groups had only one thing in common: their desire "to make money." All that was supposed to matter in Chicago was making it. But black Chicagoans discovered that at least one other thing bound the rest of the city's people together: whiteness. Chicagoans drew the color line. A black man could not cross it no matter how much money he made, and he had less of a chance to make it than anybody else.[42]

White people of all ethnic stocks agreed with Italian-American journalist Luigi Barzini, who called for rigid segregation in an article in *Corriere D'America* (a New York paper printed in Italian "because," the Chicago *Defender* claimed, "most of its readers can't decipher the English language"). "The Negro cannot be absorbed," Barzini declared, "without creating a nation of mulattoes." The *Defender* carried a translation of Barzini's statement to show "how quickly those who are welcomed to our shores fall in line with the American brand of prejudice. When they acquire this," the editor concluded, "they evidently feel that they are pure Americans—100 per centers."[43]

One of Chicago's most famous citizens, Al ("Scarface") Capone, used to say "I'm no Italian." Capone, a self-made man who climbed to the top of the ladder of organized crime in Chicago, was American-born and proud of it. The city's gangland leaders, as the *Defender* noted, "were privileged to live wherever they choose to purchase homes . . . every community was opened to them." Johnny Torrio and "Greasy Thumb" Jake Guzick lived in South Shore, Terry Druggan had a Gold Coast duplex, and many other underworld notables resided in restricted "American" communities. Capone's home was in Park Manor, a peaceful middle-class neighborhood immediately south of the Black Belt. He put the title to the house in his mother's name, but it was very much his castle, with foot-thick reinforced concrete walls and steel-barred bombproof windows. For years Capone's neighbors on the 7200 block of Prairie Avenue included several businessmen, three police officers, and a Presbyterian minister. In 1927–28, when the Park Manor Improvement Association restricted the area against undesirables, Theresa Capone signed the covenant for her son.[44]

People talked of Park Manor as a Swedish or Irish neighborhood, and realtors advertised it as "American," but like other white communities it was ethnically mixed. Old-stock Americans and people of twenty-six nationalities shared the three-quarter-square-mile territory of the Improvement Association, and they got along together very well. The Improvement Association held its meetings at Park Manor Congregational Church, but the president was an Irishman named M. J. Connelly, who worshipped at St. Columbanus Catholic Church. Park Manor residents paid no more for their housing than many people trapped in the Black Belt paid for vastly inferior accommodations, but there was little danger that blacks who could afford it would move into the area. As the pastor of the Congregational Church noted with satisfaction, there were a lot of Irish Catholics living in Park Manor. "If the restriction of the district can't keep them out," he said in 1928, "the Irish will."[45]

When I move
Into a neighborhood
Folks fly.

Even every foreigner
That can move, moves.

Why?

The moon doesn't run.
Neither does the sun.

In Chicago
They've got covenants

Restricting me—
Hemmed in
On the South Side,
Can't breathe free.

But the wind blows there.
I reckon the wind
Must care.

—Langston Hughes, "Restrictive Covenants."

PART III ❧

The Business Creed and the Color Line: The Limits of Constructive Reform

Some people have suggested taking a vacant piece of property and building it up for colored occupancy, but there is the biggest hubbub raised when any such attempt is made. People complain: "You will ruin this whole neighborhood! You will ruin the street car line! Everything out in that neighborhood will be ruined all along the street, because if you build up a colored neighborhood in any particular location nobody else will want to go out that way." So that I have come to the point where I say there is no solution. I can't do anything. I'd have been willing to put in a million dollars in property anywhere there would have been a chance to get 5 per cent on my money. There isn't any use in doing a thing that isn't economically sound.

—An unnamed businessman, probably Benjamin J. Rosenthal, cited by the Chicago Commission on Race Relations in *The Negro in Chicago* (Chicago, 1922), p. 225.

The World War I housing crisis and the terrible riots that climaxed it stirred reformers to do something constructive about their city's housing problem. For two decades and more they had investigated and publicized conditions, lobbied for restrictive building codes, and played watchdog over inspectors and aldermen to compel law enforcement and prevent enfeebling amendments. Yet they had not enlarged the stock of habitable dwellings that poorly paid workingmen could afford. And they had not kept white people and black people from fighting savagely over the available supply. Negative reform had its limits, and the reformers knew it. Similarly, the restrictive activities of realtors and property owners to seal black Chicagoans inside the Black Belt did not succeed in heading off the destructive racial clash that everyone wanted to avoid. Segments of the power structure that had not always been congenial to calls for change before now agreed that it was time to do something.

More than at any time since the heyday of George M. Pullman's experiment with his model town, businessmen became boosters for reform. The Chicago Real Estate Board, following the lead of the National Association of Real Estate Boards, endorsed zoning and city planning. And the board finally announced its support of housing reform, after years of denying that Chicago had a housing problem. As one realtor remarked, it was no longer possible to obstruct reform "with good grace." By supporting it, realtors would be in a better position to influence and even direct it. Businessmen concurred with reformers who argued that better housing for both races would mean better race relations. "We intend to undertake the solving of the Negro housing problem," a spokesman for the Association of Commerce and the Real Estate Board announced after the riots. "Decent homes must be provided for colored people in a section which is congenial to them." With businessmen behind reform, veterans of the housing movement looked forward to the postwar period as one in which constructive action would be possible. Charles Ball, of the Health Department, so pessimistic in 1917, attended the 1918 Conference of the National Housing Association with renewed hope. "The reconstruction era," he told the assembled delegates, would be "the time to advance."[1]

As the decade unfolded, Chicago did advance noticeably. The Chicago Commission on Race Relations, appointed to study the riots, set a standard in race relations and counseled the city to settle its housing problem by "constructive means." A Zoning Commission drafted a comprehensive ordinance, which the city council enacted into law. The resurgent Chicago Plan Commission embarked on a stupendous program of civic improvements. While the planners ignored housing altogether, the reform regime of Mayor William Dever took a promising step toward remedying that defect by establishing the Chicago Housing Commission. During Mayor Dever's term, the city reopened the Municipal Lodging House. Chicago got its first model housing projects in the course of the decade as well, three of them, one built in 1919–20, the other two in 1928–29. One of the projects completed at the end of the decade was "for Negroes," a belated implementation of the Riot Commission's recommendation for "better Negro housing."[2]

These advances, though impressive, were limited. The factors that set the limits on constructive reform were the same ones that governed the allocation of housing and the arrangement of neighborhoods in Chicago: the business creed and the color line. According to the business creed, housing was a commodity for private enterprise to provide at a profit. Those who could pay enough got good houses; people with too little money got inferior houses. If the worst-housed neighborhoods proved to be a danger or a disgrace to the larger community, then the public could take appropriate action, such as sending in police or providing public services. Some action, however, was beyond the scope of public authority because it belonged to the sphere of private citizens, acting either philanthropically or on a business basis. Restrictive legislation, zoning, and city planning were within the scope of government. Building, selling, and managing houses fell within the private domain, and it was all business, not philanthropy. Constructive housing reform was fine, if it was profitable. The color line consigned black people to black districts. If they could pay for good housing they were entitled to it, but it had to be segregated. As the Hyde Park–Kenwood Property Owners Association put it, "The place for a Negro aristocrat is in a Negro neighborhood." All constructive effort was bounded by the limits of privatism and racism.[3]

Two of the people most influential in the reform efforts of the twenties were Mary McDowell and Julius Rosenwald. Mary McDowell headed the University of Chicago Settlement in Packingtown, Back a' the Yards. Rosenwald was the multimillionaire president of Sears, Roebuck. He was also one of America's foremost philanthropists. The Rosenwald Fund, his main outlet for giving, contributed heavily to "Negro education" and "Negro welfare." Miss McDowell was largely responsible for the creation of the Chicago Housing Commission, and she had a hand in building all three of the model housing projects. Rosenwald served on the Riot Commission and exerted considerable control over the Housing Commission. He built the "colored" project, and he played a part in putting up the others. Years before the war they both had realized the inadequacies of negative reform, and they attempted to build model housing projects. Their unsuccessful prewar experiments foreshadowed what would happen in the postwar reconstruction era.[4]

In 1912, hoping to take advantage of a recent survey showing how horrible the housing Back a' the Yards was, Mary McDowell tried to win financial backing for a model tenement on the same block as the settlement house. She wrote to several wealthy businessmen, all of whom were generous patrons of settlement work, asking whether such a project should be run "on a basis of philanthropy or business." All of her respondents answered "Business." One of them explained:

> There is no use in housing a few people out of hundreds of thousands needing better homes unless you can show somebody how he can get a reasonable return by following your example—and build decent themselves—Don't mix business and philanthropy. . . .

Allen B. Pond, a noted architect and a veteran housing reformer, wrote:

> . . . it is not wise to try to build tenements as a matter of philanthropy. . . . A tenement is only justified on the theory that it is expected that it will pay its way and be a practical demonstration of the possibility of building paying tenements.

One businessman advised her that nothing less than a 4½ to 5 percent profit would "lead others to build. Even if you show how it can be done on a 4% basis." Allen Pond agreed that "a scheme which does not work out as well as this" could not "justify itself as an experiment in housing."[5]

Miss McDowell persuaded two wealthy Chicagoans to buy the parcel of land she had chosen. Then she made plans for a three-story building with forty flats for families and a dormitory for "young unmarried foreign men." Her hope was to rent New City Tenement to "the most needy" unskilled workers in the neighborhood and still pay her investors 4 ½ percent. Seven people, including Julius Rosenwald, agreed to invest $5,000 each if she could raise the rest of the needed $100,000 from other sources. For five years she tried to raise the money by promising potential investors that the project would be operated "on a business basis." The big packinghouses were willing to contribute $100,000 "as an investment" in model housing, but the money did not go to Mary McDowell's project. Either the packers did not want to put their money into an enterprise directed by the doughty settlement worker, or Miss McDowell turned down the money for fear that packinghouse control would discredit the project in the eyes of working people. In any case, the packers and Miss McDowell did not get together. She scaled the plans down to thirty apartments in an effort to reduce the required capital, but the money was not forthcoming. When the war broke out and she was still far short of the needed funds, she simply gave up the project.[6]

Later she acknowledged that she could not have carried through the plan without failing in her obligations to the investors, or raising the rents beyond the ability of unskilled workers to pay, or both. She never did admit that all the time she had been talking about an all-white project. Thousands of unskilled "colored workers" labored in the stockyards, but "no colored people lived back of the yards." Of all packinghouse workers, the blacks needed housing most—particularly housing within walking distance of their jobs. But Mary McDowell's neighbors on Gross Avenue would never have stood for a tenement open to blacks, nor would her potential investors. She evaded the issue by calling the project a tenement for her immigrant neighbors in Packingtown instead of a building for badly housed employees of the packinghouses. She felt that she could not violate the color line even if she had tried to.[7]

In 1914, while Mary McDowell was struggling vainly to construct her white project, Julius Rosenwald, one of her pledged subscribers, decided to build a model tenement "for colored people." The Great Migration to Chicago was just getting under way, but black people were already the worst-housed people in the city, by far. Rosenwald commissioned plans for "a high grade, modern apartment house" to accommodate the highest-income Negroes, people discontented in the mean streets of the Black Belt but barred from desirable districts occupied by whites. In 1916 he acquired a parcel of land at the northeast corner of 32nd and Vernon Avenue, a block that had been all-white until 1911 and was still mostly white through 1915. The site was thus in a section of the Black Belt that Negroes were still consolidating as the exodus of whites continued. If the area was made more attractive instead of being allowed to deteriorate, it was possible that ambitious blacks would be satisfied to halt their expansion there.[8]

The project that Rosenwald planned to erect was three stories high with sixty apartments of two and three rooms. To net a 5 percent return on the $125,000 investment, he expected to charge rents of $18 to $38 a month. When it became clear that the required rents were beyond the means of better-paid black families, Rosenwald killed the project. Unlike Mary McDowell, he took the demise of his plan in stride. A dozen years later, at a ceremony to mark the opening of "the Rosenwald," a 421-unit project "for Negroes," he talked philosophically about the earlier, aborted project:

> . . . it couldn't be done then and give returns. I made up my mind that unless the building could be built and rented on a business basis there was no virtue in putting it up. It would do more harm than good to rent it for less than market value. It would not be fair competition.

While Mary McDowell had doubts about the business creed and the color line as applied to housing reform, Julius Rosenwald believed devoutly in them both.[9]

Their premonitory excursions into model housing revealed the primacy of private enterprise and racial segregation in constructive reform. The emphasis on proving that a reform would produce a profit remained paramount throughout the twenties, and so did the tacit insistence on preservation of the color line.

CHAPTER 9 ❧

The Riot Commission and the Dual Solution

Let us in the future spend less time talking about the part of the city that we cannot live in, and more time in making that part of the city that we live in beautiful and attractive.
—Booker T. Washington, cited in Emmett J. Scott and Lyman Beecher Stowe, *Booker T. Washington, Builder of a Civilization* (Garden City, N.Y., 1916), p. 40.

We would advise our friends in Chicago to watch narrowly the work and forthcoming report of the Interracial Commission appointed by the Governor of Illinois after the late riot. The Commission consists of colored men who apparently have a much too complacent trust in their white friends; of white men who are too busy to know; and of enemies of the Negro race who under the guise of impartiality and good will are pushing insidiously but unswervingly a program of racial segregation.
—W. E. B. DuBois, "Chicago," *The Crisis* 21 (January 1921): 102.

THE IMMEDIATE REACTION OF MANY WHITES TO THE RIOT WAS TO DEMAND more rigid segregation. The city's leading business and realty publication, *The Economist*, claimed that there would have been no riot if Chicagoans knew "how to deal with negroes" the way Southerners did. In one of its rare editorials on anything besides business, *The Economist* argued that "the two races should be segregated as to their residence localities just as they are in southern cities." Actually, Chicago could have given Southerners lessons on residential segregation. There was probably no Southern city in which blacks were so segregated as they were in Chicago. *The Economist*'s editors were unaware of their city's achievement. They went on to say that if residential separation of the races did not forestall further "war between white and colored people," then "possibly also we should have jimcrow cars in Chicago." The street fighting had barely subsided when bombers began threatening Negro homeowners again.

The Hyde Park–Kenwood Property Owners' Association stepped up its campaign against "promiscuous scattering of Negroes." There was renewed agitation for a racial zoning law despite the Supreme Court's ruling. The Chicago *Tribune* spoke for most Chicagoans when it insisted that "white and black will not mix."[1]

It was against this background of bloodshed in the streets and shrill insistence on segregation that Governor Frank O. Lowden promised to appoint a biracial commission to study the causes of the rioting. The Chicago Commission on Race Relations, to which Lowden appointed "the best representatives of both races," assembled a large research staff and labored for a year and a half before issuing its massive report. *The Negro in Chicago,* published in the fall of 1922, looked beyond the riot itself and the immediate background of the clash to examine the growth of black Chicago and the uneasy response of white Chicagoans to the "city within a city."[2]

The commissioners could find no "ready remedy" to racial disharmony. They roundly rejected the simplest solution of all, the one that most whites surveyed by the staff favored: "segregation, even to the extent of colonization in Africa." Instead, the commissioners recommended a series of steps that they hoped would lead toward a "just and orderly" adjustment "by each race" to "the other's needs and aims." Among these steps were the protection of blacks using public accommodations, including beaches and streetcars; the extension of social service facilities "to the Negro community"; and the provision of "better Negro housing without segregation."[3]

Set in the context of strident clamoring for intensified segregation, the commission's report reads like a judicious, subtle, but deliberate plea for integration. The men who directed the staff's research and drafted the text of *The Negro in Chicago* were Graham Taylor's son Graham Romeyn Taylor, a social worker and a respected analyst of urban problems, and Charles S. Johnson, the pioneer black sociologist, who was then a student working under Robert Park's tutelage at the University of Chicago. So free is the volume of overt anti-Negro bias that some historians believe it to be not a collaboration but "Johnson's work." Scholars of race relations, struck by the commission's refusal to approve segregation, have concluded that the commissioners were condemning it. Actually, they denounced only "forcible segregation." In doing so, they were not endorsing the goal of a racially integrated Chicago. The commission stood for something quite different: the peaceful accommodation of white Chicago and black Chicago.[4]

Ever since the housing shortage had become critical in 1917, concerned Chicagoans had been searching in vain for a formula for racial compromise that would simultaneously mollify black grievances and relieve white anxieties. The Commission on Race Relations hit upon that formula. Black people needed housing and white people were willing to provide it, but only on the condition that blacks submit to segregation. While Negroes had no objection to living among their "race brothers," they would not settle for second-rate housing, and they refused to surrender their right to live wherever they chose. Whites understood, as the black press observed, that it was "utterly useless" to try to segregate the blacks smoothly and peaceably without the collaboration of the blacks themselves. But efforts to collaborate always broke down. The whites invariably misconstrued the blacks' readiness to discuss the housing problem for willingness to be restricted within "metes and bounds." The Negroes then countered by demanding that the whites renounce the goal of segregation. With that the negotiations would end.[5]

After years of abortive attempts at racial accommodation, the white and black members of the Riot Commission found a way to renounce "segregation" and still respect the universal white phobia against integrated neighborhoods. The postriot clamor for stricter segregation was only half of the context in which the commission operated; the other half was the long-thwarted effort of realtors and black spokesmen to settle their differences over housing.

The first group of whites who tried to strike a bargain with the blacks was the Real Estate Board committee that drew up the 1917 plan to stop blacks from "invading" white areas. The committee members expected "colored citizens" to cooperate with them, as they were dealing with "a financial business proposition and not with white prejudice." They wanted to protect white property from the damage that they were sure "negro occupation" would inflict, but they recognized that the blacks had to have housing. They were looking for some "feasible, practicable, and humane method" to supply Negroes with houses and still keep white neighborhoods white.[6]

Black businessmen and realtors met with the white group to work out an agreement. In deference to the blacks, the white realtors dropped their original scheme to push a segregation ordinance through the city council, and they offered to support a major building program in the Black Belt. Apparently the black realtors left the first meeting convinced that they had won significant concessions from their white counterparts. Accounts in the white press made it clear, however, that the whites were willing to do without a racial zoning law only because they thought that the Negroes had pledged to segregate themselves.[7]

It was incumbent upon the white committeemen to assure the Real Estate Board and the white public generally that any plan they agreed to would restrict the movement of blacks as effectively as legislation could. Accordingly, they reported that the blacks were positively "anxious" to live "by themselves." They attributed the following statement to George H. Jackson, a prominent black realtor, and said it represented the viewpoint of the blacks who met with them:

> We do not want to live in the same block with whites if we can help it, because it is not conducive to our happiness. But we want to live in decent neighborhoods [with] decent homes, good schools, good churches, and on lines of good transportation.

At least one black man at the meeting had said something to that effect, but Jackson, who later served on the Riot Commission, denied that he was the one.[8]

The Negro negotiators were mortified by the story, which the *Tribune* ran under the headline NEGROES OFFER HOUSING SWAP WITH WHITES. Even if the blacks had been willing to forfeit their freedom of residential movement (a freedom they enjoyed in name only), they could not afford to be identified in the press as accomplices to segregation. It would have been a different matter, perhaps, if the whites had quoted them as having said, "We stand by our right to live wherever we choose; it so happens that we choose to live among ourselves, when the accommodations are adequate." As it was, the blacks came out sounding too much like tools of the whites. They had no choice but to attack the whites for misrepresenting their position. Subsequent meetings ended in bitterness on both sides. The whites, confident that the blacks could not turn down the offer of loans, mortgage assistance, and "modern houses and apartments," insisted that the black realtors cooperate with the Real Estate Board to place black clients only in "sections where Negroes predominate." The blacks refused to be parties to a "segregation movement," while the whites chided them for impeding "harmony in housing."[9]

In the fall of 1917, several months after the breakdown of negotiations between the white and black realtors, T. Arnold Hill, secretary of the Chicago Urban League, appealed to the city's business magnates to construct model housing "for negro men and women." Bemoaning the fact that blacks had to pay high rents for housing which whites had discarded, Hill said, "we ought to have houses built for us." This was no demand for unhindered access to developing areas of the city. Hill was asking only that civic-minded capitalists give families "in the negro district" the chance to occupy new dwellings "built especially for them." He couched his request in terms that would not antagonize whites, yet he avoided saying that Negroes wanted segregation.

Nothing came of Hill's appeal. By the time he spoke, Julius Rosenwald had already abandoned his model project for "colored people" as unprofitable, and residential construction was grinding to a standstill. For the next year, blacks and whites battled over the limited housing stock.[10]

In 1919, at the height of the housing conflict, Chicagoans looked forward to the resumption of building and a reduction of interracial tension. Once again blacks and whites considered ways to house blacks without conflict. Resuming T. Arnold Hill's initiative, Charles S. Duke, a civil engineer whom the Riot Commission would later commend as "a well-educated and fair-minded Negro," wrote and circulated a short book with the lengthy title *The Housing Situation and the Colored People of Chicago, with Suggested Remedies and Brief References to Housing Projects Generally*. Duke, who lived in the West Woodlawn enclave, recited the familiar conditions that plagued blacks in search of housing and emphasized the uniqueness of the black housing problem: "the entire colored population," not just "the unfit," were confined to "the slum and the ghetto."[11]

Duke condemned prejudice and said that white Chicago owed it to black citizens to abandon "all attempts at racial segregation." Nevertheless, he managed to win widespread praise from whites who were anxious for a "constructive" resolution of the housing conflict. Duke explained that black families would continue to try moving to areas "where they know their presence is not desired" until the Black Belt had better homes. Agitation on the part of white organizations to segregate blacks simply incited them to test their "freedom of movement." Duke advised the property owners' associations to stop insisting on the segregation of "undesirables" and start investing money in the reconstruction of "those sections where the colored population was most numerous and whence the undesirable newcomer often hailed." If blacks could have "decent living conditions" in the Black Belt and respite from segregationist attacks, they would choose to remain where they were, and white citizens could consider their own communities secure from "the possible presence of colored neighbors."[12]

Unlike T. Arnold Hill of the Urban League, Duke did not look to white investors to solve the housing problem for the blacks. Pure paternalism, he said, would not advance the race. Black businessmen needed the opportunity to develop. Black realtors handled only about one-fourth of all real estate transactions involving blacks, and they wanted a larger share of the business. One of the charges that black participants in the 1917 negotiations with the Real Estate Board's committee had made was that the whites were proposing a realty bonanza in the Black Belt with the intention of excluding "members of the Race" from the profits. Duke argued that the solution of the housing problem would have to be achieved "by the colored people themselves and among themselves." He repeatedly mentioned the Pyramid Building and Loan Association as a likely instrument for transforming "the district most largely occupied by colored people." The Pyramid, founded in February of 1919, was the city's first "colored" building and loan association. Duke's book reads like a brochure for the Pyramid Association, whose president was George H. Jackson, the one black participant of the 1917 meetings who would later serve on the Riot Commission. Jackson probably paid Duke a fee for writing the book.[13]

Duke did not maintain that black entrepreneurs could accomplish a solution without any aid at all. To succeed, he said, they would need the active support of "those large and influential clubs of businessmen and manufacturers of the city who unselfishly concern themselves in all matters that affect Chicago's welfare." "A serious and honest effort must be made on the part of our abler citizenry, both white and colored," Duke insisted, "to develop and beautify our present centers of colored population."[14]

The white response to Duke's book was swift. *The Housing Situation* appeared in April. In May the Cook County Real Estate Board, which, like the Chicago Real Estate Board, barred black realtors from membership, resolved to bring together representatives of the Chicago Real Estate Board, the Association of Commerce, and "other civic organizations" to "cooperate with the leaders of the colored people in working out a suitable method of housing the colored race." A month later the Union League Club's committee on public affairs began "working quietly" to eliminate whatever conditions were to blame for the terror bombing of Negro houses in white territory. The conditions, of course, were the housing shortage in the Black Belt and the refusal of whites to let blacks move out.[15]

White leaders seemed to sense that exclusion and intimidation in themselves would not relieve neighborhood tensions. As the Chicago *Herald Examiner* had remarked just before Duke's book came out:

> One of the things that make a "Chicago Plan" essential is the Negro. It is impossible to put down 80,000 people within the limits that formerly held 25,000 to 40,000. The Negro has to go somewhere; he has to live somewhere; he has to get his recreation somewhere.

In May even the *Tribune* exhorted Chicagoans to find some "common sense" way to house the blacks. In June the newspaper cautioned the Hyde Park–Kenwood Association to avoid tactics that might provoke a "clash." The *Tribune* still saw nothing wrong with a frank avowal of segregation, but it advised the Hyde Parkers to quit calling black people "undesirables."[16]

Some leaders of the Hyde Park–Kenwood Association now claimed that they had favored "conciliation" all along. They hoped that white institutions would make loans to Black Belt residents. If Negroes had a "place to go," the Hyde Parkers were sure, they would "segregate themselves." At an association meeting in Hyde Park one speaker declared:

> It is our duty to help the Negro, to uplift him in his environment, mark you, not ours. But it is not our duty, now mark this, it is not our duty as I see it, nor is it according to the laws of nature for us to live with him as neighbors on a social basis.

With bombs shattering Negro residences at the rate of one every two or three weeks, blacks were looking for an honorable way out of the housing impasse. Even the most antagonistic whites were interested in indulging them, if indulgence could turn back the "colored invasion."[17]

In the spring of 1919 it was clear that some kind of deal was in the offing. In June a group of blacks requested the Bureau of Industrial Housing of the U.S. Department of Labor to give them expert advice on how to get a construction program under way in Chicago. With capable counsel from outside the city, the blacks hoped, they would approach the local "big men" from a position of strength, or at least of minimized weakness. The bureau agreed to help, but the man it assigned to assist the blacks was a former Chicago realtor, Charles Bixby. In 1917, the last time the whites had tried to impose a housing compromise on black realtors, Bixby had been one of the Real Estate Board's chief spokesmen.[18]

Instead of working with the blacks, Bixby immediately called a conference between "the prominent negroes" and representatives of "the prominent white organizations." At the meeting a large group of blacks sat looking on as Bixby turned over the chair to the Real Estate Board's representative, Lewis M. Smith, who proceeded to deliver a lengthy address on "the necessity of properly housing our colored population." Smith was the man who had chaired the Real Estate Board's committee on residential "invasion" in 1917. Upon concluding his remarks, Smith called on Bixby, who proposed the formation of a housing corporation to rehabilitate and rebuild the Black Belt. According to Bixby's account of the meeting, a "majority of the colored people" supported his proposal and agreed to authorize a biracial committee to implement it.[19]

The blacks did not really participate in the conference—they observed it. The whites made the proposal and then signaled the Negroes to approve it. While some blacks balked, most went along. Charles Bixby, who was supposed to be *their* man, was the Real

Estate Board's. This was interracial cooperation with the whites in clear control.

Complying with the decision of this conference, the Urban League appointed black members to a biracial committee, and the City Club appointed the whites. The committee came to nothing. When repeated meetings produced no results—or no results satisfactory to the whites— the committee stopped functioning. Meanwhile, Bixby's tenure with the Department of Labor ended in July. When the rioting broke out at the end of the month, the Real Estate Board and the Association of Commerce hired him to continue working on the Black Belt reconstruction plan. The realtors' and the businessmen's organizations were in charge of the movement to rebuild "the colored district," but the other "prominent white organizations" that had approved Bixby's proposal—the Union League Club, the City Club, and the Chicago Woman's Club—supported the movement wholeheartedly as a "constructive" response to a critical situation.[20]

All of the groups behind the Black Belt plan joined in taking additional constructive action in response to the rioting as well. They sent delegates to a public assembly of concerned citizens who gathered at the Union League Club as the street warfare was winding down. Graham Taylor of Chicago Commons presided over the meeting. The realtors, the business leaders, the industrialists, the professional men, and the club women in attendance united with the city's leading social workers to petition Governor Frank O. Lowden to appoint a blue-ribbon commission to investigate the disorders and recommend ways "to prevent a recurrence." The participants at the Union League Club meeting embodied all the power and prestige of Chicago's elite. They were the sort of people whom Governor Lowden, the millionaire son-in-law of George M. Pullman, knew and trusted. They may have been the only sort of people whose opinion truly mattered to him. The assembly carried great weight. Within three weeks of the appeal the governor announced his appointments to a biracial Commission on Race Relations.[21]

Remarks that Governor Lowden reportedly made to newsmen during the riot indicated that his own solution to racial conflict was remarkably like that of the business leaders. Providing black people with "proper housing and recreation facilities," he said, would eliminate "the cause of rioting." Accordingly, he maintained that "the great necessity" was to improve "the colored belt" and arrange for its orderly expansion. White men working by themselves could not settle "such questions as those of restricted districts," the governor knew. But if they cooperated with "the real leaders of the Negroes," he was confident that they could reach an understanding on which areas "the colored race should occupy" and which areas "would be reserved for the white race." Lowden added that their agreement would have to be "tacit": Official segregation of neighborhoods was unconstitutional, and many blacks objected to the word *segregaton.*[22]

Shortly before Governor Lowden made his appointments to the Riot Commission, the Real Estate Board and the Association of Commerce announced their plan for transforming the Black Belt into "a housing section for colored people that cannot be equaled in any part of the country." The organizations, backed by "some of Chicago's wealthiest men," intended to form a real estate improvement corporation capitalized at $3 million. This corporation would multiply the housing stock in the Black Belt through a program combining conversion of old structures with construction of new ones. By cutting up large apartments into small flats and by replacing "whole blocks" of frame shacks with modern multistory buildings, the corporation could accommodate a great many more people in *the existing* "colored district." More economical use of ground space would eliminate overcrowding and even permit the development of a "high class section" of cottages and apartments within territory already occupied by blacks. Because "industrious Negroes" did not depreciate property when they stayed among their own kind, President Ivan O. Ackley of the Real Estate Board predicted a tidy return on the investors' outlay. "It is not a philanthropic move," Ackley said. "It will be an organization for profit." Besides making money, moreover, the program would "settle the housing problem" and thereby "dispose of 90 percent of the race difficulties."[23]

The plan appealed to business leaders, who now began to estimate the economic damages inflicted by the riot at "easily more than $3,000,000." Building up the Black Belt would *cost less* than withstanding another riot, it would pay a profit, and it would protect white property. The plan also had the support of "leaders in the colored race," or so the Real Estate Board's president claimed.

And the board's president had succeeded in talking about the program at length without saying the word *segregation.*[24]

The Black Belt build-up scheme showed promise, but while Negro leaders did not attack it, they did not acclaim it, either. The Real Estate Board and the Association of Commerce wanted their open endorsement. Late in August, Charles Bixby arranged to meet privately with five "prominent colored people" whom he considered "representative of their race." These black men were: an unnamed officer of what Bixby called "the colored YMCA"; the Urban League's T. Arnold Hill, a longstanding advocate of improved "negro housing"; Charles S. Duke, whose book on housing "the colored people" had favorably impressed white realtors; realtor George H. Jackson, whom Bixby and other white realtors had quoted in 1917 as a proponent of separate sections for black people; Rev. Lacey Kirk Williams of Olivet Baptist Church; and Dr. George Cleveland Hall of Provident Hospital, popularly known as "the Colored people's hospital."[25]

Bixby outlined the reconstruction plan and asked the black men to endorse it. They declined, he said, on the ground that "it would not be wise for them to lend their names to it." But, Bixby claimed, they acknowledged that the plan "would do much good for their district" as well as "stabilize the white districts contiguous to their territory." And he extracted a statement from them to the effect that "the colored man did not want to invade the white districts" if there were "ample sanitary places" in "the colored district." On the basis of that meeting, the white business leaders believed that black leaders supported the program even though they could not embrace it publicly. The support seemed to be authoritative because three of the black men at the meeting—George Jackson, Reverend Williams, and Dr. Hall—had just been named to membership on the Commission on Race Relations. They comprised half of the black representation on the commission.[26]

The promoters of the Black Belt program received additional endorsements at the end of August, when the coroner's jury and the grand jury issued their reports on the rioting. Both juries believed that the blacks "would voluntarily segregate themselves" if provided with "proper housing." The grand jury stated that "the present neighborhood known as the 'Black Belt' could . . . be made a decent place to live in for a much larger population than it now accommodates" with the help of "leading public citizens." And the coroner's jury named the Real Estate Board and the property owners' associations as the appropriate citizens' groups to "attack" the housing situation.[27]

In the fall the program's sponsors broadened its scope to include housing for white workingmen as well as for "colored." The building corporation now planned to engage in two separate undertakings: rehabilitation of the *existing* "colored" areas to accommodate the "colored population," and home construction in new subdivisions to help the "foreign-born population" disperse from the old congested districts. Segregation was still the essence of the plan.[28]

The Hyde Park–Kenwood Association endorsed the plan with enthusiasm and with its characteristic lack of tact. Association officers invited black property owners to a parley in October and asked them if a $3 million program would be a sufficient inducement to get Negroes to leave Hyde Park–Kenwood "exclusively to the white population." When the officers told newsmen that the blacks had offered to keep "to themselves" in exchange for "suitable quarters," Negro realtor and politician Oscar De Priest retorted that black people would never agree to surrender their rights for a few million dollars in mortgages.[29]

Then, one night in November, handbills titled "Every Colored Person Must Leave Hyde Park" turned up on the doorsteps of black people living on the contested streets that bordered Hyde Park. The message was this:

> We colored people are no longer wanted in the district by the whites. We have been invited to move into that district [the Black Belt] as outlined by the Chicago Association of Commerce, with the knowledge of Gov. Lowden. . . . White people have always taken good care of us and in return let us show our appreciation by segregating ourselves.

The *Defender* traced the handbill, which was signed "Colored Housing Committee," to John P. Bowles, the treasurer of the Hyde Park–Kenwood Association. Bowles, a livestock commissioner, lived just west of Kenwood, on the 4300 block of Vincennes, which was starting to "go colored." Like many officials of the association, he was a Catholic and therefore free to live wherever he could pay the going rate. Shortly after Bowles wrote this note, he moved into Kenwood;

a few years later he moved to 6840 South Shore Drive, an exclusive apartment house opposite the South Shore Country Club, of which he was a member.[30]

The support of aggressive segregationists did not discredit the program to rebuild the Black Belt. Some of the most prominent businessmen in the city assumed direction of the corporation organized to carry out the scheme. The eleven directors, all white, were:

Harry H. Merrick—president, Chicago Association of Commerce

Louis T. Jamme—vice-president, Chicago Association of Commerce

Ivan O. Ackley—president, Chicago Real Estate Board

Byron Kanaley—president, Mortgage Bankers' Association

Frederick W. Upham—president, Consumers Company

B. F. Affleck—president, Universal Portland Cement Company

Herman Hettler—president, Hettler Lumber Company

W. R. Abbott—general manager, Illinois Bell Telephone Co. (by 1922 he would be president)

Col. Nathan William MacChesney—past president of the Illinois Bar Association, counsel for National Association of Real Estate Boards and Chicago Real Estate Board (eight years later, in 1927, he would draft Chicago's model restrictive-covenant form)

Col. Abel Davis—vice-president, Chicago Title and Trust Co., and member, Chicago Plan Commission

Harry Eugene Kelly—lawyer, director of Union League Club

Six or more of these men were Protestants, as befitted so influential a group. But at least two directors were not: Byron Kanaley was a Catholic, and Colonel Davis was Jewish.[31]

The corporation began meeting in November, at about the time that the Riot Commission started deliberating in earnest. All of the corporation's directors were pillars of propriety, well-to-do and civic-minded. Two of the men were deeply involved in the work of the Riot Commission. Colonel Abel Davis acted as fund-raiser and treasurer for the commission, which had to depend on the largesse of businessmen because it had no budget of its own. And Harry Eugene Kelly, the development corporation's vice-president, was one of the *members* of the commission.[32]

Governor Lowden appointed the Riot Commission in the interests of interracial peace. He viewed segregation as a means of keeping the peace, much as Chicago businessmen viewed it as a means of protecting property. Lowden understood, better than the realtors did, the importance of forswearing segregation *de verbo* in any movement to solidify it *de facto*. His mistake was in announcing his insight to newspaper reporters, who may have attributed somewhat blunter language to him than he actually used. The governor's embarrassment was minor, in any event. The *Broad Ax*, a black newspaper with a small and dwindling circulation, lambasted him, but the number one "race" publication, the *Defender*, made no mention of his remarks, and blacks raised no general uproar. Lowden named Robert S. Abbott, the *Defender*'s owner, publisher, and editor, to the Riot Commission. Abbott proved helpful in minimizing embarrassment to the commission later on. There was widespread and persistent suspicion among blacks that the commission would recommend a program of segregation, even compulsory segregation, but the *Defender* ignored it, except to dismiss it.[33]

In January 1920 the *Broad Ax* exposed one of the white commissioners, William Scott Bond, as an executive of the Hyde Park–Kenwood Property Owners' Association. Bond, a prominent Real Estate Board member who resided in Hyde Park, explained that the Property Owners' Association had used his name without permission, and he compelled them to strike it from their roster. Whether or not he had been a *member*, as distinct from an officer, of the association, Bond did not say. Nor did he state whether he supported the Real Estate Board's stand against "colored invasion." And the *Defender* did not ask him. It accepted his disclaimer without question.[34]

The story about Bond broke at a time when terrorists were throwing bombs at an unprecedented rate and the Hyde Park–Kenwood Association's pronouncements were growing more bellicose. In February two members of the commission, one black, one white, went before the City Club to warn its members of the dangers of destructive tactics. The black commissioner was Dr. George Cleveland Hall (one of those who had conferred with Charles Bixby on rehabilitating the Black Belt). Dr. Hall explained that blacks, infuriated by "the lawless aggressions" of the property owners' associations, had formed an organization to defend themselves. If the lawlessness did not stop, Hall declared, the white and black groups were bound to clash. Francis W. Shepardson, the white commissioner, contrasted the dangerous opposition of the racial organizations with the "constructive" collaboration of the biracial commission. Shepardson, a former University of Chicago history professor, was an aide to Governor Lowden and the acting chairman of the commission. He had selected the other commissioners for Lowden: He could speak with an air of authority. He assured the audience that racial conflict would subside if housing, recreation, and community agencies in "Negro residential areas" could be brought up to par with facilities in "white residential areas."[35]

Shepardson described the plight of the "respectable" black family unable to escape the "vicious" slum environment. "Segregation that throws all negroes into one vicious neighborhood," he said, was unsatisfactory. What he advocated in its place was "intelligent segregation that will permit the negro [i.e., the respectable, middle-class black] to live among his own kind whom he prefers [i.e., other middle-class blacks]." Driving home his point, Shepardson said:

> The negro does not desire to scatter himself over the entire city. But he desires a clean place to live. It is up to us to evolve ways of making his section of the city clean.

The *Defender* maintained a discreet silence about Shepardson's speech. The white press reacted favorably. The *Daily News,* whose owner-publisher, Victor Lawson, was on the Riot Commission, ran an account of it under the headline REBUILD "BLACK BELT," PLAN OF RACE BOARD. The headline echoed the title that the *News* had placed over its glowing report of the initial announcement by the Real Estate Board and the Association of Commerce: REBUILD "BLACK BELT," REALTY MEN'S PLAN. The verbal coincidence could not have been more apposite.[36]

Shepardson's solution to Chicago's race conflict was the same as Governor Lowden's: separation of the races. Except for his use of the term "segregation," however, Shepardson came very close to paraphrasing the position Charles Duke had taken in his book on housing for "colored people." And weeks before Shepardson spoke, black Alderman Louis B. Anderson had restated the black position, reducing it to the absolute minimum. Anderson made the obligatory reference to Negro rights. The black man, he said, had "the same right" to live in a modern apartment building as the white man, provided he was "financially able." But the alderman went on to say that "most Negroes would prefer to live in a district exclusively inhabited by people of their own Race." Going further, he said, "The Colored man has no desire to mix indiscriminately with the whites, but he must have a roof over his head."[37]

Alderman Anderson explained that "the colored man," contrary to the apprehensions of white people, was not "desirous of intruding himself upon the Caucasian." But there were so few "decent, sanitary flats" in the Black Belt that "colored families" were "compelled" to seek quarters "in so-called white neighborhoods." The implication was clear. Blacks would settle for separate housing if it was attractive and if it was not forced on them outright. In the same statement, Alderman Anderson denounced the Hyde Park–Kenwood Association. The alderman published his views in Riot Commissioner Abbott's newspaper, the *Defender.* Apparently he was trying to flash a signal to the commission.[38]

Shepardson and the other white commissioners eventually got the message that people like Duke, Alderman Anderson, and several of the black commissioners had been trying to transmit for years. In its final report, the commission studiously avoided commending segregation (even as the Black Belt reconstruction corporation had evaded using the term in its prospectus). The commission condemned segregation by "force" or by "proscription" (just as Shepardson had criticized unintelligent segregation). It then went on to recommend segregation without calling it by name.[39]

The power structure that summoned the Riot Commission into existence, dominated its deliberations, and paid its expenses was the same power structure that took upon itself the task of building up the Black Belt to make it hold all of black Chicago. As sociologist Arthur Waskow has written, the commission "ended, as it had begun, in the hands and with the support of the most substantial, powerful, and honored men of the city." But these men supported the commission's recommendations not only because they feared future riots, as Waskow concludes, but also because the recommendations were compatible with their own designs for black Chicago. And the recommendations bore the stamp of approval of several leading Negro citizens.[40]

The commission exposed the industrial exploitation of Negroes, detailed the extent of job discrimination, and urged capital and labor alike to give blacks "an equal chance with whites." This was something that Chicagoans had never been willing to do, but it was something that responsible people acknowledged ought to be done. Even the *Tribune*—in its editorial against "mixing" white and black— said that the races should "live socially distinct but industrially cooperative." The commission exposed discrimination in government institutions and in public facilities—discrimination that the laws of Illinois forbade—and the commissioners came out for compliance with the laws. Yet *The Negro in Chicago* did not criticize private institutions that provided separate facilities for blacks; in fact, it commended their example to organizations that did not serve blacks at all. And the commissioners did not advocate integrated housing and integrated neighborhoods.[41]

The commissioners suggested that economic discrimination had prevented Negroes from "using their own capital" to solve "their own housing problem." The implication was that integrating blacks economically would help them to segregate themselves residentially. The commissioners drew a distinction between areas of "adjustment," where Negroes could live undisturbed, and areas of "opposition," which they could not enter without resistance. By favoring "adjusted" areas over "contested" districts, the commissioners *seemed*, at some points in the text, to be approving mixed neighborhoods, "in which whites and Negroes have become accommodated to each other." In fact the so-called adjusted neighborhoods were not mixed communities at all but instead were ghettos inside larger districts (black Englewood, black Morgan Park, the great Black Belt itself) or ghetto borderlands where expansion "was ultimately looked upon as . . . natural and expected" (areas in the process of being added to the ghetto). The commissioners endorsed not integration but extension of the ghetto—if and when necessary—"without friction or disorder." While the report detailed the violent activities of the property owners' associations, it was silent about the long segregation campaign of the Real Estate Board. Along with its statements against intimidation and bombing, the commission was restating, in careful, coded language, the more candid resolutions of the realtors.[42]

The commissioners worded their recommendation on housing with the utmost care:

> Our inquiry has shown that insufficiency in amount and quality of housing is an all-important factor in Chicago's race problem; there must be more and better housing to accommodate the great increase in Negro

> population. . . . This situation will be made worse by methods tending toward *forcible* segregation or exclusion of Negroes, such as the circulation of threatening statements and propaganda by organizations or persons to prevent Negroes from living in certain areas, and the lawless and perilous bombing of houses occupied by Negroes or by whites suspected of encouraging Negro residence in the district.
>
> We therefore recommend that all white citizens energetically discourage these futile, pernicious, and lawless practices, and either cooperate in or start movements to solve the housing problem by *constructive* and not destructive methods. [Italics added.]

Held against the background of the long effort to settle the housing dispute, the statement is easy to decipher. It was not segregation the commissioners condemned but *forcible* segregation, and the solution they urged was not open housing but better *Negro* housing. This, in essence, was the same solution the grand jury and the coroner's jury had recommended. And it was just what Riot Commissioner Harry E. Kelly and his fellow directors in the Black Belt construction corporation had promised to provide: buildings, not bombings; better houses for Negroes, in Negro areas; and better houses for whites, in white areas. This was constructive, but it was a dual solution.[43]

W. E. B. DuBois, the vigilant editor of the NAACP's journal, *The Crisis*, had charged that the Riot Commission included "enemies of the Negro race" who would push "insidiously but unswervingly" for "a program of segregation." But the seven white commissioners all professed deep friendship for "the Negro." Five of these men were active promoters of "Negro betterment." Kelly, as mentioned, was a leader in the campaign to build up the Black Belt. Edward Osgood Brown was president of the NAACP's Chicago chapter. Edward Addison Bancroft and Julius Rosenwald were both trustees of Tuskegee Institute. Rosenwald, moreover, was the nation's premier donor to Negro institutions. And Francis Shepardson's suggestions for solving "the Negro problem" so impressed Rosenwald that the philanthropist personally picked him to take over the direction of the Rosenwald Fund in 1921.[44]

DuBois's indictment was wrong, but only in one particular: The men who were pushing for segregation were *friends* of the Negro race. With such friends, blacks might have felt, they had no need of enemies. But if the white commissioners *had* been enemies, the riot report would have been a very different document.

As it was, the report presented a detailed picture of the wretched conditions under which "the entire population, good and bad," lived in the Black Belt. It exposed in relentless detail the full ferocity of the white onslaught against families who tried "to secure better living conditions." It avoided recommending compulsory segregation and only hinted that blacks would readily segregate themselves. From start to finish the report dealt with the problems of black people seriously, and it paid respect to their aspirations. *The Negro in Chicago* is not the book that Charles S. Johnson would have written on his own, but his scholarship informed the text and made it a sociological classic. Johnson educated and influenced his collaborator Taylor and the white commissioners, and he strengthened the black commissioners in their effort to wrest every concession they could from their white counterparts.[45]

All seven of the white members of the commission endorsed the giant study. Only one of the six black commissioners, attorney Edward H. Morris, declined to do so. The white commissioners all wanted what was "best for the Negro," and like most men of their position in society, they were confident that they knew what was best. At least three of these men—William Scott Bond, Francis Shepardson, and Julius Rosenwald—lived in Hyde Park–Kenwood. They knew how much Negro freedom white people could tolerate. The white commissioners approved the report because it did not actually overstep the limits of white tolerance. The black commissioners went along with it because the analysis and recommendations reached all the way to the outermost limits of white tolerance.

Given the desperate need for more and better housing, on the one hand, and the pervasiveness of white hostility to Negro neighbors, on the other—two conditions that the report documented definitively—the black commissioners were in no position to get any biracial group to come out unequivocally for the freedom of black families to live wherever they chose. No local group with white membership, including the NAACP and the Urban League, had ever demanded more on behalf of Chicago's Negroes than the Riot Commission did. That was enough to make the commission's recommendations, if not altogether satisfactory, at least acceptable to most blacks. The dual solution was the only constructive one being offered.

CHAPTER 10 ❧

Garden Homes: A Project for "White People"

The colored man is asked to live decently and keep clean when all the conditions are against him.
—Benjamin J. Rosenthal, *Reconstructing America Sociologically and Economically* (Chicago, 1919), p. 28.

He does not ask you to take him into your home and entertain him,— you have a right to select your social acquaintances,—but he does ask that he be given the right to live respectably and comfortably. . . .
—Ibid., p. 29.

THE GRAND PLAN TO RECONSTRUCT THE BLACK BELT DID NOT MATERIALIZE. By the time *The Negro in Chicago* was published in 1922, the corporation organized to do the job existed only on paper. It had not built or remodeled a single building. There were two reasons for this. First, Illinois law limited the operations of real estate improvement corporations to building *new* structures on *vacant* land. There was no way under the law for a corporation to repair or demolish buildings; it could acquire only vacant tracts, not built-up properties. The Black Belt and bordering strips were practically devoid of vacant space, and the corporation's backers had no intention of opening up land in outlying areas to "colored." The corporation was going to build for blacks on cleared land in the Black Belt or it was not going to build for them at all. When attempts to amend the law in the 1921 legislative session failed, the plan to provide "better Negro housing" was doomed.[1]

Even if the legal obstacle had been removed, there was another factor that would have blocked the reconstruction program. The building boom that began in 1921 eased the housing crisis, allowing the Black Belt to expand into adjacent areas as whites abandoned them. From the standpoint of white real-estate interests, the need for a Black Belt program was no longer pressing. The corporation dropped its plan to develop subdivisions for white workingmen as well. With a full-scale boom under way, building new homes for lower-paid workers was not feasible (increased construction costs put new houses beyond their reach) and building model housing for better-paid workers was neither necessary (the regular real estate market was supposed to take care of them) nor acceptable (competition against the regular market violated the business creed). So the corporation did nothing—for blacks or for whites, either.

Although the Real Estate Board–Association of Commerce corporation accomplished nothing, another real estate improvement corporation closely associated with it succeeded in erecting a model housing project for "white people" in 1919–20, before the building boom began. This project, Garden Homes, was Chicago's first model housing enterprise. Five of the eleven directors of the unproductive realtor-merchant corporation also served as directors of the corporation that built Garden Homes. The man who conceived the project, Benjamin J. Rosenthal, played a key role in launching the Black Belt reconstruction program. Garden Homes also had ties with the Riot Commission. Several people connected with the project attended the meeting that petitioned Governor Lowden to appoint the commission. The Riot Commission's treasurer, Col. Abel Davis, handled Garden Homes' finances. And one of the principal patrons of the project was Riot Commissioner Julius Rosenwald.

Benjamin J. Rosenthal, the man responsible for the construction of Garden Homes, was a wealthy Chicago businessman with a wide range of merchandising, realty, banking, and investment interests. A Reform Jew who leaned toward Christian Science, he belonged to all of the proper businessmen's commercial and civic associations, and he shared the meager reform goals of progressive businessmen: law and order, and honest, efficient, economical government. But Rosenthal had broader goals that the common run of moneybags progressives did not share.[2]

In his book *Reconstructing America Sociologically and Economically*, published early in 1919, he advocated a nationally enforced minimum wage (a "living wage" plus "a margin of safety") and government-supported systems of compulsory insurance. A businessman at bottom (the paramount need of America, he believed, was a merchant marine second to none in the world), he justified the reforms he favored in conservative terms. Social justice was the only sure defense against "bolshevism"; good wages would sustain "good times"; paying labor a living wage would boost industrial production and reduce the costs of maintaining "jails and hospitals and insane asylums." [3]

A Wilsonian Democrat who harbored none of Woodrow Wilson's conscious antipathy for blacks, Rosenthal asked capitalists to give "the colored man" an equal chance in industry. "If you will not do it in the name of humanity," he urged, "then do it in the name of economy, for it is an economical essential, that everybody be given the opportunity to produce the best he can. . . ." Rosenthal believed that workmen, black and white, needed good housing. A worker "crowded in a badly ventilated, badly lighted, unclean house in a congested neighborhood," he argued, could not be "efficient" on the job. He went so far as to suggest that if trade unions or "public-spirited citizens" did not supply adequate housing, then "the government itself" might have to. Rosenthal entertained radical measures, but his goals were conservative. A decent home for every worker, he believed, would be an antidote to industrial unrest.[4]

In the spring and summer of 1919, Rosenthal sought support for a plan to build model housing on a massive scale. He wanted to make provisions for Chicago's "more poorly paid people who [were] badly housed," especially Poles, Lithuanians, and Italians. "The foreign population," he told potential investors, lived in "filth and squalor." Moreover, the immigrants were "segregated . . . and exploited by their coreligionists." Their isolation kept them ignorant of American institutions. Rosenthal thought that housing these people properly would be a way to Americanize as well as to shelter them. He contemplated several large projects. "People of various nationalities" would live in each of them. One of his main objects was to break down ethnic isolation. He had no intention of building separate projects for Italians, Poles, Jews, and so on. He wanted to mix the ethnic groups and encourage them to mingle as much as possible. Model homes, he hoped, would improve the "physical and moral well-being" of the people, teach them thrift, make them "loyal to our country's flag," increase their "efficiency," and render them "happy, contented wage-earning people." [5]

Rosenthal's goals were nothing if not ambitious. He envisioned ten thousand homes in forty to fifty developments of two hundred to three hundred houses each. He intended to buy vacant land and develop it; recover the purchase price by selling lots along the periphery for business purposes; and eliminate "waste, water, profit, and overhead expense" by buying materials in large orders paid for in cash and by organizing his own labor force. Then he would construct attractive but cheap homes for sale at cost over long terms. Finally, as the development returned the original investment, he would select new sites and begin anew. To prevent "speculative dealing," Rosenthal would exercise first option when a workman wished to sell his home. If the worker had not finished paying for his house, he would get back the total amount he had paid. If he owned it outright, he could sell it back at the market price. In this way, "the benefits of increased values would be bestowed on the persistent man who sticks to his determination to become a home owner." [6]

Rosenthal planned to choose the foreign workers who would inhabit his projects with the advice of "the settlement house workers in the badly housed districts." He wanted to be sure to reach the people who needed the housing most. Married men with two or more children would get preference. The settlement workers would inspect the dwellings of all applicants. No workman would be allowed to purchase one of the new houses unless the "expert investigators" certified that his present home was "unfit for family life." The new homes would sell for $3,500 to $4,000, although they would be worth considerably more. The workingmen, though ill-housed and low-paid, would have to be able to make down payments of $350 to $400 and then pay as much as $20 monthly. A worker who made his payments regularly could own his home clear of encumbrance in fifteen years. In the meantime, his payments would have provided him with fire, health, and unemployment insurance as well as life insurance equal to the unpaid portion of his house, "so that in the event of death, the estate of the deceased will receive the home." [7]

It was not too difficult for Rosenthal to rally supporters round his cause. His plan reflected a sentiment dear to "housers," realtors, and Americans generally: The home should be a house. The ideal of the National Housing Association was "A City of Homes," and homes meant single-family dwellings on individual plots owned by their occupants. At the end of the world war, the U.S. Department of Labor launched an Own Your Own Home campaign in which builders and realtors across the nation enlisted. Both the Chicago and Cook County realtors' boards had Own Your Own Home committees, and Rosenthal took pains to assure them that his program would not conflict with theirs. "We are in no way in competition with realtors," he explained. His program would supplement the general Own Your Own Home campaign by building for "a class of workers who would never be reached by the average real estate developer." Not only would his plan not invade the field of commercial realtors, Rosenthal claimed, it would actually "stimulate the general home-buying movement." [8]

In July, when Rosenthal announced the formation of the Chicago Housing Association "To Improve Housing Conditions in Chicago and to Encourage Small Wage-Earners to Acquire and Own Their Homes," he had the blessing of the realtors. Most of the association's members were major figures in commerce, industry, finance, and construction. The association also included some of Chicago's "best known social workers": settlement leaders Mary McDowell, Graham Taylor, and Harriet Vittum, and University of Chicago social work professor Sophonisba P. Breckenridge. Labor had one representative, Simon O'Donnell, the president of the powerful Building Trades Council. And the membership of Charles E. Wacker, chairman of the Chicago Plan Commission, imparted a kind of civic seal of approval to the undertaking.[9]

Eight individuals and companies joined Rosenthal in underwriting the expenses of the association and its holding company, the Chicago Real Estate Improvement Corporation. Together they advanced $600,000 to the corporation on the understanding that they would get their money back, plus 6 percent interest, once the corporation had succeeded in marketing its stocks and bonds. Among the financial backers were employers of thousands of foreign workers living in the wretchedly housed Back a' the Yards district: Morris and Company, Swift and Company, J. Ogden Armour, and Thomas

E. Wilson, the major meat packers, and William Wrigley, Jr., whose chewing-gum factory and warehouse were half a mile north of the Yards. Of all the workingmen, those whom Rosenthal wanted to help most of all were the men who toiled for the big packers in the slaughterhouses.[10]

Acclaim for the program was not quite unanimous. Millionaire philanthropist Julius Rosenwald had misgivings and invested only reluctantly. Rosenthal contended that the proposition was neither commercial nor charitable. The workers would buy the homes at cost, but they would pay for what they received, and the cost would include interest due the investors. Rosenwald rejected this notion of "mixing business and philanthropy." He particularly disliked Rosenthal's plan to let settlement workers screen prospective buyers and pick out "the proper persons" for the projects. "This being a business proposition," Rosenwald argued, "it would be a mistake to even attempt to select the people who are to occupy these homes." Somewhat grudgingly, Rosenwald matched Rosenthal's outlay of $100,000. Although he was willing to risk his money, he would not risk his reputation. Rosenwald declined membership in the Chicago Housing Association, and he refused to let Rosenthal mention his name in connection with the program.[11]

Mary McDowell was dubious on two counts. Like many settlement workers, she was troubled by the foreign workman's lust for a house and lot of his own. The thrift that a man imposed on his family in order to buy a home was not always "a blessing," she thought. "Too often" it was "a curse to the family and not good for the community." Moreover, her dismal experience with the model tenement Back a' the Yards was a fresh memory. And the business magnates with whom she had been unable to cooperate before—the meat packers—were playing a major role in this project. Miss McDowell agreed to serve on the Chicago Housing Association's "advisory social service committee" despite her misgivings.[12]

The site Rosenthal picked for his first housing demonstration was on the South Side in the sparsely settled Chatham area. He managed to acquire forty acres of muddy prairie land at the submarket price of $2,000 an acre. The tract, between State Street and Indiana below 87th Street, was the northern half of a parcel whose southern boundary was a tremendous train embankment combining the tracks of three freight railway lines. The tracks ran beneath the site and then turned northward, thus flanking it on two sides, south and west, at a distance of two blocks. The land in between, like most of the surrounding territory, was unoccupied. Built-up Chatham, which Rosenthal perceived to be on the verge of a boom, was several blocks to the north and east. Rosenthal never mentioned the railroad tracks and the unused industrial property when he talked about his project. He pictured Garden Homes as part of the expanded residential Chatham of the future.[13]

Planning for Garden Homes was still in its preliminary stages when the race riot broke out at the end of July. The rioting forced Rosenthal to consider what his association should do about Negro housing. At first he thought it would be enough to build some future project for "Negro families" provided the "initial demonstration" proved successful. But now the words he had written in *Reconstructing America* came back to haunt him: "Colored people," compelled by "prejudice" to "live in a prescribed district," suffered "the worst housing conditions." If that were true, what justification was there for giving *whites* first priority? Moreover, Garden Homes was supposed to be for steel workers and packinghouse laborers, and one-fourth or more of all black men who had jobs worked at the mills or the Yards. Again, what excuse was there for making Garden Homes a *white* project? Troubled, confused, Rosenthal sounded out Graham Taylor of Chicago Commons settlement house on "the advisability of selling to colored people only" instead of "to white people as originally intended." Significantly, Rosenthal did not raise the possibility of admitting whites and blacks alike, on the basis of need. The occupants of Garden Homes would be "white people" or "colored people only": The third alternative probably did not even occur to him.[14]

Graham Taylor's response was cautious. Negroes "certainly needed it most," he said, and building houses was a "constructive" response to "race strife." However, he did not know if the 87th Street location was "well adapted for a negro population." Any "new residential districts for negroes," he said, should be placed where they would not "arouse race antagonism." Taylor believed that it would be unwise "to scatter the negro population" unless it could be done "without mixing the races." The day he wrote his reply to

Rosenthal's inquiry, Taylor (who had presided over the meeting that petitioned the governor to appoint a Riot Commission) wrote a column on the riots for the Chicago *Daily News.* The "first need" of the city's Negroes, he said in that column, was "adequate and decent housing." [15]

While physical planning for Garden Homes proceeded, Rosenthal began to work closely with the men who were drawing up the Black Belt reconstruction program. He was probably responsible for altering that program to include the development of white subdivisions along with construction of "decent houses for colored people in a section which is congenial to them." A spokesman for the Association of Commerce announced that the Black Belt housing corporation would "cooperate closely" with Rosenthal's group, and the *Daily News* reported that Rosenthal was ready to "merge" his project with the Black Belt program.[16]

Now Julius Rosenwald became apprehensive. The site for Garden Homes was four miles south of the Black Belt, and therefore not "congenial" to black occupancy, but by coincidence it was nearby the small black community called Lilydale, which was on the other side of the railroad embankment (see Maps 10.1 and 10.2). Evidently, Rosenwald feared that Rosenthal might consider the proximity of the project to Lilydale as justification for making it "colored." Rosenthal assured Rosenwald that Garden Homes would be for whites. Rosenthal remained interested in both the "plan for the black belt" and his own project, but he knew that it would be improper to merge the two. "They will not mix," he promised. He did not tell Rosenwald that he had already agreed to become a director of the Black Belt rebuilding corporation. Later he turned down the directorship with the explanation that it "might hurt his project." Four of the directors of the Chicago Housing Association did go ahead and accept directorships on the Black Belt corporation in November. With the confusion cleared up, Julius Rosenwald did not object.[17]

Several black families, misled by the publicity about a merger of the white and black programs, applied for places in Garden Homes. They were informed that the area was not "congenial" to them. One white couple who applied for a home demanded Rosenthal's personal pledge to refuse admittance to "colored." The couple lived at the Beveridge Apartments at 26th and Calumet, an area that

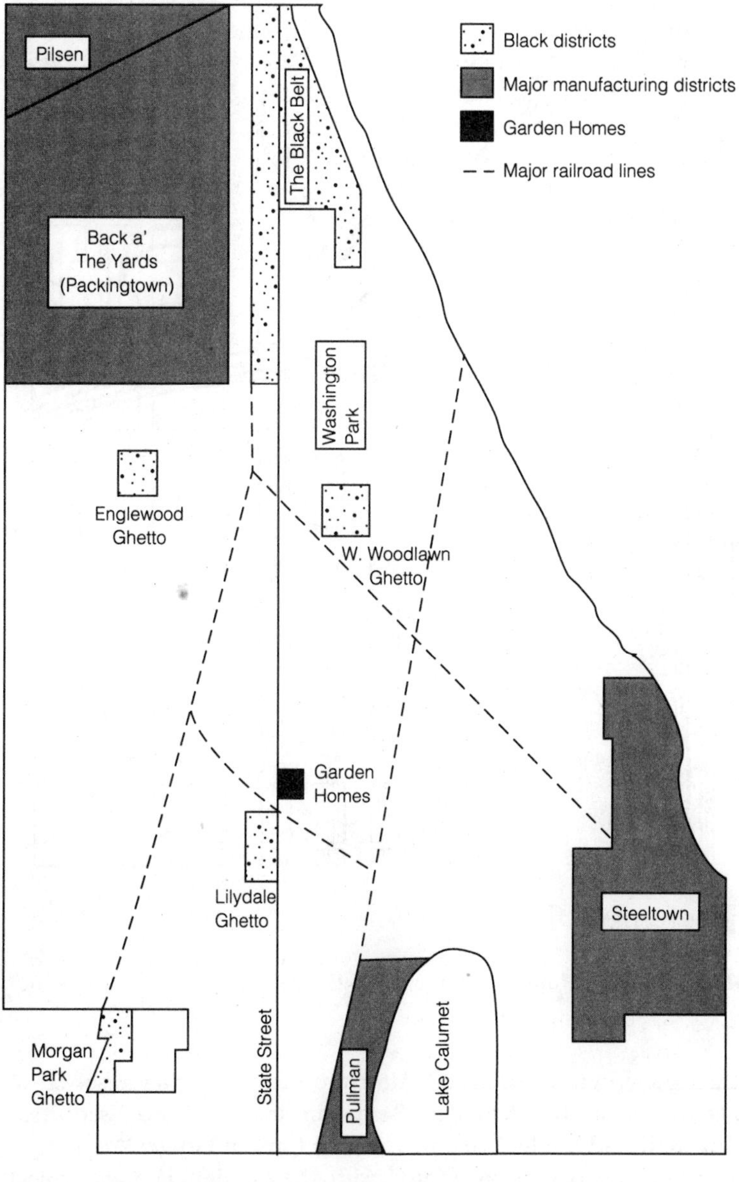

MAP 10.1. **Location of Garden Homes.**

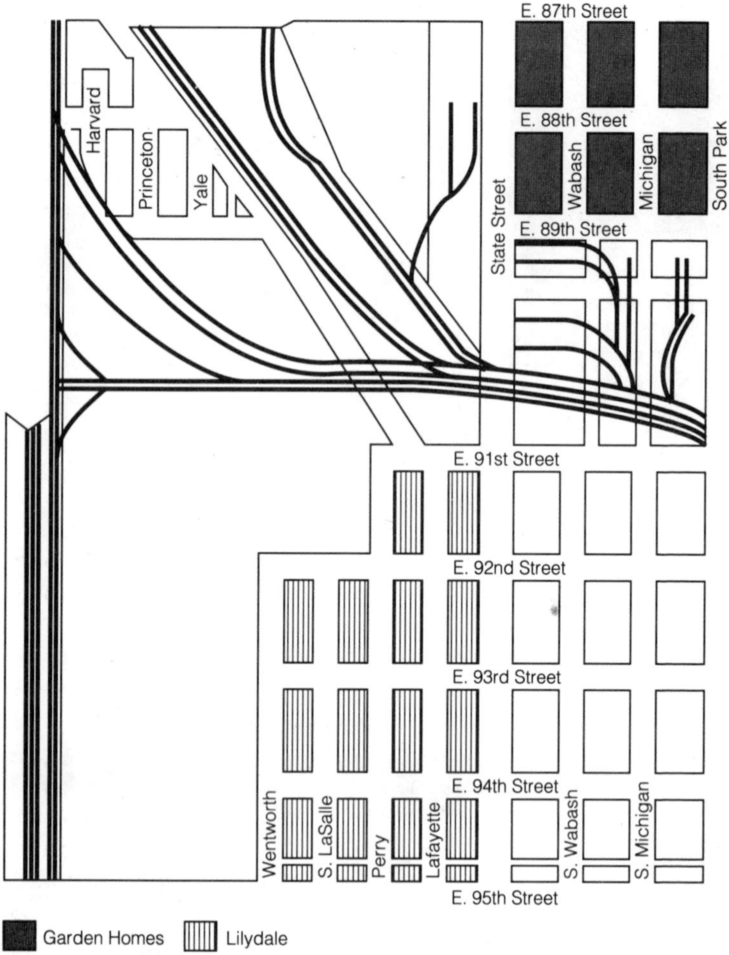

MAP 10.2. Garden Homes (base map: *Olcott's*, 1933).

"had gone over to colored." After the race riots, they resolved to get away from the Black Belt. Benjamin Rosenthal promised them that he would not let black people into Garden Homes.[18]

All of the people associated with the Garden Homes project were white, and most of them were businessmen. It is not surprising that the consensus was to exclude Negroes. The striking fact is that the consensus was unanimous. Rosenthal failed to get a single word of support when he suggested the possibility of making Garden Homes "colored." The social workers and the one businessman who had a national reputation for benevolence toward black people joined the others in discouraging him. Originally, Julius Rosenwald had urged Rosenthal to sell the homes "to anyone who wants to buy them," because business was supposed to be business. Clearly, Rosenwald had not meant anyone who was black.[19]

In the autumn of 1919, once it was settled that the workingmen of Garden Homes would be white, work on the project began. Rosenthal had intended to build 250 houses, but to keep the enterprise within safe economic limits, he scaled the number down, first to 225, then to 200, finally to 175. The plan, which the architect drew up at a nominal fee, called for 133 detached bungalows and 21 duplexes—154 buildings with 175 dwelling units. The street pattern was a simple gridiron dividing the acreage into six square blocks (see Map 10.2). All of the houses were on Wabash Avenue, Michigan, and the west side of Indiana, leaving the lots along State Street and 87th free for business use.[20]

With this stark layout, the overall plan could not claim to be innovative, but this was not a serious defect. In a way its very ordinariness was an asset: To the extent that Garden Homes looked like just another subdivision, its occupants were spared the stigma often attached to project dwellers. The building and lot plans allowed for amenities as well as necessities. Although there was a uniform floor plan, there were seven different exterior designs to prevent "sameness of appearance" while ensuring "artistic unity." The houses, some made of brick, some stuccoed, were all fireproof. They all had five rooms: a living room and dining-kitchen area on the ground floor, three bedrooms upstairs, plus a bathroom on the upper floor and a basement equipped with washtubs and furnace. Every room had direct access to air and sunlight. The lots were 30 feet wide and 162.5 to 200 feet deep. "This provision of lots of unusual depth," wrote the editor of *Real Estate News*, "is a striking feature of the plan, which looks to encouraging home gardening on a considerable scale." The plan included installation of utilities, grading—but not paving—of the streets, and considerable landscaping. The work crew planted shrubs and trees in the parkways, privet hedges along the sidewalks, flowers and decorative shrubs about each porch, and poplar trees in all of the backyards.[21]

For a workingman to be able to buy a house in such a subdivision for $3,500 to $4,000 would have been a great bargain. However, the poorly paid foreign worker with $400 to put down for a house was a rarity. Moreover, Garden Homes was four miles from the steel mills, six miles from the stockyards, and nine miles from the factories that fringed the downtown area. To live at Garden Homes, the worker would have to have been able to afford a daily round trip on the streetcar, a trip that would have lengthened his already oppressively long workday.[22]

As it turned out, the houses sold for considerably more than $4,000. Rosenthal cut expenses wherever he could, sometimes obtaining 50 percent discounts on materials that were zooming in cost, but weather delays and climbing labor costs drove the price of the houses persistently upward. By the spring of 1920 it was clear that the houses could not sell for less than $4,200. Any prospective resident would need to have "a fairly good income," Harriet Vittum informed the members of her applicant-screening committee. She made no direct reference to the obvious problem, that the purpose of the project was to house low-income families. As the weeks went by, expenses continued to mount. Instead of recruiting immigrants in need of Americanization, the Chicago Housing Association advertised the project in the English-language newspapers only and promised first consideration to American citizens. Over a thousand families applied, but the social workers' committee did not screen their applications or inspect their current lodgings. Rosenthal and his building manager interviewed the applicants and made all of the decisions. As a rule they picked the people with the highest incomes.[23]

By mid-August 1920, Rosenthal had completed the selection process and the first families moved into Garden Homes, but they still did not know exactly how much they would have to pay for their new houses. None of the buildings was actually completed. Those on Wabash and most of those on Michigan required little more than finishing touches, but considerable work remained to be done on most of the thirty-five houses on Indiana. Rosenthal assured the first settlers that they would not have to pay more than $5,300, but when the contracts were finally drawn up in September the price was $5,700, with $570 to be paid down and over $42 in monthly installments thereafter. All of the settlers were stunned by the amount, yet all but a few signed. "What the hell else could we do?" one of them said over four decades later. "Where else was there to go? No place. Christ!" [24]

The project did provide 175 houses for families who probably could not have bought them otherwise, at least for so little as $5,700. But it did not noticeably improve housing conditions in Chicago, and it enabled few small-wage earners to acquire and own their homes. Garden Homes was almost a parody of Benjamin Rosenthal's best hopes. Rosenthal had planned to shelter poor laborers from badly housed industrial districts such as Back a' the Yards and South Chicago; to Americanize Poles, Lithuanians, Italians, and other foreigners; to save Catholics and Jews from exploitation by their coreligionists; and to build enough homes, ten thousand if necessary, for "every worthy, industrious and thrifty working man now badly housed." Instead, the people who settled Garden Homes were relatively well-paid workers. Two-thirds of them had blue-collar jobs, but only 13 percent or so worked in the stockyards and in the South Chicago steel mills. The neighborhoods they left behind were not the dingiest tenement areas. They came primarily from "the zone of emergence" beyond the slums—such neighborhoods as Englewood and Woodlawn—where rents were getting too high and Negroes were getting too close.[25]

Seventy-one percent of the homeowners were immigrants or natives born of foreign parents, and people of twenty-one ethnicities moved to the community, but the leading nationalities were Irish, Swedish, British Canadian, German, and English. The Poles, Lithuanians, and Italians, for whom Rosenthal had intended the project, totaled only 11 percent of the foreign stock. Protestants may have outnumbered Catholics and Jews combined by as much as three to one.[26]

Garden Homes turned out very differently from what Rosenthal expected, and it was the only project he was able to build. Early in 1921 he announced that rising costs would make it impossible to reproduce homes like those in Garden Homes for less than $9,500.

Fifty thousand Chicagoans were still "living in unspeakable, indecent and improper conditions," Rosenthal said, but his association was at "the end of its resources" and powerless to help. Rosenthal was also unable to refinance the project. He had promised to return the money his backers had advanced him, plus interest, within a year or two, but by 1926 he had repaid only three-fifths of the principal and only a portion of the interest.[27]

Despite his disappointment, Benjamin Rosenthal took satisfaction from the fact that he had built a community. He believed it to be "a very happy and prosperous one, as well as a healthy one," and the early settlers seem to have shared his glowing estimate. They paid far more for their houses than they expected to, but they would have paid more elsewhere in the city, if they could have bought homes at all. Later arrivals got bargain prices, too, even though the project had serious need of funds. In 1922 Rosenthal sold houses appraised at $8,500 for $7,000. The project manager lived in one of the homes, and Rosenthal visited Garden Homes periodically. On Thanksgivings he sent every household a turkey, at Christmas he presented every family with a small gift, and on the Fourth of July he was guest of honor at the Garden Homes Improvement Association's annual Pageant of Progress.[28]

The people did not consider him a Lord Bountiful. They thought him kind, not arrogant; they liked and respected him. "He was a wonderful Jew, a wonderful man," one Irish Catholic woman recalled. Of the development itself she said, "It was the grandest community, the loveliest place. Ah, Garden Homes, it was wonderful." Anyone who thought that the project was somehow substandard had only to go two blocks south, across the tracks, and behold the tumbledown shacks of jerry-built Lilydale. Compared to the black enclave, Garden Homes was an Eden.[29]

Turnover was brisk in the twenties. Half of the original settlers—and a number of later settlers as well—were probably gone by 1930. Some "lost their homes," but others moved on to more substantial neighborhoods. Among those who stayed there was "terrific spirit." Coping with the unfinished houses, the unpaved streets, and other common hazards of the pioneer experience drew the people together. Surrounded by swampy wilderness, they turned to each other for social life.[30]

Every household belonged to the Garden Homes Improvement Association. Most of the families worshipped at Garden Homes Church, across the street from the project. The Methodist pastor, who lived in the project, downplayed denominationalism and treated the whole community as his congregation. The youngsters, except the Catholic children who went to a parochial school half a mile away, attended a portable branch of a public school, which, such as it was, they had virtually to themselves. The church doubled as a community center, with games, meeting rooms, and plenty of planned fun. There were clubs and activities for all age groups. A third-generation Irishman raised in Garden Homes believed that "the main thing Mr. Rosenthal wanted to do was show us turkeys and the polacks, lugans, dagoes, and everybody else, that we could all live together without knocking each other's heads in." Other old-time residents remembered Garden Homes as "a friendly community" with "no distinctions, no bigotry." [31]

By 1927 or 1928 the people had succeeded in getting their streets all paved. The shrubs and trees were growing nicely, and the place seemed to be thriving. However, not everything was rosy in the small preserve of bungalows and gardens. The business lots on State Street and 87th remained vacant except for a candy store, a butcher shop, a grocery, and one lot on which somebody put up a house. The space to the north and east of the project was still mostly empty acreage, although Chatham's built-up frontier had edged a little closer. On the other sides the gap between Garden Homes and the railroad tracks was now filled, but with factories, warehouses, and more train tracks, not homes. Benjamin Rosenthal had located his model housing project on a buffer zone dividing Chatham's pleasant residences from its somber industrial fringe.[32]

There was little the community could do to tenant the commercial property, draw residential Chatham nearer, or shut out the sight and sounds of the factories and the freight trains. But the neighborhood was able to guard itself against one threat to its security: invasion by "any negro or negroes." In 1929 the Garden Homes Improvement Association filed a restrictive covenant with the county recorder of deeds. The document, which covered the whole area, required the signatures of owners of 75 percent of the property frontage to make it operative. Every homeowner in Garden Homes, including the pastor of the church, signed it. In addition, Rosenthal's development corporation signed for one lot, and the Salvation Army signed for four. Absentee owners of four parcels failed to participate, so overall coverage fell just short of 100 percent. In effect, the covenant was unanimous. It testified, in its way, to the communal spirit of multiethnic, tri-faith, and resolutely all-white Garden Homes.[33]

❧

Postscript. For almost thirty more years, Garden Homes remained a pure-white preserve. In the mid-1950s the community found itself caught in a pincers movement between Lilydale to the south and the Black Belt, which was moving from the north through Chatham. In the spring of 1956, a black family moved into the community. Within weeks someone set fire to their house. Police investigated the arson at 8800 S. Indiana but made no arrests.[34]

CHAPTER 11 ❧

The Housing Commission and the Dual Program

Don't mix business and philanthropy.
—W. F. Dummer to Mary McDowell, 1 July 1912, Mary McDowell Papers, CHS.

Whites and blacks will not mix any more than fire and water.
—Chicago *Post,* 31 July 1919.

AT THE END OF 1921, SEVERAL MONTHS AFTER BENJAMIN ROSENTHAL announced that the Chicago Housing Association was abandoning its program to build nearly ten thousand homes for workingmen, he joined a distinguished group of Chicagoans in forming the Public Committee of Fifty on Housing. Besides Rosenthal, there were four members of the Chicago Housing Association on this committee—settlement workers Graham Taylor, Harriet Vittum, and Mary McDowell, and Col. Abel Davis of Chicago Title and Trust Co. Other social workers took part in drafting the committee's platform, among them Jane Addams of Hull-House. "The single aim" of the committee, as stated in their original platform, was "to further adequate housing for the small-wage earners of Chicago." However, the committee's members took the position that they had to have the support of "the interests directly concerned with the financing, building and renting of houses." To obtain that support, they revised their modest platform, even to the extent of giving up their goal. "The single aim of this Committee," their substitute statement read, "is to encourage the building and owning of homes in Chicago." [1]

Given the aim of the Chicago Real Estate Board's Own Your Own Home Committee (which became a permanent division of the board in the twenties), the Public Committee of Fifty was superfluous. The building boom could proceed full blast without its encouragement. The committee accomplished nothing, lapsing into inactivity almost at once. For the next five years there was no organized movement concerned with the housing of low-paid working people. Influential Chicagoans had their minds on other things. One was the much-stalled city plan; another was a long-awaited comprehensive zoning law. Forward-looking citizens saw planning and zoning as devices to propel Chicago into the front ranks of America's progressive and prosperous cities.

Once the war was over, the Chicago Plan Commission drove full speed ahead on a dazzling series of projects to improve the central business district, streamline the city's trade and transportation network, and beautify the lakefront. By ceaseless boosting, the Plan Commission dispelled the city's lingering "suspicion that beauty did not pay." The city plan did not provide for housing projects. Because it took "the public domain" as its field, the commission later explained, "housing was thereby automatically excluded." One big, glossy brochure pushing the commission's agenda claimed that Benjamin Rosenthal's project was part of "the city beautiful plan" to eliminate the city's slums, but boosters of the plan usually said that the commission's projects would help housing only indirectly, by jacking up property values.[2]

In 1919 Alderman Ulysses S. ("U.S.") Schwartz assured the Hyde Park–Kenwood Association that planned lakeshore improvements would help them save the South Side from neighbors who were not "desirable." Four years later Charles H. Wacker, chairman of the Plan Commission, predicted that lakeshore projects such as a forty-mile superdrive stretching from the northern suburbs to "the South Shore Country Club" would "greatly increase property values" all along the way and make the South Side "more desirable for residence and business." *This* was the sort of magic that stirred men's blood.[3]

Extending its reach, the Plan Commission worked closely with the Chicago Regional Planning Association, which the City Club created in 1923 to develop a comprehensive plan of highways, parks, and utilities for the metropolitan area. The commission made no little plans, and regarding housing it continued to make no plans at all. Even so, the National Housing Association urged other cities to study the Chicago Plan Commission's record and "go and do likewise." The commission was not totally indifferent to the social dimensions of planning—it knew very well what the white South Side wanted to be saved from, for instance. But its staff, made up of engineers and architects, did no social research. When the local committee drawing up plans for the federal census of 1930 asked if the commission would care to procure census data, the reply was, "We have no particular use for it."[4]

Planners were interested in zoning as an enforceable brake on haphazard development, but they were not the only ones who looked forward to enactment of a comprehensive zoning law. Housers favored zoning as a means of relieving congestion and ensuring adequate air, light, and open space for every dwelling. In theory, zoning severely abridged the prerogatives of private ownership, but no one in Chicago embraced the zoning cause so ardently as businessmen, especially those who dealt in real estate. Businessmen as well as planners wanted to impose order on urban growth, and realtors had nothing against fresh air and sunshine, especially when they could turn them to a profit. The purpose of zoning, as realtors understood it, was "to protect, stabilize and increase property values." Far from threatening property interests, zoning could be a positive boon. So businessmen thought, and by thinking they helped to make it so.[5]

In late 1919 the Real Estate Board, the City Club, and the Union League Club cosponsored a conference on zoning. Setting the tone for the conference was one speaker's fervent declaration of faith: "Zoning will increase Chicago's wealth $1,000,000,000 in twenty years!" In 1921 Mayor Thompson appointed a Zoning Commission to draft a comprehensive code. Among its twenty-two members were thirteen public officials, including Charles Wacker of the Plan Commission, and nine private citizens, of whom four were realtors. One black man served on the commission to reassure black Chicagoans that the zoning law would not include segregation. The Negro representative was Charles S. Duke, author of *The Housing Situation and the Colored People of Chicago.* In 1923 the City Council enacted an ordinance based on the commission's report: The new law faithfully reflected the real estate viewpoint on zoning.[6]

The law divided Chicago into three main districts—industrial, commercial, and residential. Within each use district it set limits on the height and volume of buildings. As the realtors expressed it, the code protected "each piece of property to its highest and best use." The act invited the maximum feasible utilization of land. The space zoned for commerce and manufacturing, if developed to the utmost, could have accommodated all of the trade and industry of the Midwest. The height and volume limits would have permitted the whole population of the United States to crowd into the area zoned for residence. The narrow apartment-house strip along the lakeshore, if built up to the capacity allowed by the regulations, could have held forty-two million people by itself.[7]

Much of the land consigned to conversion to a higher and better use was in the tenement districts, which slum landlords hoped would become commercial and industrial. The ordinance zoned the areas to suit the landlords' hopes. Where displaced people could go was a question the zoning ordinance did not touch. Immigrant as well as black neighborhoods were zoned to accommodate industrial expansion, but if immigrants had to relocate, there were places for them to go, provided they could meet the rental demands. For blacks, relocation posed a special problem. The zoning ordinance did not mark off sections for their exclusive occupancy, but neither did it provide them a way to get out of a Black Belt diminished by the encroachment of "higher uses."[8]

Although the zoning ordinance laid the groundwork for a perpetual saturnalia of construction, the building boom could not continue indefinitely without glutting the real estate market. In mid-1925 the Real Estate Board announced that the housing shortage was all but over. As far as apartments of the better grade were concerned, the city was built up to capacity, and completion of single-family developments under way or contemplated would wipe out the remaining deficit in detached dwellings. The balance between supply and demand was approaching normal. Overbuilding would put realtors at a disadvantage with renters and buyers.[9]

What the Real Estate Board hoped to do was to sustain building activity at the highest level consistent with maintenance of the market equilibrium. There were two ways to do that: build to accommodate population growth and build for a previously untapped market. Population had increased at the rate of over 112,000 per year from 1920 to 1925, but in 1925 it rose by only 33,000, and after 1927 the number of people in the city actually declined. Suburban growth, which had been spectacular, began tapering off after mid-decade as well. Accordingly, the Real Estate Board turned its attention to the possibility of housing the income groups that had not shared in the construction bonanza up to that time. The board even considered new construction for lower-paid workers, black as well as white, for the first time since it put away its plans to rebuild the Black Belt and rehouse white slum dwellers in 1921.[10]

Some Chicagoans—not many—had been concerned about the plight of the ill-housed masses even while building activity was thrumming. Settlement workers knew from day-to-day experience that conditions were not getting better in the tenement districts. Many of their neighbors escaped the slums, but many others were left behind to compete for the decaying stock of houses with still others who were newcomers to the city and its miserable tenements.

Mary McDowell of University of Chicago Settlement in Packingtown was one of the few who never tired of talking up housing problems. From the 1890s on, she took part in every effort to ameliorate living conditions in the slums, including the Garden Homes project and the abortive Public Committee of Fifty. In 1923 Chicago's newly elected reform mayor, William E. Dever, appointed her commissioner of public welfare, and she resolved to make housing—like planning and zoning—a matter of official concern. Her goal was the establishment of a permanent Chicago Housing Commission.

Miss McDowell's first task was the familiar and fatiguing one of assembling evidence to prove all over again what so many surveys had already shown, that Chicago, even in flush times, had a harrowing tenement problem. It was impossible to fund a full-scale, definitive study out of the niggardly budget that the city allotted to the Department of Public Welfare. Miss McDowell decided to conduct as ambitious an investigation of housing as her budget would allow and supplement it with studies done by others. She turned to her old friends and associates at the University of Chicago's School of Social Service Administration and asked them to send their students out to survey small districts in detail, as they had before the war. The students of Edith Abbott and Sophonisba Breckenridge began once more to descend upon deteriorating neighborhoods, schedule cards in hand.[11]

One survey, which Mary McDowell especially wanted the school to do, covered the housing of black people on Federal Street south of 45th. A swarm of students canvassed house to house the seven-block stretch of Federal in 1924. The schedule card they carried was the same one used in the 1911–12 survey of Negro houses a mile and a half farther north on Federal. The figures from the earlier survey had been dismal, of course. The results of the 1924 investigation were "decidedly worse." Of the "endless dingy wooden buildings" only 14 percent were in "good" condition and over 41 percent were in "bad repair." Sleeping rooms were darker and more crowded. A higher percentage of toilets were inside apartments in 1924, but only 31 percent were in "good repair." The rental rates were double those of a dozen years earlier. More than half of the apartments rented for $20 to $40, rents which, given the shape the houses were in, were "exorbitant beyond all reason."[12]

Alice Quan Rood wrote up the survey as a master's thesis. She illustrated it with photographs which, if artless, were nevertheless devastating in impact. One picture showed a backyard piled with bricks, barrels, lumber scraps, bedsprings, boxes, cans, and other debris. Running across the yard to a ramshackle wooden porch was a clothesline, from which a man's white dress shirt was hanging. On the porch stood a woman and three small children looking over the forlorn, littered yard. In an unpaved side alley three more children were playing. The caption read: "The landlord, who lives at another address, reserves this space for junk." Another photograph showed a middle-aged woman, a younger woman, and a little girl in a cramped, windowless kitchen. The plaster had fallen from the walls, exposing cracked laths, and water was visibly seeping up through the floorboards. Water was heating in a pail on top of a big old iron stove. The women were taking turns ironing a pile of clothes. As one ironed the other reheated her cooled-off iron on the stove. "The daylight shines through these walls," the caption noted. "The sink is on the point of collapse. The rent has just been advanced three dollars." Mrs. Rood concluded her thesis with the prediction: "Things will simply explode if the pressure continues."[13]

Other surveys indicated that the supply of *decent* housing which poorer workingmen, white or black, could afford had not really increased. Buildings on land zoned for nonresidential use stood rotting while the owners tried to extract enough income to pay taxes until the time came to sell the land for "higher and better use." When houses became uninhabitable, the owners sometimes demolished them. More often they simply let the structures tumble down from decay. Buildings vacated by more fortunate families who moved into new housing were badly worn out by the time working people acquired them. Few of the benefits of what the Real Estate Board called a "normal" housing supply filtered down to the families of the unskilled and semiskilled laboring class.[14]

At the peak of prosperity, in 1925–26, an estimated two-thirds of all Chicago families lived on less than $2,500 per year. A half or more had incomes under $2,000. In the tenement districts that the University of Chicago's social work students surveyed between 1923 and 1927, four-fifths of the fifteen thousand households canvassed had to struggle along on less than $2,000, a figure that included income from the work of wives and children, from boarders, and from all other sources. According to a rule of thumb of household economy, it was unsafe for a family to spend more than one-fifth of its income for shelter. By that standard, the overwhelming majority of Chicago's tenement population could not afford to pay their landlords more than $35 a month. Study after study showed that the housing available at that price was hardly fit to live in.[15]

Mary McDowell designed the Department of Welfare's own survey to demonstrate two things: the gravity of the housing problem and the feasibility of mitigating it. *Living Conditions for Small-Wage Earners in Chicago*, written by Elizabeth Hughes with an introduction by Miss McDowell, charged that the great building boom had done "nothing for the small-wage worker and his family." The text was full of tables, photographs, and "dreary and sordid examples" to back up the charge. Housing conditions had deteriorated in the tenement districts, but the tenants were paying twice as much for cold-water flats in frame houses predating the tenement house code of 1902 than they had paid before the war. The situation of black people was especially distressing. They, along with recent migrants from Mexico, occupied the worst housing in the city, but while Mexicans paid *less* for their flats than did any other ethnic group surveyed, the blacks paid *more* than all the rest. The report, after describing an apparently hopeless situation at length, went on to claim that there was a rental market of wage earners waiting to be tapped by "profit-making enterprises in building." This was the sort of thing that the leaders of the Real Estate Board were interested in, given their perceptions of a tapering demand for middle-class housing. However, the claim was not quite consistent with the rest of the report.[16]

Miss McDowell and Miss Hughes based their claim on the fact that 44 percent of the 1,526 households in the survey paid less than one-fifth of their total incomes for rent. By the old rule of thumb, these families could afford to pay more, that is, up to one-fifth of their income. The report argued that because they were paying less than they could, they "could afford to live in better houses if any were available for them." The argument did not necessarily follow. Only 10 percent of the sample families had aggregate monthly earnings of $200 or more. They could afford to pay as much as $40 for an unheated apartment; nine out of ten families in the survey could not. Indeed, 47 percent of the families lived on less than $100 a month; for them, a $20 rental was a hardship.[17]

Mary McDowell advanced the claim of a rental market for working-class families not so much out of conviction as in desperation. She had no faith left that the housing market could make homeowners out of common workingmen, and the report stated flatly that building homes for sale to workers was no solution. The only hope was rental apartments, but after her futile prewar attempt to build a model tenement Back a' the Yards, she had little confidence in them. In 1921, reflecting on that failure, she wrote that "private interests" would never be able to solve the problem: Nothing less than "the police power of the state" would suffice. Sure that a public solution was required but aware that government would not act, she fell back on begging business interests to "do something." *Living Conditions for Small-Wage Earners* was a long plea for private enterprise to build model tenements, even though Miss McDowell had abandoned hope in such projects a decade earlier. She felt that the city had to have an official housing body, but she asked "commerce, industry and even real estate"—not the city—"to organize a Housing Commission." She knew where the power was in Chicago.[18]

In the spring of 1926, Miss McDowell called a conference of social workers and business leaders to consider the department's housing report. Newspapers acclaimed the meeting in advance, hopeful that the participants would find a way to build low-rent model tenements that would pay "a profitable return." Such a building program would alleviate the suffering of slum dwellers, one editorial observed, and equally important, it would give the construction industry "an impetus at a time when all signs point to a decline in activity." All the old hands of housing reform in Chicago beat the drum for the conference. Benjamin Rosenthal claimed that the housing situation was "worse than ever." Jane Addams, Edith Abbott, Graham Taylor, and Harriet Vittum talked about the need for apartments that would rent for $35 to $45 a month, or no more than $10 a room.[19]

The conference, which was chaired not by Mary McDowell but by Willoughby Walling, a banker who was president of the Council of Social Agencies, agreed that model tenements offered the best possibility of a solution. The delegates named a committee to study the matter and make recommendations. The chairman of this committee was Joseph K. Brittain, president of the Chicago Real Estate Board, who said that realtors were "very much interested" in developing a "practical" and "constructive" method to house workers. On this committee's recommendation the housing conference subsequently petitioned Mayor Dever to appoint a Housing Commission.[20]

Acting with the authorization of the City Council, Mayor Dever named the Chicago Housing Commission in the summer of 1926. Dever selected the commissioners with the view of bringing together two sorts of people: those who cared about the housing problem and those who knew how to get things done in Chicago. The commission itself had no power whatever. It was purely an advisory body; the City Council did not even make an appropriation for it. For a budget, it had to rely on the voluntary contributions of its own members and whatever outside donations they could solicit.

What the commission did have was a number of members who had *access* to considerable power. Of the forty-two commissioners, seven were members of the Real Estate Board. Two were bankers. Ten were officials of major industries, utilities, and commercial concerns (including Swift and Company, Armour and Company, Sears Roebuck, the Telephone Company, and Chicago Rapid Transit Company). Julius Rosenwald's son-in-law, Alfred K. Stern, represented the Rosenwald Fund, and Werner A. Wieboldt represented the Wieboldt Foundation. There were social workers, academics, and union officials on the commission as well. Their function was to provide the more influential commissioners with information and a sense of high purpose. Mary McDowell, Edith Abbott, and Graham Taylor were commissioners, as were Professor Richard T. Ely, the distinguished economist, and Professor Ernest W. Burgess, the University of Chicago sociologist. The ailing Charles Ball, dean of Chicago's "housers," had a place of honor on the commission. Mayor Dever even chose two black men as commissioners: A. L. Foster, secretary of the Urban League, and Charles S. Duke. As their permanent chairman the commissioners elected William Zelosky, vice-president of the Real Estate Board and chairman of its Own Your Own Home division. Zelosky set the tone for the commission's work in his first address to the group. "Private enterprise," he said, "will solve this problem."[21]

The Chicago Housing Commission was an official body, but it was a private group in spirit, controlled by commerce, industry, and real estate, not by government. It not only lacked a budget of its own, it had no staff and no office. In the little over a year that it existed, its members came together only four times. A few of the members took it upon themselves to act in the commission's name. None of the social workers, professors, or other "housers" was among them. Julius Rosenwald's son-in-law, Alfred Stern, the organization's secretary, assumed overall command of the commission and directed its affairs from his suite in Sears Roebuck's colossal West Side complex. Sears Roebuck, in fact, was the commission's mailing address. The other commissioners Stern worked with were William Zelosky and Joseph Brittain of the Real Estate Board. From time to time Stern dropped a note to the rest of the commissioners and Mayor Dever to let them know what the commission was doing.[22]

Stern, Zelosky, and Brittain considered three ways of cutting down on the cost of workers' housing without cutting away "a modest but proper return on capital." The first, tax exemptions or reductions on property developed for workers, they dismissed as drastic, controversial, and unnecessary unless other expedients were tried and found inadequate. The second, single-family-unit developments in outlying areas and in the suburbs, where land was less expensive, was impossible under the existing system of mass transportation. The third, large-scale apartment projects on inner-city land, was impossible under the legal restraints on real-estate improvement corporations. Because it was easier to amend the legislation covering real estate development than to supply cheap transportation to the outskirts of the city, Stern and his cohorts concentrated on changing the law.[23]

They took a bill drafted by the Chicago Real Estate Board and announced that it was the Chicago Housing Commission's own proposal. Then the Real Estate Board and the Illinois Association of Real Estate Boards declared their support for what the public understood to be the commission's bill. Most members of the Housing Commission had never seen the proposal when a state legislator introduced it in the General Assembly on their behalf. Graham Taylor, speaking for several commissioners, protested privately that Stern had been high-handed, but in public all of the commissioners supported the legislation as if it were their own.[24]

The bill enjoyed considerable support. As the Chicago *Evening Post* observed, there was nothing "radical or socialistic" about it. All it did was simplify the existing law and lift limitations that Chicago realtors had been grumbling about for years. Under the old law, real-estate improvement corporations could buy only vacant land; they could hold only forty acres of unimproved land at a time; and they had to divest themselves of their property within five years unless they improved it, in which case they could keep it for fifteen years. The new bill allowed the corporations to acquire improved as well as vacant land. It raised the amount of land they could hold to 640 acres, vacant or otherwise, and it lengthened the time they could control it to twenty-five years.[25]

"The Chicago Housing Commission has been conservative," the *Evening Post* editorialized:

> It is not urging any departure from the sound principle of private enterprise; it is not asking the state or the municipality to engage in the building of dwellings; it has launched no visionary plan or program. With its feet on the ground, it has asked merely that the obstacles to the economic use of private capital in the construction of moderate price homes be removed.

If the realtors had pushed the bill as their own, on their own, some legislators might have opposed it as special-interest legislation. The sponsorship of the Chicago Housing Commission gave the thing the aura of a social welfare measure, while the backing of the realtors reassured conservatives that it must be safe. The bill passed without significant opposition in the summer of 1927.[26]

The Chicago Housing Commission met only one time after the bill's enactment. Then it quietly faded into oblivion without issuing any formal report of its activities, accomplishments, and demise. However, Alfred Stern continued to act as a kind of one-man commission. He was determined to see private enterprise demonstrate its capacity to take care of the housing problem. At first Stern thought of organizing a supercorporation to rehabilitate sound structures all over Chicago. He also hoped to build three massive new projects, one in "each of the main divisions of the city." It would be easier to put up three projects all at once, he thought, than to announce one development and thereby set South Siders, West Siders, and North Siders to squabbling over it. For some reason he gave up the notion of a single overall corporation. He tried to make sure that separate organizations under competent leadership would build the needed projects and coordinate their efforts through him.[27]

The Estate of Marshall Field, the department-store tycoon, had been interested in putting up a project on the North Side for some time, and at least two groups had plans to build on the South Side. The Field project went ahead to completion, but both of the South Side enterprises fell through. Stern ended up turning to his father-in-law, Julius Rosenwald, to do for the South Side what Field was doing for the North. Nobody undertook a development on the West Side. Instead of one project for each of the three main divisions of the city, Chicago got a project for each of the two races.

The South Side project was the one "for Negroes." There was no shortage of men willing to back a development for blacks, provided it was both segregated and profitable. The Chicago Real Estate Board's restrictive covenant campaign was already under way in the summer of 1927. Just as realtors were interested in expanding their conventional market by building for a lower-income clientele in a slack period, some of them sensed that a "constructive" program in the Black Belt would complement their restriction policy. One of the South Side groups with plans to sponsor a project was simply out to make money. It was composed of Black Belt slum owners who wanted to prop up sagging land values around 30th and Wabash by locating a new, desirable development there. They counted on Julius Rosenwald to lend their plan both financial support and the luster of his reputation. When Rosenwald refused to contribute either money or his name, the scheme stagnated. The other group, led by architect N. Max Dunning, was altogether reputable. Dunning had "a definite constructive plan," which Alfred Stern initially approved and (so Dunning thought) agreed to support.[28]

The prospectus that N. Max Dunning drew up for his Metropolitan Housing Association is a revealing statement of the "constructive" approach to "the problem of housing the negro population." The purpose of the association, in Dunning's straightforward language, was "to effect a sensible concentration of the negro population." Dunning argued that restriction alone could not contain "the substantial element of the negro population" within the Black Belt. Unless ambitious black families could obtain decent housing at reasonable rates in the areas they occupied, they would spearhead the invasion of white territory, and the Black Belt would "expand further and further." Building up the Black Belt, Dunning contended, was "the real way to concentrate the negro population."[29]

Dunning assured prospective investors that the venture was not "charity" or "philanthropy." It was "strictly business," combining "a work for the public good with reasonable returns." Among the "men of prominence and leadership in Chicago's commercial, industrial and civic circles" who agreed to back Dunning's plan were Max Mason, president of the University of Chicago, and two members of the Chicago Plan Commission, George W. Dixon and Nathan William MacChesney. As chief counsel for the project, MacChesney almost certainly helped Dunning prepare the prospectus. MacChesney's "wholehearted support and assistance" in the "Colored Development" underscored the complementary character of the constructive and restrictive approaches to "the negro housing problem." For it was MacChesney who had charge of drafting the Real Estate Board's model restrictive covenant.[30]

Even before the passage of the new real-estate redevelopment legislation, Dunning acquired options on a square block of Black Belt property, drew up plans for an apartment project, and took bids from construction firms. When the bill became law, Dunning was ready to move ahead with his plans. Yet his project went nowhere. Alfred Stern lost confidence in the project and prevailed on his father-in-law to step in and build a Negro project properly. When Julius Rosenwald came into the picture, there was little for Dunning to do but fade out.[31]

Stern's reasons for rejecting the Dunning plan cannot be found in any surviving source, but they can be surmised. Both the site and the project design had questionable features that raised the further question of the credibility of the sponsors. Dunning and his associates were not real estate sharpers out to make a killing in Black Belt property. The question was whether black people would accept the project under their sponsorship without inquiring into their motives. For the blacks had to believe (or make themselves believe) that the constructive program was completely unconnected with the effort to restrict them.

The block that Dunning had selected ran north and south from 29th Street to 30th between Dearborn and Federal (see Map 11.1). In 1911 students from the University of Chicago had surveyed the housing there and found it deplorable. There was a case to be made for razing it and replacing it with decent buildings. However, the site was surrounded by the worst shacks, shanties, and outworn two-flats in the Black Belt. Rebuilding a single block in the very heart of the slum would not necessarily secure the project and its tenants against the conditions prevailing all around. Moreover, the gloomy embankment of the Rock Island overlooked the site from a distance of seventy-five yards. Whether any buildings, however sound, could survive the blighting effect of the railroad tracks, even if the adjoining blocks were rebuilt as well, was problematic. Decades later the Chicago Housing Authority located Dearborn Homes, "for Negroes," on the block Dunning had chosen. Today, stretching north and south for a distance of four miles, within 225 feet of the tracks, stand seven gargantuan multibuilding public-housing projects, all occupied by black people. This fact does not vindicate Dunning's choice. The Housing Authority's projects ended up by the tracks not because the sites were desirable but because nobody deemed them fit for any "higher use." Stacking so many units in the slot alongside the tracks seemed a sensible way to concentrate the black population.[32]

As for Dunning's project design, he planned fourteen identical four-story court buildings—seven on Federal, seven on Dearborn,

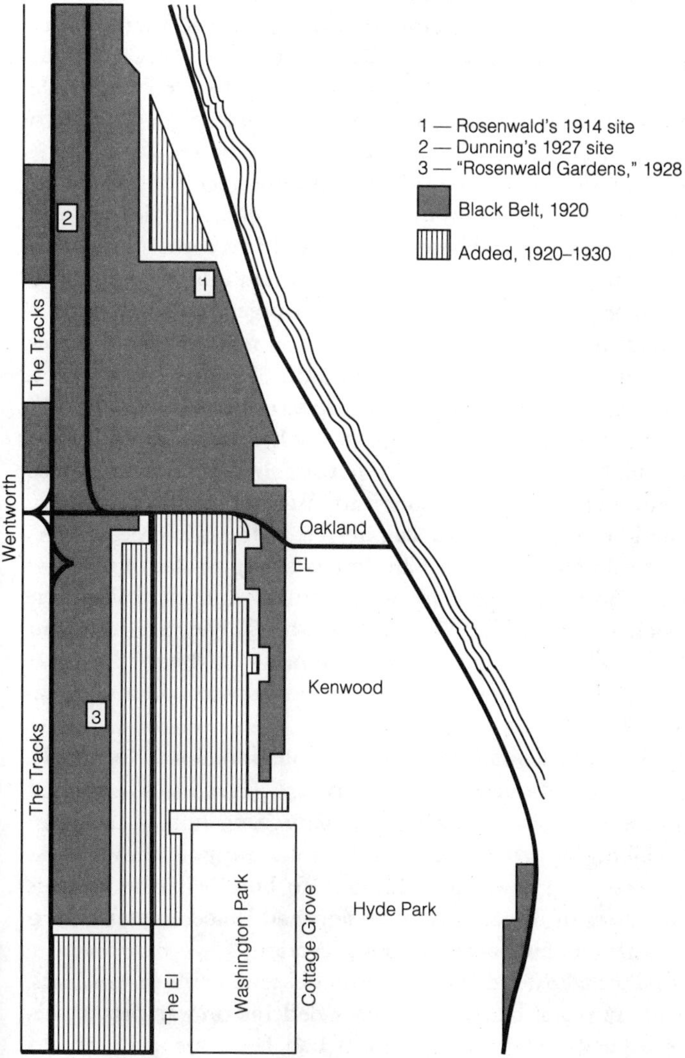

MAP 11.1. Sites of proposed "colored" projects.

with a long interior court running between the two rows of apartments, covering the old alley space. All 266 apartments had exactly the same four-room layout. The uniformity of the plan made for economy—Dunning believed that he could rent the flats for $48 a month—but it was also monotonous (though not so monotonous as the projects that rim the railroad tracks today). There was little chance that this plan would compare with the one the Field Estate was preparing "for white families" on the North Side, and Stern wanted the two projects to be not only separate but equal.[33]

A less than ideal plan, executed on an imperfect site, sponsored by men like Dunning, whom black people hardly knew, and MacChesney, whom they knew only too well as a restrictionist, was liable to stir up suspicion in the Black Belt. Dunning's project was a Jim Crow project. Alfred Stern had no objection to it on that score. The trouble was that, under scrutiny, it *looked* like a Jim Crow project. That was unsatisfactory. The South Side project needed a sponsor whom nobody would presume to scrutinize. For years Julius Rosenwald had been funding Negro schools, Negro clinics, Negro YMCAs, and Negro boys' clubs, but scarcely a soul so much as whispered that he might be doing it to institutionalize segregation. On a couple of occasions, blacks referred to the "Colored YMCA" that Rosenwald subsidized in Chicago as a "segregated, Jim Crow institution." And Clarence Darrow, the crusty white radical lawyer, told a black audience in 1927 that "the whites" had built the "Jim Crow YMCA" in order "that you may not mix with them." That was as close as anyone had ever come to calling Rosenwald a segregationist in public.[34]

Through the Rosenwald Fund and private donations, Rosenwald funneled millions of dollars into "deserving" Negro institutions and Negro branches of white institutions. Criticizing him would have been like killing the goose that laid the golden egg. Rosenwald was beyond reproach. He was just the man to build what he and his fellow members of the Riot Commission had called "better Negro housing" without being accused of segregation.[35]

Rosenwald had intended to build model tenements in the Black Belt for many years, but after he canceled his prewar project his chief contribution to housing reform had been his assistance to Garden Homes, which excluded blacks, partly because of his insistence. Now, in 1927, Alfred Stern persuaded him that the time was right to demonstrate the power of "business enterprise" to correct the deficiencies of Negro housing. A model project capably executed would pay a "business return," prove the profitability of better Negro housing, and attract additional "white capital" into building up the Black Belt. Possibly Stern appealed to Rosenwald, who was Jewish, to counter the stereotype of the predatory Jew squeezing exorbitant rents out of Black Belt tenants and ruining white neighborhoods by blockbusting. Rosenwald agreed to underwrite the project, and Stern took charge of building it. Significantly, Rosenwald elected to finance the project personally instead of drawing on the Rosenwald Fund. He wanted to make it as clear as possible that housing was not "a philanthropy," but business. The Field Estate, too, stressed that its "scheme" was not "a philanthropic project."[36]

When Alfred Stern started to work on Rosenwald's "Negro" project, planning on the North Side project was already well under way. Working closely with George Richardson, who had charge of the Field operation, Stern made up for lost time. The Field Estate had commissioned Edith Abbott of the University of Chicago to study sites for a North Side project as early as 1925. Before the end of 1927 she agreed to supervise a study of the housing needs of South Side blacks as well. In January 1928, after months of quietly negotiating to buy properties on the selected project sites for reasonable prices, the Field Estate announced its plans to the public for the first time. Julius Rosenwald's announcement followed six months later.[37]

The Field Estate planned a $4 million project on a five-acre site bounded by Sedgwick and Hudson streets on the east and west, Blackhawk on the north, and Sigel (now Evergreen) on the south. For the Rosenwald project, Stern selected the five-acre block between Wabash Avenue and Michigan Boulevard, from 46th Street to 47th. Stern expected costs to run to $2.5 million (see Map 11.1). The Field project, designed by architect Andrew J. Thomas, was larger as well as more expensive. Its ten detached buildings had 627 apartments, ranging in size from three and a half to six rooms. It also had space for twenty stores. The Rosenwald plan, drawn by the firm that had planned Garden Homes, provided for 421 apartments of three to five rooms plus sixteen stores in a series of buildings connected into one imposing structure.[38]

The two plans had much in common. The collaboration between Alfred Stern and the Field Estate man, George Richardson, was so close that the projects became almost a joint enterprise. Both designs incorporated the idea, which Andrew J. Thomas had employed in model projects in the East, of taking a whole block and arranging the buildings, which were two rooms deep, around a spacious interior garden court. Both plans provided fully heated apartments equipped with modern kitchen appliances. They both included convenient shopping facilities on the ground level, basement storage space, laundries, supervised playgrounds and recreation rooms, nurseries, and roof walks with gardens. The amenities and "social features," as the management of the South Side project later put it, were "*not only consistent with, but essential to,* sound business management."[39]

The projects also shared two drawbacks common to Andrew Thomas's model-tenement designs: steep stairwells and low ceilings. All of the buildings were five-story walk-ups. It could have been worse. In New York's Harlem ghetto, Thomas had designed a "Negro" project with six-story walk-ups. Perhaps if Thomas had been contracted to plan the "Negro" building in Chicago instead of the "white" one, he would have suggested six-story walk-ups again. As it was, a five-story climb was too much for children, for elderly people, and for anyone trying to carry groceries. The ceilings were 8 feet high instead of the 8½ feet required in Chicago's tenement house code. The City Council granted exemptions to both projects. Even with such "economy" measures as omitting elevators and reducing ceiling heights, however, the plans were impressive.[40]

Another thing that the two projects had in common was that their sponsors did not really intend them to house lower-income families. As Alfred Stern explained, it would be easy "to build good apartments, charge low rents, and accept a very small return. But this would be simply a charitable gesture and would be the surest way to warn investors away from this type of thing." And it would reinforce the belief that only "cheap, unhealthful buildings" would pay off. To make a convincing demonstration to other capitalists, it would be necessary to set rents not at a low but at a "moderate" level. The Field Estate intended to establish a $4,000 limit on family income: Applicants with higher incomes would not be admitted. But the Field project was going to be a cooperative, and a family with an income significantly lower than $4,000 would be hard-pressed to pay for an apartment. The great bulk of Chicago families lived on considerably less than $4,000 a year.[41]

Both projects cost more to build than the planners originally estimated. In the case of the Field apartments, the cost overrun exceeded 40 percent. Assembling the land proved to be a stumbling block for both enterprises. The Field site plan took in one square block and half of a small adjoining block. To consolidate the two pieces of land it was necessary to extend Hudson Street south to Sigel, slicing the smaller block in two, and then cover over the public street separating the two parcels of land that were to be joined (see Map 11.2). All of this was complicated, but it presented no problem at all. The City of Chicago sold the stretch of street that had to be covered to the Field Estate and permitted the estate to cut the small block and extend Hudson Street.

The problem came from individual property owners. When some owners got wind of the magnitude of the project and the identity of the buyer, they held out for higher prices, forcing the estate to pay three and four times the value of some of the parcels.[42]

Joseph K. Brittain of the Real Estate Board handled the buying for the Rosenwald site. Despite his precautions, owners of five buildings in the northeast section of the block figured out that one buyer was trying to assemble all of the lots in the block for a single development. They demanded more for their properties than Alfred Stern was willing to pay. Neither side yielded. As a result, the plan lost a half-acre chunk of its ground space. Most of the lots that the Rosenwald project did acquire were vacant, so the development did not have the expense of extensive demolition. But the Field site was heavily built up with aged tenements. In addition to land costs of nearly $1,212,000, the Field project had to bear the costs of clearing away the old buildings. One small savings the Field Estate did achieve: It spent nothing to help the displaced tenants locate new homes.[43]

Marshall Field Garden Apartments was completed in April 1929 at a cost of $5,679,000. The Rosenwald project, Michigan Boulevard Garden Apartments (see Map 11.3, page 266), which cost upwards of $2,700,000, opened in August 1929. The Field project, which turned out *not* to be a co-op, charged monthly rents ranging from $42 to $90. The rental range at Michigan Boulevard Garden Apartments, which people called Rosenwald Gardens or the Rosenwald, was $45 to $85 a month. The average apartment at Field Gardens

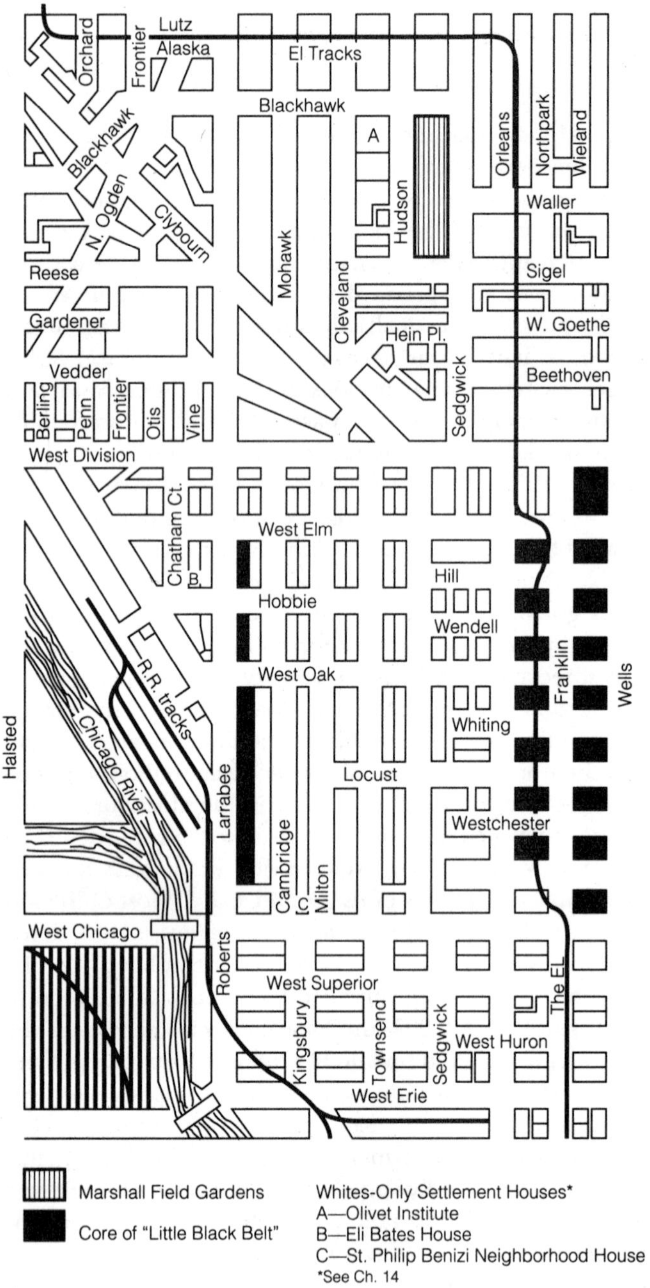

MAP 11.2. **Marshall Field Garden Apartments, "for white families" (base map: *Olcott's*, 1927).**

was four and a half rooms, a half-room larger than the average apartment at the Rosenwald, but the average rent at both places was just over $62 a month. These rents were reasonable. The 1925 Department of Public Welfare survey showed that the tiny fraction of unskilled workers who lived in heated apartments paid a median monthly rent of over $65. And without question the apartments were the best available at that price in Chicago. Reasonable, but as Alfred Stern was the first to admit, not low. Mary McDowell noted sadly, months before the projects opened, that the rents were "too high for small-income families." [44]

Even with the rents so high, the Rosenwald filled up, and a long list of people waited for apartments to become vacant. The location was as attractive as any in the Black Belt, in a section of the Grand Boulevard community that whites had maintained fairly well before abandoning it earlier in the twenties. The South Side El had a station a little over two blocks to the east. The distance between the buildings and the el was short enough for convenience and far enough for protection from most of its dirt and roaring noise. Julius Rosenwald enriched the project's surroundings by helping to bring three important Negro institutions to the area: the transplanted "Colored" YWCA and Provident Hospital, and a new public library especially (though, of course, not officially) for Negroes. As for the apartments themselves, a spokesman for Rosenwald claimed with justification that they provided "better housing than Negroes have ever had in Chicago." [45]

The Black Belt had been looking forward to the project ever since Julius Rosenwald first announced it. The *Defender* hailed it, studiously overlooking the fact that it was segregated. The paper's first report did not say that the apartments were for blacks but rather "for Chicagoans." A later article maintained that the project was open to people of "all races." The *Defender* went so far as to report that "many white families" were applying for apartments. This was an exercise in protective self-deception. If white families did apply, which is practically inconceivable, the management did not consider their applications. Yet the *Defender* called the project a first step toward wiping out " 'black belts' and slums." [46]

By treating Rosenwald Gardens in this way, the newspaper was accepting improved housing, segregated though it was, without accepting *the principle* of segregation. Editor Robert Abbott, who had

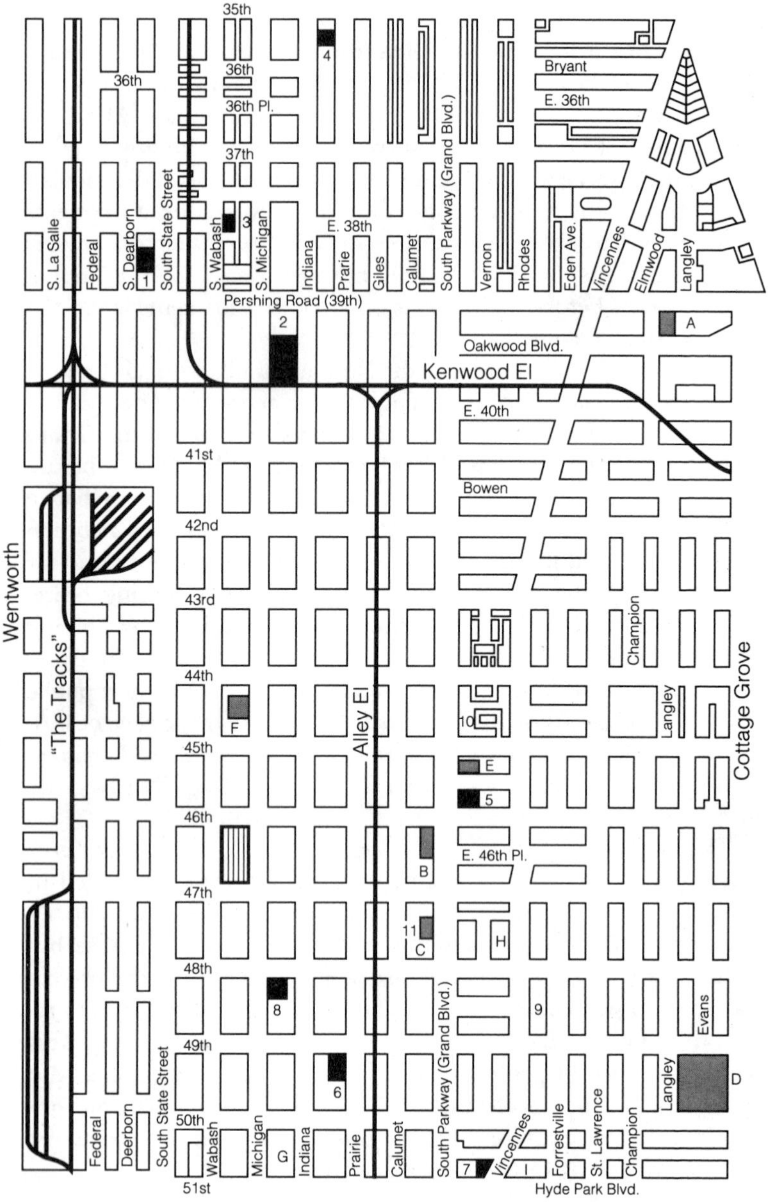

MAP 11.3. Michigan Boulevard Garden Apartments, "for Negroes" (base map: *Olcott's*, 1927).

Key to Map 11.3

Michigan Boulevard Garden Apartments ("Rosenwald Gardens")

Institutions "for Colored People"*

1. Institutional Church and Social Settlement (closed by 1919)
2. South Side Boys' Club
3. Wabash Avenue YMCA
4. "Colored" YMCA, first location
5. "Colored" YMCA, second location
6. Illinois Technical School for Colored Girls (Catholic boarding school for dependent Negro girls "regardless of creed")
7. Provident Hospital
8. George Cleveland Hall Branch of Chicago Public Library
9. African Methodist Episcopal Deaconness and Stewardess Home
10. Home for Aged Colored People
11. Mellissa Ann Elam Home for Colored Girls

White Institutions in the Black Belt*

A. Abraham Lincoln Centre
B. Sinai Temple's Emil Hirsch Center
C. Deborah Boys' Club (abandoned the area in 1930)
D. St. Xavier Academy for Girls (Catholic)
E. Illinois Home for Aged and Infirm Deaf
F. Martha Washington Home for Dependent Crippled Children
G. Chicago Home for Girls
H. Old People's Home of the City of Chicago
I. Chicago Home for the Friendless

*In 1920 the area between the "Alley El" and Cottage Grove and below the Kenwood El was still largely white. By 1930 this area was 95 percent Negro, and Cottage Grove had become the eastern boundary of the Black Belt. All of the white institutions except Lincoln Centre continued to bar Negroes. Lincoln Centre attempted an "interracial policy" with a quota on black admissions. See Chs. 13 and 14.

served with Rosenwald on the Riot Commission, proclaimed him the number one philanthropist and friend of "the Race" in America. He urged President Hoover to appoint Rosenwald to the cabinet. A black woman who read about the project in the newspapers wrote Rosenwald to thank him for his "wonderful plan for a beautiful block of flats to house my people":

> Oh how wonderful Oh how beautiful when you think of one of Gods Stewards who is not afraid to step out amidst criticism and censure and do

> what some would say the impossible for a race that it seems is a stigamato to other races just on account of the color of the skin . . . God wants more Stewards like you.

The woman lived in the 3100 block of Vernon, where Rosenwald had planned to build a model tenement before the war. She signed the letter "a very grateful race woman always able to see Gods hand in every good deed that is done for our advancement."[47]

The Rosenwald became the most coveted address in the Black Belt. People made sacrifices to live there. Even though the project drew its tenants from the black middle class, the average income of resident families in 1930 was only $2,400. That meant that the families paid, on the average, nearly a third of their incomes in rent.[48]

Before the buildings opened, Rosenwald added two black men to the corporation's board of directors. Alfred Stern hired a black office staff, and he chose a black man, Robert Taylor, to be resident manager. The management created a Board of Advisors, consisting of eleven elected tenants and three representatives of the corporation. The stated purpose of the board was to

> 1. Grant an opportunity to the tenants and Management to discuss mutual problems.
>
> 2. Justify the express confidence of Julius Rosenwald by demonstrating a high standard of living and financial responsibility.

After a year of operation, Julius Rosenwald noted with pleasure that the buildings were paying the anticipated 6 percent return on his investment. The residents paid their rents promptly, the premises were clean and orderly, and there was "little or no friction between the tenants and the management, or between the tenants themselves." The place was a showcase of decorum. Rosenwald was "especially impressed with the quiet that prevailed in the Court." He considered the enterprise a resounding success. "My faith in the Negro," he said, "is justified."[49]

Things did not work out so well at Marshall Field Gardens. Its Lower North Side site seemed favorable—within easy reach of two el stations and only a mile away from downtown to the south and the lakefront to the east. The project was so close to the opulent

Gold Coast that *Housing*, the journal of the National Housing Association, derided the Field Estate for pretending that it had reclaimed a "slum district." What the editors of *Housing* overlooked was the fact that Field Gardens was also right on the edge of a multiethnic but largely Italian slum known variously as Little Sicily and Little Hell. People who lived in the immediate vicinity could not afford monthly rents of $62, and many people who could pay that much were afraid of the surrounding neighborhood. One intersection acquired the designation Death Corner, not because of traffic accidents but because of gang killings. Moreover, black people were coming into the southern part of the district in large numbers and transforming what was once a small enclave into a "Little Black Belt."[50]

By the time Field Gardens opened, upwards of four thousand black people were living in the Lower North Side. Whites in the area hoped to contain the Little Black Belt below Division Street. The Field project, on the white side of that emerging line, cleared away "substantial housing which it was an advantage to be rid of." It was just the sort of property that landlords were willing to turn over to black tenants. Some units may have been Negro-occupied. Olivet Institute, a settlement house across the street from the project, had always drawn the color line in its neighborhood work, as had all of the area's settlements. Now Marshall Field Garden Apartments drew the line in housing reform.[51]

White people did not flock to the project. High vacancy rates plagued it from the start. Rather than fill empty apartments with black families, the management carried extensive vacancy losses. To make the project more attractive, the managers endeavored to provide a full range of community activities within the confines of the apartments. That way residents could insulate themselves from those who lived outside the oasis. This policy raised the overhead without correcting the vacancy problem. The Field Gardens did not show a profit at the end of its first year of operation, and with the onset of the Great Depression, the losses mounted.[52]

Back in 1926, when the Chicago Housing Commission was getting organized, its temporary chairman, Joseph Brittain, stated that the challenge was to house "those citizens able to pay only the lowest rents":

> It is not conceivable that a large portion of our population, upon whose existence so much of our great industrial prosperity rests, does not offer in the case of their housing a sound opportunity for permanent investment, justifying a modest but proper return upon capital.

And, added Brittain, who was then president of the Chicago Real Estate Board:

> If this is not the case, Chicago exists only by sweating this population to a level of life lower than that which should be demanded of our citizens.

Neither Rosenwald Gardens nor Field Gardens even tried to house poor people. The Field project failed to show a profit even with its middle-class clientele. And while Rosenwald Gardens appeared to be operating satisfactorily, it failed to draw additional capital into model housing. Early in the planning of the project, Alfred Stern had said that it would prove nothing unless other capitalists acted on its example. Once the hard times hit, there was no chance that that would happen.[53]

In the spring of 1931, the tenants at Rosenwald Gardens, battered by the Depression, petitioned the management to cut the rents. When the management refused, a radical black newspaper ran an angry editorial titled "Is Rosenwald Trying to Help?" The editor charged the great philanthropist with the "jim-crowing of colored people." Rosenwald funded institutions "for colored people only," the editor claimed, for the purpose of "keeping the colored man out of white institutions and to himself." Later in the year, after rioting broke out in the Black Belt, the managers of the Rosenwald building lowered the rents. Julius Rosenwald died shortly thereafter, in January 1932.[54]

Black leaders, except for a few radicals, had always spoken reverentially of Rosenwald alive, and they continued to speak gently of him dead. But for the first time, they voiced criticism of the Rosenwald Fund. In mid-1933 A. C. McNeal, the first Negro president of the Chicago NAACP, suggested that the "purpose" of the fund might be "the segregation and separation of the races" through "Jim Crow" schools, YMCAs, hospitals, and housing. By this time, even though rentals were reduced, most of "the

Rosenwald's" tenants could not make their payments without taking in boarders, who now outnumbered children in the project by almost two to one.[55]

❧

Private enterprise proved itself incapable of solving the housing problem even before the period of "prosperity" came crashing to a halt. The Depression spread the distress of being unable to pay for decent homes beyond the poorest districts to a widening circle of communities. While foreclosures and evictions were becoming everyday occurrences, solid citizens still clung to the business creed and waited grimly for conditions to return to normal.[56]

One day in August 1931 a real estate agent, accompanied by three municipal court bailiffs, went to a wretched building at 50th and Dearborn, half a mile from Rosenwald Gardens, to evict a 71-year-old Negro woman who had paid no rent for three months. When the bailiffs moved her belongings onto the street, a large crowd gathered and attempted to put the furniture back into the house. Police arrived to dispel the crowd; when the people resisted, the policemen fired at them. Three black men fell dead and others lay bleeding in the street. Three of the policemen claimed injuries as well. But law prevailed over disorder, and the aged Mrs. Diana Gross suffered the consequences of falling behind in her rent. Later in the day, amid rumors that the eviction-racked Black Belt was on the brink of revolt, the Chicago Real Estate Board issued a public statement. "We are willing to do all we can to help," the real estate agents said, "but it is impossible to compromise with what is strictly a business proposition."[57]

PART IV

The Neighborhood Role of the Settlements

Our work is needed more than it has ever been needed before, as the neighborhood becomes poorer, more foreign and more needy.

—Report of the Work of Chicago Commons for the year ending September 30, 1919, p. 1.

We did not have to meet the American prejudice against the negro . . . there were no colored people in the community.

—Mary McDowell, "Prejudice," in *Mary McDowell and Municipal Housekeeping: A Symposium*, ed. Caroline M. Hill (Chicago, 1937), p. 28.

In 1919, with the problems of postwar readjustment mounting and the prospect of social reconstruction beckoning, the veterans of the settlement movement were curiously unready for action. Jane Addams was absorbed in the world peace movement. She continued to direct Hull-House, but she had only marginal interest in neighborhood work. Physically and spiritually, she was away from the West Side much of the time. Other settlement pioneers who were still involved in neighborhood work were tired, discouraged, confused about their methods, and uncertain of their goals. They had labored hard, without clear results, to bring harmony, stability, democracy, and opportunity into community life. The tenement areas were more deteriorated than before. The settlement houses were firmly established *in* the ethnic neighborhoods, but they were not *of* the neighborhoods. The staff members for the most part did things *for* their neighbors, not *with* them. The only thing that the settlement people were still sure of was that, somehow, they were *needed.* In fact, they believed that the neighborhood people needed them more than ever. But now, more than ever, they had doubts about how to meet the need.

And then the riot came. Finally, abruptly, the settlements found themselves "face to face with the race question." They were supposed to be the institutions that, more than any others in the city, could bring "divided peoples together." All of the "foreign" districts were ethnically diverse. Every settlement staff tried, as a resident of Henry Booth House expressed it, "to develop a more tolerant feeling between the neighborhood races." But the "races" in the Booth House area, in the Jewish "ghetto" south of Hull-House, were not whites and blacks but rather Jews, Italians, Bohemians, Lithuanians, Poles, and "remnants of the disappearing Irish and German populations of an earlier day." Settlement personnel often spoke of immigrant groups as "races," and so long as the racial elements they tried to mix were whites of different ethnic stocks, their efforts met with some success. But this was no preparation at all for bringing blacks and whites together. Color was a radically different sort of race problem.[1]

During the riot it became unmistakably clear that Chicago's real "race problem" was the one involving blacks on the one hand and whites, native and foreign, on the other. A resident of University of Chicago Settlement watched helplessly as a carful of Ragen's Colts, brandishing firearms and screaming "We'll get those niggers!" sped down 47th Street toward the Black Belt. Back a' the Yards was a white neighborhood, but the packing plants had black laborers. Five black men and one white man died in street battles around the Yards. "The most atrocious murder" of the whole riot took place a few blocks from Hull-House, in another all-white area. While a rumor was circulating through the neighborhood that a Negro had killed an Italian girl, a black youngster came riding along on a bicycle. A mob grabbed the boy, bludgeoned him, stabbed him over and over again, and pumped fourteen slugs into his mangled body.[2]

There was a demand for more neighborhood work after the riot, just as there was a demand for housing reform. The postriot coroner's jury and grand jury both recommended social work with youth gangs, because of the numbers of boys involved in the rioting. The First Presbyterian Church, at 41st and Grand Boulevard in the "contested" territory, urged the provision of "good living quarters" and social settlements "for both races" in the spring of 1920. The Riot Commission issued essentially the same recommendation two years later. By that time the vicinity of 41st and Grand Boulevard was all-Negro, and First Presbyterian Church was relocated in white Woodlawn. Clearly, the church's concern was not for integration but rather for accommodation of whites and blacks in separate facilities. The Riot Commission, too, stood for a dual program, in neighborhood work as well as in housing reform.[3]

Settlement workers accepted the mandate to extend their services to blacks and work at easing racial tensions. All of the settlements operating in 1919 but one were in white neighborhoods, for white people. Settlement workers supported new settlements for the Black Belt, but they did not bring blacks and whites together in the same neighborhood centers. They proved once again that they were adept at operating across nationality barriers, but they did not overcome the color line. Most of them did not try. They had no mandate to overstep the color line, which many of them had helped to draw and hoped to hold. In Chicago, as elsewhere, the settlements stood for the unification of a segmented society, but they segregated Negroes.

The twenties was a time of tremendous neighborhood upheaval. Try as they might, settlement workers could not arrest it. They failed to establish the sort of stable "social organization" that they thought their communities required. And despite their dedication to democracy, they did not turn decision-making powers over to the people. Informally, they allowed the community will to prevail on one major question, but only one: whether or not to allow Negroes to join in settlement activities.

At the end of the decade, settlement workers were still in a muddle over the aims and methods of neighborhood work. Nevertheless, they had played a fateful role in the neighborhood transitions of the twenties, even if the exact nature of that role was never clear to them.

CHAPTER 12 ❧

"Building Better Than We Know": The Settlements and the Ethnic Enclaves

If the neighborhood about Chicago Commons were stationary, the settlement would be able to keep in touch with all the members of many families throughout a generation. But with a tremendous racial transformation and transientness of population, a great deal of work must be done with the faith that results will show some where some time.
—Report of the Work of Chicago Commons for the year, 1 October 1913 to 30 September 1914, Commons Papers, CHS.

We are building better than we know.
—Graham Taylor to Chicago Commons Board of Trustees, 20 April 1933, Commons Papers.

In 1892 Jacob Riis, the New York reformer, said that society had the choice of training the slum child "or of being slugged and robbed by him." And he argued that the first alternative was philanthropy, self-defense, and shrewd business all rolled into one profitable proposition. "No investment gives a better return today on the capital put out," Riis wrote, "than work among the children of the poor." This was the argument that launched more than a score of settlements and boys' clubs in Chicago.[1]

In 1919, just two months before the great riots, an officer of the Boys' Clubs of America told members of Chicago's City Club that the "money value" of the city's boys was about $4,000 apiece. Chicago's 250,000 boys constituted "an asset of almost a billion dollars," the speaker declared. "Of course, assets often shrink," he cautioned his audience. "When a boy ceases to be an asset to the community, he may become a liability." During the August rampage, Chicago's young men inflicted an estimated $3 million worth of damage on property. Solid citizens resolved to redouble their efforts to control the city's unruly boys. Neglect was costly. Supervision would pay.[2]

Settlement personnel had always taken "the boy problem" seriously. No part of their work seemed more important, nor more difficult, than getting hold of the boy. As the boys' worker at Abraham Lincoln Centre complained in 1915, "commercialized amusements get and hold the boys when we cannot." When the boy was little, the settlement had to outbid the nickelodeon for his attention. As he grew older there were more places where he could congregate with his friends and do what he pleased, free of supervision. It became a contest between the settlement, on the one hand, and the picture show, the poolroom, the public dance hall, and the saloon, on the other. "If we can bid higher," the Lincoln Centre worker said, "then we get the boy; if not, they get him, and sooner or later we are paying for him as a public charge."[3]

The politician, too, wanted to get hold of the boy so that when he came of age he could assume his rightful place as a loyal member of the machine. The bosses cultivated the gangs, giving the boys nickels to see a show and shoot a game of pool, bailing them out if policemen caught them playing craps, junking, ditching school, or brawling. When the boys got ambitious and threw a dance, the boss would buy tickets, help them secure a hall, and put in the fix if they wanted to sell liquor. If the boys wanted to patronize saloons, that was fine with the boss. The saloon was the main political clubroom in the tenement wards.[4]

"Every street gang in Chicago," sociologist Frederic M. Thrasher observed in the twenties, "aspires to be an athletic club with rooms of its own." Social workers believed that if a bunch of boys secured an unsupervised clubroom the battle for their allegiance was all but lost. In such a haunt the boys would not only loaf but also smoke, gamble, drink, tell "dirty jokes and nasty stories," sing vile songs, stockpile "salacious photographs," and read pornographic pamphlets ("eight pagers"), such as *Wampus Cat, Whiz Bang, Hot Dog, Jazz,* and *Smut.* The boys might do worse. Social workers knew of stag parties with live, nude entertainers; sex orgies involving one girl and as many as thirty boys ("gang shags" or "mattress parties"); masturbation races ("circle jerks"); and mass rape ("gang bangs"). The athletic clubs had little to do with conventional sports.[5]

If a gang proved its worth to a boss (by hustling up votes, passing out flyers, putting up signs, tearing down opponents' posters, perhaps slugging an occasional overzealous worker for the other side or casting a ballot in place of some registered voter who had not made it to the polls), he would sometimes show his appreciation by setting up a storefront for "the boys." The Ragen A. C. on Halsted Street was the home of Ragen's Colts, the palace guard of Cook County Commissioner Frank Ragen. Colt alumni included not only mobsters but also "aldermen, police captains, county treasurers, sheriffs, and so on." Mary McDowell charged, and the Riot Commission sustained her, that the Colts enjoyed total immunity from the law when they burned, looted, maimed, and murdered during the riots.[6]

Settlement workers regarded gangs like the Colts as beyond salvation. What they hoped to do was to attract the children's play groups to the settlement and instill them with the proper ideals before they grew into full-fledged gangs. In their competitive struggle with the picture shows and the dance halls, the settlements employed both restrictive and constructive tactics. Housing reformers attempted to regulate all tenement construction through building codes, and they built model tenements as well. In much the same way, neighborhood workers tried to police the theaters and the dance halls, and they showed suitable movies and sponsored proper dances, too.

Within five years of the opening of the first "five-cent theater" in Chicago, reformers led by Jane Addams secured passage of America's first municipal movie censorship ordinance. Hull-House was one of the first settlements to offer free screenings of model educational films for the edification of neighborhood youngsters. But on Saturday afternoons, when the settlement viewing room was practically empty, thousands of youngsters sat watching blood, thunder, and romance on the screens of local movie houses. The bland fare offered at the settlements was never serious competition for the theaters. Jane Addams called the cheap show "the house of dreams" and soon admitted that for the family, and especially for children under fifteen, the movie was the main neighborhood center, filling even more of a place in their lives than the saloon did for the adult male.[7]

Censorship did not stop the proliferation of theaters. In 1909, when the ordinance went into effect and the license fee for small theaters doubled, the city had 405 cheap movie houses. Five years later there were 380 licensed theaters and another 300 or so that operated without a license. The early theaters were small storefront enterprises. Most had magic-sounding names such as the Palace, the Bijou Dream, and Rosebud. But there was one called the Community, one called the Neighborhood, and there were several called the Home. The settlements were dealing with the first movie generation. Even youngsters who were "regulars" at the settlement house spent more time at the movie house. And the social workers thought that what the children watched in the shows, even after police censors snipped away hundreds of thousands of feet of film, was trash.[8]

In the twenties the number of theaters fell below 400, but this was the age of the colossal movie palaces with two thousand to three thousand seats. The audience was vaster than ever. In 1926 there were nearly as many seats in the shows as there were in the public schools. The great movie palaces in outlying retail districts added a new dimension to the problem of the picture shows. Before, the movie house was a neighborhood institution. Children walked to the show in packs. Going to the show was a gang function. At fourteen or fifteen, young people turned their interests toward the dance hall. Now the movie palace was a place to ride to on a streetcar or in a car. At fourteen or fifteen, adolescents left the local movie house to the youngsters and paired off with a "date" to travel to the high-class theater or went with a pack to pick up girls. For teenagers the new movie palace, all glitter on the outside but dark inside, offered many of the same opportunities as the dance hall.[9]

Social workers were alert to the danger. In 1926 Jessie Binford of Hull-House, director of the Juvenile Protective Association, declared that city adolescents were learning about "sex and affection and marriage" not at home, at church, or in school but at the show. "There is no more perplexing problem," she said, "than that of the movies." If the young people acquired anything valuable at the settlements, the neighborhood workers feared, they lost it at the movies.[10]

The public dance hall was at least as popular with young people as the movie theater, and even more "perilous." Early in 1911 the JPA estimated that the city's 328 dance halls attracted as many as 86,000 young people between the ages of fourteen and eighteen on peak nights. The proprietors permitted not only "the grossest and most dangerous forms of 'tough' dancing" but "open embracing as well," the JPA's investigators found, and they sold liquor to people of tender years. The settlements sponsored dances as much to "enforce standards" as to attract the young. Staff members patrolled the floor to uphold the proprieties. They expelled individuals or couples "under the influence of liquor," kept the lights turned up bright, and closed early. In the postwar period the dance halls followed a pattern similar to that of the movies. The number of halls diminished, but spectacular ballrooms at a distance from the tenement areas drew more and more patrons from all over. A new feature of ballrooms in the twenties was their connection with bootleg booze.[11]

More than ever, the settlements wanted to put the commercial dance halls out of business. For staff members, struggling with the crowds at the settlement dance became a trying ordeal. Unlike settlement movie shows and other activities, the dances did draw crowds, including large numbers of people who never came to the settlements for anything else, because the price was lower than at any commercial dance hall. Liquor was not for sale, but young men would smuggle in their own or arrange for a girl to slip a flask into her purse. The dance became a duel of standards between the young people and the social workers. The staff tried to bring members of settlement clubs into the enforcement procedure, and sometimes this tactic helped. Still, the stage was always set for a free-for-all.[12]

The settlements picked the stodgiest bands available and directed them to play the most sedate waltzes and fox trots. Personnel would circulate among the dancing couples to pry ardent couples apart. The dancers wanted to be Sheiks and Shebas. The staff wanted them to be ladies and gentlemen. "No shaking of the body—absolutely none" was the standard settlement rule. But no matter how tepid the music was, the girls would "shimmy" and "shake it," and the boys would "rub it up," "bump," and "sock it in." One series of dances at Northwestern University Settlement ended in a shambles when the crowd refused to obey the directives of the monitors. Harriet Vittum, the head resident, stopped the music, mounted the bandstand, admonished the audience, and stood mortified as the boys responded by "making vulgar sounds with their lips." (This was her euphemism for what the kids called "lip-farting.")[13]

Chicago Commons felt that it was making some progress with its monthly dances. Beginning in 1926, the staff permitted the senior boys' and girls' council to run an annual dance. The purpose of the Shy Kom Dance was to prove that the young people could enforce the settlement's standards on themselves once a year. These dances were relatively decorous, for which the staff was gratified, but still "the moral tone was not upheld." And staff members were disappointed to keep finding flyers like this one:

> Whoopee! For a Riot of Fun follow the crowd to the Third Annual Mammoth Frolic and dance sponsored by the Bachelor Sportsmen at the New Grand Hotel . . . Saturday Nite, Feb. 1st, 1930. Music by Eudora Singing Night Hawks.

The Bachelor Sportsmen were members of the Commons senior council. The band was one of the hottest combos out of the Black Belt. Compared to the Shy Kom Dance, the frolic promised to be like Hellz-appopin.[14]

Youth work in general, and boys' work in particular, was full of disappointments and dilemmas. No settlement really had enough space and enough staff to accommodate all of the boys in its district. Graham Taylor wrote in 1919 that the Commons had never been able to handle more than 500 of the 5,000 boys who lived in the half-square-mile area around Grand and Morgan. It was necessary to make more room somehow, he said, both to help the boys and "to protect public safety." Two years later he reported that stricter scheduling, better staffing, and rearrangement of space allotments would make it feasible to enroll as many as 1,000 boys. Yet that optimum figure still left four out of five boys around the Commons "with nowhere else to go" but the streets and such "destructive agencies" as picture shows and poolrooms. And the Commons never enrolled 500 boys again after 1921. In 1928 the total number of boys using the Commons was about 400, of whom only 280 paid dues and attended regularly.[15]

Another problem was whom to let in. If the staff imposed one code of conduct on all, would the tougher kids come as well as the upwardly mobile, ambitious types? And if the tough "element" was welcome, would status-conscious parents allow their children to attend? Gang members, if given entry, might try to take over the settlement. If excluded, they might do what twenty Polish boys did when a settlement "canned" them. They vowed "to do away with the settlement which was notified to this effect. . . . They stole balls from the settlement, broke gymnasium windows, and put fake notices on the bulletin boards, but did not cause any serious trouble." Some gangs that used a settlement as a common enemy to solidify their own cohesion went further. They broke windows and locks, invaded the buildings and engaged in "orgies of rough-housing," smashing furniture, pool tables, cue sticks, and lamps, and breaking toilet fixtures. Sometimes they vandalized the social workers' cars, and occasionally they beat up a staff member. More often they attacked individuals and groups who wanted to enter the settlement.[16]

Excluding the rougher kids meant not having a chance to manage them at all. But including them did not mean that they could be controlled either. Frederic M. Thrasher described the "bedlam in a settlement" that tried to reform a gang of fifteen boys by letting them hang out in its gang room. Thrasher observed the boys for several weeks. Always, instead of adapting to the rules laid down by the staff, they threw the place into "pandemonium." "The noise was deafening," Thrasher noted. The boys were constantly chasing each other all over the room and all over the building. "They could not hold steady long enough to play a game of pool; at about the third shot, the balls would begin to fly."[17]

Most settlements quickly gave up with boys like these. The staff would "can" them and call on the police to protect the building from retaliation. Boys' work definitely centered on boys who would not make too much trouble. Chicago Commons tried much harder than any other settlement to work the "problem" boys into the program. The effort wore down the staff and left scars on the building. Sometimes staff members were scarred as well. More than one boys' worker had to face down a challenge from the best fighter in a group, and a few times the showdowns ended in slugfests. The Commons was probably the most vandalized settlement in the city. Graffiti covered the walls and steps, and as a sociology student noted in 1931, "the portable equipment of the settlement disappears constantly; apparently nothing small enough to be put under a coat can be kept."[18]

In a neighborhood like the one around the Commons, even the "good boys" were pretty tough, and they always outnumbered the roughnecks in the program. The majority helped the staff to keep the "delinquent" minority in check. Still, some Commons workers got fed up with the harassment they took from the troublemakers. In 1928 Karl Borders, the head boys' worker, said that the settlement should stop trying to reform delinquents and "idiots." He recommended that the Commons concentrate on boys with intellect and ambition, "souls thirsting for the waters of life," and provide them "a haven in a barren land."[19]

The Commons did not give in to Borders's disillusionment, but it drew the line against incorrigibly unruly boys. It expelled them and relied on the police to make them submit. Expulsions were always provisional. If a boy agreed to "conform to the rules of the house," he could return on probation. As Lea Taylor, Graham Taylor's daughter and his successor as head resident, put it in her dismissal notes to the boys, "The Board of Trustees of Chicago Commons is a group of business men who are responsible for the property and management of the work." The trustees could not tolerate destruction of the property.[20]

All of the settlements drew the line on conduct, though none of the others drew it so loosely as the Commons did. But none of them drew any ethnic line. All neighborhoods had at least some ethnic mixture, and all settlements accepted whites of any nationality. Olivet Institute on the Lower North Side, on the edge of "Little Sicily," held street meetings in three languages besides English to draw people to its activities. The settlement house in Burnside, where twenty-two different ethnic groups lived intermingled in an area of twenty-two blocks, may have barred some individuals on the basis of behavior, but it had members from each of the twenty-two groups. The dominant ethnic group in an area often tried to treat a settlement as its exclusive preserve, but no staff let any neighborhood group dictate its admissions policy.[21]

Chicago experienced its first noticeable influx of Mexicans in the twenties. No settlement house in the city turned them away. Although the groups who customarily used the settlements usually grumbled about the admission of Mexicans, the staffs of all the settlements in the neighborhoods affected by the migration integrated them into their programs. At Hull-House the Italians received the Mexicans "almost as a group of their own countrymen" at first. But, as Jane Addams recorded in *The Second Twenty Years at Hull-House,* the Italians slowly turned against the Mexicans. For one thing, "the Mexicans mingled freely with the negroes," who came into the district below 12th Street at the same time that the Mexicans were moving in. Moreover, "many Mexicans were of dark skin." A large Latin Club, made up of Mexican and Italian young men, split in two after bad blood developed. Finally, a group of Italians threatened to withdraw from the settlement unless Hull-House denied access to Mexicans. Their reason was that Mexicans were "people of color." The settlement refused to give in to the threat. Mexicans, Italians, and people of more than two dozen nationalities continued to use the place.[22]

Working "dark-skinned Mexicans" into the routine at University of Chicago Settlement proved to be more of a problem, but the staff surmounted it. Mexicans began moving into Back a' the Yards in noticeable numbers in 1924. The established residents, particularly the Poles, seemed to harbor "a dislike for the Mexicans," an observer reported, "similar to that which they have for Negroes." Soon "chasing Mexicans" became "the chief sport" of neighborhood gangs. Sometimes the outnumbered newcomers fought back. The conflict reached its climax in 1926, when "a couple of Mexicans" fired a pistol into a crowd of thirty boys who were throwing rocks at them, and one of their shots killed a Polish youngster. Throughout the period of tension that followed, Mexicans, singly or in groups, were welcome at the settlement. For a long time the staff was afraid to allow *groups* of Mexicans to use the building when Polish and Lithuanian groups were using it, but by 1928 this seemed "perfectly safe." Each nationality group in the neighborhood viewed itself proudly as "a white race," a sociology student noted in 1928; gradually, grudgingly, the people were coming to regard Mexicans as another white group.[23]

In part the settlements' open-door policy reflected the fact that the ethnic enclaves were heterogeneous. Not only settlements but also most youth gangs had mixed membership. Frederic Thrasher, who made an exhaustive study of gangs in the twenties, found that 5 percent were "American-white," 45 percent were "dominantly or solidly of a single nationality group," 7 percent were "Negro," and the rest were "mixed." The settlements and the gangs had territorial constituencies. Because the turf was polyglot, so were they. Still, the open-door policy represented a conscious decision, and the neighborhood folk had little or nothing to say about it. If the majority had been allowed to rule, the Commons would probably have been all-Italian, Northwestern University Settlement all-Polish, and several other settlements would have been one-nationality sanctuaries as well. It was not that way, because, as Lea Taylor told the delinquents expelled from the Commons, the boards ran the settlements. The neighborhood people did not.[24]

In 1919 Graham Taylor and other settlement leaders were hoping to begin anew the task of community organization. They hoped to start boys off at the kindergarten level and lead them up the ladder of responsibility to positions at the top of neighborhood life. The behavior of the neighborhood workers belied their professed belief in grass-roots democracy. They talked about experimenting with new institutions such as kindergartens and playgrounds and then cheerfully surrendering them to the public. In practice this always meant turning facilities over to government bureaucrats, not to neighborhood people. The boards continued to deny representation to the neighborhoods. When head residents of settlements retired, the people had no say in selecting their successors. In 1922 Graham Taylor relinquished his office as head resident at Chicago Commons. He retained his ominous title of "warden" for the rest of his life. The person who took over directing the Commons program for him was his daughter Lea. She had been raised in the Commons building, except for summers in suburban Winnetka. She considered the neighborhood her real home, and by 1922 she had lived there longer than the great majority of area residents. All of this did not change the fact that she came to her post by heredity, not by democratic selection.[25]

Increasingly after 1920 the settlements filled staff openings with college students majoring in sociology or social work. Neighborhood people were available for staff work, especially in recurring periods of slack employment, but the settlements thought that they were poorly qualified. As Graham Taylor said, the settlement worker had to be able to interpret the tenement world and the world outside, one to the other. Neighborhood people knew only the world of the neighborhood, he thought; they lacked the required background and training. Despite Taylor's bias, Chicago Commons entrusted neighborhood residents with staff responsibility more than any other settlement did.[26]

Typically, settlements screened out local people from positions of authority and shunned them even as volunteers. In January 1929, a speaker at a meeting of the Chicago Federation of Settlements addressed his coworkers on the subject of volunteers. He said that while no volunteers were "worth very much," he had most success with "young business men, especially young bankers." A wealthy banker on his board of directors furnished him with a supply of eager volunteers. The banker would select "a likely young man from his force" and urge him "to get in touch with the world of affairs by leading a boys' club." Without fail the young man would take the hint and go forth to lead a boys' club both to do good and to advance himself "in the banking business." Along with aspiring businessmen, college students and young society women were the mainstays of the volunteer cadres.[27]

Nothing alienated the settlements from their neighbors so much as the issue of Prohibition. In the early days, the settlements had recognized not only the potency and the harmfulness of the saloons but their social value as well. The saloon was the poor man's club, among other things, and the settlement workers acknowledged that wiping it out with nothing to replace it would be both unfair and unfortunate. But the settlements came to view themselves as offering a man everything he could decently want in the way of a substitute for the saloon. Once, the reformers were content to police saloons, raise their licensing rates and thus decrease their number, and set up coffee shops and clubrooms to compete with them. These were weapons similar to the ones they used against the slum building, the movie, and the dance hall. People who enjoyed indulging their thirst socially could live with regulation, and they could take the settlement coffee shop or leave it. But Prohibition gave them no choice. It abolished the saloon, abolished all liquor. It was a curse, wished on them by the settlement workers.[28]

The settlements thought that they could take drink away from their neighbors, make them lump Prohibition, and still organize them into community associations. The notion was preposterous. Most of the "community organizations" that settlement workers helped to establish in the postwar period were nothing more than local councils of social agencies. No one belonged to them but the functionaries of public and private institutions: schools, clinics, libraries, police stations, charitable agencies, and sometimes churches. The councils attempted to coordinate the efforts of all the forces, mainly from outside the community, which were trying to control it. Two organizations, which called themselves "community councils," tried to do something more. The settlements that were involved in setting up these two councils viewed them as bold undertakings.[29]

Mary McDowell of University of Chicago Settlement was the main organizer of the Community Council of the Stock Yards District. The council was novel in a few ways. It included business establishments among the agencies on its board, and it invited "civic leaders and interested citizens" to take individual membership. Its geographic base was wide as well, covering about ten square miles. In structure the organization was actually a federation of several smaller councils. Within the overall council's territory were the communities of Bridgeport, McKinley Park, New City, the built-up portions of Brighton Park and Gage Park, and the white-occupied sections of Armour Square and Fuller Park. The council's eastern boundary, running four and a half miles north to south, was Wentworth Avenue, which marked the westernmost limit of the Black Belt.[30]

The council's scope was big, but its operation proved to be anything but bold. In practice, representation was institutional, after all, and eventually the dominant institutions in the council, as in the Stock Yards District, were the packinghouses. Working people had practically no influence in the organization. The figurehead president of the council throughout the twenties was a Methodist Episcopal pastor named Warren N. Clark. Reverend Clark was an inveterate joiner, with active membership in seven Southwest Side organizations besides the council: five Masonic chapters; the Lions Club; and Warren G. Harding Lodge No. 1053 of the International Order of Odd Fellows. As Saul Alinsky, who organized a very different sort of community organization in Back a' the Yards in the thirties, would later charge, the only people who attended the monthly meetings of the old district council were "professional people from the University of Chicago Settlement House and a number of Protestant ministers."[31]

The Lower North Community Council was organized "from the bottom up," on paper. The goal of the organizers in 1919 was to enroll five thousand dues-paying members dedicated to making a single, well-ordered community out of the Gold Coast and the adjoining slums. However, Eli Bates House, Olivet Institute, and the other agencies promoting the program could not convince the people of Little Hell that the council was not "merely another bit of patronage and uplift." Within a year or two it was clear that the council represented the Gold Coast, not the whole Lower North Side. A handful of executives determined policy; "a paid secretary and paid social workers" then carried it out. The bulk of the budget came from Gold Coast donations. The proceeds from an annual benefit, "one of the smartest affairs of the social season," provided the balance.[32]

The council concentrated on keeping up property values in the lakeshore district of the community. It did little to improve conditions near the river, in Little Hell. Yet the council's fund campaigns emphasized salvaging the slums. For, as Harvey Zorbaugh observed in *The Gold Coast and the Slum*, many rich people would not give money unless they "could feel that they were uplifting the slum mother speaking her broken English, and the little ragamuffin on the street." The Lower North Community Council was a community council in name only. It was more like a council of social agencies, except that the member organizations had little control over the executive committee, which was responsible not to them but to the Gold Coast. That was a technicality, however, because the Gold Coast dominated the boards of the agencies anyway.[33]

Some settlements attempted to organize men into neighborhood associations somewhat like the old community clubs at Hull-House and the Commons. The results were meager. Eli Bates House, a sponsor of the Lower North Community Council, also engineered a small organization called the Italian Progressive Club. Apparently the object was to draw the *leadership* from bankers and attorneys who had formerly lived in the neighborhood and recruit the rank and file from "the more promising of the younger generation." The Bates House staff hoped that those leaders would educate and uplift the followers. The settlement had no plans to develop a viable political organization from the club.[34]

Throughout the twenties, Chicago Commons tried to build a strong "betterment association" among the Italians. The method was somewhat like that used by organizers at Bates House, but the goal was political as well as social. Glenford Lawrence, the "men's worker" at the Commons, tried to enlist the aid of the best-known, most respected Italians in the city. With their help, he organized the businessmen and professional men in the Commons neighborhood into the Italian-American Progressive Club. Continuing to work from the top down, he directed the local "leaders" to appeal to "the young man, who has not been here long and who is still in the 'formative period of life,'" and also the young man who had been formed through years of participation in the programs of the Commons. The neighborhood's "future leaders," Lawrence thought, would come from these young men.[35]

The men's organization at the Commons went through many changes, of leadership, of name, and of stated purpose. Membership vacillated between 150 and 500. Yet Glenford Lawrence was ever optimistic. In 1923 William E. Dever, the "Commons Alderman" of the era when the settlement was a power in ward politics, ran for mayor of Chicago and won in a landslide. He swept his old home ward, and the Commons took heart. Of course, Dever had swept most of the city's wards. The Commons staff believed that their ward, the Thirty-first, like all Chicago, was ready for reform again. In the aldermanic elections of that year, Stanley Adamkiewicz, a longtime foe of the settlement, made his weakest showing since he had gone to the City Council in 1917.[36]

When the next aldermanic elections came around, the Commons felt ready to go back into ward politics. In 1925 an officer of the settlement's Italian-American association ran for alderman with the full backing of the settlement. The candidate, Gerard M. Ungaro, was a successful attorney who had lived in the neighborhood all his life. He had been part of the Commons program since his kindergarten days, and he was the first neighborhood person to win a place on the volunteer staff. In the past, several Italians had made the race to represent the ward in the City Council, and the settlement had opposed every one of them. Now the Commons proudly offered Ungaro to the neighborhood as the settlement's choice. The neighborhood's response? They rejected Ungaro overwhelmingly. "He made a clean-cut campaign," Lea Taylor wrote in the annual report for 1925, "but [he] had little chance against the Pole running for reelection." Ungaro finished with less than 22 percent of the vote. A year later he moved out of the neighborhood, miles away, to the edge of the city.[37]

The Commons had miscalculated, to put it mildly. Dever won big in 1923 not because of a groundswell for reform but because the Democratic organization was behind him, the Republican opposition was divided, and he was against Prohibition. The Commons people backed him, though he was "wet," because they knew he would enforce the law. Many people voted for him confident that he would let the booze flow freely. As mayor, he cracked down on violators of the law. His performance endeared him to prohibitionists, but it ruined his chances for reelection. When the Commons endorsed Gerard Ungaro, it was the kiss of death for his campaign. Similarly, when the staff "worked hard to turn the tide of neighborhood opinion" in Mayor Dever's favor in 1927, the result was "a large vote for the other side." Dever did badly everywhere in his old home ward, but in the precincts at a distance from the settlement he managed to salvage 44 percent of the vote. Near the Commons, where the staff concentrated its effort, he received an appalling 27 percent of the ballots cast.[38]

To work in a settlement over a long period of time was to experience disappointment and defeat over and over again. In 1928 the aged reformer Graham Taylor, having witnessed the recent humiliation of his old friend Mayor Dever, the defeat of young Gerard Ungaro, and then Ungaro's departure from the neighborhood, reflected gloomily on the "political deterioration" of "the city centers." The problem was the same one that had been vexing him throughout his tenure at Chicago Commons. The neighborhood's "better informed and experienced citizens," the "standbys" of settlement activities, always moved away, leaving vacancies for "hordes of new comers." As Taylor had lamented years earlier, the deterioration would go on and on unless the settlements could "actually hold people" where they were, "notwithstanding the increasing disagreeableness of the surroundings." The only hope was to make the ambitious, rising element of the neighborhood "stay put." The settlement's role was "to settle," to keep movement to a minimum and thus induce stability.[39]

Yet the people who stayed in the neighborhood did not necessarily stay put. There was a kind of permanent, floating population that was always there, but never at one spot for any length of time. The Commons tried to keep track of local "problem families" for United Charities, recording on a case card any occasion when crisis overtook them. The cards show that these poor, trouble-ridden people moved, not far but often, keeping a step ahead of a rent or bill collector, getting a better place when they had the money or a cheaper one when they didn't. For most families there is a different address for every contact they had with the settlement. Whether the caseworker saw them five times in five years or in five months, she would find them at five different places. To take just one case that is not extreme: One family that the settlement encountered eight times between 1914 and 1930 was living in a different flat each time. Six of their addresses were in three adjoining blocks. The seventh was one block away from this strip; the eighth was one block over from the seventh. The family kept moving back and forth, never getting anywhere. There was one month when the settlement worker saw them twice: They were at two different addresses. They were transient, but they were practically stationary.[40]

The settlement's regular clientele, in contrast to the charity families, tended to leave the neighborhood when they moved. Most of them *did* move. And, like Gerard Ungaro, the more attached they were to the Commons, the farther they seemed to go. In 1928, for instance, the most dedicated settlement club was the Lightnings. Its twelve members emulated the aggressive businessman who supervised them. They became "so identified with the settlement ideals" that they began "to class themselves with the settlement workers rather than with the neighborhood people." By 1932 all but one of the Lightnings lived outside the neighborhood. Of the eleven young men who left, the one whose home was *closest* to the Commons lived four miles away. These young men represented the most "stable" group in the neighborhood, from the settlement's viewpoint, yet they were the most mobile.[41]

There was no way to make the population stick to one spot. The people in the area around the Commons, and in all settlement neighborhoods, were in "an incessant state of migration." A 1915 survey showed that one-third to one-half of the families in the blocks around the Commons moved every year. That did not change; the continuity of change was the one thing that was constant from year to year. Nothing else was permanent and predictable.[42]

It was not only the people of the tenements who were on the move. In 1918 Taylor had complained of the terrific turnover rate among settlement workers. The settlements were in a poor position to preach stability when their own households were always in flux. By 1934, when Chicago Commons celebrated its fortieth anniversary, nearly nine hundred residents had come and gone. In forty years, the Commons staff had undergone the equivalent of nearly forty complete turnovers. Everyone was in motion.[43]

The real neighborhood role of the settlements was not to stop people from moving away. That kind of stability was impossible to impose. The settlements stabilized their neighborhoods by helping people who were upwardly mobile to make their move. The tenement districts were not static "urban villages." They became staging areas where a succession of newcomers arrived, acquired the means of advance, and then departed. The process always disturbed Graham Taylor. But even as he regretted the transiency of his staff members, he boasted of their "forthgoings" into new positions and new fields. He took pride, too, in the alumni of the Commons clubs who achieved success and made substantial homes for themselves.[44]

In 1933 a one-time volunteer worker wrote to Taylor to assure him that the settlement's work produced results, after all. The volunteer, Newton Jenkins, attended a reunion of "60 or more fine young men" who had belonged to settlement clubs eighteen years earlier, during Jenkins's time of residence. "They grew up through surroundings which seemed almost impossible," Jenkins wrote. They had gone on to take "their places in the best citizenship of our city, as lawyers, doctors, dentists and business men." The message encouraged Taylor. Thinking on it, he wrote to the Commons trustees to tell them of his rekindled hope. "We are building better than we know," he said.[45]

In the tenement districts, there was never much visible evidence of reform in housing. If anything, the houses in the old neighborhoods seemed to get worse. To see the effects of reform, it was necessary to go out to the newer neighborhoods, where houses were going up in compliance with the codes. Similarly, to witness the results of neighborhood work, one had to trace the people who "graduated" from the settlements to their new homes. Settlement workers, instead of reversing the inevitable process of mobility, were moving with it, helping it along, even when they thought they were battling it. They helped prepare the tenancy for the growing zone of workingmen's homes.

Settlements had always tried to help their foreign neighbors ascend the ladder of success. When people had freedom of residence, they tended to move out of the neighborhood when they moved up the ladder. The opportunity to move, as Charles Zeublin wrote in 1894, was "the open sesame" for the inhabitant of the slums. It meant that his enclave was not a ghetto.[46]

Nothing revealed the real role of neighborhood work so clearly as the special approach the settlements took toward blacks. At the same time that settlement workers were assisting in the dispersal of people from the ethnic enclaves, integrating them into the metropolitan neighborhood system, they were cooperating to close Negroes off in a circumscribed corner of the city.

CHAPTER 13 ❧

Settlement Workers and Blacks: A "Valid Difference"

The Negro race in America . . . needs justice and is given charity.
—Declaration of Principles of the Niagara Movement, 1905.

The man who insists upon consent, who moves with the people, is bound to consult the feasible right as well as the absolute right. He is often obliged to attain only Mr. Lincoln's "best possible," and often have the sickening sense of compromising with his best convictions.
—Jane Addams, "A Modern Lear," *Survey* 29 (2 November 1912): 136–37.

AMONG SOCIAL WORKERS AND REFORMERS, NONE WERE MORE CONSCIOUS OF Negro conditions than the leaders of the settlement movement. No other group of whites was so concerned about blacks nor so free of contempt for them. If the settlement workers were not ready to treat Negroes the same as other ethnic groups, then no white Chicagoans were.

Jane Addams, loyal to the abolitionist tradition of her father, wanted to restore the spirit of the Emancipation Proclamation. Her notion of "the race life" encompassed all kinds of people. She thought that Chicago, like "conglomerate America," was richer for the variety of its inhabitants. To her, the only race that mattered was the human race. Yet she did not underestimate how much race counted with the "white races" generally. She put the blame for "race antagonism" squarely on "the so-called 'superior races,' " whom she accused of injustice and wanton wastefulness. Racists deprived the larger culture of the contributions that minorities might make, she thought, and they squandered the limited fund of democracy.[1]

In an effort to estimate "the waste" involved in "the denial of opportunity and free expression" to Negroes, she drew up a list of Negro attributes in 1913. She included a "unique and spontaneous" sense of humor, "persistent love of color," "executive and organizing capacity" (exemplified by "the head waiter in a huge hotel or by the colored woman who administers a complicated household"), and the gifts of eloquence and rhythm, which contributed "the only American folksongs." It was a list that many a racist could have endorsed if she had concluded by claiming that Negroes could dance and run fast, too, instead of insisting on minority rights, as she did. Miss Addams believed that every group had special qualities that were cultural, not racial, and most of the traits she catalogued were modest ones, regardless of the ethnic group under consideration. The fundamental human qualities, she believed, were universal. Blacks were different not because they had special gifts or innate defects but because they had borne and continued to bear unique burdens.[2]

Miss Addams, though mindful of the exploitation and humiliation of immigrants in America, did not think that they had experienced anything comparable to slavery and the segregation which succeeded it. Negroes who moved North met obstacles to employment more formidable than those that immigrants had to face. And without explicitly commenting on the contrast between a Black Belt and an ethnic neighborhood containing four or five major groups "and many another nationality," she did call attention to the "complete segregation of the Negro in distinct parts of the city."[3]

Jane Addams began her career in social work ministering to an all-Negro clientele. A few years before she founded Hull-House she served as a volunteer at the Johns Hopkins Colored Orphan Asylum in Baltimore. Apparently the segregation of her little charges did not puzzle or disturb her, and she never again worked closely with blacks as clients. But when the "call" went out in 1909 for whites to sponsor a national organization for "the advancement of colored people," she responded. She was a founding member of the NAACP, and later she helped to establish Chicago's Urban League. Other Hull-House personnel helped to bring the plight of Negroes to the attention of whites as well.[4]

At the Chicago School of Civics and Philanthropy, Edith Abbott and Sophonisba Breckenridge directed studies of delinquency and housing which emphasized the special hardships that the "color line" imposed. Louise de Koven Bowen, the most generous and steadfast supporter Hull-House had, wrote the Juvenile Protective Association's pamphlet, *The Colored People of Chicago*, contrasting the successful assimilation of the "enterprising young people" from immigrant families with the discrimination against "colored young people, however ambitious." Mary McDowell, who left Hull-House to take over University of Chicago Settlement, joined Jane Addams in the founding of the NAACP. Along with Miss Addams, Miss Breckenridge, and Miss Abbott, she participated in the activities of the Chicago Urban League. She shared Jane Addams's dream of a civilization that would give "every group—black and white, Jew and Gentile, people of all nations—freedom and tolerance," and she believed that the dream was "worth fighting for."[5]

These women, however, spoke for only a minority of Chicago's settlement workers. In fact, their attitude was not widespread even at the movement's leadership level. The settlement journal, *The Commons*, in its limited coverage of the Negro "problem," reflected the majority viewpoint. With the exception of contributions by Jane Addams and a few others, articles in *The Commons* did not deal with denial of opportunity to Negroes. The emphasis was rather on the defects of blacks. Most contributors to the journal implied what one commentator, Henry Bruère, very clearly expressed: assimilation was for whites only.

Bruère was well known for his work in Boston settlements, and he went on to renown as director of New York City's model Bureau of Municipal Research. In 1904 he was experimenting with the application of settlement techniques to the management of industry in Chicago, where he enjoyed a close association with settlement leaders. In this period, when industrial laborers suspected management of luring Negroes North for use as strikebreakers, Bruère argued that the place for Negroes was in the South, where they could develop under the tutelage of Negro educators such as Booker T. Washington of Tuskegee Institute.[6]

In his article on industrial education, Bruère chastised "negroes" for making a "fetish" out of education. After "long years of comfortable slavery," he wrote, blacks looked upon education not as training for work but rather as a means to protect themselves from work. They had to learn that "mere education does not furnish a man with a living wage." Schools should teach the "negro" to "do those things for which the community is willing to give him wages in return." Negroes, stuffed with self-importance, continued to seek places in clerical work and in the learned professions, where "the white does not wish the service of the negro." Thwarted down home, blacks turned northward. Bruère thought that it was time to teach them to look to Southern employers and landlords. Southerners wanted "to employ the negro as a mechanic or farmer," he contended, "and if he can render skilled service in positions of this character it will reward him adequately."[7]

Industrial education on the Tuskegee model was valuable, wrote Bruère, because it indoctrinated the ambitious black man in a crucial truth:

> He cannot foist himself upon the older race, simply because he can read or write as well as his white neighbor. . . . He must be prepared to yield the community such service as it demands of him.

Because manual training schools were "raising the tone of the negroes" while reducing their aspirations to realistic levels, they deserved both "the confidence of the black race and the respect and support of the whites." These schools proceeded from the one principle that could guide blacks from a condition of "dependent inferiority": "the principle of self-development for the negro." Bruère was careful to distinguish self-development from assimilation. Assimilation was "that great principle" by which America was able to absorb "uneducated and largely unskilled people from the lower strata of European civilization." Blacks constituted a race so "foreign," Bruère believed, that they "cannot be raised by a process of assimilation."[8]

Graham Taylor, editor of *The Commons* and founder of Chicago Commons, also hoped that the sort of work done at Tuskegee Institute would keep the Negro population down on Southern farms. The prospect of a black influx into Northern cities pained him. He admired the "absolute honesty" of white Southerners confronted with "critical questions relating to the Negro." Like Jane Addams, he professed to believe that "all foreign-born" brought "rich and varied" cultures from the Old World to the New. Unlike her, he thought that some ethnic groups might be too "discrepant" to assimilate readily. Yet he kept the faith that all immigrants could ultimately be absorbed. No where, however, did he praise the heritage of Negroes, and he never talked of assimilating them.[9]

Taylor recommended Nathaniel Shaler's book *The Neighbor* for its treatment of "the tremendous immigrant issues and race difficulties in America." Shaler's "'way out' of the American difficulties," Taylor lamented, would offend those who lacked his expertise and "insight into the necessary and natural limitations and variations of races of men." What Shaler proposed was limitation on immigration while the immigrants already here were being assimilated. For "the negro," he advocated "certain added disfranchisement." Taylor emphasized that the book's distinctive merit was its understanding of problems associated with ethnic minorities, "more especially the negro."[10]

Taylor credited the author of *The Neighbor* with a "broad conception of and faith in human nature" and sympathy for people "generally condemned or despised." Reverend Taylor claimed as much for himself. He admitted to no "race prejudice," and he dreaded "race strife." Riots of the sort that rocked Springfield, Illinois, in 1908 would recur, he feared, unless the "resources of law, education and religion" were brought to bear on the condition of urban Negroes. He blamed American civilization for abandoning the "helpless" Negroes of the North to their own "feeble resources for self-help" and allowing them "to become in large part so depraved."[11]

Those who felt as Jane Addams did avoided such words as "depraved." They were "friends of the Negro," if the Negro had any friends, and they styled themselves as such. But they frankly conceded the shortcomings of black Chicagoans. Comparing the adjustment of immigrants and Negroes to urban life, Jane Addams was struck by Negroes' "lack of inherited control."[12]

Despite her use of the word "inherited," Miss Addams was not talking about genetics. European immigrants, it seemed, managed to maintain some semblance of "social traditions . . . worked out during centuries." While adherence to Old World customs could deter the immigrant's "progress" in the New, she wrote, it was "largely through a modification of these customs and manners that alien groups are assimilated into American life." She assumed, on the other hand, that slavery had cut Negroes off from the tribal civilizations of Africa. It followed, then, that the "traditions and taboos which control the relations between the sexes and between parents and children" must inevitably have been lost. Conceding the commonplace charge that "colored girls yield more easily to the temptations of a city than the Italian girls do," she rejected the explanation that Negro girls were innately promiscuous. Italian fathers traditionally guarded the honor of their daughters, she observed, while the fathers of black girls seemed to be "quite without those traditions." To her, the difference was not one of race but rather, in the case of blacks, "the lack of social restraint."[13]

Jane Addams and those few who were of like mind were unwilling to let Negroes, who appeared to have no heritage of self-control, carry on in cities without any controls at all. But then, so were Graham Taylor and the majority of settlement workers. Lacking Addams's sympathy for blacks, Taylor still wanted to constrain them, and not only by the force of law. Jane Addams knew that "legal enactment itself" did not amount to social control, but so did he, and he joined her in urging the extension of education, religion, and philanthropy into black Chicago.[14]

After the riot of 1919, Taylor presided over the assembly that called for the appointment of a race relations commission. Mary McDowell argued that Chicago could not be "a well-governed city" so long as it had "a segregated group within its boundaries." Taylor may well have agreed that *complete* segregation of Negroes made for disorder. In 1930 Jane Addams pinpointed the danger inherent in "complete segregation": It tended to put Negroes "outside the immediate action of that indispensable but powerful social control which influences the rest of the population."[15]

The difference between the minority position and the prevailing one was largely a matter of feeling and tone. In policy it was barely discernible. Graham Taylor did not dispute Louise de Koven Bowen's charge that Negroes were crowded into the most wretched houses in Chicago. He was president of the Chicago School of Civics and Philanthropy when the pioneering studies of Negro housing were done there. He admitted the unfairness of forcing slum conditions upon "both the better and the worse Negroes . . . and their children too, indiscriminately." He went so far as to concede that the "better" Negroes should be allowed to disperse from the solid Black Belt into several scattered colonies for "colored people only." That was as far as anyone would go: Neither Mrs. Bowen nor any of the others asked for more than adequate, wholesome housing "for the colored people." In 1929, during the drive to cover white communities with restrictive covenants, Jane Addams made no protest. She merely noted that "the subject of segregation" was "confused" with "real estate values," and she indicated that she did not know what "the practical solution" might be.[16]

Graham Taylor, fearful that any dispersion of Negro families, even into segregated satellites, would excite "race antagonism," was reluctant to let blacks move out of the Black Belt. So was everyone else. It was "a sort of settlement creed," as Jane Addams put it, that "social amelioration" could be achieved by "gradual modification" only. She abhorred neighborhood conflict as she did international warfare. Her pacifism was not only global but local. Graham Taylor did not condemn all war, as she did, but he believed devoutly in peace at the neighborhood level.[17]

For Mary McDowell to use such a word as "fight" to describe her campaign for racial tolerance was uncharacteristic. In fact, her effort consisted mainly of getting women's clubs to deliberate (or at least delegate committees to deliberate) on race relations and then trying to coordinate the results, if any, through an overall committee. She took the work seriously, and though it commanded much of her time and energy for the last fifteen years of her life, it accomplished nothing tangible. It did not even get the women's clubs integrated.[18]

There is no evidence that Miss McDowell's Inter-racial Cooperative Committee ever tried or intended to integrate women's clubs or anything else. The committee convened after the 1919 riot to promote mutual tolerance and peace in race relations. The fact that Chicago was spared a reenactment of the scenes of 1919 may well have satisfied the committeewomen that they were accomplishing something. If the hardening of the color line in the twenties dismayed them, they did not show it.[19]

Because Jane Addams and Mary McDowell were among the founders of the NAACP, many of their contemporaries accused them of favoring "social equality" between the races. Scholars of race and reform have treated them as integrationists. But while they opposed racism, they did not advocate integration. One white

Chicagoan, Clarence Darrow, did stand forthrightly, unreservedly, for across-the-board racial equality, but in this as in much that he did, he deviated far from the norm. Neither the local nor the national white leaders of the NAACP pressed for "absolute political and social equality" for blacks. They challenged "forced segregation" and demanded recognition of "the legitimate rights of the Negro." In 1920, when black militant W. E. B. DuBois stated in the association's journal that social equality was "just as much a human right as political or economic equality," he threw the board of directors into a crisis. Florence Kelley, Jane Addams's great friend from the pioneer days at Hull-House, threatened to resign from the board unless the association repudiated DuBois's statement.[20]

Miss Addams and Miss McDowell always avoided the language of social equality scrupulously. Along with Louise de Koven Bowen and a handful of others, they tried to better the lot of Negroes in an era when blacks were the men farthest down in America. They defended blacks at a time when such books as *The Negro: A Menace to Civilization* enjoyed wide circulation and a measure of scholarly acceptance. When Progressives such as Woodrow Wilson were recommending segregation as the ideal way to secure "justice" for Negroes, and Theodore Roosevelt was blurting "all coons look alike to me," these women were struggling for racial tolerance. They made demands on behalf of blacks that Graham Taylor and the rest did not make. Still, they asked for nothing that Taylor could not have tolerated. Mary McDowell and Jane Addams probably looked forward to the day when blacks would enjoy political and economic equality with whites and hoped, then, finally, to confront and overcome social inequality, someday. But so long as they lived, they took their stand for political and economic equality. There they drew the line.[21]

So carefully did McDowell, Addams, and Bowen circumvent the issue of social inequality that there is only one reference to it in their published works, and even that is less than direct. In *The Colored People of Chicago* Mrs. Bowen pointedly asked her city to grant its black citizens everything *but* social equality. She came down hard on Chicago for the way it treated Negroes. "The life of the colored boy and girl," she complained, was "circumscribed on every hand" by race prejudice. With "the door of opportunity shut in their faces," Negro youths sank into delinquency and crime. Mrs. Bowen warned Chicagoans to end discrimination before the "ever increasing number of idle and criminal youth" swelled beyond controllable limits. Until blacks received "fair treatment," she insisted, there would be no lasting peace. "The colored man" would settle for nothing less than his "civic and economic rights," Mrs. Bowen was sure, and she was certain that he wanted nothing more. The black man demanded equal treatment before the law, access to employment, and admission to public institutions and accommodations. He wanted "preventive institutional care and proper education for negro youth," and he desperately needed additional sanitary housing. Grant him all that, she urged, and "the colored man" would be satisfied. "He does not," Louise de Koven Bowen assured white Chicagoans, "resent social ostracism."[22]

That was all she wrote, but it was enough to show how far the racial idealism of the minority went. Settlement workers, at least the best of them, were realists as well as idealists, and their speciality as social workers was to appreciate neighborhood realities. These women were the best, and they knew that neighborhood realities militated against the mixing of blacks and whites in settlement houses.

The settlements followed the color line, and in this they were conforming to the standard procedure of Chicago's social welfare institutions. And the settlements, more than most agencies, had reasons for doing so that practically all social workers considered compelling. The administration of social service in the city, as a committee of social workers observed in 1930, reflected "the general separation of the races in social contacts." Wherever "the question of social contacts" arose, race discrimination was the rule, and the rule applied in social work as it did in everything else. When services could be dispensed to individuals or families from an office or right in the recipient's home, social agencies could process Negro cases like any others, without offending white sensibilities. But if there was a possibility that whites and blacks would meet and mix while being served, the tendency was to exclude Negroes, serve them at a special time or in a separate section, or provide whole facilities exclusively for their use in Negro neighborhoods.[23]

Illinois legislation forbade public agencies to discriminate, and they followed the law where it did not violate the unwritten mandate to keep the races separate. Publicly funded services such as at-home aid to the blind, deaf, and handicapped were available to anyone, almost without regard to race. Public officials could not keep Negroes out of the County Hospital or the Municipal Tuberculosis Sanitarium, but they did their best to locate and administer clinics and dispensaries, parks and playgrounds, swimming pools and beaches, libraries, schools, and other facilities in a way that would hold the mingling of blacks and whites to a minimum.[24]

Private welfare agencies were free to discriminate, and most of them did. A committee that conducted a survey of services available to Negroes in 1930 found that only 264 of 809 private agencies devoted so much as 1 percent of their budgets to "service to Negroes." Most of these either served blacks exclusively or furnished them "separate service." Of the remaining agencies, some were "inaccessible" to Negroes because of their distance from the Black Belt. Others, located near Negro districts, restricted their services to the "local neighborhood only." Many agencies founded by ethnic or sectarian groups "to serve their own people only" claimed to bar not only Negroes but everyone from outside the group as well. "A still greater number ostensibly offer their services to the entire community," the survey revealed, "but exclude only Negroes." [25]

Like their public counterparts, private agencies rendered service on the basis of need where the chances of racial collision were remote. For the most part, what the 1930 survey designated as "service agencies" did not discriminate. What these agencies had in common was that they could render their services without bringing their clients into close contact with each other. Some organizations, such as fund-raising and investigating bodies, had no clients of their own. Referral agencies had clients but often served them without seeing them, handling an application card or dealing with other social workers instead. Other agencies worked out of headquarters or branches or in clients' homes. Visiting nurses, for example, ministered to black as well as white households, and the Juvenile Protective Association made investigations on behalf of white and Negro children, without drawing whites and Negroes into avoidable association. Any family in distress could go to an office of the United Charities for relief. If black and white applicants happened to meet, their contact was unlikely to go beyond passing in a corridor or sharing a waiting room. Even this sort of interracial encounter was rare, however, because Negroes went to United Charities branches near the Black Belt, whereas most whites applied to offices "inaccessible" to Negro areas.[26]

If interaction had to be more intense or more prolonged than it was at a relief station, agencies tried to keep Negroes apart from whites altogether. Thus, a Negro who made the trip to one of the clinics that the Chicago Tuberculosis Institute maintained in the suburbs could get treatment, and if he wanted information he could attend the institute's special sessions on "Negro health." But he could not have a bed in the institute's sanitarium if his life depended on it. Similarly, the Protectorate of the Catholic Women's League hunted up jobs and "transient accommodations" for "unattached women and young girls of any race or creed" but referred black clients only to homes for Negroes. Catholic boarding houses were segregated less by religion than by race: While non-Catholics were often admitted, Negroes, Catholic or not, were excluded if there was no room for them in buildings for blacks. The lodging referral service was available to all, but the accommodations were for whites or for Negroes, not for both.[27]

While employment services generally helped Negroes to find "suitable" positions, "sheltered workshops," which put the unemployed to work and sometimes trained them for outside jobs, did not "employ" blacks. Even Goodwill Industries, founded by the Methodist Episcopal Church in 1920 to give sheltered employment to the handicapped, would not assist disabled Negroes, even though its workshop was just a few blocks west of the Black Belt. Such organizations as the Salvation Army and the Christian Industrial League, an outlet for the charitable urges of Chicago's Presbyterians, did not begrudge Negroes "salvage," clothing, and food, but they drew the line at lodging them. Only white women and children were allowed in the Salvation Army's residences. The Salvation Army's "industrial homes," like the Industrial League's Hotel Monroe, harbored homeless men who paid for their keep from their earnings in sheltered workshops on the premises. Negroes were barred. Soup they could get, and shoes, even salvation, but not shelter.[28]

Segregation was marked in any place where clients had to be quartered. In 1912 Ida B. Wells-Barnett, a Negro leader for whom the Chicago Housing Authority would one day name a "colored" project, complained that not only the Salvation Army but also the YMCA, the YWCA, and the Mills hotels excluded Negroes but welcomed "every other class" to their lodgings. "Even the Women's Model Lodging House announces that it will give all women accommodations except drunkards, immoral women and negro women." The situation did not improve. In 1926 some social workers, disturbed by the total absence of temporary shelter for "colored women with young children," conferred with the directors of two boarding homes, one located near the Lake Street black district, the other in the South Side Black Belt. The superintendent of the Chicago Women's Shelter, on west Adams Street in the same block as the all-white West Side YMCA and YWCA, "expressed herself decidedly to the effect that the Chicago Woman's Shelter could not care for colored cases." The shelter's few earlier experiences with such cases, she said, had all been "unsatisfactory." There was no room "for colored" at the Sarah Hackett Stevenson Memorial Lodging House, either. This institution for "needy women and children" was at 24th and Prairie, near the Black Belt's border but on the black side of the line. The president of the lodging house board "urged the proposition that the colored population should consider providing special care for their own people." Four years later, "cheap lodging" for black men and boys was still "entirely lacking," and the few facilities available to single women and girls were exclusively Negro.[29]

Hospitals, sanitariums, convalescent homes, and homes for the aged maintained the color line as meticulously as boarding homes did. The hospitals that did care for Negroes usually accepted them only as emergency cases or outpatients. To get a hospital bed a black had to go to a public institution or one of three all-Negro hospitals. The Chicago Home for Incurables in Hyde Park would admit "no mental or contagious cases"—or Negroes. Seventeen aged-care homes refused to accept blacks in 1930, even though four of the institutions were in the Black Belt. One, the Illinois Home for Aged and Infirm Deaf, had opened at 45th and Grand Boulevard in 1923, when all but a few whites had conceded the "contest" for the block to the Negroes moving in from the west. It inaugurated its whites-only policy in a neighborhood that was no longer white. The other homes were older, continuing to cater to whites as they had before Negroes overtook their surroundings.

The James C. King Home for Aged Men, at 360 E. Garfield Boulevard, limited its service to "native or naturalized male citizens of the United States." The home was not "inaccessible" to blacks territorially, and the stated restriction did not apply to them, but they were excluded along with aliens, although they were native sons.[30]

The color line proscribed even children. The Juvenile Protective Association reported in 1913 that the usual practice of children's homes and boarding schools was "to refuse colored children, with the cryptic utterance, 'We have no room.'" Lawrence Hall, an Episcopal institution on the far North Side, was typical. Since the 1870s it had housed dependent boys of any religion or nationality. "Only colored," its administrators stated in 1932, were "barred." The suburban Park Ridge School, which received public funds to house and train dependent girls from Chicago and environs, paid a Negro orphanage in the city to put up "colored girls" in 1913 rather than admit them to Park Ridge. The school's managers were sure that "this segregation" was "equally valuable to both sets of children." A similar school for Chicago-area boys, located in Glenwood, Illinois, set up a quota for Negroes instead of a separate branch. In 1913 fifteen of its 515 inmates were black. Two decades later Park Ridge was still open to children regardless of nationality or creed, with "only colored barred," but it had abandoned the branch for blacks. Its counterpart, the Glenwood School for boys, had dropped its quota. Like Park Ridge and Lawrence Hall, Glenwood School now turned away all Negro children.[31]

A few child-placing services were willing to process Negro cases, but only ten institutions in 1930 would accept black children. One of the places open to Negroes claimed to receive "both races freely, solely on the basis of need," but the rest imposed quotas or boarded only blacks. Fifty-six children's homes were exclusively for whites. Many of these homes served "special groups" such as Jews or Danish Lutherans, but even Negroes who met the qualifications for admission were denied. The Chicago Junior School in Elgin, Illinois, took "Protestant boys" and gave them a home, education, and "ideals of right living." On the South Side, in Oakland, only three short blocks east of the Black Belt's border, the Illinois Protestant Children's home cared for "dependent Protestant children." Neither place would take in a Protestant child who was not white, it went without saying.[32]

The Illinois Protestant Children's Home was representative of institutions in communities at the edge of the Black Belt. They disregarded the needs of Negroes as a matter of course. Sometimes an institution tolerated a few blacks while its vicinity was safely white and then, when Negroes moved close, curtailed its quota. The Chicago Foundling Home at Madison and Wood maintained a quota until the district to the north, the Lake Street area, became solidly black. After the spring of 1930 the Foundling Home, its own block and the adjacent streets now threatened, would "no longer admit the colored."[33]

Even after neighborhoods changed from white to black occupancy, institutions established earlier for whites commonly continued to refuse Negroes service. Child-serving agencies were as likely to persist in exclusion as those for adults. By 1930 there were practically no whites left around 51st and South Parkway except for the residents of the Chicago Orphan Asylum, a home for "children in need" established in the 1840s. The asylum had moved from its old quarters near 23rd Street to escape black neighbors. Overtaken again, it kept barring blacks as it always had. A few years later it fled once more, this time to the all-white preserve near the University of Chicago. It was far more common for facilities in changed neighborhoods to uphold the prohibition against Negroes or to abandon the area than to admit newcomers.[34]

The barriers were not lowered for sick and handicapped children. Hospitals and sanitariums that barred black adults made no exceptions for children, and facilities especially for children were just as rigid. The Ridge Farm Preventorium, a free, nonsectarian home and school for "undernourished, pre-tuberculous girls," excluded no one—except Negroes. The Martha Washington Home for Dependent Crippled Children was established in 1925 at 44th and Michigan, a district that had recently succumbed to Negro "invasion." The institution may well have been located where it was to aid white property owners in a futile attempt to retake the area and restore it to white occupancy. Whether or not the home was part of a white counterattack, it did stand as a reminder to the neighborhood that the whites, though departed, were still supreme. Completely surrounded by Negroes, it nevertheless barred black children.[35]

An older establishment, the Home for Destitute Crippled Children in Hyde Park, claimed to treat anyone in need "regardless of race, color, or residence." No other branch of the University of Chicago's clinics made such a claim. There was no limit on the number of Negro children treated as outpatients, but 101 of the Home's 107 beds were reserved for whites. An affiliate, the Country Home for Convalescent Crippled Children of the University of Chicago, had room for 120 children. All but 2 percent of the patients at the Country Home were free cases, and every child was white.[36]

Infant and day nurseries, kindergartens, and recreation centers did not board their charges, but they did bring them into close contact. Some of these places suffered little children of both races, but they usually accommodated the black children separately. The great majority tolerated no Negroes. In several cases, Negroes withdrew from agencies rather than submit their children to "separate service." Their alternatives then were inferior segregated facilities or nothing.[37]

Organizations that sponsored group activities were careful to keep whites and Negroes as far apart as possible. The Boy Scouts and Girl Scouts set up separate troops for Negroes. The YMCA from 1913 and the YWCA from 1915 maintained "colored" branches. "This racial segregation," the 1930 survey of social services reported, "is especially true of camps, of which only a very few accommodate both races at the same time in the same camp." The Scouts, the YMCA, and the YWCA ran segregated camps. Whether a scout troop operated from a Protestant or a Catholic church, a synagogue, a parochial or a public school, white children of any faith were usually admitted, whereas black children of any denomination were automatically rejected and referred to Negro troops. Catholics and Jews were welcomed at the nondenominational yet Protestant Young Men's and Women's Christian associations, whereas Negro Protestants were not. Organizations and social centers administered under the auspices of Protestant denominations generally excluded their black coreligionists, except in separate branches. Interdenominational organizations did the same.[38]

Most social group work followed the color line strictly, if not quite candidly. The Prairie Club, founded in 1908 to promote outdoor recreation, was frank enough to preach what most organizations practiced. It stipulated that its activities were "open to white people of any nationality or creed."[39]

Because "colored people were discriminated against in existing institutions," the Juvenile Protective Association reported in 1913, they attempted to develop facilities of their own, even though they lacked the financial resources to sustain a separate welfare system. First the Negro Fellowship League, and then the Chicago Urban League, tried to coordinate the delivery of services and to extend the range of services available. Negroes managed to establish homes for the aged, lodging houses, children's homes, community centers, and even hospitals, but they had to struggle to keep these places going. Two decades of determined effort produced only meager gains. In 1930 thirty-one or thirty-two agencies run "by Negroes for Negroes exclusively" were in operation, but nearly half of them were "unorganized," unincorporated, or lacking directors or budgets. Whites helped these agencies along, and they supplied additional segregated facilities as well. But the agencies for Negroes remained inadequate and overburdened. Some services were still nonexistent for Negroes in 1930. These included, besides shelter for men and boys, convalescent and maternity home care, foster care, lodging for unwed mothers, sanitarium treatment for tubercular patients able to pay, and accommodation for women and girls "undergoing treatment for gonorrhea, in an infectious stage, but not requiring hospitalization."[40]

The Commission on Race Relations, appointed after the 1919 riot, criticized the illegal discrimination that persisted in public institutions, but it had nothing but praise for private agencies that served Negroes separately. It commended the YMCA, the YWCA, and other organizations for "extending their work to the Negro community" and urged their example on other groups. While the commission encouraged white philanthropists to support Negro projects, it placed the main burden of providing social service to Negroes on the blacks themselves. Without any reference to the refusal of most welfare organizations to assist Negroes, the commission left it largely up to "the Negro community" to extend or establish "the necessary social agencies." The commission admonished blacks to contribute more freely to social agencies for "their group" and also to "general social agencies." When the head of the boarding home that turned away black women and children exhorted Negroes in 1926 to build shelters of their own, she was reiterating the commission's recommendation.[41]

Social workers considered the separation of the races to be natural and necessary, but they did not mean it to be absolute. Those interviewed in 1930 deplored not only the inferiority of

Negro social service but its "complete isolation from the organized social forces of the white community" as well. Unlike the Commission on Race Relations, the 1930 committee on Negro social service concluded that blacks were contributing all they could to welfare work among their own, and it was not enough. Negroes had neither the funds nor the skills to operate agencies at standards acceptable to white professionals. To get contributions from whites, an agency practically had to have the endorsement of the Association of Commerce, which ignored organizations not recognized by the Council of Social Agencies. The council insisted upon standards, and to achieve standards, an agency needed white contributions.[42]

The Negro agencies were trapped in a vicious circle of inadequacy. And, as the survey of 1930 reported:

> If they have any kind of a following of their own, and see a need to which they sincerely believe the white community is indifferent, they feel impelled to go ahead without endorsement. Meanwhile there is an instinctive withdrawal from contact with organized social work,— a feeling that they are not approved nor welcome, mixed with a determination to accomplish their own aims without help.

The 1930 committee appreciated "the shrewd understanding" that Negro social workers had of clients of "their own group," but it was not ready, as the Riot Commission had been, to leave Negro social service to the blacks themselves. It wanted to bring Negro social work under the control of the organized white community.[43]

This committee (its full name was the Joint Committee on the Survey of Agencies Serving the Negro Community) had a peculiar genesis. The Juvenile Court of Cook County had long been unable to find foster homes for Negro children in its custody. In 1928 the court created a special placement bureau to secure shelter in boarding homes for unwanted black children. Stymied in its efforts—no foster homes willing to accept blacks met the court's standards, and no homes up to standard would accept blacks—the bureau approached the Council of Social Agencies about the problem of supplying services to Negroes. In 1930 the council, in collaboration with the placement bureau and the University of Chicago, set up the committee to study the problem.[44]

The committee had six members: the director of the Council of Social Agencies, Wilfred S. Reynolds, who acted as chairman; Louis E. Evans, director of the special placement bureau; Jacob Kepecs, superintendent of the Jewish Home Finding Society; Raymond S. Rubinow, an officer of the Rosenwald Fund, which helped to finance the survey; Edith Abbott, of the University of Chicago's school of social work; and A. L. Foster, of the Urban League, the lone black member. This group was not disposed to find fault with segregated service for Negroes.[45]

Most members of the Council of Social Agencies practiced segregation. While the Jewish Home Finding Society did not bar Negroes, it did not serve them: It handled only Jewish cases. The University of Chicago's all-white clinics and hospitals had recently joined with the Rosenwald Fund to expand and upgrade Provident Hospital "for Negroes." The university's original Lying-In Hospital was at 51st and Vincennes, a mile northwest of the campus-hospital complex. When that area started to "go black," the university closed the facility and opened a new one near the campus in Hyde Park. Provident Hospital, meanwhile, had long been looking for a replacement for its decrepit old building. The university turned over the vacated installation on Vincennes to Provident. Under an arrangement worked out in 1929, black doctors trained at Provident would receive degrees from the university's medical school, and black applicants at the university's hospitals could conveniently be referred to Provident. The scheme was calculated to keep residents of the Black Belt, where A. L. Foster lived, separate from the people of Hyde Park–Kenwood, where four of the five white committee members resided.[46]

The white committee members were not about to censure the institutions that they represented, and A. L. Foster, however much he resented the patronization of segregationists, could not afford to spurn them. "The white man will give you Provident Hospital to keep you from Billings [University of Chicago Hospital]," an embittered black man would complain in 1935. "He spends money to keep Negroes from association with white people. It doesn't mean that without Provident you can get Billings." The unavailability of services to Negroes, and the marked inferiority of what was available, concerned the whites because they wanted neither to ignore the welfare of Negroes nor to make room for them in white agencies.[47]

The committee's staff surveyed all social agencies in the city "excepting those that, according to their own statement, serve only certain groups such as Jewish, Bohemian, Lutheran, etc., and those whose type of work is not city-wide, but serving local neighborhoods, in which no Negroes reside." This procedure exempted such organizations as the Jewish Home Finding Society and most settlement houses from scrutiny. The survey did cover most of the city's hospitals. Although the staff discovered that the overwhelming majority "refused Negro cases," the committee did not urge all-white hospitals, such as the University of Chicago's, to start treating blacks. The medical facilities already available to them were "fairly adequate," the committee concluded. "Negroes must learn to use them more."[48]

Services other than medical, the committee conceded, were desperately inadequate. It urged white agencies administering services that involved no social contact to "widen their services to Negroes." All remaining gaps in service were to be eliminated, but not by the Negro community alone. It was essential, the committee felt, "to discourage the well meaning but undesirable attempts on the part of the Negro group to meet these needs." The way to accomplish this goal was to have the Council of Social Agencies, utilizing the Urban League as its agent, assume overall coordination of agencies serving blacks. Negroes would then have the benefit of an expanded number of agencies that were for blacks, and largely staffed by blacks, but supervised, accredited, and funded by whites, who would educate Negro social workers in "principles of social work." Services to blacks were to be separate and subordinate, but not substandard. Making them standard was the most effective way to make them at once subordinate and separate. The committee not only drew most of its budget from the Rosenwald Fund, it also adhered to the fund's guiding rule: "White leadership in Negro welfare."[49]

The committee did not expect settlement houses in neighborhoods bordering on black districts or containing Negro enclaves to open their doors to blacks. The "whole aim" of neighborhood work, according to the committee, was "the bringing together of persons in voluntary social groups." Government-supported agencies could insist on "including Negroes on a non-discriminatory basis," the survey maintained, because of the weight of the law. Service agencies handling individuals or families case by case could do so as well. Even institutions such as orphanages, where some social contact among clients was inevitable, could make a nondiscriminatory policy and enforce it. Their clients, even if served in large numbers, were treated as individuals, not as members of voluntary groups, and especially if the service was free the recipients would have no choice but to "accept the policy of the management." The policy and program of a neighborhood center, however, depended largely on the "attitude of those served." There was no good reason for a referral agency to discriminate, but a settlement house could not "afford to insist upon admitting Negroes."[50]

"If, in spite of leadership to the contrary, the white members refuse to come if Negroes are included," the committee argued, "the executives are helpless. Negroes are in the minority; the organization cannot continue to live with their membership alone; and if the insistence upon admitting Negroes results in the breakup of the organization, no end has been accomplished." There was a difference between a public institution or a "service agency" that banned Negroes and a settlement that did so, the survey committee concluded. And it was, the committee maintained, a "valid difference."[51]

"Valid difference": It was a new name for a distinction that social workers had been making for decades. In 1913, when Mrs. Bowen observed that blacks encountered race prejudice "even in day nurseries and dependent homes," she was making an implied criticism of institutional discrimination. Yet she applauded the YMCA for establishing its branch for "colored men and boys." The "Y," unlike some of the segregated institutions she cited, did not receive public funds, thus it broke no law; more important, it carried on work with voluntary social groups, whereas the rest did not. Regarding neighborhood work, Mrs. Bowen's discretion verged on deception. She stated that four settlements were located "in or near the neighborhoods of colored people." As she well knew, in 1913 there were nine settlements within easy walking distance of black districts. Four were for blacks. The other five were for whites; she did not consider them "near" the black neighbor-hoods because of the social distance separating blacks from whites in adjoining areas. Mrs. Bowen simply assumed that the distance was prohibitive. And she thought it best to be silent about that assumption, at least in a pamphlet published for a biracial audience.[52]

Years later the Commission on Race Relations drew the same distinction. In a list of social agencies "convenient for use by Negroes," the Riot Commission included public facilities, United Charities offices, and other service agencies a mile or more away from black districts. The list omitted settlements unless they were inside "the Negro residential area." The commission's research director was Graham Taylor's son Graham Romeyn Taylor, who had grown up at Chicago Commons and served on its staff. The Commons was not far from the Lake Street Negro area, though the settlement had virtually no contact with the enclave. Taylor recruited his staff "as far as possible from social workers of both races"; at least one-third of the white investigators were settlement workers. On the 1930 survey committee, Edith Abbott, who began her career at Hull-House, represented not only the University of Chicago but also the settlement point of view. All of the staff members were Miss Abbott's students.[53]

No one suggested that inability to accommodate blacks in white settlements warranted indifference to Negro needs. In 1913 Louise de Koven Bowen noted the "urgent need" for more "colored social workers" trained in "the best method of Charitable administration." Later the Riot Commission exhorted whites and blacks alike to support agencies for "the instruction and encouragement of Negroes in better living." And while the 1930 survey committee absolved "individual social workers and agencies" of accountability for discrimination in neighborhood centers, it urged "development of equal service for Negroes." The reason that the 1930 committee could state directly what Mrs. Bowen and the Riot Commissioners had said so circumspectly was that the committee issued no report to the public. Because it addressed its recommendations straight to the leadership of the philanthropic establishment that had summoned it into being, it could afford a measure of candor.[54]

Jane Addams, Mary McDowell, and Mrs. Bowen agreed with Graham Taylor and the majority of white settlement workers that Negroes should have separate settlement houses to serve them. Indeed, all social workers adhered to Jane Addams's conviction that the existence of the color line did not justify whites in "withholding from a colony of colored people those restraints and customs which can only be communicated through social understanding."[55]

CHAPTER 14

The Color Line in Neighborhood Work

Men and women whatever their race or creed, ought to understand one another and help one another. That is what neighborliness means. . . . If neighborliness is really to be understanding and helpful it must get rid of prejudices.
—S. J. Duncan-Clark, speech at fortieth anniversary of Chicago Commons, 3 May 1934, in Graham Taylor, *Chicago Commons through Forty Years* (Chicago, 1936), p. 314.

A group of businessmen in this old section of Chicago is making a serious effort to bring to the growing boys of this district an opportunity to grow to young manhood as honorable, useful, members of our community. . . . The plan of operation is to enlist all white boys . . . [in] wholesome activities.
—Irving N. Klein to Max Goldenberg, fund-raising letter for Old Town Boys' Club, 10 January 1929, Goldenberg Furniture Co. Papers, CHS.

BLACKS, ISOLATED FROM MOST SETTLEMENTS AND REBUFFED IN THOSE THEY lived close to, tried to develop their own. Whites engaged in "colored settlement work" as well, because they feared that it was "dangerous" to neglect it altogether. Blacks found it nearly impossible to sustain their projects, however, and whites committed just enough resources to Black Belt settlements to ensure a "margin of safety" in neighborhood relations. The black settlements in Chicago were always few, always separate, and always unequal.[1]

In the early days, none of the better-known settlements except Chicago Commons was within a mile of a black enclave. The Lake Street Negro district was a short walk away from the Commons, on the other side of the Northwestern Railroad's tremendous embankment. The Commons did not turn away "the few Negro families" who approached it. But while staff members went to great lengths to recruit Italians and Poles into the settlement's programs, they did nothing to attract blacks.[2]

University of Chicago Settlement employed black women as domestics. Hull-House hired Negroes to work in the Coffee Shop kitchen, and a black man managed the shop for several years. In 1918 Northwestern University Settlement appointed "an educated Negro" to head its boys' department. For the next twenty-five years, "he was probably the only Negro in the area." Mary McDowell and Jane Addams entertained prominent Negroes at settlement dinners. Their neighbors were not pleased about this, but they acknowledged that the settlement houses were also homes whose residents were entitled to choose their company. W. E. B. DuBois and other black speakers addressed citywide audiences at Hull-House and University of Chicago Settlement. And on returning from her frequent NAACP conferences, Jane Addams, if her "cosmopolitan neighbors" inquired where she had been and what were her views, would tell them, taking care not to argue with them nor impose her views on them.[3]

From time to time Northwestern University Settlement's summer camp accepted a few black children at the request of child-placing agencies (something Hull-House did not do until 1938), but the camp personnel always segregated the black children. The Hull-House boarding club for working girls was always for whites only. A few settlement workers believed that boarding homes were among the institutions that could afford not to discriminate, because boarders in separate apartments had minimal social contact. But the Jane Club of Hull-House was a cooperative. Miss Addams left as much of the management as possible up to the young women. They determined the admissions policy, and they kept the Jane Club segregated from its beginning in 1891 until it closed nearly fifty years later.[4]

Until 1900 there were no settlements for black Chicagoans. Between 1900 and 1916 black and white sponsors opened at least nine settlements in the Black Belt and black satellite districts. By the time of the great riot of 1919 all of them had disappeared but one, which folded a few years later. Seven more "Negro" settlements were started in the years after the riot. Although six of them seem to have survived the decade, only one of them had anything like a full-scale program in 1930.

The settlements founded by the blacks themselves were the poorest equipped, the most severely underfinanced and understaffed, and the shortest-lived. In 1900 Rev. Reverdy Ransom launched Institutional Church and Social Settlement on Dearborn near 38th Street. Ransom and his successors worked to make it the foremost "social settlement in the world" for blacks, and they were able to approximate the usual assortment of settlement activities, but it was a tremendous struggle. By 1913 few traces of the program remained, and by 1919, if not before, the settlement was gone. Ransom took pride in the fact that his settlement was not only for Negroes but "founded by Negroes" as well. But Institutional could not make it alone. Even with some help from Jane Addams, Mary McDowell, and Graham Taylor, it never was what Ransom had hoped it would be: the Negro equivalent of "a Hull-House or Chicago Commons."[5]

Other blacks who ventured into settlement work had even less success than Ransom. Richard R. Wright, Jr., a clergyman with a University of Chicago divinity degree, started Trinity Mission at 18th and Dearborn in 1905 "to elevate the real poor and needy colored people." Trinity Mission lasted only a few years. Another so-called settlement closed down almost as soon as it began. The Negro Fellowship League, organized in 1910 by Mrs. Ida B. Wells-Barnett, included settlement work among its many projected activities. A forerunner to the Urban League, Mrs. Barnett's organization tried to run an employment agency for blacks and to coordinate Black Belt social services. For a while it maintained its own lodging house and a reading room. At about the time its settlement program on State Street was getting under way, Mrs. Barnett was forced to disband the league for lack of funds. Something called Enterprise Institute was holding night classes on State Street in 1913; it was a measure of the meagerness of settlement facilities for Negroes that Louise de Koven Bowen listed the institute, with its "150 pupils," as a settlement house.[6]

Whites were aware that black Chicago lacked adequate settlement service. In 1904 Mrs. Celia Parker Woolley, a Unitarian minister descended from New England abolitionists, explained the "crying need" for a settlement in the Black Belt:

> Hordes of colored people are coming up from the South, the majority of whom are ignorant, dissolute and idle, falling easily into vicious and crimi-

nal ways. The rapid increase of such an element lowers not only the standard of the colored population in our midst, but of our common citizenship, and threatens the well-being of the whole.

Instead of offering to aid the struggling Institutional Church and Social Settlement, Mrs. Woolley founded a black settlement of her own.[7]

To do its work properly, Mrs. Woolley believed, a Black Belt settlement had to be more than a neighborhood center for blacks. It must be a place where "whites and blacks" could meet across "the color line" to discuss their differences with frankness, justice, and good will, for the influx of newcomers was bound to heighten white prejudice against all blacks and aggravate race antagonism dangerously. Mrs. Woolley wanted both to insulate "educated colored people" from the poorer blacks who were pouring into the Black Belt and to introduce them to influential whites who could then reassure the larger community that Negroes were not all degenerates. Summoning the best-known Negro figures in the city to support her plan, she opened Frederick Douglass Center early in 1905.[8]

Originally, Mrs. Woolley talked of teaching "industry, honesty and thrift" and "right living" to individuals who sought "aid and counsel" at the center. Once the actual program got going, however, there were no activities to attract recent Negro arrivals who might yearn for uplift. The center's clientele was already uplifted. "The best whites and blacks" met there to enjoy recitals, forums, lectures, symposia, concerts, dinners, and teas. Topics discussed ran the gamut from *Adam Bede* to "Why I Am a Vegetarian." The clubs were study clubs and the classes, except for one on sewing, were strictly academic. The members of the Young People's Lyceum were mainly "high school and college attendants [and] holders of unusual positions" in commerce and industry. The students, secretaries, and clerks in the Lyceum, one Negro newspaper reported caustically, were "something above the average among the young of our race."[9]

Douglass Center stood for more than "amicable relations between the white and colored people." The center's bylaws called for "just" interracial relations and "equal opportunity" for blacks "in their civic, political and industrial life." Lest anyone mistake the center's position for militancy, Mrs. Woolley promised to nurture "a persuasive rather than a litigious spirit." She would not "foster weakness or the sense of grievance" among blacks. And to make it crystal clear that the center did not stand for *social* equality, Mrs. Fannie Barrier Williams, the main Negro assistant to Mrs. Woolley, stated that their purpose was to diminish "separation of the races" only "in their non-social relations."[10]

Some Negroes attacked Mrs. Woolley for ignoring "the neediest and poorest class of colored people." Unlike the settlements founded by blacks, Douglass Center was located east of State Street, just past the tracks of the South Side Elevated. For some years the "alley el" had marked the "grand dividing line" between the Black Belt and the white Grand Boulevard community, where Mrs. Woolley had lived before starting the settlement. "Very few Afro-Americans" lived on Wabash south of 30th Street, the editor of the *Broad Ax* complained. The supposedly black settlement was on a largely white street. Few blacks went beyond the el tracks except to go to work in white people's homes. The center, charged the *Broad Ax*, was a club where whites patronized social-climbing Negroes without affording "the slightest practical benefit to the great mass of the Afro-Americans residing in this city." Some blacks also resented the way Mrs. Woolley and the other whites dominated the blacks on the center's board and staff. The main Negro assistant at the center, Mrs. Fannie Barrier Williams, countered the criticisms with the frank admission that the settlement was "not organized to do slum work." It was involved instead in ghetto work. Douglass Center's contribution, she said, was to get "well-disposed white people . . . to know and respect the ever increasing number of colored people who have earned the right to be believed in and respected."[11]

Despite the attacks of the *Broad Ax*, the center did command the loyalty of "the cream" of black society in Chicago. The whites who participated most actively in the center's program included Jane Addams, Mary McDowell, and Edith Abbott, the settlement workers most sympathetic to black Chicagoans. Julius Rosenwald was the most prominent of several contributors who resided in the lakefront community east of the Black Belt. With all its support from distinguished blacks and whites, the center might have been expected to outlive Mrs. Woolley. But after she died in 1918, the Urban League, dominated by the same whites and blacks who had sustained Douglass Center from its inception, assumed management of it, only to let it fade away as such. The league made the building its new headquarters.[12]

Mindful of the animosity toward Mrs. Woolley and "her colored followers," other whites and blacks moved into Negro settlement work more warily. Mrs. Fannie Emanuel, a black woman who had conducted classes at Douglass Center, struck out on her own in 1908 to establish Emanuel Settlement on south Federal (then called Armour) Street, hard by the cindery embankments of the Rock Island Railroad. This was a run-down, "congested district of colored people." The program was nothing like Douglass Center's. There were youth clubs, classes in domestic science and manual training, a kindergarten, a free dental clinic, and an employment bureau. The settlement claimed to have "a few whites," but in classes, not on the staff. "We bar no one," Mrs. Emanuel said, "although our work is chiefly among colored people." The *Broad Ax* had charged that any poor black who "should happen to stumble into the Frederick Douglass Center, and ask for a few pennies or dimes . . . would be turned down cold by the best, the most exclusive, and the wealthiest Afro-Americans in this city." Emanuel Settlement was one of the few settlements in Chicago where a person could get "relief." The settlement carefully avoided the condescension that permeated Douglass Center. Instead of shunning what Mrs. Williams called "slum work," it tried to stir "neighborhood pride" in the Black Belt. With little or no support from whites, the settlement folded in less than five years.[13]

On the West Side, whites were anxious to provide "a place of recreation and congregation for the Negroes" in the "colored tenement section" wedged in between the Northwestern Railroad's belt of tracks and the Lake Street El. The nearby public park with its projected recreation center was for white West Siders, who hoped that the park system would establish, in addition to the Union Park Center, "a complete all-year-around recreation center for the colored people." Negroes gave no support to petitions for separate public facilities, however, and no public center for blacks was approved. Blacks did not object when a group of whites led by Judge Frank Sadler opened a private center, Charles Sumner Settlement, in 1908. The settlement offered blacks assembly rooms, classes, a free dispensary staffed by "two colored physicians," and "some relief."[14]

At about the time Sumner Settlement opened, another settlement "limited to the Colored" went into operation a block away. The initiative for founding Wendell Phillips Settlement purportedly came from a group of twenty blacks, largely from the West Side district. Their stated object was to have a settlement run for blacks and by blacks. However, they had circumspect white encouragement from the beginning, and by the time the board of directors organized in 1908 it was clear that the leadership was white. The president of Wendell Phillips was Judge Sadler, founder of the neighboring Sumner Settlement. Jane Addams and other settlement workers from the white West Side were on the board as well. The settlement served only blacks, though the board claimed from time to time that the clientele was mixed. Initially all of the staff members were black; later a few white social workers took up residence. White sponsorship was not so overt as it was at Douglass Center, but whites provided the bulk of funds from the start. Judge Sadler and the directors of Sumner Settlement quietly shut down operations and transferred their support—and control—to Wendell Phillips. After 1912, when Sumner closed, 25 percent of the Phillips budget came from one donor, Julius Rosenwald, the principal patron of Douglass Center.[15]

By 1919, after nearly two decades of settlement activity in the Black Belt, some eight settlement houses had come and gone. They had all been separate and either second-rate or subordinate to white control. Wendell Phillips, the only one remaining in 1919, was all three. Within two years of the great riot, blacks founded six more settlements. The Community Center on the Lower North Side did not take hold, and later attempts to establish something in its place failed. Four of the five new settlements on the South Side were church centers maintained by Negro congregations. Three of these appear to have stayed open through the twenties, but none of them resembled a substantial white settlement in physical plant or program.[16]

Of the settlements founded by blacks after the riot, the most durable was South Side Settlement House at 32nd and Wabash. It started in 1920 as Community House under a black organization called the South Side Community Service. Seven years later it changed its name and began a long and determined effort to develop a full program accredited by social agencies and schools of social work. That effort was unsuccessful: It was all the settlement could do to stay open.[17]

The rhetoric of South Side Settlement was "non-racial": Its services were open to all "racial groups" who cared to partake. Yet the clientele was black, and the settlement itself was a testament to black pride. The board of trustees was always overwhelmingly black, with only one or two whites serving at a time with forty or more Negroes. The founder and head resident, Ada S. McKinley, was black. Her settlement was the only member of the Chicago Federation of Settlements "fully staffed by colored people." South Side Settlement was "of the people and for the people" of the Black Belt. Resolved to prove that Negroes were capable of "self-help," the settlement relied almost entirely upon blacks for contributions.[18]

The main financial supporters were black businessmen led by Jesse Binga, the banker. The Depression devastated these businessmen and nearly destroyed South Side Settlement. By late 1930 it had no budget and no organized activities. Ada McKinley pressed on, saved the building from foreclosure, and restored some semblance of a program. Against staggering odds, the settlement survived and held on to its independence, but with woefully inferior facilities.[19]

South Side Settlement staved off collapse without the assistance of whites. Wendell Phillips Settlement succumbed in the twenties despite its dependence on whites. Apparently, blacks were slow to accept Phillips as an authentic center. With whites outnumbering Negroes on the board by six or seven to one, the settlement seemed to be an intrusion. West Side whites, for their part, lost interest in maintaining a private center for blacks after Negroes gained admittance to the public center at Union Park. For undisclosed reasons, Julius Rosenwald cut off his contributions and withdrew his representative from the board of trustees. The settlement languished after that, and in 1922 the board turned it over to the Urban League, which tried running it for a year and then gave up.[20]

A year later Jane Addams, Mary McDowell, Sophonisba Breckenridge, and four residents of white West Side settlements, reconstituted the Wendell Phillips board and tried to salvage the settlement. Their efforts seemed promising for a while. The neighborhood was "just beginning to appreciate the value and necessity of the Wendell Phillips Settlement" when the board was compelled to terminate the program in 1925. The Phillips Day Nursery bought the settlement's facilities and continued to struggle for survival. Near the end, community hostility toward the settlement was more evident than appreciation. A gang of "older boys" descended upon a settlement dance, "shot out windows before the police could arrive and stripped several of the girls of their clothing."[21]

For another five years or so the settlement board sponsored a "community center" at the neighborhood's black public school. Whites felt that the center, open two nights a week, raised the Negroes' "morale" and "improved [the] behavior of the young people." No one claimed that the school center substituted adequately for a settlement. After the Phillips Settlement closed, Graham Taylor, who had been one of its patrons, tried to interest white philanthropists in building a boys' club on the West Side, "where a large colored population had little or nothing done to help them help themselves." The Union League Foundation for Boys' Clubs, of which Taylor was a board member, did open a West Side club in 1927, one block north of the black district, but it barred black boys.[22]

By 1930 there were no settlements for blacks in the old Negro enclaves on the West Side, the Lower North Side, Englewood, Lilydale, and Morgan Park. In the Black Belt itself the South Side Settlement House and a few church centers were hard-pressed to provide any activities. The closest thing to a full-fledged settlement for blacks in the city was a club affiliated with the Union League Foundation for Boys' Clubs, which also ran two clubs for whites only. The South Side Boys' Club was founded in 1925 by utility tycoon Samuel Insull and a group of men "who felt that something ought to be done for the underprivileged boys who were a constant source of trouble along a part of Grand Boulevard." In 1925, Grand Boulevard was near the eastern border of the Black Belt. The Boys' Club was located four blocks west, on Michigan Avenue, closer to "the heart of [the] colored district." The purpose of the club was to instruct "colored boys" in "citizenship and respect for law." The founders did not talk, as Celia Parker Woolley had, of equal opportunity for blacks. They hoped "to create in the minds of young boys right attitudes and sounder thinking on the various problems they will face at a later time."[23]

The club's staff was black, and the board of trustees included representatives of "the better group of citizens, both colored and white," but whites dominated the board. Among the white backers of the club were two realtors who took leading parts in the Chicago Real Estate Board's campaign to cover white neighborhoods with restrictive covenants. The club had the best equipment any neighborhood center for blacks ever had. One problem the boys who used the club's extensive facilities would "face at a later time" was the wall of covenants excluding them from the neighborhoods where their benefactors lived. The covenants were upheld by law, which these boys were drilled to respect.[24]

❧

The settlements for "colored people" never had the capacity to provide black Chicago with adequate, much less *equal*, service. Several white settlements were in a position to relieve the strain on black centers by opening up their own doors to blacks who lived close by. The expansion of the Black Belt brought Negroes within reach of many neighborhood centers. A number of settlements stood only a block or two beyond black districts. Several were in "mixed" areas, that is, neighborhoods which contained a "colored section." Others served neighborhoods safely remote from the "colored problem" until the spreading Black Belt engulfed adjacent areas. Some saw their own immediate neighborhoods overtaken.

Along the rim of Negro areas those settlements that did not shut down or move away either excluded blacks altogether or contrived some way to accommodate them separately. In the neighborhoods that changed, a few options were open to the stranded settlements. They could remain in the area and resist the "invaders"; they could run and resume work elsewhere; they could adjust to their new neighbors in some fashion; they could resign themselves to serving blacks exclusively; or they could simply close. All of these were options that settlement workers hoped they would never have to consider. Settlement workers evaded "the race question" in their own settlements until neighborhood transition brought them "face to face" with it. Then they almost always chose, in one way or another, to follow the color line.[25]

A space of a few blocks was, physically, easy walking distance, and the usual range of effectiveness for a neighborhood center was several blocks in any direction. Nevertheless, settlements in white territory adjacent to the Black Belt rarely reached beyond the residences of their white neighbors. For all the good they were to the Negroes living nearby, they might as well have been closed down or located miles away.

On the South Side, just beyond the western border of the Black Belt, four settlements were founded between 1900 and 1915. Two of them fronted on Wentworth Avenue. Both passed out of existence before 1920. If they were abandoned because Negroes were pressing too hard from the east, the experience of the two remaining settlements suggests that their white sponsors gave them up needlessly. St. Rose's Social Center, founded in 1915, was only a block west of Wentworth on 25th Street. Bethlehem Settlement, dating back to 1900, worked to improve "neighborhood conditions" around 53rd Street; it was less than a block from Wentworth. Bethlehem and St. Rose's carried on their programs undaunted by the black presence because, as the Commission on Race Relations reported, the whole section along Wentworth south of 22nd Street was so hostile to Negroes that they not only found it impossible to live there but exposed themselves to danger "even by passing through."[26]

Suppose that a black youngster had wanted to go to St. Rose's Social Center. To reach it, he would first have to leave the heavily built-up Negro blocks. Once he passed State Street he entered a no-man's land of factories and warehouses with only a scattering of homes. This stretch ran a few short blocks to the high train embankments of the Rock Island. After crossing the industrial wasteland, he would have to walk through the dark, wide underpass, then get past a public park called Hardin Square. This park was on Wentworth but ran east, not west, and therefore fell on the so-called Negro side of the boundary line. The whites from around St. Rose's claimed possession of the park, which had an average daily attendance of about eight hundred whites in 1920. If he got past the park, he would then have to cross the Wentworth line and pass between two facing rows of bungalows, two-flats, three-flats, and apartment buildings, all occupied by whites, largely of Italian stock. That last block of housefronts, open windows, crowded stoops, and swarming sidewalks would have been the hardest. If somehow he made it to the settlement, the Catholic nuns who ran the place would almost certainly have turned him away, perhaps calling for police to protect him from the fate awaiting him as he tried to make his way back to the Black Belt.

St. Rose's was for "the community," and this community, which the dominant Italians shared with people of more than twenty-five nationalities, was relentlessly white. The settlement had no explicit policy of barring blacks, but they did not use the place. Nor did they use the public parks west of the train tracks. Speculating on why Negroes stayed away from the public recreation centers, which were officially open to all, by law, the Riot Commission reasoned that "fear was probably a large factor." The commission did not report on the all-white settlement houses across the "dividing line," because it did not consider discrimination by private agencies to be an issue. One may safely conclude that if blacks feared to cross the line to use public facilities where they were entitled to protection from park police, then fear was a factor in their refusal to venture over to settlement houses guarded only by neighbor-hood gangs.[27]

Bethlehem Settlement was even closer to Wentworth than St. Rose's was, but the territory around it was "protected" by a group of gangs known collectively as the Shielders. The celebrated Ragen's Colts, whose home turf was farther west, claimed jurisdiction over the area as well. The gangs enjoyed a long and spirited rivalry over the question, which of them could intimidate Negroes more. Between them the gangs, whom blacks called the Mickies on the mistaken assumptions that there was just one of them and that everyone in it was Irish, denied Negroes access to the public parks and recreation centers in the vicinity. The neighborhood had no dominant ethnic group: In 1920 the Irish ranked third among twenty-one nationalities in the area. It was not an Irish neighborhood, it was a white man's neighborhood. Of 3,979 people in the twelve-block section west of Wentworth between 51st and 55th, 3,978 were white. The area was no place for Negroes, who were packed densely into the tenements on the other side of the tracks. Whatever the feelings of Bethlehem's supervisors, they had to reckon with the overwhelming sentiment of the neighborhood, which "didn't allow niggers in." Bethlehem Settlement was out of bounds to blacks. Everyone who used it was white.[28]

Farther west than St. Rose's and Bethlehem, but still within a half-mile of the Black Belt, the Salvation Army launched its settlement work in 1921. To get to Salvation Army Settlement a Negro would have had to leave the black district, cross the industrial wasteland, get through the Rock Island underpass, make his way through the tier of white communities along Wentworth, then pass beneath a second broad bank of railroad tracks, only to emerge in Bridgeport, a tough multiethnic working-class community. With its ten Catholic parishes, Bridgeport was difficult ground for the Salvation Army to work in. With two entrenched gangs, the Dukies and the Hamburgs, both of which were prominent in mobbings of blacks during the riots, Bridgeport was dangerous turf for blacks. The settlement was intended for and used by whites only. Later in the twenties the Salvation Army set up a separate facility in the Black Belt, on the premises of the South Side Settlement House. Black families living near Wentworth north of 32nd Street were actually closer to Salvation Army Settlement than to the dispensary at the Negro settlement, but they found the outlet in the Black Belt to be far more "convenient."[29]

The communities west of the Rock Island line were notorious for their rough-and-ready approach to race relations. In communities of more refinement, people gasped in distaste, if not horror, at the way the rowdies kept Negroes from crossing the line. The attitude in workers' neighborhoods was probably closer to awe. Yet the railroad embankment, with its singular reputation, was not the only boundary. On the east the Black Belt encountered a succession of lines that held for varying lengths of time until Cottage Grove was firmly established in the twenties, and every Negro satellite district was circumscribed as well. No white area bordering on a black district welcomed Negroes into its social centers.

East of the Black Belt, across Cottage Grove, where expansion of the Negro section was blocked in the 1920s, stood genteel Hyde Park. It was not a typical settlement neighborhood, as the ladies of the Hyde Park Juvenile Protection League explained on opening Hyde Park Center in 1909. League leaders described Hyde Park as "a good residence locality (in which is located the University of Chicago) with the exception of four to six blocks" alongside the Illinois Central tracks. There, in a troublesome strip of boarding houses, saloons, pawnshops, cabarets, gambling joints, and other dubious haunts, the league placed its center, the better to battle the district's baleful influence. The center confined its service to the area east of Cottage, so there was no question of letting in denizens of the Black Belt. But it happened that within Hyde Park itself, in the very section where the center and the saloons were vying to fill the leisure hours of the impressionable and the unwary, there was "quite a large colored population . . . employed mainly as waiters in nearby hotels."[30]

The "Lake Park Avenue colony" was the largest of a few Negro boarding house areas in Hyde Park. In 1910 the colony numbered over four hundred. In the next ten years the figure dropped by almost half, due to the campaign of white property owners to drive the blacks out. Though the few children of the dwindling black colony could have been admitted to the center without inundating the place, the staff refused to accept them. After Negroes protested for more than a year the center relented. But shortly after the center admitted some Negro children, it closed, probably because of community opposition. Its successor, the Hyde Park Neighborhood Club, opened in 1919 in a block with no Negroes. Like the center before it, the club led children from east of Cottage in "activities of a social nature." Black children living in Hyde Park were excluded.[31]

A Negro had no more chance of taking part in settlement activities in middle-class Hyde Park than he did in the tough neighborhoods along Wentworth. Wherever black districts were located within walking distance of settlements, the story was the same: Blacks were supposed to stay back where they belonged, in the isolation of their own enclaves.

There were two settlements within a few blocks of the black district in Englewood. One, Neighborhood House, had a reformist staff, active in trade union, child labor, and other movements at the city, state, and national level. Of all Chicago settlements, it went farthest toward sharing powers of decision with the people of the neighborhood. The other, Ogden Hills Boys' Club, was under the firm control of "prominent Chicagoans" concerned more with training the children of the poor than aiding their working parents to improve their position. One thing Neighborhood House and the conservative boys' club had in common was that their neighborhood work stopped where the neighborhood stopped, at the line between white Englewood and black Englewood. Neither admitted Negroes into their activities.[32]

Two settlements served the "underprivileged community" of South Chicago. Both were within a half-mile of the miserable row of shanties and rooming houses called the Strand, where several hundred Negroes lived. The blacks of South Chicago were so few in number that the settlements could have accommodated them without fear of being overwhelmed. But South Chicago Neighborhood House (Baptist) and South Chicago Community Center

(Congregational) were both preoccupied with the problem of gaining acceptance in an overwhelmingly Catholic area. Community Center invited "the 37 nationalities represented in the neighborhood" to attend. Neighborhood House broadcast a policy of "no restrictions to any nationality or creed," and both settlements made a special effort to attract Mexicans. To win over the Catholics, the settlements opened their doors wide to everyone except Negroes. Community Center kept blacks out of regular activities and refused to care for Negro children in its day nursery. But in summertime, when the regular program was largely suspended, Community Center sometimes accepted up to 10 percent Negro enrollment in classes. No Negroes used South Chicago Neighborhood House at any time of year.[33]

On the West Side, the old Negro section along Lake Street had the benefit of the modest facilities at Wendell Phillips Settlement from 1908 to 1925. After Phillips folded, the neighborhood, grown from 3,000 to about 7,500, had infrequent use of a public school plant, but it had no neighborhood center. Blacks gained access to the public center at Union Park, despite the white people's stand "that as long as they could keep the colored people away they were going to do it." Though blacks did not use the park in proportion to their numbers in the area, they still accounted for 40 percent of attendance in 1920. Whites were able to evade interracial interaction, nevertheless. The adults and older children who used the center at night had "a tacit understanding" with their Negro counterparts: "on certain nights all the attendance would be black and on other nights it would be all white." During the day, when youngsters frequented the park, black and white children played in separate groups. According to the park director, this segregation was "voluntary": "Negroes," he said, "had a tendency to separate from the whites." When whites called blacks "such nicknames as 'Smoke,'" he believed, "they did it in a friendly spirit." Blacks avoided the swimming pool or confined themselves to a small section of it, he added, because it was "the natural impulse of the colored people" to be "afraid of the water." (Riot Commission investigators reported that once when a black boy strayed from the Negro section of the pool, white boys grabbed him and held him underwater until, "when he came up, he was gasping for air.")[34]

The reason that blacks did not come to the center in greater numbers, the park's director contended, was that facilities for youngsters over ten years old and for adults were inadequate. Such facilities abounded at settlements just beyond the black enclave. But the whites, who could segregate blacks within the public center but by law could not shut them out, were able to "keep the colored away" from the settlements.[35]

Chicago Commons, north and east of the Lake Street colony and within walking distance, was the best known and best equipped settlement in the district. While the Commons made "no distinction" among neighbors, it drew its southern boundary of service at the great belt of railroad tracks that separated it from the Negro district. There were times before 1920 when a black child belonged to a class or club, but as the enclave edged eastward, closer to the settlement, black attendance went down instead of up. One Negro was registered at the settlement in 1928, another in 1930. The latter was a little girl who went to the Commons camp but did not attend the settlement itself. The other Negro probably did not belong to a social group either. In 1928–29 several "Negro boys of various ages" asked admission to the settlement. The boys' department formed them into a separate group—the only one associated with the settlement that was not age-graded—but did not register them, include them in the general program, or even mention them in the Commons' annual report. Presumably a boys' worker met with them *away* from the building. Neighborhood workers were in touch with seven black families in 1928, three in 1929, and four in 1930. Probably they made "home visits" to these families or conferred with some other social workers about them, instead of counseling the blacks at the settlement. Year after year the Commons counted people from sixteen to twenty ethnic groups among its thousands of members, but "No Negroes."[36]

Two other longstanding settlements north of the enclave had no discernible contact with it at all. Neither Erie Chapel Institute nor Emerson House expressly prohibited blacks, but both confined their work to the area above "the natural boundary" of the railroad tracks. Both were Protestant settlements, both were resented by Catholics who lived nearby, and by the late twenties both were searching for ways to reach "a larger constituency." Neither considered extending its boundary southward, where the residents were Protestant. "To cross the railroad," a sociology student reported in a survey of Emerson House, "meant to find one's self in the West Side colored area." Emerson House was just across the tracks from the densest part of the black district, closer to the homes of many black West Siders than Wendell Phillips Settlement had been. By the time Phillips closed there were about two hundred blacks living *north* of the railroad barrier, in the blocks adjoin-ing Emerson House. The settlement continued its efforts to befriend the white people of "forty nationalities" who lived in the vicinity, and went on ignoring the blacks.[37]

In 1927 the Union League Foundation for Boys' Clubs founded a club near Emerson House, less than a block from the Negro colony, as noted earlier. The club claimed to serve "underprivileged boys" who lived within a "radius of five blocks." The club actually served whites who lived north of the railroad barrier and whites who lived south of it in the area along the southern border of the black enclave. Union League Boys' Club "refused service to Negroes" who lived in the gap between the two white communities, that is, right in the center of the club's designated service area.[38]

South and west of the Lake Street enclave there were six more neighborhood centers—five Protestant-administered, one secular. The oldest of the Protestant settlements, Forward Movement, closed down before 1919 but continued to run a summer camp, which "refused service to Negroes." The secular settlement, the Off-the-Street-Club, was maintained by the Advertising Council of Chicago to "provide an opportunity for all individuals of the neighborhood to grow and develop mentally, physically, spiritually, and socially." It, too, "refused service to Negroes."[39]

Of the four Protestant settlements that remained in operation, two expressly excluded blacks, although both were open to white people of any creed. Another did not *bar* Negroes from attending, but its clientele of people of over twenty nationalities was still entirely white. Two of these settlements were within two blocks of the black boundary; the other was *on* the boundary line, but on the "white" side of the street. The fourth Protestant settlement in the area was on the boundary line, too, but on the north or "black" side. The Chicago Evangelistic Institute on Washington Boulevard was the only settlement in the area that did "Negro work." Although the institute was within the Negro section, the square block on which it stood remained all-white, and the institute's center, called Friendship Hall (complete with gym, kindergarten, manual training room, and three clubrooms), was "for white people." Negroes were not admitted. "For colored members of the community," the Institute rented a room in a building one block north. The room, which had no equipment, bore the name The Wayside. Chicago Evangelistic Institute reported to the Council of Social Agencies that it operated "two neighborhood centers," one "for white people" and one "for colored." The centers were separate, but hardly equal.[40]

Altogether the settlements in the white ring around the Lake Street section of blacks had eight auditoriums, six gymnasiums, one swimming pool, fifteen domestic science and manual training rooms, seventy-nine clubrooms (exclusive of The Wayside), and other facilities scarce or unavailable in the black enclave. Like the boarding homes, children's homes, and other welfare institutions in the area, these facilities, open to the settlements' neighbors, were "available" only to white people.[41]

Farther south on the Near West Side, between the Congress Street elevated line and the gigantic belt of railroad tracks and yards beginning at 15th Street, the settlements worked for many years undisturbed by local manifestations of the color question. This was the territory of Hull-House, of the great immigrant "colonies," and of the famed Jewish "ghetto." Until the 1920s few Negroes lived there. Then, in the twenties, that part of the area south of 12th Street and east of Loomis went from zero percent Negro to over 60 percent. Jews fled the "ghetto," and blacks replaced them. By 1930 the strip between Maxwell Street and 14th Place was solidly black, and the whole section below 12th Street appeared to be well on its way to becoming all-Negro. The settlements north of 12th Street found themselves on the edge of a new black belt. The settlements south of 12th were inside it.[42]

The five settlements in the border area reacted to their new situation in one of three ways: flight, total restriction, or pretended openness. The Chicago Hebrew Institute, renamed the Jewish People's Institute (JPI), decided in 1922 to follow the exodus from the old neighborhood to the new promised land out by Douglas Park. The transfer to a splendid new plant three miles west began in 1927, and by 1930 it was complete. The great old buildings on Taylor Street, still the property of the JPI and just a block away from the streets overtaken by blacks, were stripped and allowed to slip into decay.[43]

The two Protestant settlements stayed behind and concentrated their work on special segments of the population. Firman House, dating back to 1900, decided in 1930 to aim its program at the Mexicans who had been coming into the neighborhood in increasing numbers. Firman House had never accepted blacks; now it made its ban formal. Everyone was welcome, especially Mexicans, but Negroes were excluded as a matter of policy. Garibaldi Institute, opened in 1921, labored strenuously to win over the neighborhood's Italian Catholics. It turned away no one except Negroes. A Catholic settlement, Madonna Center, a little over four blocks north of 12th Street, was farther away from the blacks than were the other settlements. There was little danger that a black person would stray so far from the "colored section" to ask admission, especially when Protestant settlements closer by denied him. But to be on the safe side, Madonna Center went on record as "refusing service to Negroes." Neither the Jewish settlement, nor the Protestant settlements, nor the Catholic settlement violated the color line.[44]

The only border settlement that made a pretense of serving Negroes was Hull-House. Now only a few blocks away from a sizable concentration of blacks, Hull-House went on much as it had before, exuding interracial good will but including almost no Negroes. The Jane Club continued to deny apartments to black women. A new nursery school, opened in 1925, set a racial quota "to be representative of [the] neighborhood." For this purpose the staff redefined the neighborhood as stopping at 12th Street, thus guaranteeing that only a few of the one hundred children would be black. For forty years at Hull-House 16th Street was the southern boundary of boys' work, and boys from the old "ghetto" had "flocked" to the settlement. Now the staff redrew the line at 12th Street, cutting the Negroes off from the area of service. In 1927 Jane Addams invited a group of black women to organize themselves as a "Negro mothers' club." Every year thereafter the Hull-House yearbooks pictured this club as evidence "that Negroes were taking part in the program." In fact, the club took no part in activities "for the general community." The members were not on the regular mailing list; they were invited to "their meeting only." Their children came "the same night," if they came at all, and played in a room by themselves.[45]

The border settlements that did not abandon the neighborhood tried to conduct themselves as if the Negroes pouring in south of them were not there. For the six centers in the old "ghetto," the influx of blacks was harder to ignore. None of them managed to stay where it was and carry on business as usual. Brotherhood House, which opened in 1920 for the benefit of "all nationalities," closed down in 1926. Maxwell Street Settlement, the pioneering Jewish settlement in the city, also folded. Another Jewish settlement, the American Boys' Commonwealth (ABC), began work in 1918 on the assumption that the district would remain heavily Jewish. When the blacks moved in, the ABC moved out. In 1930 it opened its new quarters far west of the "ghetto," within a block of the transplanted Jewish People's Institute. The Boys' Brotherhood Republic, whose motto was "There are no bad boys," led the way to the far West Side. In its new surroundings, to which the JPI and the ABC were shortly drawn, the Boys' Brotherhood Republic set a "quota of not over 10% Negro," who were admitted not to the settlement itself but to a summer camp, where they received "separate service." The 10 percent figure seemed liberal, because the relocated settlement was "far from any Negro neighborhood." Indeed, it was as far as it could get.[46]

Newberry Center, located in the part of the "ghetto" that blacks overtook most quickly and most thoroughly, responded to the inundation in a novel way. It split in two. The center had originated as a Methodist mission to Germans and Bohemians. When the neighborhood changed in the 1890s, the center adjusted itself to the Jewish newcomers, gradually coming to think of itself "as having a distinctive mission to the Jews," with "the dual function of serving their needs—physical and social—and of converting them to Christianity." The response of the neighborhood Jews ranged from "coldness" to "definite hostility." Friction was open. Vandalism and broken windows were common. When the Jewish population moved out, the center debated whether to stay in the area and minister to the Negroes or to pursue the Jewish migration. The decision was to do both.[47]

The head resident packed up most of the center's movable equipment and most of its staff and opened a new center in 1930 near the other fugitive settlements. Marcy Center, as the transplanted institution was called, was not welcomed by the Jews it hoped to convert. Jewish organizations warned children to "stay away." A well-equipped dispensary, which had been moved from the old center, was underused: People injured nearby, including children, "refused to be taken to the Marcy Center clinic for treatment." Meanwhile, back in the "ghetto," a skeleton staff remained in the old building and tried to adjust to its new neighbors.[48]

Newberry Center, what was left of it, was one of two neighborhood centers that stayed behind. Along with Henry Booth House, it opened its doors partway to blacks but went to great lengths to keep them a minority in settlement activities. Both settlements kept blacks separate from whites: Blacks used different parts of the buildings or came at special hours. And both settlements changed their boundaries of service to include the maximum number of whites in their potential constituencies. By 1930 Booth House, which had looked forward optimistically to building brotherhood between the "neighborhood races" when the races were whites of different nationalities, was still successful in keeping Negroes out of most activities. Only 16 percent of its budget went to work "for Negroes." Newberry Center was less successful. Over half of its budget went into "Negro work." Although the races stayed apart in the center's building, the whites who continued to come were "mostly Mexican," a fact that made the staff wonder if their settlement was biracial or "colored." The blacks, however, had no doubt that they were receiving separate service in a dual program. They were on one side of the color line; whites, including the Mexicans, were on the other.[49]

In 1929, a time when some settlements were fleeing the old "ghetto" and others were shutting down, a group of local merchants banded together to open a new neighborhood center. Anxious to hold white families—and shoppers—in the area, the businessmen called on "one hundred kindly men" to donate one hundred dollars per year to help "all white boys" in the area to "stay good and make good," and equally important, to stay put and make good customers. "CAN YOU THINK," read their form letter, "OF A BETTER INVESTMENT?" The merchants committee, headed by Irving N. Klein, had Catholic, Protestant, and Jewish members, one of whom was a trustee of Hull-House. They raised twice as much money as they asked for, and in 1930 they opened Old Town Boys' Club at 1300 Newberry, a block inside the Negro section. Within a year it had over a thousand members, including a large number of Mexicans, but no blacks.[50]

One other Negro enclave was within reach of social settlements, and by the Riot Commission's account, blacks in the Lower North Side were "welcomed" in the community's public recreation centers and private settlements alike. Unfortunately, this finding reveals more about the commission's racial attitudes than it does about the neighborhood's treatment of Negroes. The Lower North Side's centers, public and private, were segregated. As the commission knew, the area had two public recreation centers, a large one a few blocks from the black section and a small one right at the enclave's edge. The large center was virtually for whites only. The small one, where attendance was 85 percent white, tolerated "Negro groups" if they came at "special hours," when whites were not using the place. According to the park director, this arrangement satisfied both "the desire of the Negroes to be by themselves and also the objection of the white girls who had protested having Negro girls in the same gymnasium classes with them." As for the settlements, there were three of them. They all discriminated against Negroes, as the commission must have known.[51]

Eli Bates House was the only one of the settlements that the commission named. At one time, the commission reported, "a club of Negro young men" had been registered there. "A few Negro children" had "come to the kindergarten" and a group of black boys had used the gym, apparently, although the report did not say so, when whites were not using the facilities. Some Negro families had "asked settlement residents for advice," although black adults took no part in settlement programs. During the riot, Bates House issued a circular "deploring race hatred and appealing for order and fairness." On the whole, the head resident told the commission's investigators, Bates House never had "much contact with the Negro group." In the twenties, as the population in the black district mounted and spilled over its old confines onto blocks closer to the settlement, Bates House held its contacts with blacks to a minimum. Less than 1 percent of its budget went into "Negro work" in 1930, and at least one settlement program excluded blacks outright. The workshop, which employed jobless adults, accepted no Negroes. When the settlement made a "community survey" a few years later, it counted "only white population." As far as Bates House was concerned, blacks were not part of the community.[52]

While Bates House had almost no contact with its black neighbors, the other settlements had absolutely none at all. The Italian Catholic Church, St. Philip Benizi, never admitted blacks to its community center, although all neighborhood whites, not just parishioners, were invited. The most prominent Lower North Side settlement, Olivet Institute, also excluded blacks completely. Olivet's policies toward immigrants, on the one hand, and blacks, on the other, furnish an arresting example of the difference the color line made in neighborhood work.[53]

Olivet Institute, like Bates House, was a Protestant settlement that claimed to make "no effort to proselytize." Nevertheless Rev. Norman Barr, the mercurial Presbyterian clergyman who founded Olivet in 1898 and dominated it for forty years, wanted the settlement to be "a Christ to its community, ministering His truth." Barr regularly referred to the Lower North Side as his "parish." It was hard terrain for a Presbyterian to till. When he began his ministry there, Scandinavians and Germans were the leading ethnic groups. Though they were mostly Protestant, few were Presbyterians. By 1910 the population was overwhelmingly "foreign born," with Germans and Italians predominant among "twenty-four distinct nationalities." Negroes had come into the area and ranked eighth among the ethnic groups. "Romanism and the Lutheran form of Protestantism," Barr reported, were "almost the exclusive religious types." As the neighborhood kept changing, Barr moved the institute a few blocks away and redrew "the boundaries of the parish" to exclude the eastern half. Within the constricted boundaries, he wrote in 1920, "99% of our community is of the most recent European importation and 95% nominally Roman Catholic." By redrawing the "parish" limits Barr had eliminated the black concentration along Wells Street, but hundreds of blacks who lived on Larrabee were within the altered bounds, and nearly all were native Protestants. Barr omitted them from his calculations because he had no place for them in his community.[54]

Reverend Barr was no champion of immigrants. He accepted "the peoples of foreign tongue" into his community only because he believed that he could change them. He detested them as they were. Their ideas and habits were "un-American," he thought, and their religious convictions were "prejudices," not beliefs. In 1924 he went before a South Side klavern of Chicago's Ku Klux Klan to preach a sermon titled "Knights of the Ku Klux Klan, Save Us." Whether or not Barr was a Klansman himself, he believed with the Klan that America was Protestant and had to remain so. He took his stand on the Lower North Side for "one hundred per cent Americanism." However, he believed that Americans could be made, regardless of where they had been born. The children of immigrants were natives, and their parents were not doomed to remain aliens. They could all become Protestant Americans.[55]

Barr did not shut out immigrants from Olivet. Far from it. He did everything he could to lure adults to citizenship classes and to services at what he called "our Italian Church." For the children, besides clubs and recreation, he ran year-round Bible classes. Olivet Institute was proselytizing all of the time, and as Barr assured Presbyterian contributors, with some "success." The stationery on which he corresponded with donors bore the letterhead "Help Olivet Institute Americanize and Christianize Its Community." The rock upon which Barr built his ministry was his faith that he could take the foreigners and transform their "moral complexion." Blacks, though they were native Protestants, were indelibly nonwhite. Barr excluded Negroes from all of Olivet's programs, and he restricted the settlement's property holdings against them as well. In 1933, two years before the local property owners' association mounted a massive drive to cover the area all around the Lower North Side's "Little Black Belt" with restrictive covenants, Olivet restricted its real estate from "the use or sale of premises to negroes." Later in the decade, when the settlement sold three lots and the buildings on them, the realtor and the buyers were all Italian-Americans. To immigrants in Olivet's "parish" the settlement was an extremely condescending ally, but to blacks it was a straightforward, implacable enemy.[56]

Finally, there was the great Black Belt itself. In the course of its expansion between 1910 and 1930 it had overrun the neighborhoods of three white settlements, putting the tolerance of neighborhood workers to the ultimate test. One settlement moved away, one stayed behind and kept excluding Negroes. The other one really tried to make its program "inter-racial": No settlement in the city or anywhere in America made an effort that was comparable, or even close.

Deborah Boys' Club and Sinai Temple were Jewish institutions that fled the Near South Side between 1912 and 1918, when that area was being absorbed into the advancing Black Belt. They took up new quarters a block apart on fashionable Grand Boulevard (later South Parkway, now Rev. Martin Luther King, Jr., Drive). Sinai's new temple, with its center "for the community," was just north of 47th Street. Deborah Boys' Club was below 47th, which whites hoped would stand as "a breakwater" against the Negro tide. In the twenties the blacks came flooding in. Sinai Temple's neighborhood went under first, then the breakwater crumbled, and the area around Deborah Boys' Club was inundated. In 1930 the Boys' Club moved far away, to the Northwest Side. Sinai Temple tried to follow its fleeing congregation into Hyde Park–Kenwood, but when a deal to sell the buildings "to the colored" for $425,000 fell through in 1927, the temple was marooned.[57]

Sinai had to stay where it was. Sinai's Community Center, renamed for its late illustrious rabbi, Emil Hirsch, stayed open, but it was closed to the local community. Jews from Hyde Park and other white communities continued coming to the center, which also became a meeting place for citywide liberal groups, such as the Chicago chapter of the Women's International League for Peace and Freedom. The Negroes who lived all around the center and were excluded were not kept out because they were gentiles. Many Protestant and Catholic youngsters went to the center with their Jewish friends. Rabbi Emil Hirsch had been one of six white Chicagoans to sign the "call" to form the NAACP, but the center named for him closed its clubrooms, gymnasium, and swimming pool to "colored people" because they were "colored."[58]

Of the South Side settlements in neighborhoods that changed, only Abraham Lincoln Centre stood its ground and still gave an inch to the incoming blacks. More than any settlement in the nation, and all but alone among settlements in Chicago, it struggled to serve blacks and whites on an "inter-racial" basis. Its failure cautioned all settlement workers against tampering with the color line.

Abraham Lincoln Centre began in 1905 as an extension of the neighborhood program conducted by the Unitarians of All Souls Church. There was no congregation in the city more liberal than All Souls. Two black families attended services there at a time when "no other church or meeting place under white auspices had Negro members"—but that was also a time when no blacks lived nearby, and the Negro members had to travel a considerable distance to reach the church.[59]

Lincoln Centre was meant to be, one founder said, "a factory, a factory where men were made." Indeed, the building bore an industrial aspect. Seven stories high, built of brick, it dominated the corner of Langley Avenue and Oakwood Boulevard, dwarfing every building within a mile. A block to the east ran Cottage Grove, the western edge of the exclusive preserves known as Oakland and Kenwood. A block north, at 39th Street, the car barns of the Chicago surface lines formed a kind of barrier between the center's genteel surroundings and a tenement district to the north and west, inhabited by transit workers and other small-wage earners, "many of them German, Irish, and Jewish." Beyond this tenement area, farther north and west, was the South Side's teeming black district.[60]

The center, like the congregation that spawned it, was avowedly liberal. Above its doorway, carved in stone, was the motto of All Souls Church: "Here let no man be stranger." It opened its facilities to the tenement dwellers as well as to the residents of Oakland and Kenwood, and the directors took pride in the "mixing" of classes, denominations, and nationalities in its program. But even though the center had excellent recreational equipment, the staff stressed "cultural" activities that drew attendance mainly from its own boulevard and the fashionable addresses east of Cottage Grove. And while the center was absorbed in its forums, recitals, classes, and lectures, the tenement district to the north and west was being added, section by section, to the Black Belt.[61]

Lincoln Centre had never excluded blacks who asked admission to its activities. In 1905 "one old darkey" partook in a gardening project. Two years later the kindergarten enrolled "one colored child." In 1912 Jenkin Lloyd Jones, pastor of the Church and "dean" of the center, emphasized the principle that it was wrong to draw lines of class, religion, nationality, or race. Jews and gentiles, blacks and whites, Jones said, were welcome. One staff member, noting the expansion of the black districts and perhaps trying to soften the blow of Jones's hard doctrine, assured the trustees that the center could defend "colored people" from "unjust discrimination" without becoming "the shining buckle in a black belt." He explained that "the car barns and the boulevards" barricaded the center from the area to the northwest. There was no question, he said, that the barriers would "hold."[62]

The boulevards and the car barns, however, failed to hold. The Black Belt spread eastward from the "alley el" past Grand Boulevard, around the car barns, and over Oakwood Boulevard itself. By 1920 the black district extended across Cottage Grove above 32nd Street, and from 32nd all the way south to 50th blacks held patches of territory up to Cottage Grove. "The big, bad Grove," as Negroes would come to call Cottage, was the new eastern boundary dividing black and white Chicago, and Abraham Lincoln Centre stood on the black side of the line, with "colored neighbors" on its own street and on all blocks to the north, west, and south. The new line at Cottage, unlike earlier barriers, was not about to give way. For more than two decades it would hold firm, separating the center from its accustomed constituents in the white territory just a block away.[63]

The center, holding fast to its policy of excluding no one, met increasing difficulty in its efforts to retain whites in activities. As late as 1912 a handful of "black and brown pickaninnies" could use the building without strong opposition. But in 1919, after the staff admitted black children into the game room, white children avoided it, and white adults complained that they were being crowded out of the center by the fifty blacks who were enrolled. During the riot that summer the staff risked white hostility by harboring a number of Negroes, and the center stood accused of forcing "social equality" on the community.[64]

The staff and the trustees denied that they believed in social equality, insisting that they were merely trying to keep faith with the principles of Jenkin Lloyd Jones, who had died in 1918. They could not do that if they slammed their doors on "proper, responsible negroes." Moreover, in the wake of the rioting, they wanted to promote interracial peace. They hoped to continue concentrating their work on whites, and they emphatically did not wish to minister exclusively to blacks. Of course it was impossible to publicize their position without offending Negroes. But the goal of interracial peace and brotherhood could serve a larger goal, the retention of whites in the program. For one could not have an interracial program without including members of the white race. So the center consecrated its program to the interracial ideal.[65]

The catch, and it was a formidable catch, was that the center's rhetoric alienated the whites, who felt increasingly that the center belonged to an ideal, and to the trustees, and to the blacks, but not to them. Few whites in Oakland and Kenwood were attracted by the center's appeals for interracial fellowship. Abraham Lincoln Centre was caught: It espoused interracial principles partly to prevent its program from becoming all-black, and it drove away the whites because it insisted on interracial principles.

For a time the center achieved the appearance of interracial activity. The staff (with what appeals there is no way to tell) strenuously recruited whites to its program, and although it added "a colored man" to work part-time on "the race problem of the neighborhood," it did nothing to encourage black participation. Groups using the facilities controlled their own memberships and supervised their own functions. As a result, Negroes were kept so much to themselves that the Riot Commission reported that Lincoln Centre was operating a "separate branch" for Negroes within the main building. For years the white enrollment actually grew, and blacks did not apply in great numbers for admittance to the immense "factory" with its white directors, white personnel, and white cultural program.[66]

The trustees tried to adhere to interracial principles regarding admissions to classes and activities that the staff itself directed. The only program that the staff did not attempt to desegregate was the summer camp, which white and black children attended in separate sessions. In 1929, against enormous pressure, the staff publicly reaffirmed its opposition to "any segregation," and a year later, though the summer camp was still segregated, the dean, Curtis Reese, condemned racial discrimination as "an evil of the first rank." These actions accelerated the withdrawal of the whites, which had been pronounced since 1922. In that year, All Soul's Church abandoned Oakwood Boulevard for the South Shore community, where the bulk of its membership had moved and where, for another forty years, any black man or woman except domestics would be strangers. The center stayed behind, and by remaining, became "the shining buckle of the Black Belt" that its directors so fervently hoped it would not become.[67]

In 1932 the staff had to face the fact that whites, although enrolled in large numbers, seldom used the center. A few whites still came in groups of their own and kept scrupulously to themselves, but participation in activities directed by the staff was "almost completely colored." The program was not interracial in any real sense. Indeed, it was barely biracial. The center, even though it was within a block of a populous white district that had once enjoyed its facilities and still (so the staff thought) had need of them, was in danger of becoming "entirely colored." To forestall that eventuality, the staff resorted to a system of "controlled registration." Now all departments imposed a maximum quota of "ten per cent colored." This meant that each black applicant had to wait until nine whites signed up for an activity before gaining admittance. Abraham Lincoln Centre was learning that it was one thing to mix rich and poor, native and foreign, gentile and Jew. Trying to mix blacks and whites was something else.[68]

❧

In the main, settlement houses served blacks separately or they did not serve them at all. Most settlement workers, like most reform-minded people and most Chicagoans, generally, were racists or, if not, they were conformists: They went along. The minority whose attitudes were not overtly racist believed in equality for Negroes, but not *social* equality. They wanted to improve the condition of black Chicagoans, and they felt that they did their part. They gave money and other aid to black organizations, including black settlements. They did "what they could" to help Negroes "help themselves." They often had the support of the racists in their efforts, however. And, like the racists, they drew the line at integrating blacks into the work of their own settlements.

But the settlement creed demanded more than just bringing people together in voluntary groups. It called for bringing different *kinds* of people into harmonious relationships. Every settlement for whites served people from more than one ethnic group, because all neighborhoods were multiethnic. Even the Jewish settlements in the old "ghetto" served Jews of many nationalities, and some of them served gentiles as well. Non-Jewish settlements, in turn, welcomed Jews. Serving a mixed ethnic clientele was never an easy task, but no settlement excluded members of one ethnic group at the insistence of the neighborhood's largest group. Settlement workers learned how to deal with ethnic segmentation in their neighborhoods. They would or could not cope with the segregation of blacks. They reinforced it.

Neighborhood workers found that, while they were unable to prevent population turnover in their neighborhoods, it was possible to keep them from "turning black." None of their programs stopped white families from moving away, but their racial policies helped prevent Negroes from moving in. They barred blacks from their own centers and supported separate agencies in the Black Belt to maintain the line dividing the ghetto from white Chicago. Alert to the dangers of completely segregating the blacks from the organized forces of the white community, settlement workers moved to bring black social workers and black projects under white supervision and control. In the white settlements they exerted control, too, but their purpose was assimilation. Their purpose in controlling the black settlements was segregation.[69]

Chicago settlements, from the most liberal member agencies in the Federation of Settlements to the most conservative boys' clubs, followed the color line in neighborhood work. Neighborhood workers, whether they were anti-Negro like Rev. Norman Barr or pro-Negro like Jane Addams, were deeply implicated in making and maintaining the black ghetto in Chicago. A young Southern black man who migrated to Chicago in 1927 took a long, hard look at Black Belt neighborhood work. He worked for a while at the South Side Boys' Club and "hated it," but he learned a great deal from the "kind of dressed-up police work" he did there. His name was Richard Wright. The experience he had at the Boys' Club gave him the outlines of a character taking shape in his mind, Bigger Thomas—"*what had made him and what he meant.*" At the Boys' Club, Wright recalled after the publication of *Native Son*,

> I had an opportunity to observe Bigger in all of his moods, actions, haunts. Here I felt for the first time that the rich folk who were paying my wages did not really give a good goddam about Bigger, that their kindness was prompted at bottom by a selfish motive. They were paying me to distract Bigger with ping-pong, checkers, swimming, marbles, and baseball in order that he might not roam the streets and harm the valuable white property which adjoined the Black Belt.[70]

Conclusion: The Slum and the Ghetto

What effect do bad living conditions actually have on the lives of the poor? It is impossible to say—so interwoven are all the difficulties of human beings whose lives are a constant struggle to maintain decent homes on the small earnings of the poor.
—Edith Abbott, *The Tenements of Chicago, 1908–1935* (Chicago, 1936), p. 485.

Why they make us live in one corner of the city?
—Bigger Thomas in Richard Wright's novel *Native Son* (New York, 1940; reprint ed., New York, 1966), p. 23.

IN THE TIME AROUND 1880, CHICAGO REFORMERS SET OUT TO IMPROVE "THE housing of the working people" until it finally would be fit to live in, a goal that seemed to them modest, attainable, intolerable *not* to attain, and unforgivable, *unthinkable*, if it could not be done. Yet for five decades they and their successors would find that no amount of effort they could muster could bring this goal within reach. Housing reform and neighborhood works produced few visible improvements in the slums. So long as people stayed poor, they could not afford houses fit to live in. There was no way to make a profit on decent homes if the poor inhabited them. And the fact was that the mass of workers, for all that they toiled, were poor and mostly stayed that way for the bulk of their working lives. So the tenement districts remained the great poverty districts of the city, where the residents did their best to make clean and comfortable homes for their families out of structures that were unsound, unsanitary, and unsafe. For reformers such as Jane Addams, to know some families like these was enough to keep the faith. But generally, trudging through the dingy streets of these rundown districts was a dismal and disheartening, even dismaying, ordeal for the housing advocates.

To see any effects of their efforts, reformers had to go beyond the slums. In the growing "zone of emergence," houses conformed to minimum standards. Many of the people who lived in the zone of emergence had started out in the tenements. By fierce determination, by hard work, and sometimes by accepting the aid of settlement workers, they made their way out of the slums. Because the zone of emergence was open to whites of all nationalities but closed to blacks, reformers tried to build up the Negro ghetto with housing and social services (a program that complemented the restriction campaign of white property owners). Looking at the well-housed inhabitants of the broad bungalow belt and the fortunate few who lived in the one model project in all of the Black Belt, reformers could assure themselves that their work was accomplishing something, though not all that was needed.

Some reformers were able to maintain a hearty optimism even in the face of the misery concentrated in the slums. Mrs. Fred A. Moore, a veteran "houser" who chaired the Woman's City Club's influential housing committee, was one of these. The World's Fair commemorating the centennial of Chicago was scheduled to open in 1933. A businessmen's committee was planning to make the lakefront "gloriously beautiful" in time for the Fair, wrote Mrs. Moore to Lea Taylor, president of the Chicago Federation of Settlements, in early 1929. "What about our 'back yard'? Do we wish to show these insanitary, unhealthy areas to the world?" Certainly Mrs. Moore did not want to. She had something in mind. Wouldn't it be fitting, she asked her committee at a luncheon meeting in March, if "our slums could be redeemed before the Fair is held"?[1]

The committee thought it was a marvelous idea. Within a month Mrs. Moore had improvement associations and chambers of commerce mobilized to support her campaign. Between April and the end of the year the Building Department, jolted into action by Mrs. Moore, demolished over two thousand unfit buildings. The Building Commissioner pledged himself to "eliminate" all "slum districts . . . before the World's Fair opens."[2]

The demolition drive lost some steam in 1930. Mrs. Moore, not discouraged, adjusted her timetable. Instead of redeeming *all* of the city's slums before the Fair started, she decided, it would be sufficient to take care of the slums "adjacent to the exposition grounds." The district happened to be the part of the Black Belt abutting on Oakland, the northern "gateway" to Hyde Park–Kenwood. In 1931 the Hyde Park Kiwanis Club announced a plan of action that it had ready in case the Building Department failed to raze the Negro district. Responsible Hyde Parkers would "form a trust to buy up land now occupied by unsightly houses between 31st and 39th Streets, and convert it into parking space" for the Fair.[3]

Meanwhile, the Great Depression struck. As early as 1927 settlement workers had encountered exceptionally high unemployment among their neighbors. Around Chicago Commons one person out of four "usually employed" was "absolutely without work" by February 1928. Of course the settlements were used to the "day-by-day misery" of the tenement dwellers. By 1931 the chronic misery of the slums was acute, and it was spreading all across the metropolis. Now if settlement workers went to the zone of emergence, instead of witnessing some signs of their own success, they saw evidence of their defeat.[4]

In 1931 President Herbert Hoover, acknowledging the nationwide crisis, called a conference on housing in America. This was an unprecedented opportunity for reformers to make their case. And it proved what a mottled case they had to offer. The president appointed several committees to study the housing problem, and Chicago "housers" were prominent among his choices. Alfred Stern, Julius Rosenwald's son-in-law and the man who directed the building of Rosenwald Gardens "for colored people," chaired the committee on large-scale projects. George Richardson, who had charge of the Marshall Field Gardens development for whites, was a member of Stern's committee. Architect N. Max Dunning, who had planned to locate a "colored project" next to the Rock Island tracks in the Black Belt, was an adviser. Several other people involved in Chicago's segregated projects participated in the president's conference. There was also a committee on "Negro housing"; its research was under the direction of ex-Chicagoan Charles S. Johnson, the black sociologist whose scholarship the Chicago Commission on Race Relations had exploited when it recommended a dual program of housing reform and neighborhood work for whites and blacks. Mrs. Irene McCoy Gaines, a black Chicagoan appointed to the Negro housing committee, received unofficial instructions to make only "constructive" recommendations, "practical suggestions" that would actually "improve conditions," and not—this was implicit—agitate the question of segregation.[5]

It was obvious that President Hoover was not inviting participants to speak with no restraint, but he opened up a forum to them. If ever there was a time and place for housing reformers to speak out, this was it. And all they could bring themselves to recommend were policies in line with the business creed and the color line. "Slums," the President's Conference decided, "cost money." The conference came out strongly for "wiping out slums," and it entrusted the task to business with the warning that if business did not rid the cities of slums, government would have to. "The choice lies with business." Brave words. Echoing the coded language the Riot Commission had employed a decade earlier, the conference recommended better housing and "welfare agencies" for "Negro sections." If business and philanthropy ever got around to supplying houses and social services for the poor, they were supposed to build up the Black Belts. It was all very familiar. The President's Conference simply preached the business creed to exorcise the slum; to deal with the ghetto, it prescribed the color line.[6]

In Illinois, too, the chief executive responded to the housing emergency of 1931 by naming a commission to study the matter. The chairman whom Governor Louis Emmerson selected for the Illinois Housing Commission was Alfred Stern. No one in Chicago or in the state believed more firmly in the business creed and the color line. Edith Abbott, the veteran neighborhood worker and housing reformer, also served on the Housing Commission. She had long doubted the ability of private enterprise to house "the great mass of earners." The Depression convinced her that direct government intervention in housing was necessary, and she set out to make Stern "see the light." She tried very hard to move him from his opposition to public housing, but he would not budge. She made no attempt to convince him that housing should be open to blacks and whites alike, and not just in segregated projects, but equally.[7]

Fifty years of working in the tenement neighborhoods, claiming to be neighbors to the poor, preaching democracy and opportunity, investigating and publicizing conditions, lobbying for new codes, and playing watchdog over their enforcement, and what did the reformers have to show for it? Over seventy settlement houses and boys' clubs, all but a handful for whites only and the rest serving blacks exclusively, controlled by trustees and administered by staffs whom most neighborhood people regarded as outsiders; three segregated housing projects, built by "private housing companies" for residents whose incomes were well above those of most tenement dwellers; a tenement ordinance that was largely unenforceable in the tenement districts, because the residents were too poor to pay the "economic rent" for housing built to minimum standards. There were some improvements in the tenements, but the most important change, according to Edith Abbott, could not be credited to housing reform or to neighborhood work but to the replacement of the horse by the motor vehicle, and thus the gradual disappearance of "the filthy stables and the dreadful manure heaps." The slums, she said, remained slums. What she did not say was that the most appalling slum of all, the Black Belt, remained a ghetto.[8]

For all of their efforts, and they were considerable efforts, after all, housing reformers and neighborhood workers had not been able to unmake the slum, and, like it or not, they had helped to make the ghetto. By 1931 most of them reluctantly admitted that private enterprise would not be able to solve the housing problem, but only a handful of them agreed with Edith Abbott that it was time to move beyond the limits of the business creed and advocate government aid to the ill-housed. And while many, even most, social workers believed that it was wrong to segregate Negroes in any publicly supported institution, few, if any, were willing to follow the logic of that position across the color line if housing were ever to become a governmental enterprise. The public housing that the reformers could foresee would have to allow space for black families and white alike, because it was *public*, but only in separate units, because they did not believe that the races should mix, or if they did believe it, they were not ready to come out and say so. This was the legacy of half a century of reform. The best-meaning people of the middle classes—those who cared the most for the working class, for the poor, for the immigrants, for the African-Americans, these reformers who wanted jobs for the jobless and houses for the homeless and prosperity for all—were still stalled in 1930 by the business creed and still stymied by the color line.

APPENDIX A ❧

Standard Form, Restrictive Covenant *(abridged version)*

Drafted for the Chicago Real Estate Board by Nathan William MacChesney of the Chicago Plan Commission, 1927

AND, WHEREAS, THE PARTIES HERETO FEEL THAT THE RESTRICTIONS AND covenants hereinafter imposed and created are for the best interests of all the parties hereto and of the property hereinbefore described.

IN CONSIDERATION of the premises and of the mutual covenants hereinafter made, and of the sum of Five Dollars ($5.00) in hand paid to each of the parties hereto by each of the other parties hereto, the receipt of which is hereby acknowledged, each party as owner of the parcel of land above described immediately under his name, does hereby covenant and agree with each and every other of the parties hereto, that his said parcel of land is now and until January 1, 1949 and thereafter until this agreement shall be abrogated as hereinafter provided, shall be subject to the restrictions and provisions hereinafter set forth, and that he will make no sale, contract of sale, conveyance, lease or agreement and give no license or permission in violation of such restrictions or provisions, which are as follows:

> 1. The restriction that no part of said premises shall in any manner be used or occupied directly or indirectly by any negro or negroes, provided that this restriction shall not prevent the occupation, during the period of their employment, of janitors' or chauffeurs' quarters in the basement or in a barn or garage in the rear, or of servants' quarters by negro janitors, chauffeurs or house servants, respectively, actually employed as such for service in and about the premises by the rightful owner or occupant of said premises.
>
> 2. The restriction that no part of said premises shall be sold, given, conveyed or leased to any negro or negroes, and no permission or license to use or occupy any part thereof shall be given to any negro except house servants or janitors or chauffeurs employed thereon as aforesaid.

The covenants, restrictions, and agreements herein contained shall be considered as appurtenant to and running with the land, and shall be binding upon and for the benefit of each party hereto and may be enforced by any of the parties hereto by any permissible legal or equitable proceedings, including proceedings to enjoin violation and for specific performance . . . and provided, further, that nothing contained in the foregoing provisos shall in any manner impair the right of any person or persons interested to enforce at all times and against all persons the restrictions in this agreement contained prohibiting the use or occupation of all or any part of said premises by a negro or negroes.

This agreement and the restrictions herein contained shall be of no force or effect unless this agreement or a substantially similar agreement, shall be signed by the owners above enumerated of seventy-five per centum of the frontage above described, or their heirs or assigns, and recorded in the office of the Recorder of Deeds of Cook County, Illinois, on or before March 31, 1929. . . .

No restriction imposed hereby shall be abrogated or waived by any failure to enforce the provisions hereof no matter how many violations or breaches may occur.

This agreement and the restrictions herein expressed may be abrogated at any time on or after January 1, 1949, by the written agreement of the owners of sixty per centum of the frontage owned by the parties who shall sign this agreement, as herein set forth, such abrogation to be effective from and after the date of delivery and recording of such written agreement. . . .

The term "negro" as used herein shall include every person having one-eighth part or more of negro blood, or having any appreciable admixture of negro blood, and every person who is what is commonly known as a colored person. . . .

The covenants, restrictions and agreements herein contained shall be binding on, and for the benefit of, and may be enforced by and against, each party hereto, his successors and assigns, and the heirs, executors, administrators and successors of them respectively.

IN WITNESS WHEREOF, the parties hereto have hereunto set their hands and seals the day and year first aforesaid.

APPENDIX B ❧

Subdivision Racial Restrictions

(The Plats Books cited are stored in the Cook County Recorder's Office, Chicago.)

1. "EACH LOT IN THIS SUBDIVISION IS FOR ALL PURPOSES PERPETUALLY restricted to the Caucasian Race." Subdivision of Lot A in blocks 1, 2, and 3 in Buckley's Rogers Park Terrace, 5 June 1928, in effect "perpetually." [*Plats Book* 261, p. 20.]

2. "No premises in said subdivision shall be sold, or leased to, or occupied by persons other than of the Caucasian race, except persons not of the Caucasian race who may be employed as household servents [sic], by persons of the Caucasian race living on same premises." First Addition to Devon-McCormick Boulevard Addition to Rogers Park, 15 February 1929, in effect until 1 January 1960. [*Plats Book* 273, p. 5.]

3. "Said premises shall not be sold, leased, or conveyed by the purchaser herein, his heirs, assigns or grantees or successors in title to any person who is not a Caucasian and neither the premises herein described nor any improvement thereon shall be occupied by anyone who is not a Caucasian." Lin-De-Lane (Marquette Park area) subdivision of S. 1/8 of N. 8/12 of south

60 acres of E. 1/2 of S. E. 1/4 of Sec. 28-38-13, 28 July 1928, in effect until 1 July 1957. [*Plats Book* 268, p. 45.]

4. "No lot or Lots in this Subdivision may at any time hereafter be sold, conveyed or leased by a grantee or grantees or by any successor or successors in title of a grantee or grantees to any person who is not a Caucasian. No lot or lots in this Subdivision nor any improvement or improvements erected thereon may at any time hereafter be occupied in whole or in part by any person who is not a Caucasian (excepting, however, person [sic] employed as servants by Caucasians). In the event that any Lot or Lots in this Subdivision shall be sold conveyed or leased by a grantee or grantees or by any of the successor or successors in title of a grantee or grantees to any person who is not a Caucasian, or in the event that any Lot or Lots or any improvement or improvements erected thereon shall at any time hereafter be occupied in whole or in part by a person who is not a Caucasian (excepting, however, persons employed as servants by Caucasians), all contract or contracts for the sale of any such Lot or Lots and all such lease or leases and all deed or deeds for the conveyance thereof shall be null and void, and the property described in such contract or contracts, lease or leases, deed or deeds, shall forthwith revert to the present owner thereof.

The interest or interests of any grantee or grantees in any Lot or Lots in this Subdivision may not at any time thereafter be transferred, assigned or conveyed either voluntary or by operation of law to any person who is not a Caucasian, such contract or contracts, deed or deeds, shall be null and void, and such Lot or Lots shall forthwith revert to the present owner thereof." David F. Curtin's Third Addition to Lincolnwood in Evanston, a suburb north of Chicago, 6 April 1927, in effect until 1 March 1937. [*Plats Book* 241, p. 36.]

5. "That no part of any of said lots or premises shall be conveyed or leased by the owners thereof, or any subsequent grantee or the successors in title to any person or persons, nor shall any improvements erected thereon be used or occupied by any person, not of the Caucasian Race." Dunas's Forest Crest Subdivision in Glencoe, a suburb, north of Chicago, 5 June 1924. [*Plats Book* 192, p. 20.]

6. "The sale of these Lots and occupancy of the buildings erected on said lots shall be restricted to members of the Caucasian Race." Branigar Brothers' Ivanhoe Park Addition to Riverdale, a suburb south of Chicago, 8 May 1929, in effect until 1 July 1935. [*Plats Book* 274, pp. 28–29.]

7. "Said premises shall not be sold or leased to nor occupied by any other than a Caucasian." Cicero Avenue, 77th St. Subdivision, owners Ralph J. Luulz and Sol Shapiro, 5 July 1927, in effect until 1 July 1957. [*Plats Book* 248, p. 19.]

Notes

KEY TO ABBREVIATIONS

AJS	*American Journal of Sociology*
Annals	*Annals of the American Academy of Political and Social Sciences*
ANP	Associated Negro Press clipping files. Materials now in Claude Barnett Papers, Chicago Historical Society
Bibliography of Settlements	*Bibliography of College, Social, and University Settlements* (5 editions—1893, 1895, 1897, 1900, and 1905; place and publisher vary)
CDNA	*Chicago Daily News Almanac and Year Book*
CHS	Chicago Historical Society
CREB *Bulletin*	Chicago Real Estate Board *Bulletin*
FLPS	Works Projects Administration, *Chicago Foreign Language Press Survey* (Chicago, 1942). Materials on file with history of Chicago Project, University of Chicago

JISHS	*Journal of the Illinois State Historical Society*
LCRC	Local Community Research Committee, University of Chicago. Material at Chicago Historical Society
MRL	Municipal Reference Library (Chicago), clipping files. Materials now at Chicago Historical Society
NCCC	*Proceedings of the National Conference on Charities and Corrections*
NCH	*Housing Problems in America: Proceedings of the National Conference on Housing*
NCSW	*Proceedings of the National Conference on Social Work*
NMR	*National Municipal Review*
Negro in Illinois	"The Negro in Illinois," files of Illinois Writers' Project of Works Progress Administration. Material at George Cleveland Hall Branch of the Chicago Public Library
Olcott's	*Olcott's Land Values Blue Book of Chicago*
SSD	*Social Service Directory, Chicago*
SSR	*Social Service Review*
UCL	University of Chicago Library
UHC	Urban Historical Collection, University of Illinois at Chicago Circle
Who's Who	*Who's Who in Chicago* (6 editions, titles vary: first three editions titled *The Book of Chicagoans;* fifth and sixth editions titled *Who's Who in Chicago and Vicinity*. Publisher of all editions is A. N. Marquis Company, 1905, 1911, 1917, 1926, 1931, 1936)

PART I THE SLUM

1. Harriet Vittum, "The House and the Delinquent Child," 1917 *NCH*, pp. 314–16.
2. Graham Taylor, "The House and the Neighborhood," ibid., pp. 306–7.
3. George M. Pullman, quoted in Stanley M. Buder, *Pullman: An Experiment in Industrial Order and Community Planning, 1880–1930* (New York, 1967), pp. 77, 156.
4. Vittum, p. 314; Taylor, *Chicago Commons through Forty Years* (Chicago, 1936), p. 21.

CHAPTER 1 TENEMENTS AND IMMIGRANTS

1. Homer Hoyt, *One Hundred Years of Land Values in Chicago* (Chicago, 1933), pp. 269–70, and table 93, p. 483; Harold M. Mayer and Richard C. Wade, *Chicago: Growth of a Metropolis* (Chicago, 1969), pp. 3–192.
2. St. Clair Drake and Horace R. Cayton, *Black Metropolis* (New York, 1945), p. 7; Bessie Louise Pierce, *A History of Chicago,* 3 vols. (New York, 1937, 1940, 1957), 2: passim; Mayer and Wade, pp. 16–54; Edith Abbott, *The Tenements of Chicago, 1908–1935* (Chicago, 1936), pp. 1–16.
3. Pierce, 2: Appendix, pp. 481–82; ibid., 3: Appendix, pp. 515–16; Ernest W. Burgess and Charles Newcomb, eds., *Census Data of the City of Chicago, 1920* (Chicago, 1931), pp. 14–21, tables 4 through 8; Hoyt, pp. 281–84; Center for Urban Studies, University of Chicago, *Mid-Chicago Economic Development Study,* 3 vols. (Chicago, 1966), 3:18.
4. James Parton, "Chicago," *Atlantic Monthly* 19 (March 1867): 338–39. Among Parton's other observations were these: the stockyards had no odor, and "colored children" had free access to public schools "and no one objects."
5. Hoyt, p. 90; Parton, pp. 338–39; eleven photographs by Alexander Hesler, 1858, and six photographs and stereographs by various photographers, 1870–71, CHS, reproduced in Mayer and Wade, pp. 102–5 and ff., p. 116.
6. Ibid., pp. 28, 54, 62–64; Hoyt, pp. 65–66, 96–98; Harvey Warren Zorbaugh, *The Gold Coast and the Slum* (Chicago, 1929), pp. 21–23, 30–31.
7. Parton, p. 339; Elias Colbert and Everett Chamberlin, *Chicago and the Great Conflagration* (Cincinnati, 1871), p. 205.
8. Ibid., p. 223.
9. Ibid., pp. 273–75; Hoyt, pp. 301–11; Zorbaugh, pp. 20–23; Abbott, pp. 17–26.
10. Colbert and Chamberlin, pp. 176, 205–6.
11. Robert Cromie, *The Great Chicago Fire* (New York, 1963 ed.), pp. 25–28; Colbert and Chamberlin, pp. 205–6; Mayer and Wade, p. 107.
12. *Report of the Chicago Relief and Aid Society of Disbursement of Contributions for the Sufferers by the Chicago Fire* (Cambridge, 1874), pp. 185–95 and 272–80. The small shacks sold for $125 exclusive of land.
13. Mayer and Wade, p. 118; Hoyt, pp. 104–11 and 427–32; Abbott, p. 171; *Working Women in Large Cities, Fourth Annual Report of the Commissioner of Labor, 1888* (Washington, 1889), p. 17.
14. Chicago Department of Health, *Report, 1878,* pp. 10–11.
15. Act of 30 May 1881, Illinois, *Laws, 1881,* p. 66; Pierce, 3: 54; Chicago Department of Health, *Report, 1881 and 1882,* pp. 28–31, 47–50.
16. Hoyt, pp. 96–97, 302–4; Buder, pp. 29–33; William T. Stead, *If Christ Came to Chicago* (Chicago, 1894; reprint ed., New York, 1964), p. 73; Miriam Beard, *A History of the Business Man* (New York, 1938), pp. 683–84; David Lowe, *Lost Chicago* (Boston, 1975), pp. 26–31; "The Windy City," in Carl Sandburg's *Slabs of the Sunburnt West* (New York, 1922), p. 3; real estate broadside, ca. 1883, for

frame houses in Englewood, CHS, reproduced in Mayer and Wade, p. 163. The average tenement rental in the 1880s was probably under $7.50 a month. The cost of the plainest houses was less than $1,000; those in Englewood, a suburban community annexed to the city in 1889, sold for as little as $900.

17. Hoyt, pp. 288–89; real estate maps in Graham Aldis Papers, UHC.

18. For praise of the Chicago School see Ray Ginger, *Altgeld's America: The Lincoln Ideal versus Changing Realities* (Chicago, 1965 ed.), pp. 323–30, 350–52, and Arthur Siegel, ed., *Chicago's Famous Buildings* (Chicago, 1965), passim.

19. Ibid., pp. 38–39; Frank Lloyd Wright to Curtis W. Reese, n.d., printed in *Unity* 141 (March–April 1955): 15; Jane Addams, *Twenty Years at Hull-House* (New York, 1910), pp. 4–5.

20. Hugh Haziel Duncan, "The Chicago School: Principles . . . ," in Siegel, ed., p. 6; ibid., p. 78.

21. Mayer and Wade, pp. 193–206; Ginger, ch. 1.

22. Residents of Hull-House, *Hull-House Maps and Papers: A Presentation of Nationalities and Wages in a Congested District of Chicago* (New York, 1895), p. 14; Carrol D. Wright, *The Slums of Baltimore, Chicago, New York, and Philadelphia. Seventh Special Report of the Commissioner of Labor* (Washington, 1894), pp. 11–15. The statistical survey included one small block on the west side of Halsted which the Hull-House maps omitted.

23. Residents of Hull-House, pp. 3–4, 15–19, 143; Wright, pp. 15–19, 23.

24. Rev. D. E. McLennan, "Chicago's Moral Jungle: A Social Study with Deductions," *Northwestern Christian Advocate* (24 April 1895): n.p., bound copy, UCL.

25. Ibid.; Residents of Hull-House, pp. 15–19, 91–143, and "Nationalities Maps" 1 through 4; Wright, passim. The Hull-House researchers verbalized, but did not publicize, their objections to the federal report at the time. Their attitude is mentioned in "What of Home Conditions in Chicago?" *Charities and the Commons* 15 (6 January 1906): 461.

26. Residents of Hull-House, p. 5.

27. Ibid., pp. 5–6,10, 94–95.

28. Ibid., pp. 9–13, 117.

29. Ibid., pp. 27–90.

30. Wright, p. 84 and table 28, pp. 567–69; Residents of Hull-House, p. 6.

31. Peter d'A. Jones, "Introduction to the Torchbook Edition," Robert Hunter, *Poverty* (New York, 1904; reprint ed., New York, 1965), vi–xxix; Hunter, *Tenement Conditions in Chicago. Report by the Investigating Committee of the City Homes Association* (Chicago, 1901), pp. 3–4. Field operations were under the supervision of a Stanford University economist named Frank Fetter, but Hunter was responsible for the overall project as well as the published report.

32. Ibid., pp. 3–4, 12, 181–84; "The Social Geography of Chicago," *Charities* 11 (4 July 1903): 3–4; Hoyt, p. 161 and table 94, p. 484; Chicago Department of City Planning, *Information Bulletin. Population Growth in the City of Chicago, 1900–1960* (Chicago, 1961).

33. Hunter, *Tenement Conditions*, pp. 12–14, 181–84.
34. Ibid., pp. 52–57.
35. Ibid., pp. 32–49.
36. Ibid., pp. 31, 103–5, 125–43.
37. Ibid., pp. 59–88.
38. Ibid., pp. 88, 100–110.
39. Ibid., pp. 80–83, 142, 186–89.
40. Ibid., pp. 88–94, 103–7, 124–25, 199–200.
41. Ibid., pp. 90, 94–99, 201.
42. Ibid., pp. 51–52, 70–71.
43. Ibid., pp. 71, 112–22, 134–38, 168.
44. Ibid., p. 149.
45. "Death Is the Reason" and "The Sixteenth Ward," *The Neighbor* 1 (June 1900): 2–3; "Life in Chicago's River Wards," *Co-operation* 2 (14 June 1902): 3–5; Hunter, *Tenement Conditions*, p. 159.
46. Hunter, *Poverty*, xxv–xxvi; Hunter, *Tenement Conditions*, pp. 14, 24, 62, 72, 108–10, 161, 178.

CHAPTER 2 MODEL TOWN AND MODEL TENEMENT: REFORM ON A BUSINESS BASIS

1. Robert Hunter, *Tenement Conditions in Chicago. Report by the Investigating Committee of the City Homes Association* (Chicago, 1901), pp. 71, 148; Jacob Riis, *A Ten Years' War: An Account of the Battle with the Slum in New York* (New York, 1900; reprint ed., abridged in Francesco Cardasco, *Jacob Riis Revisited: Poverty and the Slum in Another Era*, Garden City, N.Y., 1968), pp. 333, 341. In *Poverty* (New York, 1904; reprint ed., edited by Peter d'A. Jones, New York, 1965), pp. 185–87, Robert Hunter called tenement deaths "murder" and said of slumlords, "These men are murderers."
2. Residents of Hull-House, *Hull-House Maps and Papers: A Presentation of Nationalities and Wages in a Congested District of Chicago* (New York, 1895), pp. 42–43.
3. Robert V. Bruce, *1877: Year of Violence* (Indianapolis, 1959), passim; Bessie Louise Pierce, *A History of Chicago*, 3 vols. (New York, 1937, 1940, 1957), 3: 242–51.
4. James D. McCabe [Edward Winslow Martin], *The History of the Great Riots* (Philadelphia, 1877), pp. 3–4, 448–49; Pierce, 3: 251–52; Alfred T. Andreas, *History of Chicago*, 3 vols. (Chicago, 1884–86), 3: 589; Citizen's Association Resolution, 17 June 1878, Citizen's Association Papers, CHS.
5. Receipts signed by Mayor Monroe Heath and Police Superintendent M. C. Hickey, 1 and 20 June and 10 and 22 July 1878, ibid.

6. *New York Sun,* 9 December 1883, cited in Stanley M. Buder, *Pullman: An Experiment in Industrial Order and Community Planning, 1880–1930* (New York, 1967), p. 46.

7. Pullman's testimony, *United States Strike Commission's Report on the Chicago Strike of June–July, 1894. Senate Executive Document No. 7, 53rd Congress, 3d Session* (Washington, 1895), p. 529; William T. Stead, *If Christ Came to Chicago* (Chicago, 1894; reprint ed., edited by Harvey Wish, New York, 1964), p. 73.

8. Alfred T. White, *Improved Dwellings for the Laboring Classes: The Need, and the Way to Meet It on Strict Commercial Principles, in New York and Other Cities* (New York, 1879), passim.

9. John W. Reps, *The Making of Urban America: A History of City Planning in the United States* (Princeton, 1965), ch. 15, "The Towns the Companies Built."

10. White, pp. 16–17; E. R. L. Gould, *The Housing of the Working People. Eighth Special Report of the Commissioner of Labor* (Washington, 1895), pp. 419–22; Riis, *How the Other Half Lives* (New York, 1890; reprint ed., New York, 1957), pp. 4, 202–5, 217–22; cited in Buder, p. 44.

11. Ibid., pp. 49–54; Almont Lindsey, *The Pullman Strike: The Story of a Unique Experiment and of a Great Labor Upheaval* (Chicago, 1942), pp. 38–42; Gould, p. 329.

12. Ibid.; Buder, pp. 55–59, 74; Lindsey, pp. 42–48.

13. *Cincinnati Enquirer,* 28 June 1882, cited in Buder, p. 77.

14. Gould, p. 329; Lindsey, pp. 49–52, 71–72; Buder, pp. 69–70, 89, 124–27.

15. Ibid., pp. 94–95; Lindsey, pp. 69–70.

16. Ibid., pp. 46–47, 68; Buder, pp. 59, 70, 74, 86.

17. *New York Sun,* 9 December 1883, cited in Buder, p. 94; real estate maps in Graham Aldis Papers, UHC; block maps in Chicago Plan Commission, *Report of the Chicago Land Use Survey,* 2 vols. (Chicago, 1942–43), 2: 434–35; Gould, p. 331.

18. Edith Abbott, *The Tenements of Chicago, 1908–1935* (Chicago, 1936), pp. 160–61.

19. Ibid., pp. 160–62, 208–9; Gould, p. 330; Lindsey, p. 46.

20. Ibid., pp. 68–70; Gould, pp. 330–32; Buder, pp. 86–88.

21. Cited in ibid., p. 95; Henry Demarest Lloyd, "Pullman," unpublished article, p. 11, Henry Demarest Lloyd Papers, Wisconsin Historical Society, Madison, Wis., cited in ibid., p. 100; *New York Sun,* 9 December 1883, cited in ibid., p. 94.

22. Ibid., table 2, p. 90; Gould, p. 332; Edward F. Byrant, quoted in *Chicago Inter-Ocean,* 6 September 1883, cited in Buder, pp. 80–81.

23. In 1867 Pullman ordered that every Pullman car should have a Negro porter. See Buder, p. 17.

24. Chicago Department of Health, *Report* 1881 and 1882, pp. 28–29; Citizens' Association of Chicago, Executive Committee Minutes, meeting of 2 December 1882, Citizens' Association Papers; Citizens' Association, *Annual Report . . . October, 1883,* p. 34; Report of the Committee on Tenements for Working Classes, cited in *Report of the Committee on Tenement Houses of the Citizens' Association of Chicago* (Chicago, 1884), pp. 3–4, 9; Lindsey, p. 68.

25. *Report of the Committee on Tenement Houses,* pp. 4–7.

26. Medill's testimony before the U.S. Senate Committee Investigating Relations between Labor and Capital, 1883, cited in John A. Garraty, ed., *Labor and Capital in the Gilded Age: Testimony Taken by the Senate Committee . . .* (Boston, 1968), pp. 133–34; *Report of the Committee on Tenement Houses,* pp. 4, 9–10, 17–18.

27. Ibid., pp. 8–10, 15.

28. Medill's testimony, cited in Garraty, p. 74; *Report of the Committee on Tenement Houses,* pp. 8, 16–17.

29. Ibid., pp. 19–23 and fold-out floor plans inside front cover.

30. Hunter, *Poverty,* p. 112.

31. *Report of the Committee on Tenement Houses,* pp. 18, 20–21.

32. Citizens' Association, *Annual Report . . . October, 1884,* p. 15; Citizens' Association, *Annual Report . . . October 1885,* p. 18; Richard T. Ely, "Pullman: A Social Study," *Harper's Monthly* 70 (1885): 452–66.

33. Buder, p. 33; Ray Ginger, *Altgeld's America: The Lincoln Ideal versus Changing Realities* (Chicago, 1965 ed.), p. 42; Citizens' Association, *Annual Report . . . October, 1885,* pp. 11–18; Buder, pp. 139–40; Lindsey, p. 29.

34. Ibid., pp. 8, 29; Buder, pp. 140–42; Pullman to Andrew Carnegie, 5 May 1886, Andrew Carnegie Papers, Library of Congress, cited in ibid., p. 140.

35. Charles E. Perkins to T. J. Potter, 10 May 1886, Chicago, Burlington and Quincy Railroad Archives, Newberry Library, Chicago, cited in ibid., p. 142; Citizens' Association, *Annual Report . . . October 1886,* p. 10; Citizens' Association, *Annual Report . . . October 1887,* p. 22; Citizens' Association, *Annual Report . . . October 1888,* p. 37; Arthur J. Siegel, ed., *Chicago's Famous Buildings* (Chicago, 1965), p. 21.

36. Buder, pp. 83–85, 109, 161; Lindsey, pp. 82–83, 91–93; Ginger, p. 149.

37. Lindsey, pp. 95–100, 122–30, and chs. 8–14; Buder, chs. 12–15.

38. *Chicago Daily News,* 12 May 1894, cited in ibid., p. 168; ibid., p. 178.

39. Rev. D. E. McLennan, "Chicago's Moral Jungle. A Social Study, with Deductions," *Northwestern Christian Advocate,* 24 April 1895, n.p., bound copy, UCL.

CHAPTER 3 SETTLEMENT HOUSE AND TENEMENT HOUSE: "WITH, NOT FOR"

1. Residents of Hull-House, *Hull-House Maps and Papers: A Presentation of Nationalities and Wages in a Congested District of Chicago* (New York, 1895), p. 13. Besides Jane Addams's writings, cited below, the best introductory sources for the story of Hull-House and the settlements are Allen F. Davis and Mary Lynn McCree, eds., *Eighty Years at Hull-House* (Chicago, 1969), a documentary history; Allen F. Davis, *Spearheads for Reform: The Social Settlements and the Progressive Movement, 1890–1914* (New York, 1967); and Ray Ginger, *Altgeld's America: The Lincoln Ideal Versus Changing Realities* (Chicago, 1965 ed.).

2. Jane Addams, *Twenty Years at Hull-House* (New York, 1910), pp. 73, 89–94, 97–101, 113–27.

3. Ibid., p. 89; Residents of Hull-House, p. 190.

4. Addams, *Twenty Years*, pp. 94–109, 311–12.

5. Ibid., pp. 3–5, 99–101; Robert Hunter, *Tenement Conditions in Chicago. Report by the Investigating Committee of the City Homes Association* (Chicago, 1901), pp. 51, 62–63, 136–38, 143.

6. Ibid.; Edith Abbott, *The Tenements of Chicago, 1908–1935* (Chicago, 1936), p. 164, for "hot beds"; "Housing Survey in the Italian District of the 17th Ward," in Chicago Department of Public Welfare, *First Semi-Annual Report to the Mayor and Aldermen of the City of Chicago* (Chicago, 1915), p. 81, for "the frequency of 'can-rushing.' "

7. Residents of Hull-House, p. 177; Addams, *Twenty Years*, pp. 198–211.

8. Residents of Hull-House, p. 21.

9. Ibid., p. 85; ibid., pp. 54–58.

10. Addams, *Newer Ideals of Peace* (Chautauqua, N.Y., 1907), p. 158; ibid., pp. 157–62; Addams, *Twenty Years*, pp. 199–200; Residents of Hull-House, pp. 33–38, 58–76.

11. Ibid., pp. 7–8, 21–22, 79–82, and "Wage Maps" 1 through 4; Carroll D. Wright, *The Slums of Baltimore, Chicago, New York, and Philadelphia. Seventh Special Report of the Commissioner of Labor* (Washington, 1894), pp. 64–66 and tables 17 and 18, pp. 260–323 and 468–81, respectively. These two sources, although they employ the same basic data, seem to conflict. Carroll Wright used the wages of an earner in a full workweek in his tables; the Hull-House residents used the wages of an earner in a full workweek, *multiplied* that figure by the number of weeks the individual worked, and then *divided* the annual wages by fifty-two to get an actual weekly average. Because of the difference in method, the figures in the Government volume come out much higher, *even though* Wright counted the wages of the "breadwinner" only and the Hull-House residents totaled the wages of all family members.

12. Hunter, *Poverty* (New York, 1904; reprint ed., edited by Peter d'A. Jones, New York, 1965), pp. 1–2; Residents of Hull-House, pp. 3–4; Addams, *Twenty Years*, pp. 108, 133–34.

13. Ibid., p. 358; Residents of Hull-House, p. 190.

14. Ibid.

15. Addams, *Twenty Years,* pp. 109, 163, 171.

16. Ibid., p. 39; Residents of Hull-House, pp. 15–19, 99; Addams, *Twenty Years,* p. 98.

17. Residents of Hull-House, pp. 17–19, 57, note, and "Nationalities Maps" 1 through 4. For a detailed discussion of these maps, see ch. 5.

18. Residents of Hull-House, p. 19. The epithets apply as follows: *Micks*—Irishmen; *Dagos, Wops,* and *Guineas*—Italians; *Krauts*—Germans; *Canucks*—French Canadians; *Bohunks*—Bohemians; *Lugans*—Lithuanians; *Polacks*—Poles.

19. Residents of Hull-House, pp. 108–9; Louis Wirth, *The Ghetto* (Chicago, 1928), pp. 204–26, 146–61; Wirth, "Some Jewish Types of Personality," *Publications of the American Sociological Society* 32 (1926): 90–96; Residents of Hull-House, pp. 131–43; Humbert S. Nelli, *Italians in Chicago, 1880–1930: A Study in Ethnic Mobility* (New York, 1970), pp. 154–200.

20. Addams, *Twenty Years,* pp. 249–50; Addams, *The Spirit of Youth and the City Streets* (New York, 1909), pp. 7–16; Addams, *Twenty Years,* ch. 11, "Immigrants and Their Children," especially p. 236.

21. Ibid., p. 368.

22. Ibid., pp. 110, 170–73; Residents of Hull-House, p. 144.

23. Ibid., pp. 13, 69; Addams, *Twenty Years,* p. 368; Addams, "The Subjective Necessity for Social Settlements," in Addams, Robert Woods et al., *Philanthropy and Social Progress* (New York, 1893), p. 4; Addams, *Newer Ideals,* p. 171; Addams, "The Objective Value of a Social Settlement," in Addams, Woods et al., pp. 27–29; Addams, *Twenty Years,* pp. 97–99. The passage in *Twenty Years* is taken from "The Objective Value of a Social Settlement." In the original article, Jane Addams said the people showed "no initiative"; in her book she changed the "no" to "little."

24. Addams, *Twenty Years,* p. 369; ibid., pp. 126–27; Residents of Hull-House, p. 207.

25. Addams, "Subjective Necessity," pp. 8–9; Addams, *Twenty Years,* p. 440; ibid., pp. 105, 342–99, 427–53.

26. Residents of Hull-House, pp. 54, 166, 208–30. In the 1960s, when black people accused St. Ignatius of doing nothing for the local community, defenders of the school replied that it had *never* done much for the neighborhood, even when all the residents were white.

27. Residents of Hull-House, pp. 4, 208–30; Addams, *Twenty Years,* pp. 129–43, 312–13.

28. Addams, *Twenty Years,* p. 112; Hull-House Residents, pp. 229–30.

29. Ibid., pp. 6, 95; Hunter, p. 71, 168; Franklin J. Meine, ed., *Chicago Stories by George Ade* (Chicago, 1963), pp. 79–83, 87–91, 109–14.

30. Residents of Hull-House, p. 95; Hunter, pp. 71, 168.

31. Addams, *Newer Ideals,* pp. 175–77; Addams, *Twenty Years,* pp. 251, 323, 326; Sophonisba P. Breckenridge and Edith Abbott, *The Delinquent Child and the Home* (New York, 1912), pp. 86–87 and ch. 9; Albert E. Webster, *Junk Dealing and Juvenile Delinquency* (Chicago, n.d. [1918]).

32. Addams, *Spirit of Youth,* pp. 55–57.

33. Ibid., p. 103; Addams, *Twenty Years,* pp. 383–86; Residents of Hull-House, pp. 3, 22–23.

34. Addams, "Objective Value," p. 31.

35. Addams, quoted in Davis, xiv; Addams, *Twenty Years,* p. 132; Dorothea Moore, "A Day at Hull-House," *AJS* 2 (March 1897): 629–40.

36. Residents of Hull-House, pp. 220, 225–26; Addams, "Objective Value," p. 38; Hull-House Boys' Club Registration Book, 1907, UHC.

37. Residents of Hull-House, pp. 221–23; Addams, *Twenty Years,* p. 233.

38. Ibid., pp. 237, 358–59; Residents of Hull-House, p. 216.

39. *L'Italia,* 24–25 August 1895, *FLPS.*

40. Addams, *Twenty Years,* pp. 166–67.

41. Ibid., pp. 112, 201–4; one exposé was Nell Nelson, *The White Slave Girls of Chicago. Nell Nelson's Startling Disclosures of the Cruelties and Inequities Practiced in the Workshops and Factories of a Great City. A Graphic Account of the Slave-Grinding Process Carried on by Heartless Task-Masters. Young Girls Given Worse Treatment than Dumb Brutes. Herded Like Cattle in Foul-Smelling Lofts and Basements. A Woman's Exposure of the Bitter Hardships Suffered by Working Women. Hell-Holes Where Virtue is Laughed At and Womanhood Debased. The Continuous Tragedy of Today* (Chicago, 1888); Residents of Hull-House, pp. 43–45; Ginger, p. 228.

42. Residents of Hull-House, p. 203; *Bibliography of Settlements,* all editions, 1893–1905; Robert A. Woods and Albert J. Kennedy, *Handbook of Settlements* (New York, 1911); *SSD,* 1939; Residents of Hull-House, p. 201.

43. Addams, *Twenty Years,* pp. 214–17.

44. Florence Kelley to Henry Demarest Lloyd, 15 August 1894, Henry Demarest Lloyd Papers, Wisconsin Historical Society, Madison, Wis., cited in Stanley M. Buder, *Pullman: An Experiment in Industrial Order and Community Planning, 1880–1930* (New York, 1967), p. 251, note; Residents of Hull-House, pp. 199–200.

45. Addams, "A Modern Lear," *Survey* 29 (2 November 1912): 131–37; also see Addams, *Democracy and Social Ethics* (New York, 1902), pp. 139–49.

46. Address at Rockford College, 1931, cited in James Weber Linn, *Jane Addams* (New York, 1935), p. 387; Addams, "Modern Lear."

47. Almont Lindsey, *The Pullman Strike: The Story of a Unique Experiment and of a Great Labor Upheaval* (Chicago, 1942), pp. 208–14; Mary McDowell, cited in Woods and Kennedy, p. 69.

48. McDowell, "Beginnings," typescript, n.d., Mary McDowell Papers, CHS.

49. *Bibliography of Settlements,* editions of 1895, 1897, 1900, and 1905; Woods and Kennedy; *SSD,* 1939; *CDNA,* 1895–1918.

50. Davis and McCree, p. 21. In all of Jane Addams's writings there is scarcely a reference to the board of trustees. Hull-House was more secretive than most settlements in publishing the names of board members in circulars, bulletins, and reports.

51. Residents of Hull-House, pp. 208, 220, 225–26; Buder, pp. 125–26, 205.

52. Woods and Kennedy, pp. 65–66; "A People's Own Neighborhood Center: Neighborhood House, Chicago," *The Commons* 10 (January 1905); 43–49; "A Co-operative Neighborhood House, Chicago," *Charities and the Commons* 15 (24 February 1906): 734–35.

53. The Constitution of the University of Chicago Settlement, 1 January 1898, McDowell Papers, CHS; "University of Chicago Settlement," *University Register* (July 1893–July 1894), typed copy in Ernest Burgess Papers, UCL; Davis, p. 108.

54. "A Day Nursery for Chicago's Bohemian District," *Charities and the Commons* 15 (24 March 1906): 910.

55. Graham Taylor, *Chicago Commons through Forty Years* (Chicago, 1936), pp. 8, 19; Report of the Warden of Chicago Commons for the Year 1906, typed copy, n.p., Chicago Commons Papers, CHS; Woods and Kennedy, p. 66; *Northwestern University Settlement Yearly Bulletin, 1910,* p. 7, copy in Graham Taylor Papers, Newberry Library, Chicago; *Northwestern University Settlement Circular No. 6,* June 1896, p. 13, ibid.

56. Pat Ireland, "Factors in the Americanization of a Second Generation of Immigrant People," MS prepared as an M.A. thesis for the University of Chicago, August 1932, but never submitted, in possession of Mr. Ireland, pp. 189–90.

57. *Bibliography of Settlements,* editions of 1895, 1896, 1900, and 1905; Woods and Kennedy; *SSD,* 1939; *CDNA,* 1895–1918; Carrie Wilson of Association House, cited in "Living Issues for Pulpit Treatment. Estimates of Social Settlements," typescript, p. 203, Commons Papers.

58. Harriet Vittum, head resident of Northwestern University Settlement, form letter, 5 February 1909, Taylor Papers.

59. Joseph Stolz to J. Witkowsky, 2 November 1893, Joseph Stolz Papers, CHS; Wirth, *The Ghetto,* pp. 183, 188; Woods and Kennedy, p. 75; "Chicago To Have a Hebrew Institute," broadside, 1904, Jewish Community Centers of Chicago Papers, CHS.

60. Harry Lipsky, "Citizen Making in Chicago," *Charities and the Commons* 15 (17 March 1906): 882–84; Woods and Kennedy, p. 75.

61. Ibid., pp. 51, 68.

62. Frederick A. Lorenz, form letter, May 1911, Gads Hill Center Papers, CHS.

63. Woods and Kennedy, p. 80; Duane Van Dyke Ramsey, "A Comparative Study of Social Settlements, Neighborhood Houses, and Institutional Churches" (M.A. thesis, University of Chicago, 1929), pp. 136–38.

64. Taylor, *Chicago Commons through Forty Years,* p. 192; Northwestern University Settlement, Circular No. 6, p. 13.

65. Woods and Kennedy, p. 39.

66. "Some Reasons Why Men of all Parties Should Vote for Mary E. McDowell and Harriet E. Vittum for County Board Commissioners," n.d. [1914], Woman's City Club of Chicago Papers, CHS; broadsides in English and Polish for Vittum, 1914, Taylor Papers; Ireland, p. 159; Vittum, form letter, 5 February 1909.

67. Addams, *Twenty Years,* pp. 317, 319; Davis, pp. 151–62; Nelli, pp. 92–104.

68. Davis, pp. 163–69; Nelli, pp. 113–15.

69. A phrase from William L. Riordan, *Plunkitt of Tammany Hall* (New York, 1905; reprint ed., New York, 1963), p. 3.

70. "Facts about the Seventeenth Ward," n.d., Commons Papers; untitled sheet of statistics, n.d., ibid.; voters' registration statistics, *CDNA,* 1900–1918.

71. Taylor, *Chicago Commons through Forty Years,* pp. 70–71; Taylor, Treasurer's Statement, 1910, Commons Papers.

72. Taylor, *Chicago Commons through Forty Years,* pp. 70–71; aldermanic election statistics, *CDNA,* 1911–1912.

73. Ibid., 1912–1913.

74. Ibid., 1915–1918.

75. Report of the Work of Chicago Commons for the year ending September 30, 1919, p. 7, Commons Papers; Warden's Report of the Work of Chicago Commons for the year ending September 30, 1920, p. 6, ibid.

76. "17th Ward Community Club Constitution," n.d., ibid.; Taylor to Fellow Members of the Community Club, 5 January 1911, ibid.

77. Addams, "A Function of the Social Settlement," *Annals* 13 (May 1899): 327; Addams, *Twenty Years,* pp. 33–34, 309.

78. See Gerald D. Suttles, *The Social Order of the Slum; Ethnicity and Territory in the Inner City* (Chicago, 1968), for an analysis of social organization in what remained of the old Hull-House neighborhood in the 1960s, after the double devastation of highway construction and urban renewal. The system of neighborhood relations was essentially the same as it had been at the turn of the century.

79. Cited in Taylor, *Chicago Commons through Forty Years,* p. 202.

CHAPTER 4 THE HOUSING MOVEMENT, 1893–1917: THE LIMITS OF RESTRICTIVE REFORM

1. Mary McDowell, "Housing," typed extract from a University of Chicago Settlement annual report, 31 May 1921, Mary McDowell Papers, CHS; Jane Addams, *Twenty Years at Hull-House* (New York, 1910), p. 295.

2. Frances Buckley Embree, "The Housing of the Poor in Chicago," *Journal of Political Economy* 8 (June 1900): 369, copy in "Chicago Housing Conditions 1897–1910," a scrapbook compiled by George E. Hooker of Hull-House, UCL.

3. Jacob Riis, *How the Other Half Lives: Studies among the Tenements of New York* (New York, 1890; reprint ed., New York, 1957), p. 207; Addams, *Twenty Years,* p. 100.

4. Ibid., pp. 232–33.

5. Ibid., pp. 289–91.

6. George E. Hooker, "The Problem in the Light of Current Events," *NCH,* 1917, p. 301.

7. Graham Taylor, "The House and the Neighborhood," ibid., p. 306; Sophonisba P. Breckenridge, remarks cited in Report of Proceedings of Mass Meeting of Women to Protest against the Spoils System and Adopt a Woman's Municipal Platform, 18 March 1916, pp. 28–29, Woman's City Club of Chicago Papers, CHS; Taylor, "House and Neighborhood," p. 307; see also Sadie T. Wald, "1900–1905, Chicago Housing Conditions," *Charities and the Commons* 15 (6 January 1906): 459–60.

8. Residents of Hull-House, *Hull-House Maps and Papers: A Presentation of Nationalities and Wages in a Congested District of Chicago* (New York, 1895), p. 203; Addams, *Twenty Years,* p. 227; Northwestern University Settlement Circular No. 6, June 1896, p. 5, Graham Taylor Papers, Newberry Library, Chicago; Robert Hunter, "Housing and Reform in Chicago," *NCCC,* 1902, p. 345; Addams, *Twenty Years,* p. 283.

9. "Bad Tenements. Chicago's Need of Radical Reform," *Chicago Commons* (February 1897): 1–3; *Evanston Index,* 6 February 1897.

10. Program of Conference on Improvement of Housing Conditions, Sponsored by Chicago Improved Housing Association and Chicago Architectural Club, 20–26 March, 1900, Taylor Papers; Hunter, pp. 343–44; Embree, p. 369.

11. Hunter, p. 348; Hunter, *Tenement Conditions in Chicago. Report by the Investigating Committee of the City Homes Association* (Chicago, 1901), pp. 175–77.

12. *Chicago Tribune,* 11, 14, and 28 April 1900, clippings in "Chicago Housing Conditions"; Edith Abbott, *The Tenements of Chicago, 1908–1935* (Chicago, 1936), pp. 52–55, 65.

13. *Charities* 9 (5 July 1902): 25–26. For data on parks see *CDNA,* 1900 through 1917, and Chicago Recreation Commission, *The Chicago Recreation Survey,* 1937, vol. 1, *Public Recreation* (Chicago, 1937), pp. 93–123. Eight of the thirty-four Chicago settlements described in Robert A. Woods and Albert J.

Kennedy, *Handbook of Settlements* (New York, 1911), pp. 37–80, claimed credit for the establishment of public parks and playgrounds in their neighborhoods. After 1910, the City Homes Association and its committees existed largely on paper, so the settlement workers did the bulk of the lobbying.

14. Taylor, *Chicago Commons through Forty Years* (Chicago, 1936), p. 58; Warden's Report for 1908, Chicago Commons Papers, CHS; Abbott, p. 106; Hunter, *Tenement Conditions,* map 8, p. 57; Sophonisba P. Breckenridge and Edith Abbott, "Chicago Housing Conditions, IV: The West Side Revisited," *AJS* 17 (July 1911): table 4, p. 7. Eckhart Park, at Noble and Chicago Avenues, covered two city blocks. When clearance began in 1905, there were 200 houses on the site. Since the average number of occupants per tenement in the area was 15, it is likely that Eckhart Park displaced as many as 3,000. Pulaski Park, half a mile north of the other park, opened in 1914. The site was Hunter's "block 52." Its population in 1900 was 1,315. When Breckenridge and Abbott resurveyed the block in 1911, its population was 1,188.

15. Abbott, pp. 110–12.

16. Ibid., p. 112.

17. Hunter, *Tenement Conditions,* pp. 85–88, 165; William T. Stead, *If Christ Came to Chicago* (Chicago, 1894; reprint ed., New York, 1964), pp. 19–34, 161–63; Horner C. Fancher, chief sanitary inspector, State of Illinois, Report of the Inspection of Lodging Houses in the City of Chicago, September 30, 1899, typed copy, "Chicago Housing Conditions"; Hunter, *Poverty* (New York, 1904; reprint ed., edited by Peter d'A. Jones, New York, 1965), pp. 114–20.

18. Ibid., pp. 117–18.

19. John H. Bogue, *Proposed 'Mills' Hotel for Chicago* (n.p., n.d.), p. 2, brochure in "Chicago Housing Conditions"; statement of purpose of the Municipal Lodging House in *CDNA,* 1908, p. 461; Riis, *A Ten Years' War: An Account of the Battle with the Slum in New York* (Boston, 1900; reprint ed., edited and abridged by Francesco Cordasco as part of *Jacob Riis Revisited: Poverty and the Slum in Another Era,* Garden City, N.Y., 1968), p. 347; Hunter, "Housing Reform," p. 345; Lodging-House Committee of the City Homes Association (n.p., n.d.), n.p., brochure in "Chicago Housing Conditions."

20. Bogue, pp. 2–3; Lodging-House Committee of the City Homes Association, n.p.

21. Michael Kenna and John J. Coughlan to John H. Bogue, 23 June 1899, reproduced in Bogue, p. 7; see Herman Kogan and Lloyd Wendt, *Lords of the Levee: The Story of Bathhouse John and Hinky Dink* (Indianapolis, 1943), passim.

22. Embree, pp. 373–75.

23. Lodging House Committee of the City Homes Association.

24. "The Municipal Lodging House," *Co-operation* 1 (28 December 1901): 1–2, copy in "Chicago Housing Conditions."

25. Ibid., *Report of the General Superintendent of Police 1903* (Chicago, 1903), p. 125.

26. *Report of the General Superintendent of Police 1902* (Chicago, 1902), p. 118.

27. *Chicago Inter-Ocean,* 17 December 1899, clipping in "Chicago Housing Conditions"; sign on Reliance Hotel, gravure in Levi Z. Leiter Real Estate Album, CHS, reproduced in Harold M. Mayer and Richard C. Wade, *Chicago: Growth of a Metropolis* (Chicago, 1969), p. 226; *Re-Making Men and Material: Chicago Christian Industrial League, A Scientific Philanthropy* (n.p., n.d., [1915]), p. 13; Nels Anderson, *The Hobo: The Sociology of the Homeless Man* (Chicago, 1923), p. 28.

28. "Private Agencies Refusing Service to Negroes," list in Report of Committee on South Side Survey of Social Agencies, Chicago, 1930, n.p., Julius Rosenwald Papers, UCL; *SSD,* 1939, pp. 166–67, 178, for lists of boarding clubs, hotels, and emergency shelters, and pp. 1–164 for individual listings arranged alphabetically, with detailed information including date of founding; Ida Wells-Barnett, letter to editor, *Chicago Record-Herald,* 26 January 1912, cited in Allan H. Spear, *Black Chicago: The Making of a Negro Ghetto, 1890–1920* (Chicago, 1967), pp. 46–47; Address of John Lloyd Thomas to Merchants' Club of Chicago, 9 December 1899, reported in *Tribune,* 10 December 1899, clipping in "Chicago Housing Conditions"; Anderson, p. 8. The Christian Industrial League's Popular Hotel, for instance, was open to "men of all nationalities." A census taken one night in 1915 revealed that the 208 "homeless men" were of "twenty nationalities." See *Re-Making Men and Material,* pp. 14–16. The three places for "colored women" were the Baptist Women's Missionary Union Home, the Phyllis Wheatley home, and the "Colored YWCA," established in 1906, 1908, and 1915, respectively. See *SSD,* 1939, pp. 9, 125, and 162; also see "Private Agencies Serving Both Races, Separate Service," lists in South Side Survey, n.p.

29. Hunter, *Tenement Conditions,* p. 162; cited in Taylor, "House and Neighborhood," pp. 306–7; Francis H. McLean, "Tenement-House Reform in Chicago —Progressive Measure Before the City Council This Week," *Charities* 9 (20 December 1902): 617–18.

30. Compare two City Homes Association bulletins, *Argument on Behalf of the City Homes Association in Support of the Tenement House Ordinance . . .* (Chicago, 1902) and *Proposed Ordinance Regulating Tenement Houses* (Chicago, n.d.), with *An Ordinance Relating to the Department of Buildings and Governing the Erection of Buildings, etc., in the City of Chicago, passed March 28, 1898, and all Subsequent Amendments Thereto as in Force and Effect on September 1, 1903* (Chicago, 1903). See also McLean, pp. 617–18; Abbott, pp. 59–61, 179, 185, 212–21; Charles B. Ball, "The New Tenement in Chicago," *Charities and the Commons* 17 (October 1906): 90–96; and Ball's remarks in *NCH,* 1917, p. 354.

31. Ibid.; Abbott, pp. 59–62; McLean, pp. 617–18.

32. Graham Romeyn Taylor (the son of Graham Taylor), "Private Profit by Legislation—Its Point of Attack," *Commons* 9 (April 1904): 126; "Chicago and Her Tenements," *Charities* 10 (4 April 1903): 322. The phrase "I seen my opportunities and I took 'em" is from William L. Riordan, ed., *Plunkitt of Tammany Hall* (New York, 1905; reprint ed., New York, 1963), p. 3.

33. Abbott, pp. 59–62.

34. Ibid., pp. 62–63; "Sanitary Ills Disclosed by Hull-House Workers," *Charities* 10 (13 June 1903): 587–88; Maud Gernon, Gertrude Howe, and Dr. Alice Hamilton, *An Inquiry into the Causes of the Recent Epidemic of Typhoid Fever in Chicago. Made by Residents of Hull-House* (Chicago, 1903), UCL; "Lax Methods of the Chicago Sanitary Bureau," *Charities* 11 (1 August 1903): 100; "Chicago's Absurd Sanitary Bureau," *Charities* 11 (17 October 1903): 353–54.

35. Addams, *Twenty Years,* pp. 298–99.

36. "Next Step in Chicago's Housing Problem," *Charities and the Commons* 18 (13 July 1907): 413; Abbott, pp. 62–63.

37. Ibid., p. 64, note; Lawrence Veiller, remarks cited in *NCH,* 1916, p. 480.

38. Abbott, p. 64, note. Ball never stated his ambition directly, but the implications are clear in his actions and in his statements about the need for an independent tenement house authority. See, for example, Ball, "Health Departments and Housing," *NCH,* 1912, pp. 33–46, and "Can a Health Department Cope Adequately with the Housing Problem?" Ibid., 1919, pp. 266–72.

39. "The Old Soldiers Clause in Civil Service Laws," *Commons* 9 (April 1904): 103–104; *Record-Herald,* all issues March–April 1904, 3 September 1904, and 23 February 1905; Abbott, p. 64, note.

40. "Cost of Sanitary Inspection in Chicago," *Housing Betterment* 8 (September 1919): 66; Abbott, p. 65; Chicago Civil Service Commission, Efficiency Division, *Report on the Department of Builders, City of Chicago: Inquiry December 28, 1911–May 6, 1912* (Chicago, 1912), pp. 5–6.

41. Amelia Sears, *The Charity Visitor: A Handbook for Beginners* (Chicago, 1913), pp. 12–13, 22–24.

42. Chicago Association of Commerce Housing Committee, *The Housing Problem in Chicago* (n.p., n.d. [1912]), n.p., CHS; *Guide to City Club Housing Exhibition, 15 April June 1913* (Chicago, 1913), ibid.; *Housing Betterment* 2 (July 1913): 10; "Chicago Unites Its Forces," ibid., 3 (July 1914): 5–7.

43. Speakers' comments recorded in Merchants' Club Executive Committee Circular Report, 27 October 1906, cited in Michael P. McCarthy, "Chicago Businessmen and the Burnham Plan," *JISHS* 63 (Autumn 1970): 232; Daniel H. Burnham and Edward H. Bennet, *Plan of Chicago* (Chicago, 1909); "Houses for Poor a Huge Problem/City Plan Commission Urged to Add That Subject to Its Enterprise," *Tribune,* 8 October 1910, clipping in Taylor Papers.

44. "For Chicago's Better Housing," *Survey* 27 (13 January 1912): 1567–68; *Ordinance Relating to Buildings within the City of Chicago as Passed Dec. 5, 1910* (Chicago, 1933), p. 429.

45. *Housing Betterment* 3 (April 1904): 15–16; Ball, "Housing Progress of the Year: Chicago," *NCH,* 1917, p. 355; Wald, p. 3; Abbott and Breckenridge, "Housing Conditions in Chicago, III: Back of the Yards," *AJS* 16 (January 1911), photograph and caption, facing p. 442; *City Club Housing Exhibition,* pp. 12, 21; Ball, cited in *Housing Betterment* 6 (December 1917): 42. Thousands of rear buildings show up in the detailed block maps in Chicago Plan Commission, *Report*

of the Chicago Land Use Survey, 2 vols. (Chicago, 1942–43), vol. 2: *Land Use in Chicago.* Hundreds of them, perhaps more, have survived the combined ravages of time, New Deal slum clearance, and postwar highway and urban renewal programs and still stand today.

46. William B. Hale, vice-president of the Chicago Civil Service Reform Association, remarks at Mass Meeting of Women to Protest against the Spoils System, 18 March 1916, pp. 16–17; Graham Taylor to Charles W. Folds, 14 April 1919, Taylor Papers; "The Chicago Municipal Lodging House for Men," in *Report and Handbook of the Department of Health of the City of Chicago, 1911–1918* (Chicago, 1918), pp. 1076–81; Anderson, pp. 260–61.

47. "Cost of Sanitary Inspection in Chicago," *Housing Betterment* 8 (September 1919): 66; Abbott, p. 65; Dr. Miller, cited in Hale, pp. 16–17. Before Mayor Thompson appointed Dr. John Dill Robinson to head the Health Department, he appointed him to replace the venerable reform figure Theodore B. Sachs on the Municipal Tuberculosis Sanitarium Board. Sachs, who was the man responsible for the creation of the sanitarium, committed suicide within months of his dismissal. See Philip D. Jacobs, "Theodore B. Sachs," *Journal of the Outdoor Life* 13 (May 1916): 131–32, and Lewis W. Hunt, *The People Versus Tuberculosis* (Chicago, 1966), pp. 38–40. Reformers like Ball and the Hull-House residents considered Sachs a fatality in Thompson's assault on municipal agencies, and they deeply resented Dr. Robinson.

48. Ball, cited in *Housing Betterment* 6 (December 1917): 42; Abbott, pp. 479–80; Hooker, "Problem in Light of Current Events," p. 303.

49. Hunter, *Tenement Conditions,* p. 162.

PART II THE GHETTO

1. Robert Hunter, *Tenement Conditions in Chicago. Report by the Investigating Committee of the City Homes Association* (Chicago, 1901), pp. 12, 71, 181–83.

2. Alzada P. Comstock, "Chicago Housing Conditions, VI: The Problem of the Negro," *AJS* 18 (September 1912): 241–57; Sophonisba P. Breckenridge, "The Color Line in the Housing Problem," *Survey* 29 (1 February 1913): 575–76.

3. Ibid.

4. Benjamin J. Rosenthal, *Reconstructing America, Sociologically and Economically* (Chicago, 1919), pp. 28–29.

CHAPTER 5 THE OUTLINES OF THE GHETTO

1. Alderman Louis B. Anderson, "Facts Show We Came Here First and Are Here to Stay," Chicago *Defender,* 7 February 1920.

2. St. Clair Drake and Horace Cayton, *Black Metropolis* (New York, 1945), pp. 32–45; Allan H. Spear, *Black Chicago: The Making of a Negro Ghetto, 1890–1920* (Chicago, 1967), pp. 5–6; William M. Tuttle, Jr., *Race Riot: Chicago in the Red Summer of 1919* (New York, 1970), p. 160.

3. For factors facilitating or retarding "the movement of ethnic groups into the life of the community" see W. Lloyd Warner, *Yankee City* (one-volume ed., abridged; New Haven, 1963), pp. 355–425; Oscar Handlin, *Boston's Immigrants: A Study in Acculturation* (2d ed., rev. and enlarged; Cambridge, 1959), pp. 51–70, 88–92; Handlin, *Fire Bell in the Night* (Boston, 1964), p. 97; "Comparing the Immigrant and the Negro Experience," in *Report of the National Advisory Commission on Civil Disorders* (Washington, 1968), pp. 143–45; and Edward C. Banfield, *The Unheavenly City* (Boston, 1970), pp. 55–59, 67–69, 78–85.

4. *U.S. Census Reports,* 1850–1900; Ernest W. Burgess and Charles Newcomb, eds., *Census Data of the City of Chicago, 1920* (Chicago, 1931), tables 7 and 8, pp. 20–21; John M. Allswang, *A House for All Peoples: Ethnic Politics in Chicago, 1890–1936* (Lexington, 1971), pp. 14–19; Cayton and Drake, pp. 8–20, 33–34.

5. Robert S. Abbott in *Defender,* 5 March 1927.

6. Cayton and Drake, pp. 35–45; Spear, pp. 5–7; "White and Black in Chicago," editorial in Chicago *Tribune,* 3 August 1919.

7. Spear, pp. 7, 29; Tuttle, pp. 112–13; Stanley Buder, *Pullman: An Experiment in Industrial Order and Community Planning, 1880–1930* (New York, 1967), pp. 17, 79–81, 219, and table 2, p. 90. Buder provides an "ethnic profile" of Pullman without commenting on the exclusion of blacks.

8. Cited in Eric F. Goldman, *Rendezvous with Destiny: A History of Modern American Reform* (New York, rev. ed., abridged, 1956), p. 30; cited in Buder, pp. 184 and 219.

9. The phrase "think of themselves . . ." is borrowed from Nathan Glazer and Daniel Patrick Moynihan, *Beyond the Melting Pot: The Negroes, Puerto Ricans, Jews, Italians, and Irish of New York City* (Cambridge, 1964), pp. 10, 12, where it is used concerning ethnic, not racial, consciousness. Edgar Litt wrote in *Ethnic Politics in America* (Glenview, Ill., 1970), p. 4, "for there to be 'brothers there must also be others.' "

10. Bertram Wilbur Doyle, *The Etiquette of Race Relations in the South* (Chicago, 1937).

11. Richard R. Wright, Jr., "The Negro in Chicago," *Southern Workman,* 35 (October 1906): 557.

12. Spear, tables, maps, and commentary, pp. 14–17. Tuttle reproduces Spear's maps, pp. 68–73, and refers to data, p. 163. For residential data, see *Broad Ax,* beginning in 1899, and Chicago *Defender,* beginning in 1905, especially from 1909 on. The Urban League's study is cited in detail in Chicago Commission on Race Relations, *The Negro in Chicago: A Study of Race Relations and a Race Riot* (Chicago, 1922), pp. 135–36, 187–92, hereafter cited as Riot Commission.

13. David A. Wallace, "Residential Concentration of Negroes in Chicago" (Ph.D. dissertation, Harvard University, 1953), cited in Karl E. and Alma F. Taeuber, *Negroes in Cities: Residential Segregation and Neighborhood Change* (Chicago, 1965), pp. 53–54.

14. Residents of Hull-House, *Hull-House Maps and Papers: A Presentation of Nationalities and Wages in a Congested District of Chicago* (New York, 1895), p. 17; Grace Abbott, "A Study of the Greeks in Chicago," *AJS* 15 (November 1909): 380; Milton B. Hunt, "The Housing of Non-Family Groups of Men in Chicago," ibid., 16 (September 1910): 156; Natalie Walker, "Chicago Housing Conditions, X. Greeks and Italians in the Hull-House Neighborhood," ibid., 21 (November 1915): 315–16; Edith Abbott, *The Tenements of Chicago 1908–1935* (Chicago, 1936), pp. 93–100.
15. Burgess and Newcomb, *Census Data 1920,* table 52. There were sixteen census tracts along Wentworth between 22nd and 63rd. Only one had fewer than nineteen ethnic groups represented within its limits. The average number of nationalities per tract was twenty-three. The Irish ranked first in one tract and second in five others. Poles ranked as high as fifth in only one tract. Yet the Riot Commission, Drake and Cayton, Spear, Tuttle, and others have called the territory Irish-Polish.
16. Interview with Rose Mary Lee Philpott (my mother), spring 1972. Her sister Dorothy Lee Nelson, interviewed in the summer of 1973, remembered the presence of other ethnic groups, especially Swedes. My Aunt Dorothy married a "Swede" (actually he was Danish), but he was not from Columbanus parish, and his mother was Irish, as my mother was quick to point out. The statistics are in Burgess and Newcomb, *Census Data 1920,* tracts 450–451, table 52, pp. 539–40; Burgess and Newcomb, *Census Data of the City of Chicago, 1930* (Chicago, 1933), tracts 885–886 and 888–889, tables 1, 2 and 3; *U.S. Sixteenth Census,* 1940, *Special Report. Population and Housing Statistics for Census Tracts and Community Areas, Chicago, Ill.,* tracts 885–886 and 888–889, tables 1 and 3; Morgan S. Odell, field director, "United Religious Survey of the Greater Grand Crossing Area," a report by the University of Chicago Divinity School, December 1929–January 1930 (typescript), n.p., Ernest W. Burgess Papers, UCL.
17. Robert Hunter, *Tenement Conditions in Chicago. Report by the Investigating Committee of the City Homes Association* (Chicago, 1901), p. 184; Bernice Davida Davis, "Housing Conditions in the District of Burnside" (M.A. thesis, University of Chicago, 1924), pp. 7–8; Burgess and Newcomb, *Census Data 1930,* community area summaries, community area 47, tables 1, 2 and 3; Edith Abbott, pp. 76, 151–55.
18. Jane Addams, "The Objective Value of A Social Settlement," in Jane Addams, Robert A. Woods et al., *Philanthropy and Social Progress* (New York, 1893), p. 28. When she repeated this passage in *Twenty Years at Hull-House* (New York, 1910), pp. 97–98, Miss Addams dropped the words "more or less." Residents of Hull-House, pp. 3–9, 15–17, and "Nationalities Maps" 1 through 4; Carroll D. Wright, *The Slums of Baltimore, Chicago, New York, and Philadelphia. Seventh Special Report of the Commissioner of Labor* (Washington, 1894), p. 23. The federal report lists data for an additional block immediately west of Halsted between Taylor and 12th streets. The four nationalities maps cannot be reproduced because the cost is prohibitive.

19. Residents of Hull-House, pp. 15–16; Edith Abbott, pp. 81–83; Joseph Parot, "Ethnic versus Black Metropolis: The Origins of Polish-Black Housing Tensions in Chicago," *Polish American Studies* 29 (Spring–Autumn 1972): 18–21.

20. Residents of Hull-House, pp. 8–19, 22–23; Carroll D. Wright, p. 26. The federal enumerators listed 696 "blacks" and 429 "mulattoes, quadroons, and octoroons." On the Hull-House maps they are all "colored people." It is most likely that the two "colored people" who lived west of the river were not visibly "black," but mulattoes, quadroons, or octoroons. Blacks appear in 56 lots, of which 23 are all-black.

21. Hunt, pp. 153–54; Stanley Lieberson, "Comparative Segregation and Assimilation of Ethnic Groups" (Ph.D. dissertation, University of Chicago, 1960), pp. 176–79; Grace Peloubet Norton, "Chicago Housing Conditions, VII: Two Italian Districts," *AJS* 18 (January 1913): 510–511 and 531; Humbert S. Nelli, *Italians in Chicago,* 1880–1930 (New York, 1970), pp. 23–28; "Housing Survey in the Italian District of the Seventeenth Ward," *First Semi-Annual Report of the Department of Public Welfare to the Mayor and Aldermen of the City of Chicago* (Chicago, 1915), pp. 74–75. The closest thing to an all Italian block in Chicago was the east side of Plymouth Court between Polk and Taylor streets. In 1912, of 123 households, 118 were headed by Italians. But "the neighborhood as a whole," Grace Norton noted, was "a polyglot territory" (Norton, pp. 510, 531). Nelli found only one other linear block that was nearly so Italian (23 of 26 homeowners were Italians) in the period 1880–1930. In the five blocks of Little Sicily surveyed by Norton, Italians constituted 53 percent of the population. One block was 90 percent Italian, another was 62 percent, but in the remaining "Italian" blocks Italians were a minority (with percentages of 48, 24, and 12). Lieberson's segregation indexes showed Italians to be more segregated from native whites than blacks were in 1910. The Italian index was 68, which means that 68 percent of the foreign-born Italians would have had to change their residences to another ward in order to have Italians spread evenly among native whites in all wards. The index for blacks was 67. By 1920, the index for blacks was up to 76, while the Italian index was down to 57. Lieberson's indexes are misleading for two reasons. First, the geographical units of analysis, the thirty-five wards, are unsuitable; they are too few, too large, and too irregular in shape to make differences of 1 to 10 meaningful. Second, Lieberson's indexes do not show the segregation of Italians from non-Italians or the segregation of blacks from nonblacks. Even if Italians were somewhat less likely to live within a few blocks of native whites than blacks were, they were not segregated by themselves. They lived intermixed with whites of many nationalities. Blacks, on the other hand, lived with blacks.

22. Clarence Darrow, "Little Louis Epstine," originally published in *The Public* in 1903, in Arthur and Lila Weinberg, eds., *Clarence Darrow: Verdicts Out of Court* (Chicago, 1963), p. 383; Louis Wirth, "The Ghetto," *AJS* 33 (July 1927): 57–71, reprinted in Albert J. Reiss, Jr., *Louis Wirth on Cities and Social Life* (Chicago, 1964), p. 94; Robert E. L. Faris, *Chicago Sociology,* 1920–1932 (San Francisco, 1967), biographical statement following Preface, n.p.; *Who's Who in Chicago,* 1936.

23. Dr. Liebman Adler, quoted in Wirth, *The Ghetto* (Chicago, 1928), p. 172; ibid., pp. 189–93, 201–5. See also Maurice H. Krout, "A Community in Flux—the Chicago Ghetto Re-Surveyed," *Social Forces* 5 (December 1926): 273–82; Wentworth Abraham Goldberg, *Jewish Population of Chicago, 1931* (Chicago, 1934); Philip P. Bregstone, *Chicago and Its Jews. A Cultural History* (Chicago, 1933).

24. Hunt, pp. 149, 157–58; Edith Abbott, p. 75; Hunt, p. 157.

25. Edith Abbott, pp. 133, 136, 140; Davis, p. 8.

26. Richard Wright, "Introduction" to Drake and Cayton, xix.

27. Burgess and Newcomb, *Census Data 1930,* tables 1, 2, and 3. Part of Little Sweden on map 12 is in the community of Park Manor, which my mother, the Irish woman from St. Columbanus parish, remembered as all-Irish.

28. Ibid.; Edith Abbott, p. 104. Stanislawowa covered 34 contiguous census tracts; the Black Belt covered 50. It should be noted that the 86 "Negro" tracts shown in map 12 had an average of nearly 15 nationalities represented in them. This does not mean that the Negro tracts were ordinary mixed areas. It simply means that the small white populations inside larger black areas were ethnically mixed, like white populations elsewhere. The average would be higher were it not for the negligible white totals in so many of the tracts. For example, tract 581 in the Black Belt had a population of 4,219, of whom 97 percent were black. The 51 foreign-stock whites living there were from 15 "countries." Where the white percentages in the Negro tracts were larger, there were usually more nationalities represented, and whites and blacks occupied separate areas within the tracts, i.e., a black area and an ethnically mixed white area.

29. Residents of Hull-House, p. 96.

30. See Parot, pp. 15–16, and Sam Bass Warner, Jr., and Colin B. Burke, "Cultural Change and the Ghetto," *Journal of Contemporary History* 4 (October 1969): 173–88. I have drawn on these interpretations without agreeing with them fully.

31. Wirth called "the ghetto" both "a geographical area" and "a state of mind." See *The Ghetto,* xi and passim.

32. Elizabeth A. Hughes, *Living Conditions for Small-Wage Earners in Chicago* (Chicago, 1925), p. 7; Anita Edgar Jones, "Mexican Colonies in Chicago," *SSR* 2 (Fall 1928): 579–81; Mark Riesler, "The Mexican Immigrant in the Chicago Area During the 1920's," *JISHS* 66 (Summer 1973): 144–45.

33. Manuel Bueno, "The Mexicans in Chicago," a student paper, n.d. (1924 or 1925), Burgess Papers; Charles S. Newcomb and Richard O. Lang, *Census Data of the City of Chicago, 1934* (Chicago, 1934), supplement table 4, p. 668. The 1930 census volume does not sort Mexicans out from "other races." The supplement in the 1934 volume does. Davis, table 1, p. 8; Edith Abbott, p. 136.

34. Businessman cited in Paul S. Taylor, *Mexican Labor in the United States: Chicago and the Calumet Region* (Berkeley, 1932), p. 225; ibid., pp. 82–83, 109–10.

35. "Black, Brown and White," in William Broonzy, *Big Bill Blues: William Broonzy's Story as told to Yannick Bruynoghe* (London, 1955), pp. 56–59.

CHAPTER 6 DRAWING THE COLOR LINE

1. Fannie Barrier Williams, "Social Bonds in the 'Black Belt' of Chicago," *Charities* 15 (7 October 1905): 44.
2. Chicago Commission on Race Relations, *The Negro in Chicago: A Study of Race Relations and a Race Riot* (Chicago, 1922), pp. 107–8, hereafter cited as Riot Commission.
4. Chicago *Record,* 5 May 1897, cited in Negro in Illinois; Chicago *Inter-Ocean,* 12 February 1902, cited in ibid.; Ernest W. Burgess and Charles Newcomb, eds., *Census Data of the City of Chicago, 1920* (Chicago, 1931), table 52.
3. *The Economist,* 8 August 1908.
5. Chicago *Defender,* 1 November 1919.
6. *U.S. Twelfth Census,* 1900, vol. 1, *Population,* part 1, tables 30 through 32; Richard R. Wright, Jr., "The Economic Condition of Negroes in the North v. Recent Improvement in Housing among Negroes in the North," *Southern Workman* 37 (November 1908): 601.
7. Ibid., p. 602.
8. Ibid., p. 603.
9. William D. Neighbors, "The Colored Real Estate Men on South State Street Are Not Transacting as Much Business as They Should—Several Prominent White Real Estate Firms Are Growing Rich at the Expense of the Colored People in General," *Broad Ax,* 23 February 1918; *Defender,* 1 November 1919.
10. *Inter-Ocean,* 19 August 1900, cited in Negro in Illinois.
11. Ibid. For the subsequent Negro "invasion" of Vernon Avenue from 31st to 36th streets, see Wright, p. 608; Riot Commission, pp. 109 and 136; interview with Miss Grace Garnett, 30 July 1941, in Negro in Illinois; ad for 3331 Vernon in *Broad Ax,* 3 August 1907.
12. Ads in *Defender* and *Broad Ax,* beginning in 1906; *Defender,* 7 March 1931; Neighbors.
13. Edith Abbott, *The Tenements of Chicago, 1908–1935* (Chicago, 1936), pp. 382–92; George W. Whitehead to R. G. Soderstrom, 14 March 1929, and Whitehead to Victor A. Olander, 4 April 1929, Victor Olander Papers, CHS; Riot Commission, pp. 8, 135, 252, 272.
14. A realtor on 35th Street, interviewed in Robert Bussian and C. E. Wilson, "Study of an Area in Transition," student paper, March 1930, p. 38, Ernest W. Burgess Papers, UCL; Alzada P. Comstock, "Chicago Housing Conditions, VI: The Problem of the Negro," *AJS* 18 (September 1912): 241–42.
15. Wright, Jr., p. 608; Riot Commission, pp. 107–11, 35–36, 140, 212–15.

16. LCRC, "History of Woodlawn Community, Chicago," 1927–29, Doc. 5, CHS.
17. Anthony Downs explains the role of "the whites who aren't there yet" in *Urban Problems and Prospects* (Chicago, 1970), pp. 35–36, 73–74, note 22; LCRC, Doc. 5 and Doc. 1, p. 16; Burgess and Newcomb, *Census Data 1920,* table 52.
18. *Defender,* 10 May 1913; Louise de Koven Bowen, *The Colored People of Chicago* (Chicago, 1913), n.p.
19. Ibid.; *1970 Census of the Population* Vol. 1, *Characteristics of the Population* Part 15, Illinois, tables 7, 27, 28, 29, 105; 1970 *Census of the Population and Housing: Census Tracts. Chicago, Illinois SMSA,* Part 1, tables P-l and P-3.
20. Riot Commission, pp. 114–15; *Broad Ax,* 1 September 1906. The Chicago Beach Hotel alone employed over 100 blacks.
21. Ibid., 1 September 1906 and 28 August 1909; Chicago *Record-Herald,* 21 August 1909, cited by Allan Spear, *Black Chicago: The Making of a Negro Ghetto, 1890–1920* (Chicago, 1967), p. 22.
22. Ibid.; *Broad Ax,* 18 September 1909; Fannie Barrier Williams, "A Negro's View of Housing Segregation in Hyde Park," letter to editor, *Record-Herald,* 15 September 1906 (I owe this reference to Prof. David Johnson of the University of Texas at San Antonio) .
23. *Record-Herald,* 22 August 1909, cited by Spear, p. 22; Riot Commission, p. 107; *Defender,* 17 March 1917; Burgess and Newcomb, *Census Data 1920,* table 52 (the southern edge of census tract 401 plus tracts 438 through 442).
24. "Blind Pig": a saloon that operates without a license; Williams, "Segregation in Hyde Park."
25. Report of a speech by the white radical lawyer Clarence Darrow, a Hyde Park resident, to a black audience, in *Broad Ax,* 29 December 1906; George Packard, "A Civic Problem and a Social Duty," *Survey* 29 (1 February 1913): 575.
26. Comstock, pp. 245–48, 250–52.
27. Ibid., pp. 245, 249.
28. Ibid., pp. 253–55.
29. Ibid., pp. 253–57; Breckenridge, p. 575.
30. Ibid.; Comstock, p. 243 and maps facing p. 241; Wright, Jr., p. 602; Vice Commission of Chicago, *The Social Evil in Chicago: A Study of Existing Conditions with Recommendations* (Chicago, 1911), pp. 38–39; Riot Commission, pp. 342–44. In 1912 Chicago outlawed prostitution, but the vice districts remained. Harold F. Gosnell, *Negro Politicians: The Rise of Negro Politics in Chicago* (Chicago, 1935), pp. 128–29. When the Hyde Parkers closed down Henry "Teenan" Jones's saloon-casino at 56th and Lake Park, for instance, Jones went straight to State Street and opened *two* "clubs," Elite No. 1 and Elite No. 2. William M. Tuttle, Jr., *Race Riot: Chicago in the Red Summer of 1919* (New York, 1972), p. 165.

31. Comstock, pp. 255–56; Breckenridge, pp. 575–76.
32. Burgess and Newcomb, *Census Data 1920,* tables 9–10, 21, 24–26, and 34; Riot Commission, pp. 194–230.
33. Cited in ibid., p. 530; *Tribune,* 30 May 1917 and 12 July 1917.
34. *Defender,* 24 March 1917; cited in ibid., 24 August 1918.
35. *Defender,* 17 and 24 August 1918; *Who's Who,* 1926.
36. Riot Commission, pp. 361, 392.
37. Ibid., pp. 115, 251–52, 273, 279; Langston Hughes, *The Big Sea* (New York, 1940), p. 33; Frederic M. Thrasher, *The Gang: A Study of 1,313 Gangs in Chicago* (Chicago, 1927; rev. ed., 1936), pp. 16, 202; Riot Commission, pp. 117–20, 592; Arna Bontemps and Jack Conroy, *Anyplace But Here* (New York, 1966), p. 175.

CHAPTER 7 HOLDING THE LINE: VIOLENCE

1. CREB *Bulletin* 25 (18 April 1917): 313–16; Chicago *Tribune,* 10 April 1917; Chicago *Defender,* 14 and 21 April 1917.
2. CREB *Bulletin* 25 (18 April 1917): 315–16; *Defender,* 14 April 1917.
3. Chicago *Daily News,* 30 April 1917. O'Brien's ads in the *Defender* from 1918 on list more flats and houses just inside disputed territory than in solidly black areas. White property owners did not attack him as a "blockbuster," and he remained in good standing with the Real Estate Board.
4. CREB *Bulletin* 25 (15 October 1917): 551; *Tribune,* 9 June and 1 July 1917; CREB *Bulletin* 25 (21 November 1917): 624. The Supreme Court decision was *Buchanan v. Warley* 245 U.S. 60.
5. *Defender,* 22 September 1917; Chicago Commission on Race Relations, *The Negro in Chicago: A Study of Race Relations and a Race Riot* (Chicago, 1922), pp. 117–20, hereafter cited as Riot Commission. The organization called itself the Kenwood Property Owner's Association originally, then changed the name to Kenwood and Hyde Park Property Owners' Association. People commonly called it the Hyde Park-Kenwood Association, however. The text follows the popular usage.
6. *Defender,* 27 September 1919.
7. Ibid., 30 August 1919, 25 May 1918, and 27 September 1919. For the *Defender's* role in stimulating the migration, see William M. Tuttle, Jr., *Race Riot: Chicago in the Red Summer of 1919* (New York, 1970), pp. 74–82, 89–92.
8. *Defender,* 27 September 1919. For the founding of the Urban League, see Arvarh E. Strickland, *History of the Chicago Urban League* (Urbana, Ill., 1966), ch. 2.
9. Two white men, cited in Riot Commission, p. 452; Charles L. Samson to his wife Loula Jay, 17 November 1918, World War I Letters of Charles L. Samson, CHS.

10. Resident of Woodlawn, cited in Riot Commission, p. 457; Kenwood and Hyde Park Property Owners' Association, *Property Owners' Journal*, cited in ibid., p. 591; West Woodlawn woman, cited in ibid., p. 452; "A resident near Dorchester Avenue and Sixtieth Street," on the Midway opposite the University of Chicago, cited in ibid., p. 453.

11. *Defender*, 27 September 1919, 6 March 1920, and 24 May 1919; real estate ads in *Defender*, 1917–1919. Some ads were aimed directly at "newcomers." The flats listed were usually in the oldest parts of the Black Belt. More frequently ads invited application from "first class people only," "high class tenants only" and "reliable working people only." Some agents, determined to keep prostitutes out of "respectable" buildings, discriminated against single women and woman-headed families. Their ads specified "couple," "man and wife or man," "couple or man," and "man only."

12. Ibid., 1 November 1919. Names of some officers and members, including Ald. Schwartz, appear in the *Tribune*, 6 August and 22 and 25 October 1919. The Riot Commission mentioned Schwartz's affiliation, pp. 120, 210. Tuttle, p. 174, note 30, cites an Association letter from W. H. Schendorf to Fellow Members, 24 March 1919, NAACP Papers, Middle Atlantic Youth Division of NAACP, Washington, D.C.; this letter names officers. Charles E. Fox, the president, was a realtor and builder. John P. Bowles, the treasurer, was a livestock commissioner. Winfield H. Schendorf, a realtor, and J. E. Murphy, a railroad executive, were members of the executive committee. These men were Catholics. Louis Aaron and George Mayer of the executive committee were Jewish. The secretary is not named in the newspaper accounts or Tuttle's text, but the association delegated him to persuade the congregation of Temple Isaiah not to sell its building at 45th and Vincennes to blacks (*Tribune*, 25 October 1919). Therefore I assume that he was Jewish. Temple Isaiah *did* sell; the congregation merged with Temple Israel and moved to white Hyde Park.

13. *Defender*, 1 November 1919. For Carey see Joseph Logsdon, "Reverend A. J. Carey and the Negro in Chicago Politics" (M.A. thesis, University of Chicago, 1961).

14. Riot Commission, pp. 3, 53, 122–23; *Defender*, 5 June 1919 and 25 May 1918; Tuttle, pp. 175–76. The commission counted twenty-four bombings before the riot; Tuttle documents twenty-six.

15. *Defender*, 8 May 1915; *Tribune*, 3–5 May 1915.

16. *Defender*, 25 May and 1 June 1918; Chicago *Herald-Examiner*, 25 May 1918, cited in Riot Commission, p. 535; *Tribune*, 5 May 1915.

17. Riot Commission, pp. 122–23 and 536.

18. Tuttle, pp. 108–10, 137–40, 153–56, and 181–82; *Defender*, 7 June and 5 July; Riot Commission, pp. 3, 115, 123, 272–80, 536.

19. Ibid., pp. 55–57; *Tribune*, 1 July 1919; Tuttle, pp. 182, 238–41; Riot Commission, p. 57.

20. Ibid., pp. 1–2, 4–52, 655–65; Tuttle, pp. 3–66.

21. Riot Commission, p. 7.

22. Ibid., pp. 126, 571.

23. Ibid., pp. 25, 660; James T. Farrell, *Studs Lonigan: A Trilogy* (New York, 1938), pp. 73–74 of *The Young Manhood of Studs Lonigan.*

24. Riot Commission, pp. 23, 25, 660.

25. *Broad Ax,* 9 August 1919; *Tribune,* 9 August 1919; Riot Commission, p. 25 (the reference to "depredations" at 69th and Elizabeth is to the attack on Owen Harris's house).

26. Archie Motley to author 11 March 1972; countless conversations with Mr. Motley since 1966. Archie Motley is the Motleys' grandson. His father, Archibald, the noted artist, was a young man in his twenties in 1919. He has told Archie about much of this, and Archie has questioned him at my request. The late novelist Willard Motley, author of *Knock on Any Door,* was a youngster at the time his family underwent this ordeal. His account of it is in Motley, "Let No Man Write Epitaph of Hate for his Chicago," *Sun-Times* 11 August 1963.

27. Frederick M. Thrasher, *The Gang: A Study of 1,313 Gangs in Chicago* (Chicago, 1927; rev. ed., 1936), pp. 16, 184–85, 201–3; Tuttle, pp. 54–55. The Shielders protected the whole area west of the Rock Island tracks from Negro "invaders." Between 47th and 51st, the train yards extended west to Wentworth.

28. Tuttle, p. 55; Riot Commission, pp. 12–14; Mayor's Commission on Human Relations, "Monthly Report of the Executive Director" (October 1947): 16, mimeographed, CHS.

29. Sterling Morton to Wirt Morton, 11 August 1919, Morton Family Papers, CHS; Frank Justin, "Neighborhood Study Paper #3. The Race Riot," student paper, 23 February 1932, n.p., Ernest W. Burgess Papers, UCL; Riot Commission, pp. 6–7, 12–14, and 39.

30. Justin, n. p.; Riot Commission, p. 14.

31. Morton to Morton; Tuttle, p. 54; Ernest W. Burgess and Charles Newcomb, *Census Data of the City of Chicago, 1920* (Chicago, 1931), table 52. Tract 380, which exactly coincided with "the burned district," had 800 white families.

32. *Tribune,* 4 August 1919; Riot Commission, p. 15.

33. Ibid., p. 31; *Defender,* 4 June 1919. Another all-white institution, De LaSalle Institute, a Catholic high school for boys, stood diagonally across the street from the Angelus.

34. Riot Commission, pp. 6, 29–32, 597, 661.

35. *Defender,* 2 August 1919.

36. *Tribune,* 5 and 6 August 1919; the association published Fox's letter as a pamphlet titled *Your Rights and Mine: A Short Symposium on Current Events as Applied to and Effecting Realty Values in Kenwood and Hyde Park* (see Riot Commission, p. 590).

37. Riot Commission, p. 134.

38. Ibid., p. 125.

39. Ibid., p. 126; Farrell, pp. 169–70 of *The Young Manhood of Studs Lonigan.*

40. Riot Commission, pp. 3, 122–23, 126, 131, 532, 536; Tuttle, pp. 175–76. Tuttle suggests that white blockbusters believed in "giving blacks and whites equal access to adequate housing" (p. 159). That is most unlikely. H. J. Coleman was one of the blockbusters whose home was bombed. In 1953 his firm was the city's leading manager of slum properties. See *The Road Back: A Dramatic Exposé of Slum Housing in Chicago,* reprinted from the *Chicago Daily News* (Chicago, 1954), p. 4.

41. Riot Commission, pp. 124–27, 131; Chicago *Post,* 6 January 1920, cited in ibid., p. 535.

42. Ibid., pp. 119, 123, 126–27, 536; *Defender,* 10 January and 17 April 1920. The suspect, Edwin Thompson, was the nephew of John R. Thompson, owner of a restaurant chain.

43. Riot Commission, p. 127.

44. Ibid., pp. 120–24, 127–28, 131, 133–35; *Tribune,* 10 January 1920. The phrase is from Charles Fox's letter to Mayor Thompson, *Tribune,* 6 August 1919.

45. Chicago *Searchlight,* n.d., a Negro newspaper cited in Riot Commission, p. 567; ibid., pp. 152–53.

CHAPTER 8 HOLDING THE LINE: RESTRICTION

1. Chicago Commission on Race Relations, *The Negro in Chicago: A Study of Race Relations and a Race Riot* (Chicago, 1922), p. 116, hereafter cited as Riot Commission.

2. Ibid., pp. 107, 137–38; A. J. Maloney, "Morgan Park and Its Changes," reminiscences of an old settler, n.d., n.p., Negro in Illinois; T. J. Woofter, Jr., *Negro Problems in Cities* (New York, 1928), pp. 107–8; Chicago *Defender,* 24 February 1917; Chicago *Tribune,* 2 August 1917.

3. Riot Commission, pp. 108, 224–25.

4. Ibid., pp. 107, 138–39.

5. Homer Hoyt, *One Hundred Years of Land Values in Chicago* (Chicago, 1933), table 87, p. 476; Chicago *Tribune,* 21 May 1921.

6. Philip M. Hauser and Evelyn M. Kitagawa, eds., *Local Community Fact Book for Chicago, 1950* (Chicago, 1953), figures for community areas 38 and 40, Grand Boulevard and Washington Park, and the part of community area 36, Oakland, west of Cottage Grove; "Interviews" by E. Jennings and A. Williams, n.d., n.p., in Negro in Illinois, for the burning of St. Elizabeth's Catholic Church and Bethel A.M.E. Church in 1924; Kenneth M. Jackson, *The Ku Klux Klan in the City, 1915–1930* (New York, 1967), for the Bethel burning, which Jackson attributes to the Klan; "Houses," n.d., n.p., and George C. Moore, "The N.A.A.C.P.," 17 May 1941, both in Negro in Illinois, for the bombing of Temple Israel after Bethesda Baptist congregation bought it in 1925; St. Clair Drake and Horace Cayton, *Black Metropolis* (New York, 1945), p. 79, for the Bethesda bombings; *Defender,* 15 October 1927; Carroll Binder, *Chicago and the New Negro,* reprinted from *Chicago Daily News* (Chicago, 1927), p. 3.

7. George J. Williams, addressing the January 1920 rally of the Hyde Park-Kenwood Association, cited in Riot Commission, p. 124.

8. Jackson, ch. 8; Hauser and Kitagawa. The six communities were Kenwood (community area 39), Hyde Park (area 41), Woodlawn (area 42), South Shore (area 43), Greater Grand Crossing (area 69), and Englewood (area 67; West Englewood, is included here with area 68, Englewood proper). One of these communities, Woodlawn, showed a net loss of white population in the twenties because of white flight from the expanding black satellite in West Woodlawn. East of Cottage Grove white Woodlawn gained in population, but it was not growing at nearly the rate of the other white communities. Even so, population turnover was tremendous in Woodlawn proper. Newcomers poured into the area during the decade. Only 30 percent of the persons listed at Woodlawn addresses in *Polk's Street Directory*, 1928–29, are listed at the same address in the alphabetical directories for 1923 published by Polk and by Illinois Bell Telephone Co. One householder in five for whom there is a 1923 listing lived in an area that was "going black" and then moved to white Woodlawn.

9. Jackson, ch. 8.

10. Ibid., p. 126.

11. Ernest W. Burgess and Charles Newcomb, eds., *Census Data of the City of Chicago, 1930* (Chicago, 1933), community area summaries, tables 1–5; Louis Wirth and Eleanor H. Bernert, eds., *Local Community Fact Book of Chicago* (Chicago, 1950). In 1930 there was no community area where less than 42 percent of the white population was foreign-stock. The six community areas in which native-stock whites outnumbered the foreign-stock were area 9, Edison Park (48.9 percent of whites were foreign-stock), area 36, Oakland (47.3 percent), area 39, Kenwood (48.9 percent), area 42, Woodlawn (49.1 percent), area 72, Beverly (42.4 percent), and area 75, Morgan Park (44.7 percent). I reviewed the biographical sketches of "the men and women . . . who control the activities and welfare of Chicago and its environs, in all important avenues of public, private, business and intellectual endeavor" in the five editions of *Who's Who in Chicago* published from 1917 to 1936. The ads in Olcott's give the names of prominent bankers, realtors, and insurance men. See Maps 5.8 and I.1.

12. *Defender*, 31 May 1919; James T. Farrell, *Studs Lonigan: A Trilogy* (New York, 1938), pp. 279, 332, and 347 of *The Young Manhood of Studs Lonigan*.

13. Jackson, pp. 95, 99–126. Jackson's interpretation differs from the one here. Jackson believes that the Klan foundered because of an urban force it could not control: mobility. He fails to consider the relative strengths of Catholics and Jews on the one hand, and of blacks on the other. While natives could not contain the ethnics, whites *did* control the movement of blacks.

14. Harold F. Gosnell, *Negro Politicians: The Rise of Negro Politics in Chicago* (Chicago, 1935), p. 32; Drake and Cayton, p. 382.

15. See Clement E. Vose, *Caucasians Only: The Supreme Court, the NAACP, and the Restrictive Covenant Cases* (Berkeley and Los Angeles, 1959), pp. 1–29.

16. Riot Commission, pp. 116, 175; Arthur Weimer and Homer Hoyt, *Principles of Urban Real Estate* (New York, 1939), pp. 285, 310; Harold Cahen, "Validity of Anti-Negro Restrictive Covenants: A Reconsideration of the Problem," *University of Chicago Law Review* 12 (February 1945): 204–5; Dunas' Forest Crest, Glencoe (suburb north of Chicago), 5 June 1924, *Plats Book* 192, p. 20, Cook County Recorder's Office. There was no single formula for the subdivision restrictions. See Appendix B for some of the variations.
17. *Corrigan v. Buckley*, appeal dismissed, 271 U.S. 323 (1926); Vose, pp. 17–19, 28. In the 1948 decision *Shelley v. Kraemer*, 334 U.S. 1 (1948) the Supreme Court declared judicial enforcement of covenants to be unconstitutional state action. *Chicago Realtor* 41 (January 1928): 64–65; ibid., 39 (December 1926): 39–40, 43; Herman H. Long and Charles S. Johnson, *People vs. Property: Race Restrictive Covenants in Housing* (Nashville, 1947), p. 12.
18. MacChesney's biographical sketch in the 1936 ed. of *Who's Who in Chicago* takes up one entire column. Only two other sketches out of 10,735 in the volume are as lengthy. He was a special assistant U.S. Attorney General in 1911–12; a "Bull Moose" Progressive in 1912, actively campaigning for Theodore Roosevelt; a member of the Republican Convention executive committee, 1908–20; and a longtime counsel for the National Child Labor Committee, for whom he drafted "many acts for social, uniform, and progressive legislation." President Hoover appointed him U.S. minister to Canada in 1932. Locally he served on the boards of several social agencies. He was a member of the Chicago Crime Commission and the Committee of Fifteen (a vice commission), as well as the Chicago Plan Commission. His wife, Lena, was active in settlement work and housing reform. For MacChesney's promotion of "constructive" efforts to "build up the Black Belt," see chs. 9 and 10.
19. *Who's Who*, 1926. Article 34 of the amended code is given in Nathan William MacChesney, *The Principles of Real Estate Law* (New York, 1927), p. 586, and in Herbert U. Nelson, *The Administration of Real Estate Boards* (New York, 1925), pp. 207–8. Both books belong to a series edited by the liberal economist Richard T. Ely. Also see Long and Johnson, p. 66.
20. Standard form of restrictive covenant, reproduced as Appendix A. *Chicago Realtor* 41 (January 1928): 69, announced that the form was ready but did not print it. The Property Restriction Associations of Englewood and Greater Pullman identified the covenants they circulated as copies of the standard form. See Archibald J. Motley Papers, CHS, for the Englewood covenant and Ernest W. Burgess Papers, UCL, for the Pullman covenant. The standard covenant covering the Washington Park Subdivision in West Woodlawn is Document 9914711, Book 25525, pp. 5–31, dated September 1927, recorded 11 February 1928, *Records of Cook County, Deeds*, in Cook County Recorder's Office. This covenant is quoted in full in *Burke v. Kleiman*, 277 Ill. App. 519 (314) .
21. Standard form of restrictive covenant. The Washington Park Subdivision covenant was one which required more than the recommended percentage of coverage: it called for 95 percent.

22. "Judge" Henry Lunt, Real Estate Board spokesman, cited in Thomas E. Hunter, "Problems of Colored Chicago," March 1930, student paper, Burgess Papers, and in *Calumet Index*, 5 December 1928, article reprinted by the Greater Pullman Property Restriction Association, copy in ibid.

23. *Calumet Index*, 5 December 1928, ibid.; *Hyde Park Herald*, 30 March 1928; "Fence Under Construction," editorial in *Vicinity News*, November 1928, clipping, Burgess Papers; *South End Reporter*, editorial, 6 December 1928, clipping, ibid.; N. W. Wiersema, President, and Harvey L. Smith, Business Manager, Greater Pullman Property Restriction Association, to "Property Owner," n.d., ibid.

24. T. W. Wysacker, "Keeping Uptown Chicago 99 44/100% Pure (White)," student paper, 30 May 1930, p. 9, Burgess Papers; also see *Calumet Index*, 5 December 1928. Wysacker, besides being a student, was a realtor whom the Central Uptown Chicago Association hired "to obtain the necessary signatures" for the covenant.

25. Ibid., p. 4.

26. *Hyde Park Herald*, 30 March 1928.

27. "Fences Under Construction"; *Calumet Index*, 5 December 1928. The associations, which claimed over 100,000 members, are listed with their officers in "Neighborhood Organizations Interested in Community Affairs," *CDNA*, 1926–1931. They are listed with their membership totals in "A Ward Redistricting Plan," n.d. [March 1931], n.p., a typed study prepared by the University of Chicago for the Citizen's Association, Burgess Papers. *Chicago Civic Agencies: A Directory of Associations of Citizens of Chicago Interested in Civic Welfare, 1927* (Chicago, 1927), lists 123 white neighborhood improvement associations, five of which give as their "object" the exclusion of "undesirables" (pp. 87, 115, 149, 168, 182). For the extent of the restricted districts, see Long and Johnson, pp. 12–33, and Louis C. Washington, "A Study of Restrictive Covenants in Chicago" (M.A. thesis, University of Chicago, 1948), pp. 4–26.

28. *Defender*, 20 October 1928.

29. Ibid., 10 March 1929; John Spilker, *Real Estate Business as a Profession* (Cincinnati, 1923), pp. 123, 128. Most texts published between 1923 and 1949 followed the formula laid down by Stanley L. McMichael and Robert F. Bingham in *City Growth and Values* (Cleveland, 1923), pp. 177–87, 201–2. McMichael and Bingham thought that the *first* generation of immigrants from "certain foreign lands" should "live in settlements by themselves until they absorb American ideals." For Negroes, *all* Negroes, they advocated rigid, permanent segregation in "established districts." "Racial Zoning," *Housing* 17 (December 1928): 297–98.

30. *Defender*, 14 May 1927 and 10 March 1929.

31. *South End Reporter*, 6 December 1928; Wiersema and Smith to "Property Owner," with list of officers and advisory committee members on letterhead; Burgess and Newcomb, community areas summaries, tables 1 and 2 for areas 47, 49, 50, and 53: Burnside, Roseland, Pullman, and West Pullman; Wirth and Bernert, data for same areas.

32. City figure calculated from ibid., table A; suburban figure calculated from Kitagawa and Karl E. Taeuber, *Local Community Fact Book, Chicago Metropolitan Area, 1960* (Chicago, 1963), tables I-3 and V-3.

33. Ibid., table V-5; Wirth and Bernert, white population data for areas 36, 39, 41, 43 and 68: Oakland, Kenwood, Hyde Park, Woodlawn, South Shore and Englewood; *Who's Who,* 1926 (for Levy) and 1936 (for Levy and Donne); *Defender,* 25 February 1928; *CDNA* 1926–1928, listing property owners' associations' chief officers; William G. Donne and Van V. Lain (president and vice-president of Englewood Property Restriction Association), form letter to "All Property owners in Englewood," 21 May 1928, listing all officers, in Motley Papers.

34. *Chicago Realtor* 41 (January 1928): 65–66, (February 1928): 28 and 31, (April 1928): 28, (May 1928): 31, (July 1928): 26 and 30, (December 1928): 5 and 17; for Boenicke and Victor Curto, *Who's Who,* 1936; "For the Advancement of Uptown Chicago," n.d., a handbill attached to Wysacker's paper, listing 189 business and individual contributors to the restriction campaign, of whom thirty are in the 1926 or 1936 edition of *Who's Who; Plats Books* 192 through 274. De Lugach's first recorded restriction was Frank De Lugach Western Ave. View, 5 November 1926, *Plats Book* 236, p. 32. He stated all subsequent restrictions in the same language.

35. Dr. A. G. Fairfix, quoted in *Defender,* 20 October 1928; "Judge" Henry Lunt, cited in Hunter, n.p.; Wiersema and Smith to "Property Owner"; MacChesney, p. 586; realtor quoted in *Defender,* 20 July 1929.

36. Archie Motley to author, 11 March 1972. The covenant reproduced in Appendix A is the one which the Englewood restrictionists sent to Mr. Motley. Willard Motley, "Let No Man Write Epitaph of Hate for His Chicago," *Sun-Times,* 11 August 1963.

37. Document 10563434, Book 27945, pp. 175–204, dated 1 November 1927, recorded 30 December 1929, *Records of Cook County Deeds,* for properties restricted by Salvation Army; "For the Advancement of Uptown Chicago," for companies and public figures supporting restriction. David H. Jackson was chairman of the Illinois Commerce Commission, 1926–28, and president of the Lincoln Park Board, 1925–27. The aldermen were James B. Waller of the Forty-third Ward and John A. Massen of the Forty-eighth Ward. See *Who's Who,* 1936, for all three. For William E. Dever, see Graham Taylor, *Chicago Commons through Forty Years* (Chicago, 1936), pp. 71, 139–40, 292. In his unsuccessful reelection campaign in 1927, Dever promised to keep Chicago "a white man's town." He warned that Negroes would swarm to the city if his Republican opponent, Big Bill Thompson, won. For the Dever campaign's "racist" tactics, see Humbert S. Nelli, *Italians in Chicago 1880–1930* (New York, 1970), p. 219, and Harold F. Gosnell, *Negro Politicians: The Rise of Negro Politics in Chicago* (Chicago, 1935), pp. 54–55.

38. *Defender,* 14 May 1927; covenant covering Washington Park Subdivision. Quotation from Horace Cayton, "Negro Housing in Chicago," *Social Action* 6 (15 April 1940): 29. The legal challenge to covenants in the thirties centered on this covenant.

39. Interviews with three landlords in Robert Bussian and C. E. Wilson, "Study of an Area in Transition" student paper, March 1930, pp. 28, 31–32, Burgess Papers.

40. Interview with manager of "H. & G. Realty Co." [Hobbs and Grubbs], in Hunter, n.p; John M. Gries and James Ford, eds., *Publications of the President's Conference on Home Building and Home Ownership,* 11 vols. (Washington, 1932), vol. 6: *Negro Housing,* pp. 179–80 and Appendix 7, pp. 258–59.

41. Interview with a property owner, Bussian and Wilson, p. 32; Kelly Miller, "Home Ownership by the City Negro," *Chicago Sunday Bee,* undated clipping [1932], ANP.

42. William T. Stead, *If Christ Came to Chicago* (Chicago, 1894; reprint ed., New York, 1964), p. 123.

43. *Defender,* 7 July 1928.

44. John Kobler, *Capone: The Life and World of Al Capone* (Greenwich, Conn., 1971), p. 18; *Defender,* 7 July 1928; Mary Letts, *Al Capone* (New York, 1974), p. 47; Document 10387098, Book 27331, pp. 46–63, dated 1 November 1927, recorded 1 June 1929, *Records of Cook County Deeds.* The covenant which Theresa Capone signed was one of sixteen, each encompassing six blocks, which covered Park Manor. Mrs. Capone signed for two adjoining properties with a combined frontage of 100 feet; her signatures are on pp. 50–51 .

45. Burgess and Newcomb, tables 1, 2, 3, and 10, for tracts 885–886 and 888–889. *There were nineteen Black Belt tracts with a range of median rentals as high as or higher than the range in Park Manor.* The Protestant minister is quoted in Morgan S. Odell, field director, "United Religious Survey of the Greater Grand Crossing Area," a report by the University of Chicago Divinity School, December 1929–January 1930 (typescript), n.p., Burgess Papers. Interestingly, the minister was under the mistaken impression that the community (which my mother, cited in ch. 5, called "all-Irish") was nearly two-thirds Irish. Incidentally, the University of Chicago Divinity School study was undertaken at the request of a Protestant church which needed more space: their problem was whether to add on to their buildings in Park Manor or move and build anew. The congregation wanted to stay *if* they had assurance that Park Manor would "stay white" for at least twenty-five more years. The University's students recommended that the church stay: the blacks would not cross "the tracks" along South Chicago Avenue for twenty-five years. The church stayed and built; the first blacks moved into Park Manor, with violent resistance, in 1946. See *Against Discrimination, Documented Memorandum No. XIV. Racial Tensions in the Park Manor Neighborhood of Chicago* (Chicago, 1948), CHS. The area did not become predominantly black until the mid-1950s, twenty-five years after the survey. This was the grace period the congregation had prayed for, and when their time had run out, they were already meeting in a new place of worship.

PART III THE BUSINESS CREED AND THE COLOR LINE: THE LIMITS OF CONSTRUCTIVE REFORM

1. Ernest Woltersdorf, "The Chicago Real Estate Board Good Housing Committee Report," CREB *Bulletin* 25 (29 December 1917): 694–95 and (6 June 1917): 406–7. Lawrence Veiller, secretary of the National Housing Association, said that the most significant development in housing in 1917 was that the "real estate interests" had "taken up housing reform." See Veiller, "Housing Progress of the Year," *NCH,* 1917, pp. 418–19. Louis T. Jamme, vice-president of the Chicago Association of Commerce and Industry, quoted in "Chicago Launches $3,000,000 Project," *Housing Betterment* 8 (December 1919): 60. Charles B. Ball, "What Are We Going to Do About It?" *NCH,* 1918, p. 350.

2. Chicago Commission on Race Relations, *The Negro in Chicago: A Study of Race Relations and a Race Riot* (Chicago, 1922), pp. xvi, 645, hereafter cited as Riot Commission; Nels Anderson, *The Hobo* (Chicago, 1923), p. 261 and Appendix A, Summary of Findings and Recommendations, pp. 265–79; Chicago Department of Public Welfare, *Annual Report,* 1924, pp. 15–22; Riot Commission, pp. 644–45.

3. *Property Owners' Journal,* 15 February 1920, cited in ibid., pp. 121–22.

4. Ibid., Appendix A, Biographical Data of Members of the Commission, pp. 652–53; *Who's Who,* eds. of 1905 through 1931; Morris Robert Werner, *Julius Rosenwald: The Life of a Practical Humanitarian* (New York, 1939); *The Julius Rosenwald Centennial: The Julius Rosenwald Centennial Observance at the University of Chicago, 15 October 1962* (Chicago, 1963).

5. See Sophonisba P. Breckenridge and Edith Abbott, "Housing Conditions in Chicago, III: Back of the Yards," *AJS* 15 (January 1911): 433–68; Questionnaires returned to Mary McDowell by Allen B. Pond, 20 May 1912, Clarence Buckingham, 24 June 1912, W. F. Dummer, 1 July 1912, and I. N. Higbie, 26 July 1912, in Mary McDowell Papers, CHS.

6. McDowell, "New City Tenement," form letter, n. d., ibid.; McDowell, form letter, 11 July 1913, ibid. The phrase "on a business basis" appears in both. Northwestern University Settlement, Workers' House Meeting, 13 October 1917, copy in Graham Taylor Papers, Newberry Library, Chicago. Participants discussed an effort "to unite the social agencies and the packing houses on a plan for model housing," and they mentioned that the packers were ready to invest $100,000. McDowell, form letter, 11 July 1913; McDowell, "Housing," typed extract from a University of Chicago Settlement report dated 31 May 1921, McDowell Papers.

7. Ibid.; McDowell, "Practice," in Caroline M. Hill, compiler, *Mary McDowell and Municipal Housekeeping: A Symposium* (Chicago, n.d. [1937]), pp. 28, 32–35.

8. Alfred K. Stern, "Decent Housing for Negroes: A Demonstration in Chicago of the Possibility of Making Negro Housing a Large-Scale Business Enterprise," *American City* 40 (March 1929): 102; "Model Houses for Negroes," *Housing Betterment* 5 (August 1916): 40–41; Riot Commission, p. 109.

9. "Model Houses for Negroes"; Julius Rosenwald, quoted in "Good Housing at a Profit: Model Apartments for Negroes One Hundred Per Cent Rented," *American City* (October 1929): 161.

CHAPTER 9 THE RIOT COMMISSION AND THE DUAL SOLUTION

1. *The Economist,* 2 August 1919; Chicago *Tribune,* 5 and 6 August 1919; ibid., editorial, date not given, cited in Chicago Commission on Race Relations, *The Negro in Chicago: A Study of Race Relations and a Race Riot* (Chicago, 1922), p. 552, hereafter cited as Riot Commission.
2. Ibid., pp. xiv, 612.
3. Ibid., pp. 451–73, 640–45.
4. John Bracey, August Meier, and Elliot Rudwick, "The Black Sociologists: The First Half Century," in Joyce A. Ladner, ed., *The Death of White Sociology* (New York, 1973), p. 15, treats the report as Johnson's book. Among other authors who regard the commission's goals as integrationist are Allan H. Spear, *Black Chicago: The Making of a Negro Ghetto, 1890–1920* (Chicago, 1967), pp. 218–19, and Arthur I. Waskow, *From Race-Riot to Sit-In, 1919 and the 1960s* (Garden City, N.Y., 1967 ed.), pp. 66–104.
5. Chicago *Defender,* 21 April 1917 and 2 August 1919. The whites were "limiting our spheres to metes and bounds," the editor wrote. "Hence the race riots."
6. CREB *Bulletin* 25 (18 April 1917): 313–16.
7. *Tribune,* 10 April 1917.
8. Ibid.; *Defender,* 21 April 1917. The *Defender* reported that the white press attributed to Jackson "what Manns said." Eugene Manns was a black realtor.
9. *Tribune,* 10 April 1917; Chicago *Daily News,* 30 April 1917.
10. T. Arnold Hill, "Housing for the Negro Wage Earner," *NCH,* 1917, pp. 309–13.
11. Charles S. Duke, *The Housing Situation and the Colored People of Chicago, with Suggested Remedies and Brief References to Housing Projects Generally* (Chicago, n.d. [1919]); Riot Commission, pp. 34, 201.
12. Duke, pp. 3–4, 6, 12–16; "The Housing of Colored People," *City Club Bulletin* 12 (18 August 1919): 169–70; "The Negro Citizen and Housing," *Housing* 8 (December 1919): 71–72. Both articles reprinted extracts from Duke's book.
13. William D. Neighbors, "The Colored Real Estate Men on South State Street Are Not Transacting as Much Business as They Should—Several Prominent White Real Estate Firms Are Growing Rich at the Expense of the Colored People in General," *Broad Ax,* 23 February 1918; *Defender,* 21 April 1917; Duke, pp. 3, 22–23, 26–28, 32–33. There had been several unsuccessful attempts to organize Negro building and loan associations, e.g., the Afro-American Building and Loan Association described in *Broad Ax,* 17 November 1906.
14. Duke, pp. 3, 5, 15.

15. *Housing Betterment* 8 (September 1919): 98; *Defender*, 21 June 1919.

16. *Herald Examiner*, 29 March 1919, quoted in *Defender*, 5 April 1919; *Tribune* editorial, date not given, quoted in ibid., 10 May 1919; *Tribune*, 30 June 1919.

17. Ibid., 28 June 1919; Riot Commission, p. 119.

18. "Report of Charles R. Bixby on Civic Real Estate Improvement Corporation of Chicago, Illinois," CREB *Bulletin* 27 (31 December 1919): 978.

19. Ibid.

20. Ibid.

21. Riot Commission, xv; Waskow, pp. 60–62. For Lowden, see William T. Hutchinson, *Lowden of Illinois*, 2 vols. (Chicago, 1957). The commissioners "representing the white people" were: Edward Osgood Brown, a lawyer, president of the Chicago NAACP; Julius Rosenwald; Harry Eugene Kelly, a lawyer, chairman of the Union League Club's Industrial Division; William Scott Bond, realtor, trustee of the University of Chicago; Edgar Addison Bancroft, a lawyer; Victor F. Lawson, owner, editor, publisher of the Chicago *Daily News;* and Francis W. Shepardson, former professor of history at the University of Chicago and director of registration and education under Governor Lowden. The commissioners "representing the Negro people" were: Robert S. Abbott, owner, editor, publisher of the Chicago *Defender;* Dr. George Cleveland Hall of Provident Hospital; George H. Jackson, realtor; Adelbert H. Roberts, a lawyer; Rev. Lacey Kirk Williams of Olivet Baptist Church; and Edward H. Morris, a lawyer and former state legislator (Riot Commission, pp. xvi–xviii, 651–53).

22. *Tribune*, 1 and 5 August 1919; *Herald Examiner*, 1 August 1919, cited in *Broad Ax*, 30 August 1919.

23. *Daily News*, 7 August 1919, MRL clipping; *Tribune*, 8 August 1919.

24. *Daily News*, 22 October 1919, MRL clipping; *Daily News*, 7 August 1919.

25. "Report of Charles R. Bixby on Civil Real Estate Improvement Corporation," p. 979; Spear, p. 174.

26. "Report of Charles R. Bixby on Civil Real Estate Improvement Corporation," p. 979.

27. Riot Commission, pp. 49–52.

28. "Chicago Launches $3,000,000 Project," pp. 59–60; "Report of Charles R. Bixby on Civic Real Estate Improvement Corporation," p. 980; Bixby, "Chicago Considers Her Housing Needs," *Housing Betterment* 8 (December 1919): 66–69.

29. *Daily News*, 25 October 1919, MRL clipping. The headline over the article was "NEGROES SAY THEY WILL QUIT WHITE ZONES/ Agree to Move if Homes Can Be Found for Them." *Defender*, 1 November 1919.

30. Ibid., 29 November 1919; *Who's Who*, eds. of 1926, 1931, and 1936.

31. "Report of Charles R. Bixby on Civic Real Estate Improvement Corporation," pp. 981–82.

32. Riot Commission, p. xvii; Waskow, pp. 67–70.

33. *Broad Ax*, 30 August and 6 September 1919.

34. Ibid., 24 January 1920; "Wm. Scott Bond Denies Association with Rowdies," *Defender*, 7 February 1920.

35. "The Race Problem in Chicago and the Governor's Commission," *City Club Bulletin* 13 (March 1920): 48.

36. *Daily News*, 25 February 1920, cited in Negro in Illinois; *Daily News*, 7 August 1919.

37. Alderman Louis B. Anderson, "Facts Show We Came Here First and Are Here to Stay," *Defender*, 7 February 1920.

38. Ibid.

39. Riot Commission, pp. 34, 201, 478–79, 518, 645. The commission cited Duke as an authority in two places and quoted "a Negro alderman" who favored "Better housing for the colored people and improvement of the district in which a vast majority of them reside. This without lines or thought of segregation."

40. Waskow, pp. 70, 100.

41. Riot Commission, p. 647; *Tribune*, date not given, cited in ibid., p. 552; ibid., pp. 146–51, 326, 644, 646. For the commission's acceptance of the color line in welfare and neighborhood work, see ch. 12, below.

42. Riot Commission, pp. 108–22, 606–11.

43. Ibid., p. 645.

44. W. E. B. DuBois, "Chicago," *The Crisis* 21 (January 1921): 102; Waskow, p. 62.

45. Waskow, p. 89; Riot Commission, pp. 116–35, 152–53, 186, 195, 622. At one point the text states that blacks had "hitherto virtually segregated themselves" (p. 227). There are several statements like the following, phrased in the passive voice: "It has been maintained that not much financing could be expected from white people unless boundaries were allotted to the Negroes," and ". . . the opinion was also given that their tendency is to remain among and near their own people." The report quoted a number of people such as a real estate broker who "disclaimed any desire to promote segregation," yet recommended "creating definite districts" as the "exclusive territory" of Negroes (p. 224). Johnson probably wrote the first draft of the text, which Taylor then edited, with considerable give-and-take between the two. "The recommendations were drafted by Taylor, Johnson, and Shepardson, and were circulated for the commission's approval" (Waskow, p. 88). The recommendations were hardly what any of the three men would have written working alone. Rather they represent an extremely delicate balance of essentially conflicting views. That the report overall can be interpreted as integrationist is a tribute to Johnson's skills as writer and negotiator.

CHAPTER 10 GARDEN HOMES: A PROJECT FOR "WHITE PEOPLE"

1. Hon. Hiram E. Todd, "Illinois Real Estate Corporations," *Chicago Realtor and Chicago Real Estate,* 24 (November 1921): 54–56. The board's lobbyists did not include this bill on their list of high-priority measures. See Frederick K. Root, "Committee on Legislation," ibid., 24 (December 1921): 7–8.

2. "Benjamin J. Rosenthal's Record," in Benjamin J. Rosenthal, *Reconstructing America Sociologically and Economically* (Chicago, 1919), p. iii; *Who's Who,* 1926, 1931, and 1936 eds.; interview with George N. Quin, a business aide of Rosenthal's, spring 1966. Rosenthal headed the Chicago Mail Order Co., he built the North American Building at 36 S. State, and he owned *Redbook* magazine for a time. He was a director of the Chicago Association of Commerce. For an extended account of Garden Homes, see Thomas Philpott, "Garden Homes, 1919–1966: The Story of a Housing Development," seminar paper, University of Chicago, spring 1966, on file at CHS.

3. Rosenthal, pp. v, 31–43, 76–82.

4. Ibid., pp. 4–7, 28–29. Rosenthal was a member of the Chicago Board of Education, 1894–1897, and chairman of the Committee on Unemployed which Mayor Thompson appointed in 1915. He also established employment committees to aid men past forty-five, "crippled people," and "colored women" who were qualified for "higher" jobs than "menial service."

5. Rosenthal to Julius Rosenwald, 18 June 1919, Julius Rosenwald Papers, UCL; John E. McEldowney, "Millions for Home Building. Chicago Housing Association Launches Huge Program to Promote Home-Owning and Foster Americanization Among Chicago Foreign Workmen/Details of Method by Which Big Men of Finance, Business and Building World Unite in Plan Looking to Erection of Ten Thousand Houses/Bond Issue to Afford Business Men and Investors Opportunity in Upbuilding of Wide Chicago Areas," *Real Estate News* 14 (October 1919): 1–7, copy in Graham Taylor Papers, Newberry Library, Chicago; Rosenthal to Rosenwald; Rosenthal, p. 29.

6. Rosenthal to Rosenwald; McEldowney, p. 4.

7. Ibid.

8. Lawrence Veiller, "Housing Progress of the Year," *NCH,* 1920, p. 328; James F. Basiger, general manager of the project, speaking for Rosenthal, cited in McEldowney, p. 6.

9. "Chicago Housing Association," typed copy of broadside, n.d. [early July 1919], Taylor Papers. This motto later appeared on the association's letterhead. The original members of the Chicago Housing Association were: Herman Hettler (president), William Grace (vice-president), Moses Greenebaum (treasurer), A. Volney Foster (secretary), James F. Basiger (general manager), Isaac S. Rothschild (general counsel), and J. Ogden Armour, Judge Bernard Barasa, Col. Abel Davis (chairman of finance committee), George W. Dixon, Dorr E. Felt, Charles W. Folds, D. F. Kelly, Albert D.

Lasker, Minnie Low, Harry H. Merrick, Simon O'Donnell, Benjamin J. Rosenthal, Julius F. Smietanka, Frederick W. Upham, Harriet Vittum, Charles H. Wacker, Thomas E. Wilson, Harry A. Wheeler, William Wrigley, Jr., Charles S. Frost, Leroy J. Kenevel, George C. Nimmons, John Paul Stafford, Emerson Bradshaw, Sophonisba P. Breckenridge, Mary McDowell, Graham Taylor, and Charles Wrigley. Later, B. F. Affleck of the defunct Black Belt reconstruction corporation became a director of the association's building corporation.

10. The backers and the amounts they advanced were: Julius Rosenwald, $100,000; J. Ogden Armour, $100,000; Swift & Co., $100,000; Benjamin J. Rosenthal, $100,000; Thomas E. Wilson, $50,000; Morris & Co., $50,000; William Wrigley, Jr., $50,000; Albert D. Lasker (the advertising genius), $25,000; Consumer's Co., $25,000. See Rosenthal to Rosenwald, 29 August 1919, Rosenwald Papers. McEldowney, p. 4.

11. Rosenthal to Rosenwald, 18 June 1919. The 5 percent return to investors, Rosenthal argued, eliminated "all charity." Julius Rosenwald to Rosenthal, 21 June 1919, Rosenwald Papers; also see Rosenwald to E. J. Buffington, 13 August 1920, ibid., in which Rosenwald said that the plan was not "feasible" because it depended on "the philanthropic appeal." Rosenthal to Rosenwald, 29 August 1919, Rosenwald Papers.

12. Mary McDowell, "Housing," typed MS, 31 May 1921, Mary McDowell Papers, CHS.

13. Rosenthal to Rosenwald, 18 June 1919; "Chicago Housing Association"; *The Economist,* 10 January 1920. Burgess and Newcomb, eds., *Census Data of the City of Chicago, 1920* (Chicago, 1931), table 52, p. 557, gives the population for tract 468 (79th Street to 95th, State to Cottage Grove) and six smaller districts within the tract. The 1920 population of the entire two-square-mile area was 5,021. Three sources show the years in which houses were built, block by block: Chicago Plan Commission, *Housing in Chicago Communities, Community Area 44* (Chicago, 1940), "Selected Housing Maps of Chatham . . . ," n.p.; Chicago Plan Commission, *Report of the Chicago Land Use Survey,* 2 vols. (Chicago, 1942–43), vol. 2: *Land Use in Chicago,* pp. 358–61, 374–77; and *Sixteenth U.S. Census, 1940. Housing Supplement to the First Series. Housing Bulletin for Illinois. Chicago Block Statistics,* table 3, tract 653.

14. Rosenthal, pp. 28–29; James F. Basiger (for Rosenthal) to Graham Taylor, 7 August 1919, Taylor Papers.

15. Graham Taylor to James F. Basiger, 8 August 1919; Chicago *Daily News,* 9 August 1919. The issue of *The Survey* dated 2 August 1919 ran an article on Garden Homes mentioning that a *later* project might be built for "Negro families." See "Constructive Housing," *Survey* 42 (2 August 1919): 674.

16. "Chicago Launches $3,000,000 Project," pp. 59–60; "Report of Charles R. Bixby on Civic Real Estate Improvement Corporation," p. 980; *Daily News,* 8 October 1919, clipping in Rosenwald Papers.

17. W. C. G. [William Graves], Rosenwald's secretary, to Rosenwald, 21 October 1919, cited James Basiger and Benjamin Rosenthal. In this memo Graves informed Rosenwald of Rosenthal's answer to "your question about the attached clipping," i.e., the *Daily News* report. "Chicago Launches $3,000,000 Project," pp. 59–60; "Report of Charles R. Bixby on Civic Real Estate Improvement Corporation," pp. 981–82. The four were Harry Merrick, Abel Davis, Herman Hettler, and Frederick B. Upham. Sometime after the Black Belt rebuilding corporation faded away, one of its members, B. F. Affleck, joined the Garden Homes corporation. Thus *five* of the eleven directors of the Black Belt corporation were closely associated with Garden Homes.

18. George A. Quin interview; interview with an original settler of Garden Homes, spring 1966.

19. Rosenwald to Rosenthal. All the social workers—Vittum, Stafford, Breckenridge, Low, McDowell, and Taylor—and at least three of the businessmen—Davis, Dixon, and Greenebaum—were members of the Chicago Urban League, whose main contributor was Julius Rosenwald. Thus many of the members of the all-white Chicago Housing Association were certified "friends of the Negro."

20. Rosenthal to Rosenwald, 18 June and 29 August 1919; *Daily News,* 25 October 1919; McEldowney, pp. 1, 4.

21. "For the Information of Prospective Purchasers of Houses in 'Garden Homes,'" broadside, n.d. [May 1920], Taylor Papers; McEldowney, p. 4.

22. In a study of unskilled and semiskilled workers, 72 percent of whom were immigrants, Leila Houghteling found that 90 percent made less than $1,700 in 1924 (a "prosperous" year) and 55 percent made less than $1,400. Sixty-nine percent of their families claimed that they had no savings at all, and of those who admitted to having some savings, only 3.3 percent had as much as $400. See Houghteling, *The Income and Standard of Living of Unskilled Laborers in Chicago* (Chicago, 1927), pp. 24–26, 112, 120.

23. Harriet Vittum to Graham Taylor, 13 May 1920, Taylor Papers. There is a copy of the detailed application form in the Taylor Papers, but all of the filled-out applications are gone from the Garden Homes files. In May, Miss Vittum still thought that her social service committee would select the first residents (Vittum to Taylor), but Rosenthal and his general manager made the choices and did whatever interviewing was done (interview with Edward Benes, spring 1966). James Basiger, the manager, informed the press that there were over 1,000 applicants; see *Daily News,* 18 August 1920, and "Workers Seek Homes at Cost," *City Club Bulletin,* 13 (23 August 1920): 172.

24. In the spring and summer of 1966 I interviewed ten original settlers of Garden Homes and four other people who moved there in the twenties. All of them wished to be anonymous. These people showed me their contracts and their payment books, and there are copies of several contracts, called Articles of Agreement, dated 1 September 1920, in the Garden Homes files of the Benjamin J. Rosenthal Estate (courtesy of the Rosenthal Estate, Chicago).

25. Rosenthal to Rosenwald, 18 June 1919; Burgess and Newcomb, eds., *Census Data of the City of Chicago, 1930* (Chicago, 1933), table 8, tract 653. Note that the figures come from the 1930 census, not the 1920 census. They provide only an *estimate* of the 1920–21 project population. There are no data for the 1920 group as such. The 1,000 detailed applications for houses in the project have disappeared from the thin Garden Homes files. The 1920 census was completed before Garden Homes was occupied (and the 1920 census tract boundaries took in a large area with a population of over 5,000; if the project *had* been occupied, its residents could not have been sorted out from the total population anyway). The redrawn tract boundaries of 1930 isolate the project population. In 1930 Garden Homes was the only built-up section of tract 653, and it appears that the census enumerators skipped over most of the fifteen or so dwellings scattered through the parts of the census tract outside the project and counted the occupants of Garden Homes as virtually the whole tract population (i.e., the project had 175 houses, and the returns showed 175 "families" in 175 "homes" or "dwellings," while voters' lists and a street directory showed other occupied houses in the area). The 1930 census figures, then, describe the Garden Homes population exactly, or nearly so. I have taken the characteristics of the 1930 population *as if* they applied to the group that settled Garden Homes in 1920–21. Interviews with original settlers indicate that the two populations were similar, except that the original group may have had a higher proportion of natives, Protestants, and white-collar workers. The March 1921 voters' registration list for Ward 9, Precinct 9, which included the project area, showed voters from only 63 Garden Homes addresses (the lists are filed with the City of Chicago Board of Election Commissioners, City Hall, Chicago). I looked up their previous addresses in the Chicago and suburban telephone directories for 1919 and 1920. The 63 addresses constitute a crude 36 percent sample of the project. None of the people whose previous addresses are listed came from the Back a' the Yards, South Chicago, the Hull-House area, or any other of the main settlement house neighborhoods. There were people from suburban Joliet, Aurora, Algonquin, and LaGrange, however. The leading neighborhoods of origin were Englewood, Woodlawn, Hyde Park, Park Manor, Kenwood, South Shore, Grand Boulevard, and Washington Park, all on the South Side; there were people from the far North Side and the far West Side as well. Three of the original settlers' families I interviewed were not on this 1921 list: one came in flight from within the Black Belt, the other two from Englewood, on the Black Belt's border.

26. Burgess and Newcomb, *Census Data, 1930,* tables 9, 2 and 3. All 175 household heads were white, but 2 of the 862 people living in the census tract were Negroes, both of them middle-aged women (table 1, p. 133). They may have lived in Garden Homes as domestics or nurses, or they might have occupied one or two of the houses outside the project. The enumerators counted only occupied dwellings; if two of the project houses were vacant, the enumerators could have counted two off-project occupied houses without affecting the total 175 "homes" or "dwellings" in the tract. Whoever these black women

were, wherever they stayed, they were gone by 1934, when the tract numbered 855 people, every one of them white. See Charles S. Newcomb and Richard O. Lang, *Census Data of the City of Chicago, 1934* (Chicago, 1934), table 4. Interviews with three original settlers, two Catholic, one Protestant. One of the Catholics thought that the Protestant percentage was 90 or higher, the other one was sure that there were always 30 to 35 Catholic families and "half a dozen or eight lovely Jewish families." The Protestant woman concurred with the latter estimate.

27. "Chicago's Housing Needs," *Housing Betterment* 10 (April 1924): 94; Rosenthal to Rosenwald, 18 June and 29 August 1919, and 8 December 1922, Rosenwald Papers; Rosenthal, "To the Stockholders of Chicago Real Estate Improvement Corporation," 13 November 1922, ibid.; William Graves to J. Ogden Armour, William Wrigley, Jr., Albert D. Lasker, and Harold H. Swift, 24 December 1924, ibid.; Graves memorandum, "RE Chicago Real Estate Improvement Corporation and Chicago Housing Association," 20 September 1926, ibid.

28. Rosenthal to Rosenwald, 8 December 1922; Articles of Agreement for 8855 Wabash, dated 1 September 1922, Garden Homes files; Certificates of Valuation by the Chicago Real Estate Board, No. 2448 (8759 Wabash), and No. 2449 (8749 Michigan), both dated 24 October 1922, ibid.; interview with original settlers.

29. Ibid. "We often bless him," another settler said of Rosenthal. For Lilydale, see ch. 8 supra, and Chicago Commission on Race Relations, *The Negro in Chicago: A Study of Race Relations and a Race Riot* (Chicago, 1922), pp. 108, 224–25.

30. All the householders and their spouses are listed in *Polk's Chicago Street and Avenue Guide and Directory of Householders, 1928–1929* (Chicago, 1928), which lists addresses street by street, house by house, and gives the name of the occupants. Only 37 of the 63 households from the March 1921 voters' registration list are shown at Garden Homes addresses in 1928; the other 26 (41 percent) are gone. In the special census of 1934, for the first time, enumerators asked families how long they had been living at their present residence. Only 48 percent of the Garden Homes families had lived there as long as ten years; from 1924 to 1934 there was a net turnover of 52 percent (Newcomb and Lang, table 2, p. 233). Comparison of voters' registration lists for March 1921 (Ward 9, Precinct 9), October 1926 and February 1927 (Ward 8, Precinct 49), and October 1932 (Ward 19, Precinct 56) indicates that many settlers who came after 1920–21 left within a few years. Interviews with original settlers and other early settlers gave evidence of the turnover as well as of community spirit.

31. Interviews with original settlers and other early settlers. One of the original settlers said, "Everybody loved everybody else. And if you ever needed to borrow anything, why, you could ask anybody, and they'd give it to you."

32. Chicago Title and Trust Co., title search reports, and Chicago Real Estate Index Co., statements of taxes and special assessments, Garden Homes files; interview with an original settler; *Polk's Chicago Street and Avenue Guide; Olcott's*, 1927 through 1929.

33. Document 10563434, Book 27945, pp. 175–204, dated 1 November 1927, recorded 30 December 1929, *Records of Cook County, Deeds,* in Cook County Recorder's office.

34. Chicago Urban League, mimeographed "working paper" titled "Reported Incidents of Racial Violence in Chicago in 1956 and 1957," n.p., n.d., p. 22. The arson occurred on 25 April 1956.

CHAPTER 11 THE HOUSING COMMISSION AND THE DUAL PROGRAM

1. "Public Committee of Fifty on Housing," printed circular, 31 November 1921, and "Public Committee of 50 on Housing," typed draft, n.d., Graham Taylor Papers, Newberry Library, Chicago. All fifty were white. Most were Protestant, but there were several Catholic and Jewish members.

2. Lloyd Lewis and Henry Justin Smith, *Chicago. The History of Its Reputation* (New York, 1929), p. 140; Chicago Plan Commission, *Annual Report,* 1933, p. 1527; "Millions for Home-Building," in *Chicago—America's Greatest Most Attractive City Burned 1871—Rebuilt as by Magic. Now Her Reconstruction Plan* (Chicago, n.d.), pp. 99–100, 104. The section on Garden Homes in the brochure was an uncredited reprint of John E. McEldowney's article in *Real Estate News* 14 (October 1919): 1–7, cited in ch. 10, supra.

3. Alderman Schwartz's speech cited in Chicago Commission on Race Relations, *The Negro in Chicago: A Study of Race Relations and a Race Riot* (Chicago, 1922), p. 210, hereafter cited as Riot Commission. See also the comments of a South Side realtor, ibid., p. 206. Charles H. Wacker, "The South Side and the Chicago Plan," *Chicago Realtor* 26 (February 1923): 5–6, 23.

4. Mel Scott, *American City Planning Since 1890* (Berkeley, 1969), pp. 210–211; "Chicago's Remarkable Achievements," *Housing* 17 (October 1928): 151–54; Eugene S. Taylor, manager, Chicago Plan Commission, to Ernest W. Burgess, chairman, Chicago Census Committee, 10 June 1929, Ernest W. Burgess Papers, UCL.

5. Jacob L. Crane, Jr., "Tentative Zone Plans, Zoning Questions and Answers," *Chicago Realtor* 25 (September 1922): 15–16.

6. Edward M. Bassett's remarks at the 1919 conference, quoted in Charles M. Nichols, "A Good Job of Zoning Will Do Wonders for Chicago," *Chicago Realtor* 25 (May 1922): 9; "The City Club and Zoning," *City Club Bulletin* 12 (22 December 1919): 249–50, and "The Zoning of Cities," ibid., 253–56; Chicago Zoning Commission, *Tentative Report and a Proposed Zoning Ordinance for the City of Chicago* (Chicago, 1923).

7. Crane, Jr., pp. 15–16; Report of Alderman Arthur G. Lindell, in Minutes of the Chicago Recreation Commission, 10 June 1943, copy in files of Chicago Housing Authority, Chicago; Metropolitan Housing Council, "Zoning and Zoning Administration in Chicago," unpublished report, 1 July 1938, in files of Metropolitan Housing and Planning Council, Chicago.

8. Zoning maps in *Chicago Zoning Ordinance with Amendments Up to and Including July 1, 1924* (Chicago, 1924), and in *Olcott's* after 1923.

9. Realtors' report cited in Elizabeth A. Hughes, *Living Conditions for Small-Wage Earners in Chicago* (Chicago, 1925), p. 17.
10. Population estimates in Homer Hoyt, *One Hundred Years of Land Values in Chicago* (Chicago, 1933), table 93, p. 483.
11. Alice Quan Rood, "Social Conditions among the Negroes on Federal Street between Forty-fifth Street and Fifty-third Street" (M.A. thesis, University of Chicago, 1924), p. 4; Edith Abbott, *The Tenements of Chicago, 1908–1935* (Chicago, 1936), presents findings from both the earlier and the later surveys, pp. 120–26 and passim.
12. Rood, p. 4; Alzada P. Comstock, "Chicago Housing Conditions, VI: The Problem of the Negro," *AJS* 18 (September 1912): 247–48; Rood, pp. 15–49.
13. Ibid., ff. p. 20. The first photograph, without the caption, is reprinted in Abbott, facing p. 124. Rood, ff. p. 23. This second photograph, without the caption, is reprinted in Abbott, facing p. 222. The other picture on the page is also by Rood. The last quote from Rood is on p. 50.
14. Abbott; see especially Esther Crockett Quaintance, "Rents and Housing Conditions in the Italian District of the Lower North Side of Chicago, 1924" (M.A. thesis, University of Chicago, 1925).
15. Albert P. Allen, "Chicago's Housing Problem," report to Chicago Housing Commission, 14 July 1927, citing Illinois Bell Telephone Co. surveys, in Taylor Papers; Hughes, pp. 3, 45; Abbott, pp. 303–10; see also Leila Houghteling, *The Income and Standard of Living of Unskilled Laborers in Chicago* (Chicago, 1927), pp. 24–86, and Hughes, pp. 44–48. One early statement of the rule of thumb is in E. R. L. Gould, *The Housing of the Working People. Eighth Special Report of the Commissioner of Labor* (Washington, 1895), p. 422.
16. Hughes, pp. 14–38, 40–43, 59.
17. Ibid., pp. 15–16, 39.
18. Mary McDowell, "Housing," typed excerpt from a University of Chicago Settlement annual report dated 31 May 1921, Mary McDowell Papers, CHS; Hughes, pp. 3–4, 39–43, 58–61.
19. Chicago *Evening Post,* 31 March 1926, clipping in William Dever Papers, CHS; *Daily News,* 17 March 1926, clipping in ibid.; *Tribune,* 11 April 1926, clipping in ibid.
20. *Daily News,* 11 April 1926, article based on press releases issued before the conference, clipping in ibid.; Willoughby Walling, conference chairman, to Mayor William E. Dever, 11 May 1926, ibid.; Joseph Brittain, quoted in *Tribune,* 11 April 1926.
21. Mayor William E. Dever, "To the Honorable, the City Council of Chicago," copy of request for authority to appoint a commission, 12 May 1926, Dever Papers; roster of members on Chicago Housing Commission stationery, copies in Taylor Papers. There is an incomplete list of members on a sheet titled "Chicago Housing Commission," n.d., McDowell Papers. William Zelosky, address at Chicago Housing Commission meeting, 3 December 1926, Taylor Papers.

22. Letters of Alfred Stern to Dever, Dever Papers, and Stern to Taylor, Taylor Papers. The incomplete list of members is the only item about the commission in Mary McDowell's Papers. The manuscripts of the other members of the commission are practically bare of materials on the commission. I found nothing in the Burgess Papers, the Agnes Nestor Papers, CHS, and the Edith Abbott Papers, UCL; there are a few items in the Victor Olander Papers, UHC.

23. Joseph K. Brittain, address at opening meeting of Chicago Housing Commission, "outlining a possible procedure for the Commission," n.d. [3 August 1926], Taylor Papers; Alfred Stern to Taylor, 22 December 1926 and 21 January 1927, ibid.; William Zelosky, addresses at meeting of 3 December 1926; Allen, "Chicago's Housing Problem."

24. "Our Legislative Activities at Springfield," *Chicago Realtor* 40 (August 1927): 15; "Real Estate Improvement Corporation Powers Are Enlarged: Home Building Made Easier," ibid., 40 (August 1927): 24; Stern to Taylor, 3 June 1927 and Taylor to William Zelosky, 7 June 1927, Taylor Papers; Stern to Dever, 3 June 1927, and Dever to Stern, 4 June 1927, Dever Papers.

25. Chicago *Evening Post,* 9 May 1927, clipping, Taylor Papers; *Daily News,* 1 July 1927, clipping, Dever Papers; "Real Estate Improvement Corporation Powers Are Enlarged."

26. *Evening Post,* 19 May 1927; *Daily News,* 1 July 1927; "Real Estate Improvement Corporation Powers Are Enlarged."

27. Stern to Dever, 21 July 1927, Dever Papers; Stern to Taylor, 21 July 1927, Taylor Papers; Stern to Dever, 1 July 1927, and enclosed memorandum, Dever Papers.

28. Interviews with Black Belt realtors and property owners in Robert Bussian and C. E. Wilson, "Study of an Area in Transition," student paper, March 1930, Burgess Papers, pp. 12, 23, 38 and 40; "Metropolitan Housing Association of Chicago," n.d., but marked "Received May 18, 1927," p. 2; in President's Papers, 1925–1945, University of Chicago Archives, UCL.

29. Ibid., pp. 1–3, 7.

30. Ibid., pp. 1, 3–4.

31. Ibid., pp. 5–7; N. Max Dunning to Max Mason, 3 June 1927, University of Chicago President's Papers.

32. The square block was one of four in Comstock's study. For the selection of public housing sites in Chicago see Martin Meyerson and Edward C. Banfield, *Politics, Planning and the Public Interest: The Case of Public Housing in Chicago* (Glencoe, 1955), and *Gautreaux v. Chicago Housing Authority,* United States District Court, E.D.N.D. Illinois, 1969. 296 F. Supp. 907.

33. "Metropolitan Housing Association of Chicago," pp. 5–6, and three architect's drawings, attached. Edith Elmer Wood, *Recent Trends in American Housing* (New York, 1931), p. 234, refers to the "Marshall Field Estate houses for white families and the Julius Rosenwald houses for Negroes."

34. Riot Commission, pp. 642–53, mentioned Rosenwald's contributions to schools "for Negroes" and YMCA branches "for Negroes" favorably. Critical blacks are cited in Allan H. Spear, *Black Chicago: The Making of a Negro Ghetto, 1890–1920* (Chicago, 1967), pp. 62, 100, and 197. Darrow's speech was reported in the *Broad Ax,* 30 April 1927.

35. Edwin R. Embree, *Julius Rosenwald Fund: A Review to June 30, 1929* (Chicago, 1929).

36. Stern, "Decent Housing for Negroes: A Demonstration in Chicago of the Possibility of Making Negro Housing a Large-Scale Business Enterprise," *American City* 40 (March 1929): 102–3; Embree, p. 29; *Michigan Boulevard Garden Apartments* (Chicago, March 1930), brochure in Ferdinand Barnett Papers, CHS; "Chicago Builds Model Tenements," *Housing* 17 (September 1928): 194–96.

37. T. V. Smith and Leonard D. White, eds., *Chicago: An Experiment in Social Science Research* (Chicago, 1929), pp. 195, 206; Stern, "Decent Housing for Negroes," p. 102; "Chicago Builds Model Tenements," pp. 197–98; *Defender,* 14 July 1928.

38. "Chicago Builds Model Tenements," pp. 195–97; Stern, "Decent Housing for Negroes," pp. 102–3; John M. Gries and James Ford, eds., *Publications of the President's Conference on Home Building and Home Ownership,* 11 vols. (Washington, 1932), vol. 3, *Slums, Large-Scale Housing, and Decentralization,* pp. 83–84, 103.

39. "Chicago Builds Model Tenements," pp. 195–97; Stern, "Decent Housing for Negroes," pp. 102–3; "The Negro Coming into His Own," *Housing* 18 (June 1929): 110–13; Gries and Ford, eds., vol. 6, *Negro Housing,* pp. 105–7; "Modern Housing for Negroes Brings Gratifying Results," *American City* 43 (May 1931): 151; *Michigan Boulevard Garden Apartments; Five Year Report of the Michigan Boulevard Garden Apartments Building Corporation* (Chicago, 1935), pp. 4–11.

40. For the Paul Laurence Dunbar Apartments in Harlem, see James Ford et al., *Slums and Housing,* 2 vols. (Cambridge, 1936), II, 742–48; "Chicago Builds Model Tenements," pp. 196–97; *Five Year Report of the Michigan Boulevard Garden Apartments Building Corporation,* p. 24.

41. Stern, "Decent Housing for Negroes," p. 103; "Chicago Builds Model Tenements," pp. 195–96.

42. Ibid., 197–98; Howard Wood, "Chicago Points Way to Slum Clearance: Private Initiative Paves Way for Rehabilitation," Chicago *Sunday Tribune Magazine,* 14 August 1938, copy of article in Lea Taylor Papers, CHS.

43. *Defender,* 14 July 1928; interview with Mrs. Dorothy Taylor, widow of Robert Taylor, manager of Rosenwald Gardens, 31 August 1966; Wood, pp. 234–36.

44. Ibid.; Hughes, p. 32. Mary McDowell, "Hovels or Homes," *Opportunity* 7 (March 1929): 74–77, 100.

45. Embree, p. 29.

46. *Defender,* 14 July 1928 and 19 January 1929. Architectural historian Carl W. Condit has written that the pleasant, thoughtful design of the buildings (despite the five flights of stairs), combined with careful maintenance, "gave them a human quality that later projects usually lacked." Condit, *Chicago, 1930–1970. Building, Planning, and Urban Technology* (Chicago, 1974), pp. 37–38.

47. *Defender,* 19 January 1929; Mrs. Anna B. Wilson to Julius Rosenwald, 10 July 1928, Rosenwald Papers.

48. Robert R. Taylor to Edith Elmer Wood, 4 March 1931, cited in Wood, p. 236; "Good Housing at a Profit: Model Apartments for Negroes One Hundred Per Cent Rented," *American City* 41 (October 1929): 161. Probably most of the married women in the project worked to help pay the rent. One of two nursery schools run by the management was open from 7:30 A.M. to 6:30 P.M. to accommodate "the mother who works." The apartments were "designed to reduce the drudgery of housework, thereby releasing the housewife for lucrative employment." See *Michigan Boulevard Garden Apartments,* n.p.

49. *Five Year Report of the Michigan Boulevard Garden Apartments Corporation,* p. 10; "Rosenwald Garden Apartments Huge Success," ANP Bulletin, 1 October 1930; Robert R. Taylor, "A Demonstration in Modern Housing," *Opportunity* 9 (March 1931): 83–84; "Modern Housing for Negroes Brings Gratifying Results." The two black men who became directors were Perry Parker, president of the Pullman Porters' Benefit Association, and George R. Arthur, executive secretary of the Wabash Avenue YMCA. The other directors were "outstanding financiers and business men": Edward C. Brown of the First National Bank; E. J. Buffington of Illinois Steel Co.; Rosenwald; Stern; George Richardson of the Field Estate; Willoughby Walling of Personal Loan and Savings Bank; Charles Swift of Swift and Co.; B. F. Lindheimer, a realtor and lawyer; and Hugo Sonnenschein, a lawyer. Seven other white men were directors while the project was in the building stage: a lawyer, an architect, a manufacturer, two bankers, a realtor, and Lloyd Steere, business manager of the University of Chicago. Ironically, it was during the project's first year of operation that Rosenwald chose to withdraw his support from the Chicago Urban League, a decision which crippled the league and, coupled with Alfred Stern's efforts to get all other major white contributors to stop their donations, nearly killed it. See Arvarh E. Strickland, *History of the Chicago Urban League* (Urbana, Ill., 1966), pp. 97–103. Rosenwald's "faith in the Negro" was nothing to take for granted.

50. "Chicago Builds Model Tenements," p. 195; Harvey Warren Zorbaugh, *The Gold Coast and the Slum* (Chicago, 1929), pp. 1–16, 43–45, 127–29, 140–81; Louis Wirth and Eleanor H. Bernert, eds., *Local Community Fact Book of Chicago* (Chicago, 1949), community area 8, Near North Side.

51. Zorbaugh, pp. 147–48, 164, 180; Documents 11706997 and 12031063, dated 1 November 1933, restrictive covenants to which Olivet Institute settlement house was a party, cited in Minutes of Special Meeting of the Board of Trustees of Olivet Institute, 29 September 1939, in Olivet Community Center

Papers, CHS; form letter of the Near North Side Property Owners' Association, 18 February 1936, and enclosed street-by-street "report of progress" on "the restriction work," CHS; Wood, p. 234. See ch. 14, "The Color Line in Neighborhood Work," below.

52. Wood, p. 235; Ford et al., II, 690; Gries and Ford, eds., vol. 3, p. 103.

53. Brittain address, p. 2; Stern, "Decent Housing for Negroes," p. 103.

54. *The Chicago Whip,* 9 May 1931.

55. McNeal, quoted in *Defender,* 8 July 1933; *Five Year Report of the Michigan Boulevard Garden Apartments Corporation,* p. 18. By 1934 there were only 150 children in the 421-flat project, and 65 percent of the tenants had roomers.

56. The number of foreclosures in Chicago rose from 3,148 in 1929 to 5,818 in 1930, reached 10,075 in 1931, and hit a peak of 15,201 the next year (Hoyt, pp. 269–70). From 1929 on, bailiffs evicted an increasing number of families. The peak year was 1932, with 3,947 evictions carried through. The number of people who waited for the bailiffs to put them out of their apartments was small compared to the number who waited until the last day and moved themselves out. In 1932 the municipal court issued 63,152 eviction writs. For the evictions, see Abbott, pp. 433–35.

57. St. Clair Drake and Horace Cayton, *Black Metropolis* (New York, 1945), pp. 85–87; Abbott, pp. 442–43; Paul E. Baker, *Negro-White Adjustment* (New York, 1934), pp. 106–9; *Tribune,* 4 August 1931.

PART IV THE NEIGHBORHOOD ROLE OF THE SETTLEMENTS

1. *All Souls Church and the Abraham Lincoln Centre Year Book,* 1920, p. 24; Statement of Purpose, Northwestern University Settlement, in Robert A. Woods and Albert J. Kennedy, *Handbook of Settlements* (New York, 1911), p. 66; Statement of Purpose, Henry Booth House, ibid., pp. 52–53.

2. Chicago Commission on Race Relations, *The Negro in Chicago: A Study of Race Relations and a Race Riot* (Chicago, 1922), pp. 55, 659, and map ff. p. 8.

3. Ibid., pp. 50–51, 643–44; Chicago *Daily News,* 15 April 1920, cited in Negro in Illinois; LCRC, "History of Woodlawn Community, Chicago," 1927–28, Doc. 4, CHS.

CHAPTER 12 "BUILDING BETTER THAN WE KNOW": THE SETTLEMENTS AND THE ETHNIC ENCLAVES

1. Jacob Riis, *The Children of the Poor* (New York, 1892; reprint ed., edited and abridged by Francesco Cordasco as part of *Jacob Riis Revisited: Poverty and the Slum in Another Era,* Garden City, N.Y., 1968), p. 130.

2. C. J. Atkinson, "Starting the Boys Right," speech printed in *City Club Bulletin* 12 (2 June 1919): 13; Chicago *Daily News,* 22 October 1919, MRL clipping.

3. Mrs. E. E. Smith, in *The Abraham Lincoln Centre All Souls Church Reports* for 1915, pp. 39 and 43.

4. Jane Addams and Mary McDowell, testifying on the politicians and "the boy problem," in Chicago Commission on Race Relations, *The Negro in Chicago: A Study of Race Relations and a Race Riot* (Chicago, 1922), p. 55, hereafter cited as Riot Commission; Frederic M. Thrasher, *The Gang: A Study of 1,313 Gangs in Chicago* (Chicago, 1927; rev. ed., 1936), pp. 452–61.

5. Ibid., pp. 234–39, 268–69, and caption under photograph, p. 459; "Stag Parties," *Juvenile Protection Association Bulletin* 3 (May 1921); Anna Zaloha, "Girls' Work 1931–1932," typed report, pp. 5–6, describing gang rapes committed near Chicago Commons by "more or less organized groups of boys and men," Chicago Commons Papers, CHS.

6. Thrasher, pp. 458–60; Riot Commission, pp. 12–14, 54–55.

7. "The Moving Picture Show," *Vigilance* 25 (April 1912): 20–21; Terry Ramsaye, *A Million and One Nights: A History of the Motion Picture* (New York, 1926), pp. 473–76; Jane Addams, *Twenty Years at Hull-House* (New York, 1910), p. 386; Addams, *The Spirit of Youth and the City Streets* (New York, 1912), ch. 4, "The House of Dreams."

8. Louise de Koven Bowen, *Five and Ten Cent Theaters: Two Investigations by the Juvenile Protective Association of Chicago, 1909 and 1911* (Chicago, n.d.), n.p.; Clarence G. Baker, "Chicago Churches Helping the Needy" (M.A. thesis, University of Chicago, 1914), p. 3; *Lakeside Directory,* 1909 through 1914; an untitled list of Chicago movie theaters, dated May 1916, in Ernest W. Burgess Papers, UCL; Addams, *Spirit of Youth,* ch. 4; Addams, *Twenty Years,* p. 386; Albert W. Webster, *Junk Dealing and Juvenile Delinquency* (Chicago, n.d. [1918]), pp. 16–18; interviews with children attending social settlements, Burgess Papers. In 1914 the *Lakeside Directory* listed 380 "5 and 10 cent theaters," but Baker counted 703 in operation. The list in the Burgess Papers is arranged by wards and, within wards, by streets. It gives the name, address, and seating capacity of 498 theaters. These shows had 224,233 seats, or about one for every two children between the ages of five and fifteen. The tenement wards had more than their share of cheap shows. Webster, an investigator for the Juvenile Protective Agency, found that getting money for the movies was the main reason that "slum" boys resorted to stealing (of 100 juvenile offenders he interviewed, 62 said that they stole because they needed money for the show). Politicians treated boys to the show to curry their favor. Only 11 of the 100 boys Webster talked to "frequented" a settlement house or a supervised boys' club. But all of them attended the movies regularly, at least once a week. Many claimed that they went every day, and several admitted to attending several times a day. Managers in the poorer neighborhoods usually let two kids in for the price of one at the last show of the day. The settlement-house children whom Burgess's students interviewed went to the show just as frequently as the "delinquent boys" in Baker's study. City children in the period 1905–1925 had as much exposure to movies as children in the period 1950 to 1970 had to television.

9. Thrasher, ch. 6, "The Movies and the Dime Novel"; Ernest W. Burgess, "Urban Areas," in *Chicago: An Experiment in Social Science Research,* ed. T. V. Smith and Leonard D. White (Chicago, 1929), p. 127; Burgess, "Studies of Institutions," ibid., pp. 163–70; Chicago Recreation Commission, *The Chicago Recreation Survey, 1937* (Chicago, 1938–39), vol. 2, *Commercial Recreation,* pp. 28–32.

10. Jessie F. Binford, *Annual Report of the Juvenile Protective Association of Chicago for 1926,* pp. 7–8; see also F. Zeta Youmans, "Opportunity Night," *Survey. Graphic Number* 58 (1 September 1927): 485–88.

11. Bowen, *Our Most Popular Recreation Controlled by the Liquor Interests: A Study of Public Dance Halls* (Chicago, 1911), n.p.; Addams, *Twenty Years,* pp. 34–50; Chicago Recreation Commission, 2: 136–39; Burgess, "Urban Areas," p. 127; Burgess, "Studies of Institutions," pp. 163–70.

12. Pat Ireland, "Factors in the Americanization of a Second Generation of Immigrant People," MS. prepared as an M.A. thesis for the University of Chicago, August 1932, but never submitted, in possession of Mr. Ireland, pp. 162–83.

13. Ibid., pp. 5–6.

14. Emil De Julio, "To the 1928–29 Joint Council," report, 15 May 1928, on the development of the Shy Kom Dance, Commons Papers; copy of flyer, ibid.

15. Graham Taylor, form letter, n.d. [1919], Commons Papers; Taylor to J. S. Cornelius, 10 October 1921, ibid.; Taylor to Rev. H. K. Booth, 3 October 1921, ibid.; series of three maps of "Constructive and Destructive Agencies" in the Chicago Commons ward (it was the Seventeenth before 1921, the Thirty-first after), dated 1912, 1921, and 1926, and untitled maps for 1921 showing "independently organized boys' clubs" and "poolrooms," Commons Papers. The "constructive agencies" are settlements, schools, churches, parks and playgrounds; the "destructive agencies" are saloons, "5¢ shows," other "theaters," poolrooms, clubrooms, and dance halls. In 1912 the destructive agencies outnumbered the constructive ones 270 to 37. By 1925, largely because of Prohibition, the ratio was down to 54:28. For membership figures see Boys' Department records, 1920–1928, and maps "Registration of Chicago Commons 1921–1922 Before Ogden Ave." and "Chicago Commons Registration 1924–5, After Ogden," Commons Papers. (Ogden Avenue was a new street which cut diagonally through the built-up neighborhood.)

16. Thrasher, pp. 34, 95, 175; typed report with handwritten title, "Assault on *Worker* CC," 4 February 1927, Commons Papers; letters of Lea Taylor to Captain Joseph Palczynsky of the Racine Avenue Police Station, 7 and 25 November 1930 and 10 November 1932 reporting thefts and vandalism and requesting special police protection for the settlement's building and grounds, ibid.

17. Thrasher, p. 85.

18. Leader of Black Pirates, "Club Leader's Report," March 1926–May 1926, n.p., Commons Papers; Chester Curtis Scott, "A Study of the Boys' Work Program of a Social Settlement in Its Relation to Delinquency" (M.A. thesis, University of Chicago, 1929), pp. 85–88; Margaret Artman, "Observations on the Causes for the Prevalence of Delinquency among the Children of Immigrants in the City Slum," student paper, December 1931, p. 37, Burgess Papers.

19. Ibid., pp. 1–2; Joe Rago, Secretary, "Minutes of the Lighting Athletic Club," 24 February 1921 to 8 May 1922, Commons Papers; Emil De Julio, president of Chicago Commons Boys' Council, to Lea Taylor, 24 November 1926, ibid.; Karl Borders, "Annual Report Boys Dept. 1928–1929," n.p., ibid.; Borders, "Boys' Department Annual Report 1927–28," p. 3, ibid.

20. Borders, "Annual Report Boys Dept. 1928–1929," n.p.; "Excluded from all activities at Chicago Commons," two lists containing ten names, 1927, Commons Papers; "Boys expelled Oct. 1931 . . . ," ibid.; numerous letters of Lea Taylor to expelled boys and to their parents, 1926, ibid. The quote is from one of these letters, Lea Taylor to Vito Partipilo, 16 October 1928.

21. Norman B. Barr to James B. Forgan, 9 July 1920, Commons Papers; Bernice Davida Davis, "Housing Conditions in the District of Burnside" (M.A. thesis, University of Chicago, 1924), pp. 6–10.

22. Robert C. Jones and Louis R. Wilson, *The Mexican in Chicago* (Chicago, 1931), p. 10; Addams, *The Second Twenty Years at Hull-House* (New York, 1930), pp. 282–83.

23. Florence Lyon Gaddis, "Conflict between Mexicans and Poles (Living near Ashland Ave. and 45th St.)," student paper, autumn 1928, pp. 4–7 and 9, Burgess Papers.

24. Thrasher, pp. 191–94.

25. Addams, *Twenty Years,* p. 312; Taylor, remarks in "Report of the Eighth Conference of the National Federation of Settlements," 1918, typescript, p. 8, Commons Papers; Taylor, *Chicago Commons through Forty Years* (Chicago, 1936), p. 252.

26. "Warden's Report of the Work of Chicago Commons for the year ending September 30, 1920," p. 5, Commons Papers, hereafter cited as Commons Report; Committee of the Chicago Federation of Settlements, *The Administration and Activities of Chicago Settlements* (Boston, 1921). A 1925 survey of settlement hiring policies revealed that 3 percent of Chicago's settlement staff members came "from neighborhood": see "Questionaire [sic] Staff Training, Experience and Salaries . . . Sent out in March 1925, by the Chicago Federation of Settlements," p. 1, Commons Papers.

27. Notes taken by Duane Van Dyke Ramsey at the meeting, reproduced in Ramsey, "A Comparative Study of Social Settlements, Neighborhood Houses, and Institutional Churches" (M.A. thesis, University of Chicago, 1929), p. 118.

28. Taylor, *Chicago Commons through Forty Years,* pp. 173–78.

29. William J. Blackburn, "Brief Report on the Organization, Program and Services of the University of Chicago Settlement for the Year 1927–28," n.d., typed report, p. 31, Mary McDowell Papers, CHS.

30. Ibid., *SSD,* 1939, pp. 56–57.

31. Minutes of Committee to Study the Significance of the Back of the Yards Neighborhood Council, 29 April 1942, p. 3, Welfare Council of Metropolitan Chicago Papers, CHS.

32. Harvey Warren Zorbaugh, *The Gold Coast and the Slum* (Chicago, 1929), pp. 204–20.

33. Ibid., pp. 195–99, 215–18, 220.

34. Ibid., p. 178, note 2.

35. [Glenford Lawrence], "Men's Annual Report 1921–2," pp. 3–9, Commons Papers, hereafter cited as Men's Report; Lawrence, Men's Report, 1925, n.p.

36. Commons Report, 1921, p. 2; ibid., 1926, p. 1; ibid., 1929, p. 6; Graham Taylor to Chicago Commons Trustees, 17 March 1926, Commons Papers; Taylor to Jane Addams, 26 September 1929, ibid.; John M. Allswang, *A House for All Peoples: Ethnic Politics in Chicago 1890–1936* (Lexington, 1971), pp. 125, 134–35; Taylor, *Chicago Commons through Forty Years*, p. 71; Taylor to William C. Boyden, 13 March 1923, Commons Papers; *CDNA*, 1924, p. 739.

37. For Ungaro see Taylor, *Chicago Commons through Forty Years*, p. 300 and *Who's Who*, 1936; Commons Report, 1925, p. 1; *CDNA*, 1926, p. 815; *Chicago Telephone Directory*, 1926. Ungaro moved to 7131 W. Altgeld Avenue, 2 1/2 miles north and 8 miles west of the Commons. His new home was within a block of the city limits.

38. Allswang, pp. 125–26, 144–46, 161, 194–95; Humbert S. Nelli, *Italians in Chicago, 1880–1930: A Study in Ethnic Mobility* (New York, 1970), pp. 228–31; Commons Report, 1925, p. 1; ibid., 1927, p. 2; *CDNA*, 1928, p. 767. Allswang and Nelli both use sample precincts from the Thirty-first Ward around the Commons.

39. Taylor to Mrs. R. W. MacDonald, 23 February 1928, Graham Taylor Papers, Newberry Library, Chicago; Taylor, "The House and the Neighborhood," *NCH*, 1917, pp. 306–7; Taylor, remarks at Eighth Conference of National Federation of Settlements, p. 7. Karl Borders, the head boys' worker, complained of a group which had been connected with the Commons for several years. "The more ambitious and higher grade boys" had moved on, "leaving a disgruntled and low grade type of boy with little or no constructive interest of any kind." The remnant became "so destructive" that Borders had to bar them from the house "with police officers present to back up the decree." They served their probation period in a "friendly" manner, and so were entitled to request readmission. Borders hoped they would not do it. "I am afraid they are practically hopeless," he wrote. See Borders, "Annual Report Boys Dept. 1928–1929," n.p.

40. Chicago Commons Inactive File, Case No. 8 (case numbers assigned by United Charities), an Italian family, Commons Papers. In eight encounters the staff found the family spelling its last name four different ways. The staff contacted the family in 1931 at the 1930 address. Between 1936 and 1942 the staff encountered the family four more times; each time the people had a different address, the last of which was one block away from the flat they had occupied twenty-eight years earlier. I use this family as an example here because it is the oldest case in the records, covering more years than the others. There are several cases which are more striking, e.g., Case No. 1165, a Polish-Italian family whom the staff checked on eight times between 1928 and 1932 at eight addresses, or Case No. 978, a Polish family whom the staff contacted seven times, at seven addresses, from 1921 to 1930—four occasions were in one year, two were in one month, and the family used at least five spellings of its name.

41. Scott, p. 68; D. Otto Nall to Ernest W. Burgess, 4 June 1932, Burgess Papers. Nall plotted the residences of boys' club members on a series of maps; he was unable to show the members of the two most active clubs, the Lightnings and the Adelphis, on the community maps, because they lived so far away. In preparation for the Commons' fortieth anniversary celebration in 1934, the staff and volunteers took old club membership lists and tried to locate the former members. In most cases, even with the clubs from the twenties, only one or two members were still living in the neighborhood. The lists are in the Commons Papers.

42. "Housing Survey in the Italian District of the Seventeenth Ward," *First Semi-annual Report of the Department of Public Welfare to the Mayor and Aldermen of the City of Chicago* (Chicago, 1915), p. 89; Nelli, pp. 47–51.

43. Taylor to Edward L. Ryerson, 13 March 1919, Commons Papers; Taylor, *Chicago Commons through Forty Years,* p. 278. There were rarely more than thirty members in residence; in some years there were fewer than twenty.

44. Taylor, *Chicago Commons through Forty Years,* pp. 248–300.

45. Newton Jenkins to Graham Taylor, 21 March 1933, reprinted in Taylor to Commons Trustees, 20 April 1933, Commons Papers; Taylor to Trustees, ibid.

46. Residents of Hull-House, *Hull-House Maps and Papers: A Presentation of Nationalities and Wages in a Congested District of Chicago* (New York, 1895), p. 96.

CHAPTER 13 SETTLEMENT WORKERS AND BLACKS: A "VALID DIFFERENCE"

1. Jane Addams, *Twenty Years at Hull-House* (New York, 1910), p. 37; Addams, "Has the Emancipation Proclamation Been Nullified by National Indifference?" *Survey* 29 (1 February 1913): 565–66.

2. Ibid. She repeated the same list, slightly altered, in *The Second Twenty Years at Hull-House* (New York, 1930), p. 399.

3. Addams, "Has the Emancipation Proclamation Been Nullified?" p. 566; Addams, "A Function of the Social Settlement," *Annals* 13 (May 1899): 336; Addams, *Second Twenty Years,* p. 396.

4. This is how Addams described the work of the Negro orphanage, where she worked in 1886: "They take little colored girls and keep them until they are fifteen, training them to be *good servants,* the children themselves expecting to be that and having an ambition for a good place. I heartily approve of the scheme." Addams to Alice Haldeman, 28 December 1886, Jane Addams Papers, Swarthmore College Peace Collection, cited in Daniel Levine, *Jane Addams and the Liberal Tradition* (Madison, Wis., 1971), p. 29. She also visited "a home for about 16 old colored women who are so interesting I mean to go there often." Addams correspondence cited in Allen F. Davis, *American Heroine: The Life and Legend of Jane Addams* (New York, 1973), p. 42. Ellen Gates Starr recalled that, whereas studying and socializing exhausted Addams in

Baltimore, "after a morning with the colored people in the Johns Hopkins home, she was actually physically better. . . ." Cited in ibid. Addams and Mary McDowell were among six white Chicagoans who answered the NAACP's "call." Two prominent ex-Chicagoans who were Hull-House alumnae, Florence Kelley and Lillian Wald, signed also. When the Progressive Party convention of 1912 excluded black delegations from the South, Miss Addams protested without success and "was assailed by the old familiar discomfort concerning the status of the colored man," but she stuck with the party and seconded the nomination of Theodore Roosevelt, who had supported the "lily-white" delegations. See Addams, "The Progressive Party and the Negro," *Crisis* 5 (November 1912): 30–31.

5. Sophonisba P. Breckenridge and Edith Abbott, *The Delinquent Child and the Home* (New York, 1912), pp. 55–56, 151–53; Breckenridge, "The Color Line in the Housing Problem," *Survey* 40 (1 February 1913): 575–76; Alzada P. Comstock, "Chicago Housing Conditions, VI: The Problem of the Negro," *AJS* 18 (September 1912): 241–57; Abbott, *The Tenements of Chicago, 1908–1935* (Chicago, 1936), pp. 117–26; Louise de Koven Bowen, *The Colored People of Chicago* (Chicago, 1913), n.p.; Mary McDowell, "Hovels or Homes?" *Opportunity* 7 (March 1929): 74–77, 100; McDowell, "How the Living Faith of One Social Worker Grew," *Survey* 60 (1 April 1928): 60.

6. Henry Bruère, "Industrial Education for Negroes," *Commons* 9 (December 1904): 612–14. For Bruère, see Davis, *Spearheads for Reform: The Social Settlements and the Progressive Movement, 1890–1914* (New York, 1967), pp. 185–86.

7. Bruère, pp. 613–14.

8. Ibid., pp. 612–14.

9. Graham Taylor, "The Southern Social Awakening," *Survey* 28 (14 September 1912): 744–45; Taylor, "Developing the American Spirit," in *America and the New Era*, ed. Elisia M. Friedman (New York, 1920), p. 234.

10. Reviewer [Taylor], "Two Significant Books," *Commons* 9 (May 1904): 222; Taylor, Warden's Report for the First Quarter of 1907, in Commons Trustees' Minutes, Commons Papers, CHS; Taylor, Warden's Reports for 1908 and 1920, ibid.

11. Reviewer [Taylor], "Two Significant Books"; Taylor, "The Riot in Lincoln's City," *Charities and the Commons* 20 (29 August 1908): 627–28.

12. Addams, *Second Twenty Years*, p. 397.

13. Ibid., pp. 397–98.

14. Ibid., p. 396; Taylor, "Riot in Lincoln's City," pp. 627–28.

15. Mary McDowell, cited in Steven J. Diner, "Chicago Social Workers and Blacks in the Progressive Era," *SSR* 44 (December 1970): 407; Addams, *Second Twenty Years*, p. 396.

16. Taylor, "Riot in Lincoln's City," p. 628; Taylor to James F. Basiger, 8 August 1919, Graham Taylor Papers, Newberry Library, Chicago; Bowen, n.p.; Addams, *Second Twenty Years*, p. 396.

17. Taylor to Basiger; Addams, *Second Twenty Years,* p. 407.

18. Caroline M. Hill, compiler, *Mary McDowell and Municipal Housekeeping: A Symposium* (Chicago, 1937), pp. 24–26.

19. Ibid.

20. See, for example, Diner, pp. 396–408, and Gilbert Osofsky, *Harlem: The Making of a Ghetto, 1890–1930* (New York, 1965), pp. 53–54, 67, 217, note 1. Davis takes this position in *Spearheads for Reform,* pp. 94–102, but modifies it in *American Heroine,* where he writes that Jane Addams "did not entirely avoid the racist attitudes of her day, but she came much closer to overcoming them than most of the reformers of her generation" (p. 129; see also p. 180). One of the white founders of the NAACP, the socialist William English Walling, did demand "absolute political and social equality" for blacks in his article "The Race War in the North," *Independent* 65 (3 September 1908): 529–34, written before the NAACP was formed. The NAACP never used such language in the period before 1930, because it connoted not only social integration generally but sexual intermingling; Walling never used it again either, at least in public. Davis, in *Spearheads for Reform,* pp. 100–102, documents the disappearance of the demand for social equality without comment. Louis T. Athey recounts the reaction of Florence Kelley to the Du Bois article in "Florence Kelley and the Quest for Negro Equality," *The Journal of Negro History* 56 (October 1971): 249–61. Years later Kelley apologized to Du Bois and said he had been right. In 1929 she refused to sponsor the housing experiments at Radburn, N.J., and Sunnyside, N.Y., because they excluded Negroes. Her fellow Hull-House alumna, Lillian Wald, also a charter member of the NAACP, endorsed the projects despite the "exclusion" policy. By 1930 Florence Kelley had reached the position that Clarence Darrow had been taking for decades, and like Darrow, she found herself out of step with most of her liberal allies. Mary McDowell's private sympathies were probably very close to the views that Darrow, and later Kelley, expressed, but she always moderated her public stance.

21. Robert W. Shufeldt, *The Negro: A Menace to American Civilization* (Boston, 1907); for Wilson, see Kathleen L. Wolgemuth, "Woodrow Wilson and Federal Segregation," *Journal of Negro History* 44 (January 1959): 158–73, and Henry Blumenthal, "Woodrow Wilson and the Race Question," ibid., 48 (January 1963): 1–21; for Roosevelt, see John D. Weaver, *The Brownsville Raid* (New York, 1970), pp. 140–42.

22. Bowen, n.p.

23. Irene Graham, "Six Months of the 'South Side Survey,' July 1 to December 20, 1930," p. 8, with records of Joint Committee on the Survey of Agencies Serving the Negro Community, in Julius Rosenwald Papers, UCL; "Report of Committee on South Side Survey of Social Agencies, Chicago, 1930," p. 2, hereafter cited as Survey of Agencies, ibid.

24. Survey of Agencies, pp. 2–5; Chicago Commission on Race Relations, *The Negro in Chicago: A Study in Race Relations and a Race Riot* (Chicago, 1922), pp. 231–56, 266–97, 334–43, 439–41, 613–19, hereafter cited as Riot Commission.

25. Survey of Agencies, pp. 2, 5, and table B, "Private Social Agencies, according to type of Service, Showing Percentage Serving Negroes," p. 4. According to the text, of 800 private agencies 261 were "accessible" to Negroes, but the figures in table B, when totaled, are 264 of 809. Among the 264 "accessible" agencies are 23 "serving Negroes, but less than one per cent," 18 whose service to Negroes was "indefinite" and could not "be measured," and an indefinite number "that have served a few Negroes in former years, but do not happen to have included any in 1929." The surveyors *exaggerated* accessibility and amount of service.

26. Ibid., pp. 2–7; lists of "Private Service Agencies Serving Negroes," "Private Agencies, White, Serving Both Races Together," and "Private Agencies Serving Negroes, Indefinite Type of Service, Can Not Be Measured," with materials of Survey of Agencies.

27. Lists of "Private Agencies, Refusing Service to Negroes" and "Private Agencies, White, Serving Both Races Together," ibid.; *SSD*, 1939, pp. 127 and 144. The Institute itself was on the second list, but its sanitarium was on the first. Hospitals were listed separately. Thirty of them expressly denied service to Negroes, and "38 hospitals not reporting," the surveyors believed, "almost certainly do not serve Negroes" (Survey of Social Agencies, table B, p. 4). The 207 agencies listed as refusing service to Negroes included only those that stated in writing that they barred all blacks. Agencies which in fact served only whites but did not admit to prohibiting blacks were omitted. Thus the list of agencies refusing to serve Negroes *minimizes* the amount of exclusionary segregation.

28. "Private Agencies Refusing Service to Negroes"; *SSD*, 1939, pp. 39, 78, 135–37.

29. Ida B. Wells-Barnett, cited in Allan H. Spear, *Black Chicago: The Making of a Negro Ghetto, 1890–1920* (Chicago, 1967), pp. 46–47; "Memorandum of conference on temporary shelter, housing and care for colored women with young children," 9 July 1926, in Welfare Council of Metropolitan Chicago Papers, CHS; "Private Agencies Refusing Service to Negroes"; *SSD*, 1939, pp. 52 and 137; Graham, pp. 5–6; Survey of Agencies, p. 6.

30. Ibid., p. 7; lists of "Private Agencies Operated by Negroes for Negroes Exclusively," "Clinics and Dispensaries Available for Chicago Negroes," and "Private Agencies Refusing Service to Negroes," with materials of Survey of Agencies; *SSD*, 1939, pp. 43, 90, 97. The Home for Incurables did not "refuse" to admit Negroes, but it was not "available" to them. The tip-off is this: the home is not on any of the Survey's lists of agencies serving Negroes, even "less than one per cent." When an agency is not on these lists, I have concluded that it excluded Negroes.

31. Bowen, n.p.; "*Lawrence Hall*, 4833 North Francisco Avenue," 21 September 1932, report in Welfare Council Papers; W. S. Brophy to Julius Rosenwald, 7 December 1913, Rosenwald Papers; Spear, p. 46; "Park Ridge School for Girls," 28 July 1932, report in Welfare Council Papers; "Private Agencies Refusing Service to Negroes."

32. Ibid., Survey of Agencies, p. 5; *SSD*, 1939, pp. 44, 92.

33. List of "Private Institutions Serving Negroes, Not Including Hospitals," footnote, with materials of Survey of Agencies.

34. "Private Agencies Refusing Service to Negroes"; *SSD,* 1939, pp. 46–47. The asylum had moved from 2228 Michigan to 5120 Grand Boulevard (later South Parkway, now Dr. Martin Luther King, Jr., Drive). Later in the thirties the asylum moved to 850 E. 58th Street. In 1940 a group promoting a settlement house "for Negroes" bought the abandoned building, which then became South Parkway Community Center.

35. "Private Agencies Refusing Service to Negroes"; *SSD,* 1939, pp. 111, 130.

36. "Private Institutions Serving Negroes, Not Including Hospitals"; *SSD,* 1939, pp. 64, 81.

37. Survey of Agencies, pp. 7–8 and table B, p. 4. Only 27 percent of these facilities accommodated blacks at all.

38. Lists of "Private Agencies Refusing Service to Negroes," "Recreation Facilities for Negroes, by Residence Areas," and "Private Agencies Serving Both Races, Separate Service," with materials of Survey of Agencies; Spear, pp. 46, 52, 100–101, 174, 227; T. J. Woofter, *Negro Problems in Cities* (Garden City, N.Y., 1928), p. 246; Survey of Agencies, p. 8. The Negro YMCA, Spear writes, was "but a shadow of the superbly equipped, lily-white YMCA in the Loop." The "small and unattractive" YWCA for "colored," according to Woofter, was "woefully inadequate."

39. *SSD,* 1939, p. 126.

40. Bowen, n.p.; Spear, pp. 101–6; lists of "Private Agencies Operated by Negroes for Negroes Exclusively," "Unorganized Negro Agencies Operating at Present Time," "Types of Service Reported Entirely Lacking for Negroes," and "Facilities Reported Inadequate for Negroes," with materials of Survey of Agencies; Graham, pp. 5–7; Survey of Agencies, pp. 5–7. See Spear, pp. 106, 169–74, and Arvarh E. Strickland, *History of the Chicago Urban League* (Urbana, Ill., 1966), chs. 2 and 3, for the Urban League.

41. Riot Commission, pp. 8, 326, 644–46.

42. Graham, p. 8.

43. Ibid.

44. Wilfred E. Reynolds (director, Council of Social Agencies) to Raymond Rubinow (officer, Rosenwald Fund), 26 April 1930, Rosenwald Papers; Graham, p. 1. The special bureau for placing Negro children was called the Joint Service Bureau: see *SSD,* 1939, p. 102.

45. Graham, title page; Reynolds to Rubinow. Edith Abbott and A. L. Foster had served together on the Chicago Housing Commission, which led to the dual housing program detailed in ch. 11, supra. Miss Abbott advised the planners of Field Gardens and Rosenwald Gardens on site selection.

46. *SSD,* 1939, p. 99, for Jewish Home Finding Agency, listed as Jewish Children's Bureau. For the provision of "adequate and modern hospitalization for Negroes" at the new Provident Hospital, see press releases dated "November __" [sic]

and 18 and 23 December 1929, ANP files; for addresses of committee members, *Who's Who,* eds. of 1931 and 1936, and *Chicago Telephone Directory,* 1930.

47. Oscar C. Brown, quoted in Ethel Harris, "Interview with the leader," 1935, among materials on "The 49th State Movement," in Negro in Illinois.

48. Graham, p. 2; Survey of Agencies, p. 7; "A Digest of Interim Report of the 'South Side Survey,' " p. 1, with materials of Survey of Agencies.

49. Graham, pp. 7–8, 10; Edwin Embree, *Julius Rosenwald Fund: A Review to June 30, 1929* (Chicago, 1929), p. 31.

50. Graham, p. 9; "Digest of Interim Report," p. 1.

51. The long statement appears in Graham, p. 9, and Survey of Agencies, p. 8. The phrase "a valid difference" is in Graham, p. 9.

52. Bowen, n.p.

53. Riot Commission, pp. 146–51, map, "Social Agencies Used by Negroes," facing p. 148; ibid., pp. xviii, 653; Taylor, *Chicago Commons through Forty Years* (Chicago, 1936), p. 251. Irene J. Graham, who directed the staff, also directed the field work for the study which Edith Abbott made to help Julius Rosenwald select a site for his Black Belt housing project. The survey listed the day nursery, nursery school, playground, and recreation facilities at Rosenwald Gardens with "Private Agencies Operated by Whites, or Whites and Negroes, for Negroes Exclusively." Miss Graham wrote a well-informed master's thesis and an article on Chicago's black people: see "Negroes in Chicago, 1920: An Analysis of United States Census Data" (M.A. thesis, University of Chicago, 1929) and "Family Support and Dependency among Chicago Negroes," *SSR* 3 (December 1929): 541–62.

54. Bowen, n.p.; Riot Commission, p. 193; Graham, p. 9.

55. Addams, *Second Twenty Years,* p. 398.

CHAPTER 14 THE COLOR LINE IN NEIGHBORHOOD WORK

1. Untitled pamphlet about Wendell Phillips Settlement, n.p., n.d. [1925], Chicago Commons Papers, CHS. One page has two pictures of black children and a large, bold-face caption, "Where Danger Stalks."

2. Chicago Commission on Race Relations, *The Negro in Chicago: A Study of Race Relations and a Race Riot* (Chicago, 1922), p. 112, hereafter cited as Riot Commission. The annual reports of Chicago Commons (titles vary) from 1906 to 1930 detail the staff's attempts to bring white newcomers into the settlement program.

3. D. E. Proctor, "The University of Chicago Settlement: A Study of the History of Its Internal Organization," student paper, n.d. [1925], pp. 43–44, in Ernest W. Burgess Papers, UCL; Riot Commission, pp. 112, 395–96; Jane Addams, *Twenty Years at Hull-House* (New York, 1910), pp. 255–56; Mary McDowell to Arthur W. Mitchell, 8 November 1934, Arthur W. Mitchell Papers, CHS.

4. "Private Agencies Serving Both Races, Separate Service," with materials of Joint Committee on the Survey of Agencies Serving the Negro Community, 1930, in Julius Rosenwald Papers, UCL, collection hereafter cited as Survey of Social Agencies; "Camps Available for Negro Boys, Girls, and Adults," ibid.; "Private Agencies Refusing Service to Negroes," ibid.; Addams, pp. 136–39.
5. Allan H. Spear, *Black Chicago: The Making of a Negro Ghetto 1890–1920* (Chicago, 1967), pp. 95–96; Robert A. Woods and Albert J. Kennedy, *Handbook of Settlements* (New York, 1911), p. 77.
6. *Broad Ax*, 30 June 1906; Spear, p. 106; Bowen, n.p.
7. Celia Parker Woolley, "The Frederick Douglass Center, Chicago," *Commons* 9 (July 1904): 328–29.
8. Ibid., p. 328; *Inter-Ocean*, 15 December 1904, clipping in Negro in Illinois; Spear, p. 104; Steven J. Diner, "Chicago Social Workers and Blacks in the Progressive Era," *SSR* 44 (December 1970): 403.
9. Woolley, p. 329; Fannie Barrier Williams, "The Frederick Douglass Center," *Southern Workman* 35 (June 1906): 334–36; weekly programs printed in *Broad Ax*, 2 December 1905 to 10 February 1906; ibid., 20 January 1906.
10. Woolley, p. 329; Williams, p. 336.
11. *Broad Ax*, 23 and 30 June, and 7 July 1906; Williams, pp. 334–36.
12. Weekly programs in *Broad Ax*, 1905–12; Spear, pp. 104, 170.
13. *Broad Ax*, 23 June 1906; Woods and Kennedy, pp. 39–40, 47.
14. Riot Commission, pp. 39–40, 273.
15. Chicago *Tribune*, 14 August 1907; Spear, p. 105; Allen F. Davis, *Spearheads for Reform: The Social Settlements and the Progressive Movement, 1890–1914* (New York, 1967), p. 95; Wendell Phillips Settlement, untitled pamphlet. Mrs. Bowen and Sophonisba Breckenridge were also on the original board.
16. Riot Commission, pp. 146–50; "Private Agencies Operated by Negroes for Negroes Exclusively," "Unorganized Negro Agencies Operating at Present Time," and "Recreation Facilities for Negroes, by Residence Areas," in Survey of Social Agencies; *CDNA*, 1900–1920; untitled Chicago Federation of Settlements pamphlets, listing member agencies, n.d. [1921 and 1925], in Lea Taylor Papers, CHS; *SSD*, 1939, pp. 113, 122, and 187–88. Beginning in 1916, *CDNA* listed Welfare League at 2136 Federal as a social settlement. At this location, it had to be a Negro settlement. Apparently it was gone by the time of the riot. Hartzell Center, founded in 1920 by South Side Methodist Episcopal Church, was gone by 1925. Olivet Christian Center, Metropolitan Community Center, and Bethesda Community Center survived the decade. Olivet Center began in 1918, but its operation was so small for the first few years that the Riot Commission did not notice it.
17. Riot Commission, pp. 148–49; *Twenty Years of Character Building, 1918–1937*, pamphlet in Mitchell Papers, n.p.
18. Ibid.; Robert L. Neal to Congressman William L. Dawson, 21 October 1948, copy in L. Taylor Papers.

19. Report of the Executive Secretary to the Board of Directors of the Chicago Urban League, 17 June 1924, in ibid.; *Twenty Years of Character Building.* The notation in "Unorganized Negro Agencies Operating at Present Time" reads, "did have settlement activities, no budget now."

20. Wendell Phillips Settlement, untitled pamphlet, listing board members for 1924–25 and "Board of Directors of Wendell Phillips Settlement," n.d. [1925–26], in L. Taylor Papers; Riot Commission, pp. 273, 279; Reports of the Executive Secretary to the Board of Directors of the Urban League, 7 March and 15 November 1922, and 15 November 1923, in L. Taylor Papers; Memorandum of Activities at the Chicago Urban League, 20 February 1924, ibid.

21. Report of the Executive Secretary to the Board of Directors of the Urban League, 15 November 1923 and 17 June 1924, in ibid.; Board of Directors of Wendell Phillips Settlement, Minutes, 18 June 1924, in ibid.; form letter to the Board of Wendell Phillips Settlement, 30 January 1926, ibid.; Thomas J. Woofter, Jr., *Negro Problems in Cities* (New York, 1928), p. 275.

22. John McClellan to Lea Taylor, 5 April 1929, and form letter from Lea Taylor, 26 May 1930, in L. Taylor Papers; Graham Taylor to Britton I. Budd, 17 December 1925, G. Taylor Papers; "Private Agencies Refusing Service to Negroes," in Survey of Social Agencies; *SSD,* 1939, pp. 144–45. The white philanthropists were leaders of the South Side Boys' Club Foundation, an affiliate of the Union League Foundation. The Urban League had asked these men to convert Wendell Phillips Settlement into a boys' club in 1924 (see Memorandum of Activities at the Chicago Urban League) .

23. Chicago Recreation Commission, *The Chicago Recreation Survey, 1937* (Chicago, 1938–39), vol. 3, *Private Recreation,* p. 56; Woofter, pp. 251–52; *The Negro Boy Problem and the South Side Boy's [sic] Club Foundation,* n.d., n.p., listing the trustees, CHS.

24. Ibid. George F. Nixon was president of the CREB in 1928, and he promoted restriction in several districts where he handled property. Frank J. O'Brien of McKey and Poague Realty was a leader in property owners' associations in Oakland, Kenwood, Hyde Park, and Woodlawn. Also on the board was Lyndon H. Lesch, who headed the University of Chicago Business Office, which helped to maintain restrictive covenants in Hyde Park, Kenwood, and Woodlawn.

25. *All Souls Church and the Abraham Lincoln Centre Year Book for 1920 and Report for 1919,* p. 24.

26. For Wentworth Center, 43rd Place and Wentworth, and Neighborhood Guild, 2512 Wentworth, see Woods and Kennedy, pp. 72 and 78–79; for the branch of Chicago Boys' Club at 3737 Wentworth, see untitled typed history of Chicago Boys' Clubs, Inc., p. 25, in Chicago Boys' Clubs Papers, CHS; see *SSD,* 1939, pp. 10, 135, for Bethlehem Settlement and St. Rose's Social Center; Riot Commission, pp. 115, 273.

27. Ernest W. Burgess and Charles Newcomb, *Census Data of the City of Chicago, 1920* (Chicago, 1931), table 52; Burgess and Newcomb, *Census Data of the City*

of Chicago, 1930 (Chicago, 1933), tables 1, 2, and 3. In both censuses 60 percent of the whites were Italian stock. The tract, numbered 314 in 1920 and 524 in 1930, was part of Little Italy, although Chinatown happened to be located in it. St. Rose's is *not* included on any of the Survey of Social Agencies lists of agencies serving Negroes. I have taken omission from these lists as evidence that agencies excluded blacks. The Survey's list of "Private Agencies Refusing Service to Negroes" included only those that stated their ban on blacks in writing. The quote from the Riot Commission is on p. 279.

28. Ibid., pp. 11–16, 39; Frederic M. Thrasher, *The Gang: A Study of 1,313 Gangs in Chicago* (Chicago, 1927; rev. ed., 1936), pp. 16, 19, 201; Burgess and Newcomb, *Census Data 1920,* table 52, tract 381. The Riot Commission, Spear, and several other sources refer to the four-mile strip west of Wentworth from 22nd to 55th as "Irish," "Polish," and "Irish and Polish." Actually, the Irish ranked third and the Poles ranked fifteenth among twenty-seven ethnic groups inhabiting the area. In tract 381, around Bethlehem, the leading countries of the foreign-born were: Sweden—354, Germany—234, Ireland—214, Hungary—200, and Russia—108. Poland, with 21, ranked thirteenth, tied with Greece. The director of the public park nearest Bethlehem said that white gangs were "keeping the colored people out of the parks," and the policeman stationed at another nearby park drove blacks away, saying that there were parks east of the tracks where "niggers ought to stay" (Riot Commission, pp. 278, 293).

29. *SSD,* 1939, p. 137; "Clinics and Dispensaries Available for Chicago Negroes," in Survey of Social Agencies. Bridgeport, an area of 2.5 square miles, had over 60,000 residents from 27 or more ethnic groups in 1920. The number of Negroes that year was 23. By 1930 only *one* (1) Negro lived in Bridgeport. See Burgess and Newcomb, *Census Data 1920,* table 52, and *Census Data 1930,* community area table 1. For the gangs see Riot Commission, pp. 11–17, and Thrasher, pp. 16–18. One of the leaders of the Hamburg Social and Athletic Club in 1919 was Richard J. Daley, mayor of Chicago, 1955–1976.

30. Woods and Kennedy, pp. 64–65.

31. Riot Commission, p. 107; Spear, p. 46; *SSD,* 1939, p. 83; Chicago Recreation Commission, 3: pp. 12, 14. For all its vaunted gentility, Hyde Park had elements resembling the gangs west of Wentworth. "A very rough element of whites congregates every night on Lake Park near Fifty-first Street," a white woman reported, "hoodlums that the colored people living there must fear" (Riot Commission, p. 307) .

32. Woods and Kennedy, p. 65; *SSD,* 1939, p. 38; Chicago Recreation Commission, 3: 49–52; "Private Agencies Refusing Service to Negroes." The Ogden Hill Boys' Club is on this list; Neighborhood House is not, but it did not serve blacks.

33. *SSD,* 1939, p. 140. The center's day nursery is listed in "Private Agencies Refusing Service to Negroes"; the quota in the summer school is noted in "Private Centers Serving Negroes, Not Including Dispensaries," in South Side Survey. South Chicago Neighborhood House is not on any of the South Side Survey lists of agencies serving Negroes. In 1936, when the settlement was under

attack for proselytizing Catholics in the area called The Bush and otherwise disregarding the neighborhood's feelings, a staff member said that the settlement was doing its part to "make the Bush white" ("South Chicago Neighborhood House," a summary of a 1936 report, in Welfare Council Papers).

34. Riot Commission, pp. 282, 285, 287. Also see Thrasher, p. 186.

35. Riot Commission, p. 278.

36. "Study of Agencies in Chicago Doing Work for Girls," n.p., 21 January 1922, report in Commons Papers (the western boundary was "Robey" [Damen], which ran north and south through the heart of the black colony); Riot Commission, p. 112; "Report of the Work of Chicago Commons Association for the Year Ending September 30, 1928," p. 13, in Commons Papers (hereafter these reports are cited as Commons Report, with year); Commons Report, 30 September 1930, pp. 12, 19; Lea Taylor to Commons trustees, 30 August 1930, Commons Papers; Karl Borders, "Annual Report, Boys Dept. 1928–1929," n.p., ibid.; Commons Report, 30 September 1928, p. 28; Commons Report, 30 September 1929, p. 11; Commons Report, 30 September 1930, p. 5.

37. Woods and Kennedy, p. 76; *SSD,* 1939, pp. 70–71; "Possible Lines of Action for Erie Chapel Institute," n.d. [March 1930], n.p., Commons Papers; "Emerson Settlement, 1757 W. Grand Avenue, From a Study by Students of Dr. Burgess," n.d. [1927–28], n.p., ibid.; "Possible Lines of Future Action, Bethany Congregational Church," March 1930, pp. 1–3, ibid.

38. *SSD,* 1939, pp. 144–45; Chicago Recreation Commission, 3: 12; "Private Agencies Refusing Service to Negroes." The club belonged to the Chicago Federation of Settlements.

39. Woods and Kennedy, pp. 49–50; *SSD,* 1939, p. 122; "Private Agencies Refusing Service to Negroes." The Off-the-Street Club was a member of the Chicago Federation of Settlements.

40. New First Congregational Church, 1613 W. Washington, barred blacks from its camp and its girls' residence. Ballington Booth Community Center, 2845 W. Washington, barred blacks from its day nursery. Neither had Negroes in its community center, either. See *SSD,* 1939, pp. 118–19 and 152–53, and "Private Agencies Refusing Service to Negroes." Chase House, 211 S. Ashland, belonged to the Chicago Federation of Settlements. See Chicago Recreation Commission, 3: 12–13, and *SSD,* 1939, pp. 17–18. It is not on the lists of agencies serving Negroes. For Chicago Evangelistic Institute, see Chicago Recreation Commission, 4, *Recreation by Community Areas in Chicago,* n.p.; *SSD,* 1939, pp. 17–18; "Private Centers Serving Negroes, Not Including Dispensaries."

41. Chicago Recreation Commission, 4: n.p., lists the facilities and equipment of all agencies.

42. In 1920 only 138 Negroes lived in the whole area (census tracts 257 through 261). In 1930 the area (tracts numbered 434 and 440 through 443) had a Negro population of 11,339. The white population in the meantime had dropped from nearly 25,000 to about 7,300, including 1,800 Mexicans (in 1930 the census counted Mexicans as nonwhite). See Burgess and Newcomb, *Census Data, 1920,* table 52, and *Census Data, 1930,* table 1.

43. Untitled pamphlets and form letters, Jewish Community Centers of Chicago Papers, CHS; Chicago Recreation Commission, 3: 12, 14–15; Meyer Levin, *The Old Bunch* (New York, 1937), p. 507.

44. Carlotta Kanouff, *"Firman House,"* Association of Commerce report, June 1937, pp. 1–2, copy in Welfare Council Papers; *SSD*, 1939, pp. 74, 76, 110; "Private Agencies Refusing Service to Negroes."

45. The Jane Club is listed in "Private Agencies Refusing Service to Negroes"; Hull-House and its Mary Crane Nursery are listed separately in "Private Centers Serving Negroes, Not Including Dispensaries." At least 160 boys from the old "ghetto" belonged to the Boys' Club in 1907: see Hull-House Boys' Club, Official Registration Book, 1907, in UHC, and Louis Wirth, *The Ghetto* (Chicago, 1928), p. 188. For the boundary changes, see Chicago Recreation Commission, 3: 12 and 14. The account of the Negro Mothers' Club is from Dewey Jones, the first black resident of Hull-House, speaking at meeting on "interracial policy and program" of Chicago Council of Social Agencies' Executive Committee, Division on Education and Recreation, 15 March 1939, pp. 7–9, Welfare Council Papers, hereafter cited as meeting on inter-racial policy.

46. Joseph Stolz to J. Witkowsky, 2 November 1893, Joseph Stolz Papers, CHS; Woods and Kennedy, p. 78; Wirth, p. 188; *SSD*, 1939, pp. 12, 161; Chicago Recreation Commission, 3: 53–58; Thrasher, p. 408; *Boys Brotherhood Republic*, booklet, n.p., n.d. [1930], CHS; "Private Centers Serving Negroes, Not Including Dispensaries," for remark on quota.

47. "Marcy Center and Its Community," typed report, 16 May 1945, pp. 1, 7–9, in Welfare Council Papers.

48. Ibid., pp. 7–9.

49. Chicago Recreation Commission, 3: 12 and 14, for altered boundaries; "Private Centers Serving Negroes, Not Including Dispensaries"; Arlington Smith, program director of Newberry Center, at meeting on inter-racial policy, p. 4. At this meeting Smith referred to the NAACP as "the Association for the Advancement of Colored Boys."

50. Irving N. Klein to Max Goldenberg, 10 January 1929, Goldenberg Furniture Co. Papers, CHS, which lists the members of the subscription committee; Goldenberg to Klein, 19 January 1929, ibid.; untitled history of Chicago Boys' Clubs, Inc., pp. 31–32, 35; "How the Old Town Boys' Club Came Into Being," n.d., report in Chicago Boys' Club Papers; Minutes of the Meeting of the Executive Committee of Chicago Boys' Clubs, 15 July 1930, ibid.; Old Town Boys' Club newspaper, untitled, 25 December 1931, in Old Town Club records, ibid. The club affiliated with Chicago Boys' Clubs, which took it over completely in 1938, retaining the whites-only policy. The original Chicago Boys' Club, opened in 1901, was in a downtown building, remote from any neighborhood. The club's policy was to help "children of all creeds and colors," and the downtown club accepted Negro boys as members until the directors closed it in 1911. From then on, the club operated from neighborhood branches, two of which were near Negro enclaves, and they never ac-

cepted blacks. See *Darkest Chicago and Her Waifs,* the club's journal, 1903 through 1911, especially "annual report" issues every January, and *Chicago Boys' Club 1912,* p. 26, in Chicago Boys' Club Papers, and "Private Agencies Refusing Service to Negroes."

51. Riot Commission, pp. 112, 276, 295.

52. Ibid., pp. 112–13; "Private Agencies Serving Negroes, But Less Than One Per Cent"; "Private Agencies Refusing Service to Negroes," for the workshop; Walter L. Kindelsperger, "Statistical Measurement in Group Work" (M.A. thesis, University of Chicago, 1940), table 3, p. 33.

53. *SSD,* 1939, pp. 134–35; "Private Agencies Refusing Service to Negroes."

54. Woods and Kennedy, pp. 79–80; *Olivet Institute, 1888–1913,* pamphlet, October 1913, pp. 22, 84, Olivet Community Center Papers, CHS; Norman Barr to James B. Forgan, 12 July 1920, copy in Commons Papers.

55. Woods and Kennedy, p. 79; *Olivet Institute, 1888–1913,* pp. 85–86; Kenneth T. Jackson, *The Ku Klux Klan in the City, 1915–1930* (New York, 1967), p. 121.

56. Norman Barr to James B. Forgan, 28 July 1923, copy in Commons Papers (Barr boasted that 190 immigrants had become citizens since the previous fall, and he expected 400 children in the summer Bible School); letterhead on Barr to Forgan, 12 July 1920; Woods and Kennedy, p. 79; "Private Agencies Refusing Service to Negroes"; Documents 11706997 and 12031063, both dated 1 November 1933, restrictive covenants cited in Minutes of Special Meeting of the Board of Trustees, 29 September 1939, pp. 1–5, Olivet Papers.

57. Chicago Recreation Commission, 3: 54; *SSD,* 1939, pp. 70, 161; Perry J. Stackhouse, *Chicago and the Baptists: A Century of Progress* (Chicago, 1933), p. 202; Chicago Recreation Commission, 3: 54; Carroll Binder, *Chicago and the New Negro* (Chicago, 1927), p. 8.

58. *SSD,* 1939, pp. 70, 101–2. The center is listed with "Private Agencies Serving Negroes, But Less Than One Per Cent"; black adults were allowed to attend the citywide conferences there, so the center claimed to be "serving Negroes." Ms. Mary Anne Sugrue, a Catholic, went swimming there frequently in the late twenties and early thirties: interview with Ms. Sugrue (my mother-in-law), 25 March 1972. In 1944 the Catholic Archdiocese of Chicago bought Sinai Temple, "the most imposing piece of church property in Bronzeville . . . and converted it into a school and community center" for the *local* community: see St. Clair Drake and Horace Cayton, *Black Metropolis* (New York, 1945), pp. 413–15, note. Sinai congregation rebuilt in Hyde Park.

59. Helen Rosenfels, "Fifty Years of a Living Democracy," *Unity* 141 (March–April 1955): 8.

60. Ibid.; Frank Lloyd Wright to Curtis W. Reese, n.d., reprinted in *Unity* 141 (March–April 1955): 15; Homer Hoyt, *One Hundred Years of Land Values in Chicago* (Chicago, 1933), map 36, "Distribution of Buildings Seven Stories High or Over, 1933," p. 243; Woods and Kennedy, p. 73.

61. Rosenfels, p. 8; Woods and Kennedy, p. 73.

62. *The Abraham Lincoln Centre and All Souls Church Annual, 1906* (Chicago, 1906), p. 28, hereafter cited as Lincoln Centre annual report, with year; Lincoln Centre annual report, 1908, p. 18 (the class had about forty other children of ten "nationalities," listed as American, English, Welsh, Scotch, Irish, German, Scandinavian, Danish, and Jewish); Lincoln Centre annual report, 1912, pp. 63, 122.

63. Maps, "Distribution of Negro Population, 1910" and "Distribution of Negro Population, 1920," in Riot Commission, facing pp. 106 and 110.

64. Lincoln Centre annual report, 1913, p. 23; ibid., 1919–20, pp. 15, 25.

65. Ibid., p. 24; Curtis W. Reese, "The Abraham Lincoln Centre Ideal," *The Abraham Lincoln Centre Year Book, 1926* (Chicago, 1926), p. 3, hereafter cited as Lincoln Centre Year Book, with year; "Annual Message of Dean Curtis W. Reese," 1930, pp. 15–16.

66. Minutes of the Board of Trustees, Lincoln Centre, 20 January and 1 March 1921, Abraham Lincoln Centre Papers, CHS; Minutes of the Staff, 6 October 1929, cited in Joan Rockwood, "Analysis of an Interracial Program: The Abraham Lincoln Centre" (M.A. thesis, University of Chicago, 1941), p. 25; map, "Social Agencies Used by Negroes," in Riot Commission, ff. p. 148; Minutes of the Board of Trustees, 3 November 1927 and 30 December 1932; Lincoln Centre Year Book, 1928, p. 21; Raymond Lee Gibbs, "The Life Cycle of Oakland Community" (M.A. thesis, University of Chicago, 1937), p. 132.

67. The camp is listed with "Private Agencies Serving Both Races, Separate Service"; Minutes of the Staff, 6 October 1929, cited in Rockwood, p. 25; Reese, quoted in Lincoln Centre Year Book, 1930, pp. 15–16; Gibbs, p. 130; Rockwood, pp. 8–9.

68. Gibbs, pp. 132–33; Minutes of the Staff, 8 March and 16 November 1933, cited in Rockwood, p. 26. The staff was discussing a policy which had been in effect since the latter part of 1932. The Board of Trustees never took official action on the quota policy, which remained "informal." The effect of the policy, for a while, was to drive Negro registration down and reverse the trend of enrollment. Black registration dropped from 485 to 178 between 1932 and 1934. In 1928, 44 percent of "boys and girls" registered were "colored"; in early 1932 about 60 percent of the youngsters were black; by 1934 their percentage was down to 25. The policy failed because whites who enrolled hardly ever visited the place. What "participation" there was remained overwhelmingly "colored." In *Settlement Houses and the Great Depression* (Detroit, 1975), Judith Ann Trolander has an excellent chapter on "The Settlements and Race Relations" in which she traces the color line in neighborhood work. She uses the example of Abraham Lincoln Centre to show that "the picture was not totally negative," contending that "Integration was the hallmark of Abraham Lincoln Centre" (pp. 137–38). It probably *was* the closest thing to "an integrated settlement" in America in the twenties and the thirties—and it was *not* integrated, which is the real point.

69. Sophonisba P. Breckenridge tried to establish a permanent program for training Negro social workers (to do Negro social work) at the Chicago School of Civics and Philanthropy. The scholarship program collapsed after two students won certificates in 1913. Both students were "placed" at the "colored" Wendell Phillips Settlement before it folded (see Diner, pp. 400–401 and 405). After that, an occasional black student won admission to the school, and a few completed the master's program. The University of Chicago's School of Social Service Administration (successor to the School of Civics) did not award a Ph.D. to any Negro until 1969.

70. Constance Webb, *Richard Wright, A Biography* (New York, 1968), pp. 107–11; Richard Wright, "Introduction: How 'Bigger' Was Born," *Native Son* (New York, 1940; reprint ed., 1966), p. xxvi.

CONCLUSION: THE SLUM AND THE GHETTO

1. Mrs. Fred Atkins Moore to Lea Taylor, 12 March 1929, Lea Taylor Papers, CHS, hereafter cited as L. Taylor Papers; Minutes of Luncheon Meeting of Woman's City Club Housing and Zoning Committee, 21 March 1929, copy in ibid.

2. "Chicago Makes Rapid Progress in Campaign for Alteration of Unsafe and Unsanitary Buildings," *American City* 41 (August 1929): 44; Report of the Housing Committee of the Woman's City Club, 28 April 1931, copy in L. Taylor Papers.

3. Meeting of the Executive Committee of the Joint Committee on Housing, 15 January 1931, copy in ibid. Mrs. Moore was a member of the executive committee. The Joint Committee on Housing represented the Woman's City Club and the City Club. Report of the Housing Committee of the Woman's City Club, 28 April 1931.

4. Lea D. Taylor to Chicago Commons trustees, 16 February 1928, Chicago Commons Papers, CHS; Edith Abbott, *The Tenements of Chicago, 1908–1935* (Chicago, 1936), p. 480.

5. John M. Gries and James Ford, eds., *Publications of the President's Conference on Home Building and Home Ownership*, 11 vols. (Washington, 1932); Nannie H. Burroughs to Mrs. Irene McCoy Gaines, 13 October 1931, Irene McCoy Gaines Papers, CHS.

6. Gries and Ford, eds., vol. 3, *Slums, Large-Scale Housing and Decentralization*, p. xiv; ibid; vol. 6, *Negro Housing*, pp. 114–15.

7. Abbott, *The Tenements of Chicago*, p. 482; Abbott to Grace Abbott, 24 November 1933, Edith Abbott Papers, UCL.

8. Abbott, *The Tenements of Chicago*, pp. 477–78.

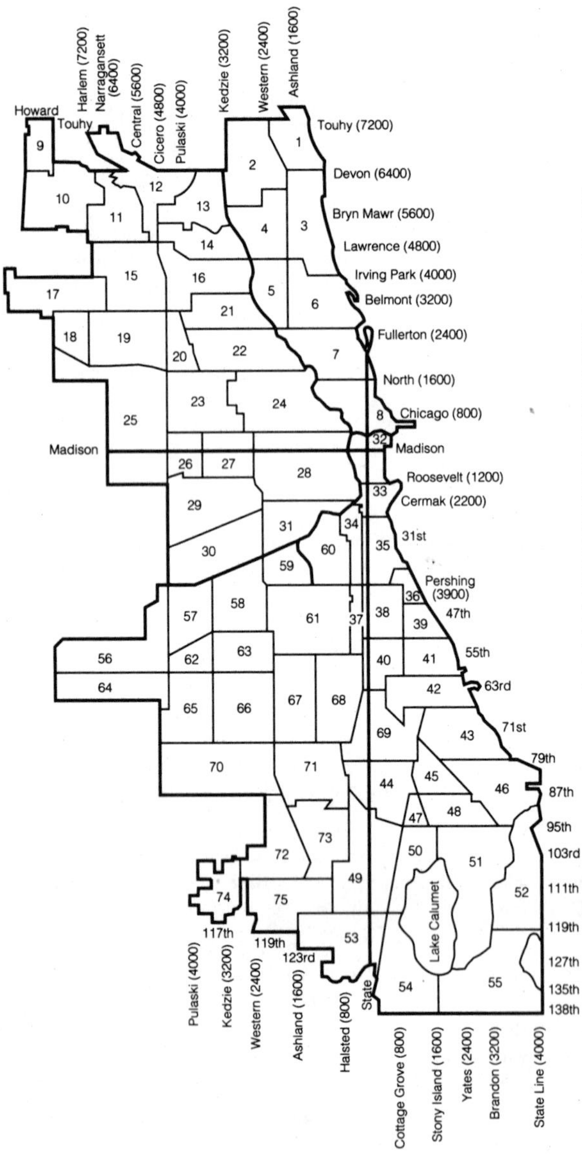

Chicago, 1930

Community Areas	Population
1 Rogers Park	57094
2 West Ridge	39759
3 Uptown	108585
4 Lincoln Square	46419
5 North Center	47651
6 Lake View	128066
7 Lincoln Park	97873
8 Near North Side	79554
9 Edison Park	5370
10 Norwood Park	14408
11 Jefferson Park	20392
12 Forest Glen	4065
13 North Park	11052
14 Albany Park	55577
15 Portage Park	64203
16 Irving Park	66783
17 Dunning	19659
18 Montclare	8500
19 Belmont Cragin	60221
20 Hermosa	23518
21 Avondale	48453
22 Logan Square	114174
23 Humbolt Park	80835
24 West Town	187551
25 Austin	13114
26 West Garfield Park	50910
27 East Garfield Park	60125
28 Near West Side	153761
29 North Lawndale	113054
30 South Lawndale	76749
31 Lower West Side	66174
32 Loop	7851
33 Near South Side	10416
34 Armour Square	21456
35 Douglas	50285
36 Oakland	14962
37 Fuller Park	14437
38 Grand Blvd.	87005
39 Kenwood	26942
40 Washington Park	44178
41 Hyde Park	48017
42 Woodlawn	66052
43 South Shore	78515
44 Charham	36228
45 Avalon Park	10023
46 South Chicago	56685
47 Burnside	3485
48 Calumet Heights	7343
49 Roseland	42985
50 Pullman	6705
51 South Deering	7868
52 East Side	16839
53 West Pullman	28474
54 Riverdale	1486
55 Hegewisch	7890
56 Garfield Ridge	6050
57 Archer Heights	8120
58 Brighton Park	47560
59 McKinley Park	22032
60 Bridgeport	53547
61 New City	86096
62 West Elsdon	2861
63 Gage Park	31555
64 Clearing	5434
65 West Lawn	8919
66 Chicago Lawn	47462
67 West Englewood	63845
68 Englewood	89063
69 Greater Grand Cr.	59474
70 Ashburn	735
71 Auburn Gresham	57604
72 Beverly	15795
73 Washington Hgts.	17865
74 Mount Greenwood	3310
75 Morgan Park	12747

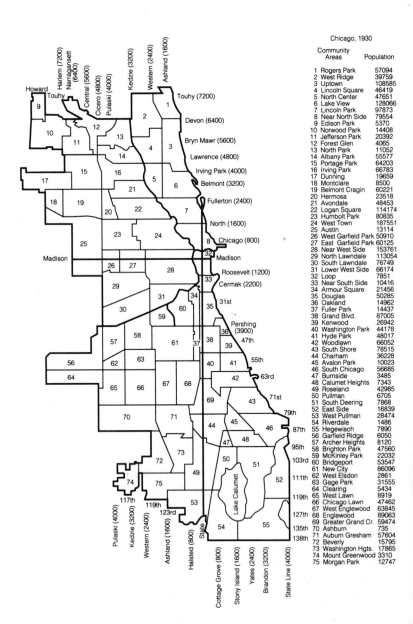

MAP I.1. Community areas of Chicago, 1930. Madison is the base line for streets running north and south, at which point house numbers start with number 1. State Street is the base line for streets running east and west. In the index, a named street will be followed by the initials N-S or E-W, for the direction in which it runs, and a number/letter designation indicating the location relative to the base line street. For example, "Wabash (N-S, 45 E)" means that Wabash runs north-south and is in the area east of State Street but west of Cottage Grove (800).

INDEX ❧